BULWER

and

MACREADY

*A Chronicle
of the
Early Victorian
Theatre*

University of Illinois Press, Urbana, 1958

BULWER AND MACREADY

A CHRONICLE OF THE EARLY VICTORIAN THEATRE

Edited by Charles H. Shattuck

To the Memory of

Harold N. Hillebrand

1887-1953

Counselor and Friend

contents

_____ I

When William Charles Macready bade farewell to his last theatre audience, on February 26, 1851, he asked to be given credit for two great efforts in behalf of the national stage — "to establish a theatre, in regard to decorum and taste, worthy of our country, and to have in it the plays of our divine Shakespeare fitly illustrated." Once at each of the great patent houses he had essayed the responsibility of management, and from each he had been forced out after a two-year trial period by what seemed to him the cupidity and even the malevolence of the proprietors. Thus, during the thirty-four seasons after his London debut, in only four seasons had he actually been in a position to effect these reforms he spoke of. Nonetheless he felt that "some good seed has yet been sown," and that "the corrupt editions and unworthy presentations of past days will never be restored."

He passed into history in the image that he coveted — "moral, grave, sublime," as Tennyson dubbed him in the official valedictory sonnet. He had become a national hero of "decorum and taste" and acknowledged champion of "our divine Shakespeare." To this day he is credited with banishing trained lions from the stages and prostitutes from the houses of the patent theatres, and with restoring Shakespeare's plays in "true" texts and in apt and beautiful mountings.

Yet there was another great effort, no less significant and far more pervasive to his career, which he did not mention on that farewell night: his sturdy promotion of the legitimate drama of his time. His self-neglect on this score was amended by others at the Valedictory Dinner three days later. In Tennyson's sonnet, which John Forster read to the assembled six hundred, are these lines:

> Thine is it that our drama did not die,
> Nor flicker down to brainless pantomime,
> And those gilt gauds men-children flock to see.

Speaking from the Chair, Edward Bulwer (by then Sir Edward Bulwer-Lytton) paid emphatic tribute to this aspect of Macready's accomplishment:

Many a great performer may attain to a high reputation if he restrains his talents to acting Shakespeare and the great writers of the past; but it is perfectly clear that in so doing he does not advance one inch the literature of his time. It has been the merit of our guest to recognize the truth that the actor has it in his power to assist in creating the writer. He has identified himself with the living drama of his period, and by so doing he has half created it. Who does not recollect the rough and manly vigour of Tell, the simple grandeur of Virginius, or the exquisite sweetness and dignity and pathos with which he invested the self-sacrifice of Ion? And who does not feel that

1

but for him these great plays might never have obtained their hold upon the stage, or ranked among those masterpieces which this age will leave to posterity?

"Those masterpieces which this age will leave to posterity"! How, a century afterwards, are we for whom the English drama of that period is a discouraging desert of dry bones — how are we to understand Bulwer's language? Was it sheer naïveté? unprincipled puffery? or merely the expectable hyperbole of an official occasion? And what are we to make of the six hundred listeners who punctuated every sentence of this passage with loud and renewed cheering? For us it is hard to remember that during the three decades after 1820 the English people believed that they were experiencing a genuine dramatic renaissance. "The tragic drama was about to revive amongst us," wrote Thomas Noon Talfourd in the preface to *Ion* (1835), "and I was not insensible to its progress. Although the tragedies of the last twelve years are not worthy to be compared with the noblest productions of the great age of our drama, they are with two or three exceptions, far superior to any which had been written in the interval. Since the last skirts of the glory of Shakespeare's age disappeared, we shall search in vain for serious plays of equal power and beauty with *Virginius, William Tell, Mirandola, Rienzi,* or the *Merchant of London.*" He excepted only *Venice Preserved* and Home's *Douglas* as serious drama of the intervening past which might be included with these. Had he written this preface a decade later he might have doubled or trebled his list of plays of comparable "power and beauty."

It is not to the purpose here to canvass the reasons why that dramatic renaissance turned out to be a failure (for that has been done well enough by Professors Allardyce Nicoll, Ernest Reynolds, and others). It is to the purpose rather to insist emphatically that it did occur, and that like any other dramatic renaissance it was a vivid and hopeful experience for those who lived in the midst of it and believed in it. In 1820 Sheridan Knowles's *Virginius,* as acted by Macready, accomplished for England what Eugene O'Neill's *Beyond the Horizon* accomplished for America exactly a century later. It caught, crudely but measurably, the spirit of the age in many of its manifestations. It set forth what was generally taken to be a valid tragic projection of the life and aspirations of its beholders. It was couched in what then seemed a refreshed and vital artistic form. It inspired a considerable flowering of other plays in its wake — initiated a dramatic renaissance which caused deep stirrings and high excitements while it lasted. We have long since rejected Knowles's meaning as limited, naïve, and dated, his verse as banal, his structure as shoddy neo-Elizabethanism. But we shall never understand the significance of Knowles and his eager successors unless we accept the enthusiasm of their audiences as quite genuine.

Along with Knowles a dozen or more authors made well-meaning contributions to the theatre Talfourd was talking about; dozens of others strove, however vainly, to give their portions too. And many of them — indeed, most — brought their plays to Macready to be performed, expecting from him not only ideal actorship but oftentimes counsel in the planning and writing as well. He was the artist, said Talfourd, "to whom all have by turns been indebted for the realization of their noblest conceptions." A pamphleteer in 1842 credited him with being "the means of introducing to the stage almost all the sterling new pieces of the last twenty years." R. H. Horne had little affection for him, yet in his *A New Spirit of the Age* in 1844 he linked Macready with Knowles as the two who "have continually exerted themselves to open new springs, or recall the retiring waters." A *Times* critic in 1845 declared that "whenever Mr. Macready was absent the poetic drama languished . . . and was called into immediate life when he returned." Whether he was in management or out of it, said William Johnson Fox in 1847, "dramatic poetry seeks his friendship." Bulwer's tribute, then, was not merely ceremonial rodomontade, but the proper assertion of a well-known truth.

Macready was peculiarly fitted, by training and temperament, to lead such a dramatic renaissance in such a time. He was proud, sensitive, intelligent, and ambitious. Though born into a theatrical family, he aspired from early boyhood to the "gentlemanly" professions of the Church or the Bar. Forced to leave Rugby School at the age of fifteen because of his father's financial collapse, and forced into the disagreeable labors of managing and performing in the provincial theatres of his father's circuit, he early learned to "hate the theatre" — that is, to hate the ignorance, slovenliness, and mindlessness of the company he must keep behind the scenes and of the audiences in front that he must pander to. Frustrated in his aspirations to escape the theatre, he worked with fanatic devotion to improve his place within it; and when, by 1820, he had in turn made his name as a leading actor in the country and distinguished himself from the pack at Covent Garden, he was ready to embark upon a more or less conscious and consistent program of transforming the theatre itself into an institution worthy of himself and his friends.

His friends, needless to say, were rarely of the profession: they *were* men of intellect. Even before his London debut he had found the delights of polite company within the social orbit of the Twiss family of Bath. In his early London years he frequented literary circles where he knew John Hamilton Reynolds, Charles Lloyd, Barry Cornwall, Mary Russell Mitford, and Richard Sheil, and he met Wordsworth, Robinson, Hazlitt, Hunt, and Lamb. He formed lasting friendships, then or thereafter, with Talfourd, Samuel Rogers, Thomas Moore, Harriet Martineau, Bulwer, Forster, and Dickens. He was a devoted admirer of Browning from their first meeting, and though their friendship collapsed after the production of *A Blot in the 'Scutcheon,* for several years they were intimates. He knew Landor, Tennyson, and Carlyle. It was to persons like these, and to distinguished scientists, artists, philosophers, and journalists that he listened for approval.

His own bent toward literature was strong, and he worked as assiduously at cultivating his mind as he did at cultivating his actorship. He developed a firm and often vivid prose style: his *Reminiscences,* though incomplete, are excellently organized and thoughtfully expressed, and the *Diaries* he kept from 1833 to 1851 are as remarkable for their controlled literacy as for their solid factual detail. He kept up his classical languages as proudly as any University man, and read fluently in Italian and French. He collected a fine library. Thoroughly conversant with the older literature and history of England and Europe, he kept abreast of the fiction, verse, and philosophical and critical writing of his contemporaries. Thus it is not surprising that as leading actor and sometimes as manager in the London theatre he should have striven to promote the drama of his time toward literary worth.

If the intellectual sterility of the theatrical profession impelled Macready to re-wed theatre to literature, its social degeneracy was an equally powerful stimulus in another way. He created for himself and scrupulously maintained the position of a gentleman. According to English statutes unrepealed from the reign of Elizabeth, an actor was a "rogue and vagabond." For Macready, who found the generality of the profession little better than rogues and vagabonds indeed, the quaint old phrase became a bitter symbol of the "half-world" of his calling and, ultimately, a goad to drive him out of it. He was an intensely moral man, honorable and upright in his business and professional relations. Among theatre folk, unfortunately, he had the reputation of being cold, arrogant, or even cruelly sarcastic, for his efforts to govern his violent temper (his one serious weakness) kept him under constant strain. Once, and once only, his temper got the better of him and he delivered his opinion of Alfred Bunn in fisticuffs instead of words, but Bunn's physical pain on this notorious occasion was as nothing compared to the racking shame that beset Macready for months afterwards. The virtues he bred in himself and that he expected in others were prudence, frugality, sobriety, reliability, dignity, self-respect. Thus, he postponed marriage until his thirtieth year because Mrs. Siddons had so advised him; at the insistence of his sister Letitia he postponed it nearly a year longer until Catherine Atkins was intellectually and socially groomed to be a worthy wife. He begot many children and educated them (as long as they lived) under strict paternal care; they were banished from the theatre. His home from 1830 to 1840 was a pleasant country mansion overlooking the Reservoir at Elstree, where driving, boating, archery, country walks, and conversation were the diversions of his distinguished guests. After 1840 he kept a splendid house in Clarence Terrace, Regent's Park. He made and saved money with such care and purpose that at the age of fifty-eight he was able to retire to a handsome old house at Sherborne in Dorsetshire, where he devoted his next nine years to reading, contemplation, and the direction of a school for laboring children. The pattern of his personal life was eminently that of the Victorian gentleman, householder, and paterfamilias, and thus in his very self he embodied all the best characteristics and domestic ideals which the heroes of the new drama gave him to project.

In yet another way he was a singularly ready exponent of the new drama: keenly aware of the social injustices of his civilization, he was politically an uncompromising republican. "Art has no politics," of course he would say, but the spirit of the age was, in the aftermath of the American and French Revolutions, the spirit of Reform, and Macready was a dedicated reformer. The very word Tory he hated. The institution and the person of royalty prompted many angry sentences in his diaries. He loathed the sight of those newspapers whose pages were filled with accounts of aristocratic "dinners, dances, marriages and such trasheries, as if the perpetuation of a race like our aristocrats were of the slightest moment." Reactionary turns of government sent him into burning rages against the agents thereof. From Virginius and William Tell to Philip van Artevelde he created many an impersonation of the defender of Hearth, Home, and the People against the brutality of tyrants. Even so seemingly innocuous a romance as *The Lady of Lyons,* as we shall see in some detail, carried in its time a burden of social significance, cheered by the liberals and damned by the reactionaries, however wrongly, for political reasons. It is obvious that Macready found such roles gratifying, and that he poured into them the zeal and heat of his own political convictions.

During his London career Macready performed or saw produced under his management nearly a hundred new plays, of which perhaps forty would be interesting to a historian of that "dramatic renaissance." A few notes will indicate the range of his activity. Including *Virginius,* he performed in six of Knowles's plays, and he employed Knowles as collaborator in a modernization of *The Maid's Tragedy,* called *The Bridal.* He helped to compose and then acted in Barry Cornwall's *Mirandola.* He acted in Mary Russell Mitford's *Julian* and assisted her in the composition of *The Foscari* and *Rienzi.* He staged four of Byron's plays: *Werner, Sardanapalus, The Two Foscari,* and *Marino Faliero.* He arranged for the stage and played in all three of Talfourd's tragedies. He performed Browning's *Strafford* and counseled Browning on the writing of *A Blot in the 'Scutcheon.* He performed or produced ten plays of T. J. Serle, including *The Merchant of London* and *Master Clarke.* He produced and performed James Haynes's *Mary Stuart,* Zouch Troughton's *Nina Sforza,* Gerald Griffin's *Gisippus,* John Marston's *The Patrician's Daughter,* William Smith's *Athelwold,* and James White's *The King of the Commons.* He prepared and performed a stage version of Henry Taylor's then celebrated dramatic poem *Philip van Artevelde.* His most important collaborative effort, of which this volume is a record, was of course that with Edward Bulwer.

———————— II

When Edward Bulwer invited Macready to call on him at the Albany, in February, 1836, to announce, as it were, the opening of his siege upon the theatre, he could pardonably expect to deliver himself *en monarque,* for his was the greatest going literary reputation of the day. At the age of thirty-three (ten years Macready's junior) he was not only the most widely read and most admired novelist in England but famous in Germany, Italy, France, and America as well. He had published ten novels in at least four distinct manners: witty novels of fashionable life like *Pelham;* Newgate melodramas — *Paul Clifford* and *Eugene Aram;* the baroque philosophical romance of *Godolphin* (as yet anonymous); and historical novels — *The Last Days of Pompeii* and *Rienzi.* His reputation was further enhanced by several volumes of verse, by his two-year editorship of *The New Monthly* magazine, by his extraordinarily acute sociopolitical analysis called *England and the English,* and by his successful five years of service as a Reform member of Parliament. The notoriety of his social life, in which he figured as a prince of the wits and dandies, entertaining lavishly in Hertford Street and gracing Lady Blessington's evenings at Seamore Place and Gore House, added a glitter to his reputation.

To his admirers his literary dexterity made him appear the heir at once of Farquhar, Fielding, Radcliffe, and Scott, and even his enemies, with the sneer of "pseudo-Byron," acknowledged his affinity to the bright generation just gone. Savage abuse was spewed at him by publishers' bullies and the Tory press — notably in *Fraser's Magazine* and *The Age* — but however painful it was to him in person it could not undermine the authority he had so remarkably achieved. He was ready now for conquest in that arena most tempting and most dangerous to all English men of letters after Shakespeare — the theatre.

The opening of Bulwer's theatrical campaign coincided with the smashup of his domestic life. During the preceding nine years his marriage to Rosina Wheeler had become a Strindbergian hell of incompatibility. When Macready first met him in Dublin in October of 1834, he had temporarily abandoned Rosina because of her supposed love affair with a Neapolitan prince. In 1836, in the very month that Bulwer called Macready to visit him at the Albany — a few days before or after — Rosina made a surprise appearance at these bachelor quarters, threw a tantrum at the sight of tea-things laid for two, and accused Bulwer of keeping a mistress. Their final deed of separation was signed on April 19. No sign of the dreadful imbroglio troubles Bulwer's first letters to Macready, however, nor is there any mention of it at this time in Macready's diaries. Doubtless Bulwer looked upon the separation as a prelude to the peace he needed for the initiation of this new career — little imagining it was really the prelude to a lifelong sufferance of hatred and public shame.

Bulwer's interest in the theatre was of long standing. In Parliament, as early as 1832, he caused to be set up a Select Committee of Enquiry into the legal foundations of the English theatre, and early in 1833 he introduced to the House of Commons certain bills aimed to correct the worst evils which the Committee had uncovered. His legislative targets were three: to establish a copyright law which would protect dramatic authors (successful); to destroy the monopoly practices by which only the so-called patent houses could legally perform "legitimate" drama (successful a decade later); to abolish the Lord

Chamberlain's prerogative of dramatic censorship (unsuccessful). In Book IV of his *England and the English* (1833), he reviewed these legal aspects of the theatre, assayed the weaknesses and achievements of contemporary dramatic writing, and recommended certain courses of thought to the "future Scott of the drama" — the pursuit of the Simple and the Magnificent. He originally wrote *Eugene Aram* (which appeared as a novel in 1832) as a stage play, a portion of which he afterwards published in *The New Monthly*. He planned a dramatic trilogy on the rise and fall of Oliver Cromwell, and actually composed the final play of the series.

By February of 1836 he had completed his romantic tragedy, *The Duchess de la Vallière*, which through Macready's agency was his first play to be acted. During the next four years he was to write and see staged four more plays, three of them (whatever we think of them today) masterpieces final for his epoch. *The Lady of Lyons* and *Richelieu* would hold the stage far beyond Bulwer's own lifetime — even into our own century; the comedy of *Money*, though less constantly popular than the other two, has actually a greater vitality and validity, being readable even today as a mirror of the early Victorian social scene.

For both matter and manner in his dramatic writing, Bulwer was strongly attracted to the French. Although in *England and the English* he could deplore the contemporary French drama as a wretched catalogue of moral atrocities and the French theatre as a battlefield desolated by the wars of the classicists and the romanticists, yet he could also imply that Victor Hugo's plays were masterpieces worthy of emulation. The July Revolution of 1830 was at first heartening to Bulwer as a political liberal, and the emergence of Hugo, Dumas the Elder, Delavigne, and others in the theatre encouraged him by example to regard the theatre as available for the infusion of republican ideas. "Romanticism is but liberalism in literature," said Hugo in the preface to *Hernani*. "Literary liberty is the daughter of liberty in politics." Bulwer had neither the temper nor the audience for such programmatic boldness, but he took courage from it. In the "Introductory Remarks" to his first collected *Dramatic Works* (1841), speaking from hindsight, he dared at last to discuss his three plays of French subject matter — *Richelieu, La Vallière,* and *The Lady of Lyons* (in that order) — as a sort of trilogy delineating the drift of political power from "the One Man" to "the old provincial chivalry" to "the People." Bulwer could then claim and advertise such political intentions, for by 1841, as it turned out, his reformist career — both in Parliament and in the theatre — was ended. Belatedly he could acknowledge his debt of idea to his French masters.

The range of his reading was, of course, much wider. From Sophocles to Schiller, from Terence to Tieck, he sought inspiration for plays. The projects from such sources which he contemplated but did not write or did not issue are tempting to the imagination.

Abruptly after 1840 Bulwer's dramatic output ceased, and to outward appearances his siege upon the theatre ended. We know from his correspondence that the ending was not as sudden as it seemed, and that for many months he combed frantically for the proper stuff for further plays for Macready. A decade later he provided a comedy called *Not So Bad as We Seem* for the distinguished amateurs of the Guild of Literature and Art, who played it successfully throughout England; in 1868 he published *The Rightful Heir* (a revision of *The Sea-Captain* of 1839) and saw it produced by Hermann Vezin; in 1869 he published a rhymed comedy called *Walpole;* his *Junius Brutus* was produced and his *Darnley* was produced and published after his death. In the archives at Knebworth House are the manuscripts — some fragmentary, some complete — of a number of other dramatic pieces. Failure of health and the necessity of living much abroad contributed to the abatement of his theatrical efforts after 1840. Macready, who was his "only" actor, became increasingly unavailable to him during this decade, being himself preoccupied with amassing money for retirement. Bulwer had found, too, that the financial rewards from playwriting were not commensurate with the time and effort expended, and he had perforce to return to the more lucrative profession of novelist. In any case he had made his conquest of the stage. His reputation as a playwright was, seemingly, unshakable, and he could leave the future of the drama to others.

III

The compulsive figure of John Forster intrudes into the correspondence and events that make up the Bulwer-Macready story, for he was an intimate of both men and a passionate enthusiast in all things literary and theatrical — even, like Dickens, a skilled amateur actor. A man of well-stocked and well-trained mind, tremendous energy, bullish opinion, and sometimes very bad manners, his greatest significance was his knack of living the lives of other people. In the words of his only biographer, Richard Renton — whose book is properly entitled *John Forster and His Friendships* —"From the beginning to the end of his career, he knew everyone worth knowing." His reputation as a historian (*Lives of Eminent British Statesmen*), a biographer (of Dickens, Goldsmith, Landor), an editor, a critic, and a bibliophile is considerable, but all these accomplishments pale beside the stimulation he provided to innumerable poets, novelists, playwrights, philosophers, actors, and artists upon whom his driving personality impinged.

Born in 1812 (hence nine years younger than Bulwer, nineteen years younger than Macready), he was already a figure of authority in the literary scene well before Bulwer's emergence as a dramatist. As early as 1830 he was contributing articles to leading magazines and had begun his Cromwell studies for the *Lives of the Statesmen* series. By 1833, at the age of 21, he was the official literary and dramatic critic of the liberal and influential weekly, *The Examiner*.

He was in correspondence with Bulwer in 1831, and within three years they were fast friends; they were to remain so, with occasional lapses over political divergences, for the rest of their lives. Forster praised and advised and directed many of Bulwer's literary exploits, and at times when Bulwer had to be absent from London, Forster served as his business manager, publishing agent, and theatrical factotum.

Macready met Forster in 1833 at Edmund Kean's funeral, and within the year got to know him well enough to declare that he was "an enthusiast; I like him." From then on he could never get rid of him. Their relations were often strained to the breaking point, for Macready was strong-willed and short-tempered and authoritarian himself, and dozens of times he was offended by Forster's aggressive interference in his professional affairs. But Forster's basic integrity, the genuineness of his devotion, and, under his crusty and often crude outward behavior, his personal warmth and tenderness always won out. Whether in wrath or in affection, Forster's name was written into Macready's *Diaries* many hundreds of times — more than any other — and of the few constant friends that Macready kept throughout the decades of his life after retirement, Forster was one.

Because of his special interest in the subject, Forster gave detailed advice on the writing of *Cromwell*. He attended the rehearsal preparations of *La Vallière*. For technical reasons the writing of *The Lady of Lyons* was kept secret from him, but he was there to cheer the results and defend it from its newspaper enemies. By an offensive act of indifference he nearly cut himself out of the planning of *Richelieu*, but he made peace in time to be useful to both author and actor-producer before it was over. He gave advice in the stage preparations and did what he could as a critic to alleviate the debacle of *The Sea-Captain*. In the affairs of *Money*, which was dedicated to him, he was from first to last a busy and effective agent in and out of the theatre, not the least of his contributions during this time being the sympathy he brought to the Macready household upon the death of his god-daughter Joan. In these and dozens of other ways Forster made himself integral to these climactic events of the theatre of the thirties and forties.

IV

The correspondence here presented, with its narrative augmentation from Macready's *Diaries*, constitutes one of the fullest records ever made of the planning, writing, and staging of a body of plays by a significant English dramatist. Here, in the very words of Bulwer the author, Macready the actor-producer, John Forster their mutual adviser, and various others, are set down the essences both of Bulwer's career as a playwright and of Macready's most sustained endeavor to restore to the theatre a dramatic corpus of literary

worth. For the general reader, to whom Bulwer's playwriting is irrevocably a
dead issue, the correspondence can mean little — its forgotten problems, false
starts, deviations, and longueurs can be but an oppression to the mind. The
student of literary and dramatic method, however, will find much in the give-
and-take of the principals to excite speculation. The theatre historian will
want to know even much more than can be here included about the critics'
reports on the original productions and the long stage history of the three
"successful" plays.

We could wish, of course, that the correspondents were Congreve and
Betterton, or Shakespeare and Burbage, that the plays under consideration
were of greater value to us today. Yet even if they were, I suspect, the fundamentals of the correspondence would not be much different. We cannot
imagine Shakespeare addressing to his performers critical anticipations of
Coleridge, Bradley, or G. Wilson Knight. He might, like Bulwer, have been
annoyed when they deleted from performance his favorite verse essays and
"poetical beauties," but he would hardly have chosen to explicate for them
those particular verbal felicities which we now take such delight in, nor his
vastier implications of theme. Like Bulwer, he might have consulted his pro-
ducer on sources and models for plays, the timeliness and propriety of certain
subjects with reference to the taste of the audience and perhaps the danger of
censorship, the choices between merry and bitter tone or comic and tragic
form, the organization of plot, the particular skills of the resident company
and the necessity of providing each performer a role worthy of his rank in the
profession, the needs of costuming and furnishing and stage arrangement, the
progress of rehearsals, the success or failure of the play just launched and
the need for alterations in it, and perhaps even emoluments. Bulwer's problems
are universal to the history of playwriting and, *mutatis mutandis,* reflect Shakespeare's problems or anticipate Bernard Shaw's. The important thing is that
in an age of letter-writing and before the age of telephony so many of his
problems got put on paper.

Bulwer approached the theatre in 1836 and 1837 with two plays ready-
made — *Cromwell* and *The Duchess de la Vallière*. The first was to collapse
in a welter of ardent but fruitless discussion. The second, after many vicissi-
tudes, was to be his maiden venture upon the stage. It failed. Out of this
rough initiation he learned many lessons. Novel-writing and play-writing, he
was to discover, were very different professions, operating under almost oppo-
site rules. As a novelist he had only to finish a book and signify so to the
publisher: "the price was down for his name"; but a play had to be approved
and bought as a play, literary reputation guaranteeing nothing. Further, in
the straitened economy of the theatre, the "price down" was but a niggardly
fraction of the price down for a novel, and it was determined by the immediate box office receipts. The novelist is a solitary and comparatively independ-
ent artist; the playwright is but one member (sometimes the least conspicuous

member) of a numerous company of artists who are all collaborating with and rivaling one another for rewards and glory. The novelist's audience is distant, silent, deliberative; the playwright's audience is immediately present, massed and contagiously sensitive, unpredictable, and instantly expressive of its pleasure or displeasure.

To get *La Vallière* staged at all Bulwer had to engage Macready's personal interest and adapt his plans to the vagaries of Macready's professional affairs; had to contend with three hostile or incompetent managers; had to suffer the vanities and shortcomings of several wrong actors; had to contend with the unexpected attacks on the supposed immorality of the play; had to accept its early failure. These were painful lessons for a proud and sensitive man, but he took them for the most part in patience.

Other lessons having to do with dramaturgic art were more constructive and hence more welcome. If Macready and Forster both found *Cromwell* inadequate, at least they had the intelligence and generosity to tell him the reasons why. As for *La Vallière*, he learned from its performance that a play must not exceed the length of an audience's power to endure it, and that if the author is depending on one great actor he had better provide that actor a controlling role. Earlier, from Macready's criticism of the first manuscript, he learned such fundamentals as that climactic scenes must be prepared for by prognosticative scenes; that "strong" scenes have to be played on-stage and not in "retirement to a chamber"; that wordless pantomime is injurious; and that suspensive plot elements must be renewed and sustained as nearly as possible to the final curtain. In lessons of this sort Bulwer was to become an eager adept.

After the catastrophe of *La Vallière* he might have quit the theatre had not Macready gone into management and begged his support. Cleverly, Bulwer elected the subject and tone of romantic comedy, and between luck and cunning he hit upon exactly the right fable — that of the noble commoner winning out against the entrenched social prejudices of decadent aristocracy. *The Lady of Lyons* was exactly consonant with the rising spirit of Liberalism in the decade. It was bound to succeed. He wrote it easily and swiftly, needing only minor technical advices from Macready. The letters surrounding it are interesting mainly for their few notes on costuming, for the long-drawn-out struggle to find a title, and for the gleeful conspiracy between Macready and Bulwer to keep the authorship a secret.

Again, to be sure, Bulwer had failed to provide his chief actor a really dominant role, for it developed that Pauline Deschappelles measurably outweighed Claude Melnotte on the stage. Again too, by the implicit Liberalism of the fable, he fell dangerously athwart the prejudices of certain reactionary critics. By its innocent charm, however, the fable triumphed. Bulwer at once achieved the eminence among dramatic writers that he yet maintained among novelists.

As Macready looked to his second Covent Garden season, Bulwer was willing to write again. Macready urged him still to pursue comedy, but along a soberer and more critical line, "touching on those unhealthy parts of our social system, which you have the power of taking advantage of for real good." He fancied for himself a role more mature than that of Melnotte — a father or elder professional man —"a keen hunter after the prizes of ambition, power & wealth, turned from his pursuit by the discovery of better things existing in the heart's indulgences." At his urging Bulwer read in Schiller's *Cabal and Love,* Marmontel, Goldoni, Macklin's *Man of the World,* Jonson's *Volpone* — but none of these took his fancy.

Not yet ready for critical comedy Bulwer turned once more to the romantic kind, extracting from a French novel an elaborate story of love and danger in the days of Richelieu. The historical setting was fortunate. Macready rejected the romantic comedy forthwith, but the flaming figure of the Great Cardinal impinged more and more upon Bulwer's attention (and Forster's, too, for he was now privy to Bulwer's dramatic plans). The romantic part of the story was reduced to mere auxiliary service. *"You* are Richelieu," Bulwer told Macready in October of 1838; "Richelieu is brought out, accordingly, as the prominent light round which the other satellites move. It is written on the plan of a great Historical Comedy, & I have endeavoured to concentrate a striking picture of the passions & events — the intrigue & ambition of that era." He wrote it twice by mid-November, first in prose and then in verse, but it did not satisfy. Macready found it "deficient in the important point of continuity of interest" and feared privately that (like *Cromwell*) it could never be made effective.

It was Macready who solved the problem, though we can never know exactly how: in an interview on November 17 Macready explained a plan of alterations which "enchanted" and "delighted" Bulwer and stimulated an over-all rewriting of the play. Even so there were painful doubts and endless labors ahead. When Macready read the play to Forster (in Bulwer's presence) that stalwart fellow delivered a crushing blow to the play and almost to the friendship: he fell asleep! Bulwer was so shocked, so disheartened, that he wanted to abandon *Richelieu,* but finding he could not, he reworked it again. In mid-December Macready read it (anonymously) to a half-dozen critical friends, including Robert Browning; their enthusiastic response did not allay Bulwer's fears, and he continued to revise it down to the first of the year. Only the triumphant greenroom reading on January 5 ended all doubts and confirmed *Richelieu* for production.

More than ever before, Bulwer concerned himself with matters of staging. He specified the exact colors and styles of principal costumes; called for scenery to express the splendor of Richelieu's household; described the several forms to serve for the "many papers used by way of writs, despatches &c." He expressed preferences in the casting, sent directives for the actors, and dictated various climactic stage businesses. In his excitement he even attempted to coach Macready — a presumption rarely dared by any other and one which strained Macready's temper.

The fact of the matter was that the actor and the author were in fundamental disagreement as to the character of Richelieu, and Bulwer fought hard to make his view prevail. Macready's conception, derived from his own democratic prejudices and bolstered by the views of Alfred de Vigny, was of a wily despot, hard, dry, and intellectual, with emphasis on his "vanity, and suppleness and craft." He wanted to make him "all vulpine," as Bulwer put it. Bulwer wanted rather to underscore Richelieu's gaiety, his "high physical spirits . . . which, as in Cromwell, can almost approach the buffoon." It had occured to him to provide Richelieu with a court jester, and though he dismissed this stale device he wanted Macready to develop Richelieu as a practical humorist. When Richelieu addresses the mob, Bulwer objected to Macready's unrelieved hauteur. "I think you snub them a little too much in the old play way," he wrote. He wanted Macready to fetch the mob along with jocular touches before cracking the whip at them. Elsewhere he called for the insertion of "a chuckle," a "jovial laugh," a "pointed slyness," a "broad humorous glance" — and at one moment to "make the point more sudden & hearty . . . & absolutely touch his ribs with the forefinger." He might as well have taught his grandmother to milk ducks. Macready, angered by the intrusion, refused to discuss such points, dismissed them privately as tokens of "low farcical point" and "melodramatic rant," clung to his own "more delicate shadings of character," and seriously doubted Bulwer's "taste." Bulwer probably never saw his Richelieu performed as he intended it, at least by Macready; but he would not bear grudges. The inflammatory possibilities of the situation were drowned in the play's overwhelming success.

To have had two successes in a row seems to have unhinged Bulwer's judgment. Now unquestionably the leading dramatist of the day, he assumed the prerogatives of that reputation and reverted to something like the overconfidence in which he first approached the theatre. Snatching up a current French melodrama he hastily worsened it into an English one, and then began to pretend it was a masterpiece. *Norman* it was called, its hero an Elizabethan sea farer. Macready was to perform it, though not to produce it, for he had now abandoned management and hired out as starring actor to Benjamin Webster at the Haymarket. His first response to *Norman* was a flat *"I do not like it."* Bulwer made desultory stabs at other subjects, then converted *Norman* from its English scene to a Spanish one and called it *The Inquisition.* By early autumn at Macready's direction he converted it to the Elizabethan scene again, called it *The Birthright* (presently *The Sea-Captain*), and shortly thereafter sold it to Webster for £600, paid in advance. Impatient of revision he rushed it into print and then anxiously suffered it to go into performance.

The financial triumph was the only reward *The Sea-Captain* was to bring him. It had a longish run, for of course Webster had to keep it on as long as possible in order to earn back his investment; and the general audience, perhaps flattered to be served melodrama from such eminent hands, appears to have sustained it. The critics, however, except for a few partisans, struck it down with reasoned argument or contempt or even outright ridicule.

Though ill and visiting the spas, from Cheltenham to Margate to Aix, Bulwer spent the summer of 1840 in concentrated endeavor to write a really first-rate play. He was now ready for social comedy, along the lines Macready had prescribed for him two years earlier. His first attempt was to be called *Appearances*—"a genteel Comedy of the present day—the Moral, a satire on the way appearances of all kinds impose on the public, you a rogue playing the respectable man—& the Intellect of the play." In early August Macready persuaded him to abandon *Appearances* and gave him in place of it the theme and outline of *Money*. He wrote *Money* while on the Continent, speedily and with assurance, and by mid-September sent it from Brussells complete.

Revisions of detail were to follow in due time, of course, but never from the first night that Macready and Forster read the play together had they the slightest doubt that Bulwer had succeeded. The inadequacy of the performers in rehearsal would cause much worry, and Macready came to detest his own role of Alfred Evelyn, but the play could hardly have failed. In the course of stage preparation, as in the writing, Bulwer emerged at last as the complete professional, sensitive to every detail of casting, dress, and *mise-en-scène*. The success of *Money* made a proper climax to his four-year career in the public theatre, and, regrettably, the ending.

During the years following, Bulwer tried again and again to bring off a play for Macready's uses, but to no avail. He read in dozens of sources. He tried *Cromwell* again. He dreamed of a satire on the Public, set forth in a story about Walpole. He wrote four acts of a society drama called *The Egotists*. He translated *Oedipus the King*. He completed a tragedy on the elder Brutus. He contemplated dramatizations of his own *The Ill-omened Marriage, The Last of the Barons,* and *Harold*. Nothing would do. Yet the many letters exchanged during the decade of the forties are full of interest for their tentative exploration, their promise, and their record of failure.

V

None of the three principals of this book of letters has been accorded thoroughgoing biographical or critical study by modern scholars. The standard work on Bulwer—reliable but critically reserved—is *The Life of Edward Bulwer, First Lord Lytton,* by his grandson, The Earl of Lytton, two volumes (London, 1913). Bulwer's early years, up to but not including his career as playwright, are expertly analyzed by Michael Sadleir in *Bulwer: A Panorama:*

I, Edward and Rosina, 1803-1836 (London, 1931). Brander Matthews' edition of the *Letters of Bulwer-Lytton to Macready* (Newark, 1911) has preserved the bulk of Bulwer's letters to Macready here printed. William Archer's *William Charles Macready* (London, 1890) is the classic biography of the actor. J. C. Trewin's *Mr. Macready, A Nineteenth-Century Tragedian and His Theatre* (London, 1955) is an excellent popular treatment of the subject. The basic materials for the Macready biography are, of course, his own records of his life and work — *Macready's Reminiscences, and Selections from His Diaries and Letters,* edited by Sir Frederick Pollock (London, 1875) ; and *The Diaries of William Charles Macready, 1833-1851,* edited by William Toynbee, two volumes (London, 1912). The only book-length study of Forster is the very informal *John Forster and His Friendships* by Richard Renton, (London, 1912).

The manuscripts of Bulwer's letters to Macready have not, for the most part, been available to me in the assembling of this correspondence. They have disappeared, presumably into the hiding places of collectors, and have eluded every effort to find them. Like the many other correspondences in Macready's possession at the time of his death, this one somehow got out of the family's hands. According to Mrs. Lisa Puckle, Macready's granddaughter, it happened not infrequently in the thirty-five years during which Macready's widow survived him that interested persons would "borrow" from her sets of letters and fail to return them. Later, such letters would be heard of as sold somewhere, especially in America. Such was perhaps the history of the Bulwer letters.

The bulk of them were at one time in the hands of Brander Matthews, for in 1911 he published 105 of them — *Letters of Bulwer-Lytton to Macready* — for the Carteret Book Club of Newark, New Jersey. Matthews' editing was far from satisfactory. It appears that he sometimes "improved" the texts from roughnesses of spelling and punctuation, and his errors of transcription (Bulwer's handwriting is difficult) were numerous. His guesses at dating the letters were often quite wrong. Nonetheless, one must be grateful to Matthews for preserving so much: the text of most of Bulwer's letters to Macready here printed, with such corrections as are obviously in order, is that of the Matthews edition.

Two of Bulwer's letters to Macready concerning *Richelieu,* unknown to Matthews, were once printed by Robert Lytton in an article in the *Fortnightly Review.* A dozen more concerning mainly *The Lady of Lyons,* likewise unknown to Matthews, have wandered off to a separate oblivion, from whence transcribed typewritten copies have emerged in time for inclusion here. One original letter, printed in Toynbee's edition of Macready's *Diaries,* is in the Library of Princeton University. Two original letters are in the Library of the University of Illinois. Two original letters and some manuscript play fragments are in the Forster Library at the Victoria and Albert Museum.

Macready's letters to Bulwer are all taken from the original manuscripts in the Lytton Archives at Knebworth House, Knebworth, Herts. There, too, are preserved all of Bulwer's letters to Forster, Forster's to Bulwer, Webster's to Bulwer, and occasional other items here included. Bulwer's letters to Webster are from manuscripts in the Harvard University Library.

When working from originals I have endeavored to reproduce as faithfully as possible all those carelessnesses of hand and idiosyncrasies of spelling, abbreviation, punctuation, and the like, which give quick letter-writing its personal flavor and sense of immediacy. "Errors" of this sort are usually let stand without editorial comment. The conventional system of italics, small capitals, and large capitals is used to represent the writers' underlining of words one, two, and three times.

All of Macready's letters, all of Bulwer's letters to Macready, and most of the auxiliary letters are printed *entire*. However, in order to avoid needless repetition and typographical clutter, the rubrics of dating, salutation, and farewell have been shorn from the texts, the essentials of identification being reduced to a regularized heading. It should be noted that many of the exchanges between Bulwer and Forster are *not* entire letters, but only relevant excerpts from letters that deal with other matters besides the plays.

I am grateful to the late Harold Hillebrand for having many years ago provided the impetus for this study; to the late Lord Lytton for having given me copies of many of the Macready letters; to Lady Hermione Cobbold, not only for permission to print the Bulwer letters but for making available to me the contents of the Lytton Archives; to Mrs. Lisa Puckle and Brigadier John Macready for permission to print the Macready letters and for kindly advice; to Professors C. C. Gullette, J. F. Heller, Leo Hughes, and Stephen S. Stanton, and to Mr. Boleslav Taborski for assistance in research; to Professors Alan S. Downer, Barnard Hewitt, Gordon Ray, and Wesley Swanson for critical advice; to Mrs. Hobart Peer, the Misses Kate and Judith Shattuck, and Mrs. Harris Wilson for preparation of the manuscript; to Professor Donald Jackson and Miss Rachel Anderson for editorial direction; to the authorities of the Victoria and Albert Museum and the Harvard University Library for permission to print manuscripts from their holdings; to the staff of the Historical Manuscripts Commission, the Houghton Library, the Gabrielle Enthoven Collection, and the Garrick Club for many courtesies.

CHARLES H. SHATTUCK, *University of Illinois, March 3, 1957*

chapter one

1834
1837

The Duchess de la Vallière
and *Cromwell*

The earliest letters of the Bulwer-Macready correspondence that have been preserved are of February and March, 1836, but the personal acquaintance of the two
men had begun nearly a year and a half earlier. The details, here summarized, are
faithfully recorded in Macready's diaries.[1]

In late October, 1834, Macready was playing a brief engagement in Dublin. One
afternoon he walked out to the Military Hospital to visit his old friends, the family
of Colonel D'Aguilar.[2] As he approached the gate, he was met by the Colonel and his
daughter setting out for a drive, and as they paused to chat, Bulwer came by. Introductions were made, and arrangements were set for a dinner party at the D'Aguilars'
two days later.

In reporting the dinner, Macready pays especial attention to Bulwer, "whom I
liked very much"; he found him "quite what Sheil[3] described him, very good-natured,

---

[1] Most of Macready's diary references to Bulwer may be found in William Toynbee's
well-indexed edition of *The Diaries of William Charles Macready*, 2 vols. (London,
1912). But Toynbee omitted numerous passages (including occasional lines about Bulwer) which had already been printed by Sir Frederick Pollock in *Macready's Reminiscences and Selections from His Diaries and Letters* (New York and London, 1875).
I shall assume that the date of the event is sufficient guidance for the curious reader
who wishes to examine Macready's original statements in their diary context.

[2] Sir George Charles D'Aguilar (1784-1855), deputy adjutant-general at Dublin from
1830 to 1841, later distinguished for leadership in military action in China, knighted in
1852. A devoted theatre-goer, he translated one of Schiller's tragedies — *Fiesko; or, The
Conspiracy of Genoa* — which was performed and published in Dublin in 1832.

[3] Richard Lalor Sheil (1791-1851), Irish lawyer, dramatist, and politician, noted for
extraordinary eloquence in the House of Commons; Master of the Mint in Lord John
Russell's government, 1846-50; British Minister at Florence at the end of his life. Macready created leading roles in five of his plays — *The Apostate, Bellamira, Evadne,
Montoni,* and *The Huguenot* — between 1817 and 1822. Macready and Sheil were
devoted friends.

17

and, of course, intelligent." During the course of the evening he urged Bulwer to write a play and was pleased to find that Bulwer's thoughts had already tended that way: "he told me he had written one, great part of which was lost, on the death of Cromwell." At the end of the party Bulwer drove him to his Dublin lodgings, expressing the hope that they might soon meet in London.

Seven months later, on May 31, 1835, John Forster brought them together again at one of his bachelor dinners, in the company of a dozen eminent artists and men of letters. "Pleasant day," says Macready, but he records no talk of playwriting. The following two Sundays Macready gave dinners at Elstree, and Bulwer was invited for June 14. But on June 9 the diary reports with a sting: "Letter from Bulwer at some length, excusing himself from dining here on Sunday. One expression in his letter I disliked — the 'honour of my acquaintance.' My acquaintance can be no honour to such a man as Bulwer, and it almost sounds like irony." The temper of this entry is habitual to Macready. It reflects both his morbid fear of "cuts" because of his anomalous social position as an actor, and his intense respect for Bulwer's enormous literary prestige. On June 19 he left his card at Bulwer's, but thereafter he pursued the acquaintance no further.

Bulwer, however, appears to have been thinking of Macready long and often. Some eight months later, on February 23, 1836, he called Macready to him to announce that he had written a play, that its hero was designed for Macready to act, and that the published book would be dedicated to him.[4] Macready's record of the visit provides us, incidentally, an amusing glimpse of the novelist in his habit as he lived. "Called on Bulwer, whom I found in very handsome chambers in the Albany, dressed, or rather *déshabillé*, in the most lamentable style of foppery — a hookah in his mouth, his hair, whiskers, tuft, etc., all grievously cared for. I felt deep regret to see a man of such noble and profound thought yield for a moment to pettiness so unworthy of him. His manner was frank, manly and cordial in the extreme — so contradictory of his appearance. He told me, after talking about the *Provost of Bruges* and recalling our conversation in Dublin, that he had written a play; that he did not know whether I might think the part intended for me worthy of my powers, for that inevitably the weight of the action fell upon the woman, that the subject was La Vallière. He handed me a paper in which I read that it was dedicated to myself. It almost affected me to tears. I could not read it. He wished me to read the play, give my opinion, and that he would make any alterations I might suggest. I appointed to see him tomorrow." The event was momentous with hope for Macready, and it occurred when he sorely needed a lift to his spirits. For two seasons he had been struggling through an engagement as principal tragedian at Drury Lane, at a time when popular taste for "the legitimate" was rapidly vitiating on a diet of melodrama, menagerie acts, and operatic spectacle; and he was serving under the managership of Alfred Bunn,[5] enduring every inconvenience and indignity which that cheerful scoundrel could put upon him. The engagement was to come to an end very soon, and in unexpected violence. But at the moment he was aware only that Bunn was hastening to break off the run of his latest

---

[4] The complimentary page, as printed in the first edition, reads: "Dedicated / to / W. C. Macready, esq., / for science and genius / unsurpassed in his profession / and / from whom the artists, / of what profession soever, / may learn that / art is the poetry of nature, / expressing / the true / through the medium of / the ideal.

[5] Alfred Bunn (1798-1860) was one of the worst managers ever to control the major houses of London. After being stage manager at Drury Lane under Elliston in 1823, he spent several years speculating in theatre management in the provinces. During the season of 1833-34 he took control of both Drury Lane and Covent Garden, a venture which failed. He continued at Drury Lane a few seasons, but by 1840 he was bankrupt. His main contribution was to the development of English opera.

hope of reasserting his actorship — G. W. Lovell's *The Provost of Bruges.*[6] Now here was Bulwer, the first novelist of the day, enlisting in his cause.

When he returned to his rooms after the performance that night he found the manuscript of *La Vallière* waiting for him. He read it at once and was pleased. "What talent he possesses!"

The next day he excused himself from the promised visit to Bulwer in order to restudy the play "very attentively" and make up notes for revision. On this day too he spoke to Manager Bunn about it — keeping the author's name secret, as Bulwer had insisted — and extracted tentative promise of royalty up to £500, payable in equal installments on the third, sixth, ninth, sixteenth, and twenty-fifth nights.

On February 25 he called on Bulwer to report — "and found him less carefully set up than on my former visit. We talked over the play, and I mentioned my objections, at the same time suggesting some remedies. He yielded to all readily except the fifth act; upon that he seemed inclined to do battle, but at length I understood him to yield. . . . He wished me to write my remarks and send them to him, for which purpose he would return me the MS." On Saturday Macready went at the job in earnest. He found himself increasingly perplexed between its "smooth" reading and its probable weakness for "effect in representation."

The play, which derives from the career of Louise de la Vallière, mistress of Louis XIV, was suggested to Bulwer by a novel on the subject by the Comtesse de Genlis.[7] The purpose of the play, like that of the novel, is not to re-create the historical facts (which are remote and unimportant enough) but to create a tragic moral struggle out of "la funeste influence d'une passion coupable sur la destinée d'une femme sensible et née pour la vertue." The action of the play, *as we now read it,* runs as follows. In Act I, Louise is shown on the eve of her departure for the Sun King's court. She is betrothed to the Marquis de Bragelone (the Macready character), a rugged old soldier and family friend. She is not in love with Bragelone, however, and puts off his affectionate addresses with vague response. The act closes at Fontaine-bleau, with Louis choosing her as his mistress, having been led to this choice through the conniving of the Duke de Lauzun, who sees in the innocent girl a tool for getting royal favors. In Act II, which takes place some while after, Bragelone, who has spent the interim in camp and battlefield and has heard rumors of Louise's fall from virtue, comes to her rescue. He persuades her to flee to a nunnery. But Louis pursues her and woos her back again. Thus far Louise's practical fortunes are ascendant. In Act III she is driven downward, practically and morally both. The wicked Lauzun has found her too honest to be useful, and abetted by the ambitious Mme. de Montespan he alienates Louise from the King. At the close of the act Louis gives public sign that Louise is abandoned and Montespan has been awarded her place. Then in the beginning of Act IV, Lauzun proposes to marry Louise himself. So vicious a liaison is the worst that could befall her, but it provides the impulse toward her moral rehabilitation: she rejects him. Then Bragelone returns, once more to labor for her salvation. By now he has become a Franciscan friar. After three scenes of Bragelone's moral haranguing, two of them devoted to Louise and one to telling off the King, he carries her away a second time to the nunnery. In Act V, Evil is dispersed and Good

---

[6] George William Lovell (1804-78), secretary of an insurance company, and playwright. *The Provost of Bruges: a tragedy, in five acts* (London, 1836) was a study of political life in the twelfth century, which not even Macready liked much, except for its republican sentiments. Bunn cut off its run after the eighth night to avoid accretion of royalty; Lovell had to sue Bunn for the £200 owing him. Lovell wrote successful plays — *The Wife's Secret* (1846) and *The Trial of Love* (1852) — for Charles Kean.

[7] Stéphanie Félicité Ducrest de Saint-Aubin, Comtesse de Genlis (1746-1830): *La Duchesse de la Vallière suivie de sa Vie Penitente,* 2 vols. (Paris, 1804).

is triumphant. Lauzun and Montespan quarrel with each other and lose the King's favor. Louis repents, pursues Louise to the nunnery, and tries again to woo her. But she is adamant in virtue: the play closes with the ceremony of her taking the veil.

Now obviously there is not much in this for Macready as actor: the action belongs mainly to Louise, Louis, and Lauzun, and the Bragelone character can only operate from the perimeter. Nonetheless Macready strove hard to help improve the play — strengthening his own role, to be sure — but generally reorganizing its construction for better stage effect. His most valuable contribution was to insist inexorably that Louis should pursue Louise the second time, to the very end of the play. Bulwer resisted this action in the name of "probability," naïvely wanting to depend upon pageant and spectacle to bring off the finale. But he capitulated. This is but the first of many instances of his taking instruction from Macready in the manipulation of stage actions.

It is perhaps a credit to the generosity and sense of both men that Bulwer offered to "give the ending" to Macready by way of a death-scene for Bragelone and Macready would not have it.

The extant correspondence commences with Macready's first critique of *La Vallière* and Bulwer's response to it. Macready is careful not to praise too much, and his suggestions for revision are vividly theatrical; Bulwer accepts correction swiftly and cheerfully except for "the grand difficulty of Act 5," where he stands his ground with all the reasons he can muster.

1. MACREADY TO BULWER, *Elstree, February 28,* [*1836*]

The more I dwell upon this play, the more reluctant I become to propose any alteration. The picture of manners it presents, the variety of its characters, the charm of its language and its truth of passion give to its perusal in its present state so lively an interest, that I distrust my judgement in trying its probable effects before an audience by the too fallible test of my experience. I have never in any previous instance so distrusted myself: all I can hope is that some, among my remarks, may be worthy your attention.

Act 1st — The abruptness of La Valliere's announcement at Court imme-diately after seeing her about to depart from her distant home is, I think, too perceptible.

The prize drawn by Montespan would be objected to. Qu. — Should not the audience be prepared in some degree for La Valliere's passion by some previous expression of her sentiments of enthusiastic and devoted loyalty — a sort of second religion in her heart, of which she readily becomes the victim?

It appears to me that the future scenes between La Valliere & Bragelone would receive an accession of interest from their engagement being more dwelt on in their parting interview: some token given would add to his motives for seeking her in the fourth act, and heighten the pathos of that scene, where he might return it to her.

Act 2nd — Might not the departure of Bragelone with La Valliere, rescuing her, as he believes he does, from shame & sorrow, be marked by stronger ex-pression of triumph and affection?

Act 4th — Qu. — Should not the meeting between Bragelone and La Valliere be productive of more striking effect? it ends by their retirement to a chamber, of which the audience knows nothing until the next act. — Two characters, in such relation to each other, at such a point of the story, could not meet without raising the expectation of the audience very high.

Bragelone's passing over the stage does not appear necessary, and is injurious to the effect of the character.

Act 5th — It is with extreme diffidence I offer my opinion upon this act: — and while I fear the too long protraction of the catastrophe, I doubt the method of concentrating the interest, which I venture to submit.
Scene 1st — I should propose to be that, which now is Scene 4th — between Montespan, Lauzun etc — heightened perhaps a little.
Scene 2nd — to be what now is Scene 5th — between Bragelone & La Valliere, strengthened, and introducing that passage of Bragelone's sorrow over her, as she is fainting in his arms — in Scene 3rd.
Scene 3d — The Exterior of the Convent — the Court passing to the ceremony, and that part of the last scene introduced, in which Lauzun gives Montespan her dismissal.
Scene 4th — & Last. The Church of the Convent —

The rites interrupted by the King's sudden entrance — He insists on speaking with her while yet it is possible, and the strength of Scenes 2 & 3 — is here introduced — he leaves her as in Scene 3d — La Valliere's request of forgiveness from the Queen is translated from Scene 1st — and the conclusion remains.

2. BULWER TO MACREADY, *Albany, Tuesday, [March 1], 1836*[8]

I have received your kind note. What you propose in the second act is already done. What you propose in the fourth I am about.

Now for the first Act. The intermediate Scene required to break the suddenness of the transition (which suddenness I acknowledge) is attended with great difficulty — not to incur the same suddenness. Two scenes only occur to me, one between Bragelone & the mother — or one between Bragelone & the King — if the last, Bragelone must not disclose his love, which is incompatible with the subsequent conduct of the Play. Should neither of these please you, can you suggest any dominant emotion or passion to call forth? I do not see my way clearly to strong effect — I don't know, in fact, what to make the talkers say! any hints would be very acceptable. Now to the grand difficulty of Act 5. After much consideration I am not able to persuade myself to the introduction of the King in the scene of the taking the Veil. Not that I care about the His-

---

[8] The ending of this letter has been lost.
Bulwer was often careless in dating his letters, and Brander Matthews' guesses, made without benefit of the external evidence now available, were generally chaotic. This letter, for instance, which Matthews buries as number X, is inevitably of March 1, 1836, and is the earliest preserved in the Bulwer series. Further corrections to Matthews' datings will usually be indicated in brackets and without comment.

torical truth. But I do not think the more sacred Law of the Probabilities would allow the evident breach of the Probable — in Louis delaying so long his interference — knowing by the Presence of the Queen & publicity of the occasion — the very day of the ceremony. Either he would come before, or I must prepare the way for him by painting his struggles in a separate Scene which the limits of the play w^d not allow. I fear too that the audience could not get over the Publicity of so great an assemblage & so solemn a scene, to an interview that should be so private. Louis would naturally ask (if he did come) to see her in another room. — Moreover, the effect is taken from the dread repose of the Ceremony, & perhaps — if Louis's grief were powerfully painted — the sympathies would be diverted to him from Bragelone & La V. Should we therefore defer his parting interview with La V., we might do it thus: Scene 1st as you suggest — Montespan, Lauzun, &c.

Scene 2. Chateau. Bragelone & La Vallière & his exclamations over La V. when insensible. Then we might introduce the King seeking her at the Chateau.

The next scene — the exterior of the Convent, Lauzun & Montespan.

Last scene as it stands.

Or else

Instead of seeking her at the Chateau there might be a scene before she takes the veil — of a cell in the Convent — and the King coming to her — followed by Scene the last. I have thought of another alteration or addition that might doubtless be affecting in itself — as it would fall in your hands. But I fear it would take from the sterner points of Bragelone's character, and mar the harmony of the Denouement. However, I mention it at present merely as a suggestion — Between the last interview of Bragelone & La Vallière and the Convent scene — Suppose that we introduce one of a burial ground in view of the convent & a gravedigger employed at a grave. — Bragelone — ill and declining — purchases that grave which is directly in front of the Convent windows. — Then, instead of ending the Play with the Present Ceremonial, to follow that scene by one of Bragelone's Death by this grave — as if he had only survived to fulfill a duty, & had no further business with life.

By curtailments as to the Queen & King. . . .

During their conference on February 25, Bulwer had been amiable about alterations, but demanding about finances. "We talked over terms," Macready relates. "He was not satisfied with Bunn's proposal, but added to that £200 down, and to be paid through the two following seasons £5 per night, after which the copyright to revert to him. This is rather a hard bargain; I do not think Bunn will concede so much." Some years before, Bulwer had put through Parliament a bill for the protection of dramatic authors;[9] he was now disposed to profit by the bill and to set an example for other

---

[9] The activities of Bulwer's Parliamentary Committee of Enquiry in 1832-33 are described in the Earl of Lytton's *The Life of Edward Bulwer, First Lord Lytton,* 2 vols. (London, 1913), I, 427-38.

playwrights to follow. Unfortunately, his ignorance of the economics and other practical realities of the theatre was now to lead him into a cul-de-sac. On March 1,
Macready again pressed Bunn for an acceptance, but Bunn "would say nothing, *until
he knew the author.*" Bunn, of course, was merely amused at the idea of taking on an
anonymous play, sight unseen, at extraordinarily dear terms. In his reminiscences,
published a few years after, he puts Macready's overtures and Bulwer's demands in
the most ridiculous light, simply by reporting them:

In the beginning of March, this year of 1836, Mr. Macready came into my room,
and with a self-satisfied smile said,

"What will you give me for a first-rate play by a first-rate man?"

"A first-rate price," said I; "and who's your friend?"

"I am not at liberty to mention names," answered he.

"Then send me the piece, and you shall have my answer in four-and-twenty hours,"
said I.

"I do not think the author will do that," rejoined he.

"Pray, have *you* read it?" inquired Pilgarlick.

"I have, and think very highly of it," answered he.

"Well, doctors, you know, may differ; and I should like to know upon what grounds
I, who have all the risks to run, am to be deprived of the same opportunity of judging
accorded to you, who are a comparative cipher in the affair," said I.[10]

The next day Macready called on Bulwer again — "and evidently came on him by
surprise; he could not well avoid seeing me; indeed he did not demur, though evidently
a little discomposed. He was in complete déshabillé — a white nightcap on his head,
looking like a head of Gay or some poet of that time — it was a picture; his busts,
papers, etc., around him, and the unornamented man of genius undandified. I told
him of Bunn's desire to know the author's name before he committed himself, and that
I could not counsel it, as I knew Mr. B_____ to be *utterly faithless and treacher-
ous.*" Macready urged him rather to let Bunn see the manuscript. But this concession,
oddly, was unthinkable to Bulwer. He would let his name be mentioned, but no more.
"He at last commissioned me to give his name to Mr. Bunn, but would not consent to
his seeing the play to judge of it; the price down was for *his name.*"

3. MACREADY TO BULWER, *61 Lincolns Inn Fields, March 4,* [1836]

The play has received a great increase of interest and power in the improvements you have made, in my humble opinion: — the scene itself between
Bragelone & his servant is Characteristic and good, but in its effect upon the
subsequent interviews with La Vallière of the greatest value: — it has heightened very much the character. The introduction in the fourth act I think most
beautiful & cannot fail to produce strong effect.— Why have we not such
works as these, instead of translations from Scribe,[11] upon our stage? — I saw
Bunn yesterday afternoon, but his mind was exhausted by its efforts on Chevy
Chase, and he could not turn to things of less moment; I was to see him after
Virginius, and then I suppose he was rapt in the enjoyment of the spectacle,
which was going on, for I could not find him.

---

[10] Alfred Bunn: *The Stage: Both Before and Behind the Curtain,* 3 vols. (London,
1840), II, 169-70.

[11] Eugène Scribe (1791-1861), the French dramatist. His opera, *La Juive,* adapted by
James Robinson Planché as *The Jewess,* was a great success at Drury Lane in the 1836-37
season. Planché was also the author of the melodramatic spectacle, *Chevy Chase,* which
Macready mentions here.

I shall endeavour to catch him this morning, or, if not, tomorrow.

I return the papers — having been extremely gratified in reading them.

Macready saw Bunn on the following day and "delivered Bulwer's proposal of his play without being looked at. Bunn refused, but said he would write to Bulwer." As Bunn reports it, "I took the liberty of saying that although Mr. Bulwer might be considered a first-rate novelist, he could not possibly be considered a first-rate dramatist, and that I declined making any such blind bargain."[12]

4. MACREADY TO BULWER, *Lincolns Inn Fields, March 5,* [1836]

I would have called on you to day, if it had been in my power, but I am driven to the very last minute in preparing to leave Town tomorrow morning.

I have seen Mr. Bunn, and stated your unwillingness to give the M.S. out of your hands dependent on the will of any person to accept or decline it: — he is averse to make a contract without leave to form his own judgement of the work. He is in possession of my sentiments on the subject, but contends for his own right of judging: at the same time he adds, that he should not be likely to treat in an ordinary manner a work of yours, and upon his suggesting the more direct course, as I must leave town, of addressing you himself on the subject, I acquiesced in it — I hope not contrary to your wish. You may therefore expect to hear from him to the effect I have mentioned. — I hope, though much doubt, that an arrangement may be made. —

He is to let me know at Bath, if the play is to be put in hand, but you will perhaps oblige me with a word of information on the subject, as one on which I am particularly anxious.

The exchange of letters between Bunn and Bulwer is stiffly resistant. They are to each other "Sir," and "Your obedient servant," and they make points at each other more like public debaters than fellow artists seeking to come to agreement.

5. BUNN TO BULWER, *Theatre Royal, Drury Lane, March 5, 1836*[13]

While I am aware that my reply to your communication made by Mr. Macready should pass through that channel to you, I have been induced, by his request & with the view of saving time, to trouble you with a direct answer.

I am flattered by your desire to produce one of your works at this theatre; & if I am not equally flattered by the prohibition attached to its production I still have no reason to complain of it. But, as during the many years I have been connected with the London stage, I have had to decide, as every manager ought, on the quality or fitness of what he produces, & has to pay for, and as the most distinguished dramatic writers of the last 25 years have invariably done me the honor to request my judgment, humble as it is, I must decline, with much respect, being the medium of placing on the Stage a work, by whomsoever written, on the composition of which I am not wished to decide.

If it should be your pleasure to allow me a perusal of the play, (as there

---

[12] Bunn, *The Stage,* II, 169-70.
[13] Original in the Knebworth Archives.

Plate 1. Edward Bulwer about 1834, shortly before he began his career as playwright.

Plate 2. William Charles Macready about 1843, from an engraving of a miniature by Robert Thorburn.

Plate 3. John Forster about 1840, from a drawing by Daniel Maclise.

Plate 4. "Hot Cross Bunn." A cartoon celebrating the knockdown fight between Macready and Bunn in Bunn's Drury Lane office on April 29, 1836.

Plate 5. The Lady of Lyons, a scene from Act II, drawn by George Scharf, from *Recollections of the Scenic Effects of Covent Garden Theatre,* London, 1839.

Plate 6. Richelieu, Act. I, Scene ii, drawn by George Scharf, from *Recollections of the Scenic Effects of Covent Garden Theatre,* London, 1839.

Plate 7. The piquet scene from Act III of *Money*. From the Lowne Collection of Macreadiana in the Library of the Garrick Club.

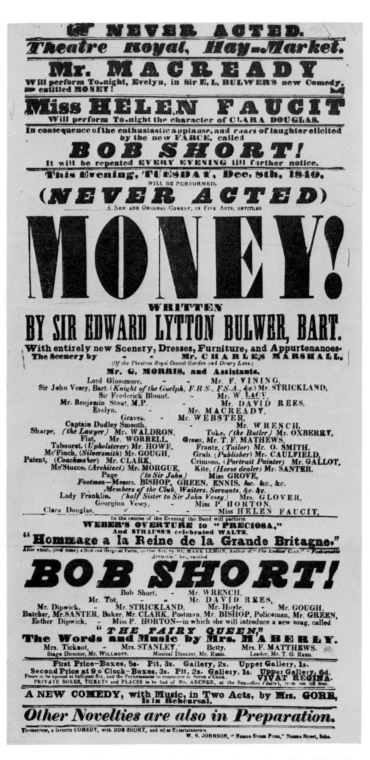

Plate 8. First night playbill of *Money*, from the Gabrielle Enthoven Collection of the Victoria and Albert Museum.

is no time to be lost in fixing Mr. Macready's next character) I hope I need not add that my high respect for your literary station would not admit of my slighting, or hastily disputing, the pretensions of the work in question.

6. BULWER TO BUNN, *Albany, March 7, 1836*[14]

Before I reply to the more business part of your letter, allow me to set both parties right with regard to a seeming misunderstanding. *I made* no communications. I rather imagine I was the person who *received* them. I had an offer from another theatre. Previous to my decision, I felt obliged (according to an old promise) to show the play to Mr. Macready, and in some measure to allow him the first choice. Mr. Macready professed himself so much pleased with the play, that he wrote me word he would speak to you, concealing my name. He afterwards called on me and made certain propositions, which I considered fair and liberal, but which I was obliged to modify in some instances, viz. to limit the copyright to the theatre to three years, and to require a certain portion of the money on giving the MS., though perfectly willing, should the play fail of an adequate run, to return it.

With regard to showing the MS. to you, sir, in your capacity of manager, while I allow it quite natural in you to wish to see the play before you produce it, yet, having in no instance since my first publication, allowed the purchaser to inspect any work of mine in MS., having always found such reputation as I may possess a sufficient guarantee for its contents; so, on the other hand, it is natural for me not to depart from a rule hitherto carefully maintained on one side, and cheerfully complied with on the other. Nor can it be from any want of respect for your judgment, or deficiency in courtesy to yourself, that I am compelled to adhere to this maxim. Had I the pleasure of your personal acquaintance, and had you not been the manager of a theatre, I might naturally have wished to benefit from the suggestions of a longer dramatic experience than my own.

I fear, as it is, that our difference upon this point will constitute an insuperable objection to the arrangements between us, unless any middle course could be suggested, which is only likely to arise from a personal interview on the matter. At present I shall take leave to consider the negotiation begun by Mr. Macready at an end. . . .

P.S.— When I consented to the request of Mr. Macready to mention to you my name, I did so on the understanding, which, no doubt, he communicated to you, that it was a strictly private and confidential communication.

7. BUNN TO BULWER, *Drury Lane, March 8, [1836]*[15]

I am favoured with your letter, and think it right to follow your own example of being explicit.

---

[14] Bunn printed this letter in *The Stage*, II, 171-72, with liberal italicizing of statements he found astonishing.

[15] Original in the Knebworth Archives.

I mean no disrespect to one party or the other when I frankly state that I would not produce a play on the opinion of *any* performer. They direct their views, generally, to an *individual* character — a manager directs his to *all*, & therefore Mr. Macready could have no "choice" beyond his acting station. I think it will be admitted that a great difference exists between the purchase by a publisher of the work of an Established Writer in one branch of Literature & the production by a Manager, of such Writer's work in another branch. The public looks to the Director as well as to the Author, & I question if he is not the most assailable — I *know* he is the most assailed. As respect the terms I beg to state that the highest given to the most successful authors are £300 for 9 nights, £100 more for the 20th & £100 for the 50th. Mr. Macready suggested some slight alteration to which there seemed to be no great objection.

But these terms imply a right, in perpetuity, to the Theatre's performing such play — If that right is to be limited, the terms would naturally and proportionably be reduced.

People are apt to attach but little importance to the perusal of a play by a Manager — but if he does his duty it is a task of great labour & responsibility. *I* seldom undertake such tasks — when I *have* done so, the performances arising therefrom have been, it may not be presumptuous to assert, successful. It will gratify me, at any time, to have a personal interview — but as it is impossible to deviate from the system upon which I, as well as my predecessors, have invariably acted, it must rest with yourself to determine what such interview shall lead to.

Mr. Macready did *not* impose any secrecy upon me, but I shall feel bound, if you desire, to maintain it.

Unquestionably Bunn was in the right to decline to "buy what the profane call a *pig in a poke*," as he jocularly puts it; and Bulwer was not even quite honest in his pretensions of having "had an offer from another theatre." After a letter or two more, Bunn tells us, the matter was dropped.[16]

By now Macready had gone to Bath to commence his Spring tour of the provinces. There on March 10, "Received a letter from Bulwer, apprising me of the expected termination of negotiation with Mr. Bunn on the subject of his play, and wishing me to impress on Mr. Bunn that the communication was confidential — also desiring to be informed of the extent of my engagement with Bunn, and whether I should be at liberty to enter into any other with Mr. Osbaldiston;[17] further inquiring as to the possibility of Morris's acceptance of the play."

8. MACREADY TO BULWER, *2 Queen Square, Bath, March 10, 1836*

It is throwing away words to comment on Mr. Bunn's proceedings, at least in one who knows the man's character as well as I unfortunately do. I particularly rejoice, that he has not seen the M.S. and will certainly, though I

---

[16] Bunn, *The Stage*, II, 173. Here and at random in his three volumes, Bunn savages the "intellectuals" who sought to impose upon the London theatre in the 1830's.

[17] D. W. Osbaldiston, manager of Covent Garden Theatre in 1836 and 1837.

decline writing to him on my own affairs, address a letter to him by this days post on the subject of the communication being considered confidential — not that an oath upon the best Bible or the most holy relic in Christendom would have any retentive power for him.

My engagement with him dates to the 27th May, which would be too late to enter upon another at Covent Garden. — As I before hinted to you, I think the costume, the nature of the interest, and the cleverness of the scenes in the play adapt it admirably for the Haymarket, where, I should imagine, it would be worth Mr. Morris's[18] while to engage his company with reference to it. I do not think any one but Miss E. Tree[19] could perform the heroine, as the stage at present stands: — if you made any arrangement with Mr. Morris (who, I should apprise you, is a dull and uninformed man) and that you still retained the wish that I should make one of your characters, I would not let the question of amount of compensation be a hindrance. I mention this, because Mr. Morris would be alarmed perhaps at the thought of having to pay me the terms I have hitherto demanded from him.

I know so little of the Covent Garden company, and what I do know is so little in its favour, that I cannot promise to offer an opinion on the expediency of entrusting a play to them.

At Exeter on March 16 Macready received the next budget of news. "Bulwer seems keen after money," he comments. "He does not let the grass grow under his feet."

9. BULWER TO MACREADY, *Albany, Monday, March [14], 1836*

On receiving your kind letter, I sent for Mr Morris, & after some conversation he agreed to write to you. He has this day called on me, much disturbed by not receiving an answer. After as frank a communication as I could obtain with him, he seemed to imagine that the salary of 30£ *per week* contingent on the success of the play was the utmost he could afford — calculating on the probability of playing the piece every night. I make his engagement with you a *sine qua non;* that settled, my own terms I shall conclude to his satisfaction. Now I know well that this salary is not adequate to your merits or celebrity & I have only therefore to request that on no consideration of personal courtesy or kindness to me, you will suffer it to influence you to the prejudice of other arrangements & the detriment of your own interests. — Perhaps you will be kind eno' to relieve the agitated mind of Mr Morris by a Yes or No — as little influenced as possible by your favourable inclinations toward myself.

Hoping to hear from you *au plutôt.* . . .

The proposed arrangements for a summer season production of *La Vallière* under Morris at the Haymarket looked encouraging for the moment.

---

[18] D. E. Morris, then manager of the Haymarket Theatre.

[19] Ellen Tree (1805-80), an important actress of leading roles at this time; made her debut at Covent Garden in 1829; married Charles Kean in 1842 and performed with him throughout his management of the Princess's Theatre, 1851-59, and on his American tours.

10. BULWER TO MACREADY, *Knebworth Park, Stevenage, Herts., March 25, 1836*

I cannot say how obliged & touched I am by your kindness, nor how completely I understand the liberal and delicate spirit which pervades it.

I conclude now that the affair is settled, as Mr Morris himself wishes the Play to appear the 1st of June. Other details you can settle with him.

Perhaps you will, by & by, inform me how long your other and more valuable engagements will allow you to remain at the Haymarket, should the play succeed.

If sufficiently encouraged by results, I shall seriously think of Dramatic composition & hope in a grander subject & the exhibition of loftier passions to embody a character more suited to your powers than Bragelone. I suppose in the casting of the Parts, Louis will fall to F. Vining,[20] & I think, with training, Webster[21] might refine himself into at least the best Lauzun we could get.

11. MACREADY TO BULWER, *Exeter, March 28, [1836]*

My answer to Mr. Morris, written at the moment I received his letter, when indeed scarcely able to write, will satisfy you on every point of yours, which reached me after the play last night.

The desire of seeing your name added to the list of those, who have raised our dramatic literature so high, has alone influenced me in my correspondence with that gentleman. I told him as much with my opinion of your play, and merely required from him the salary he mentioned to you, which, if sufficient, is barely so for my ordinary expenses.— I also stated to him the necessity there was for the production of the play immediately upon my liberation from Drury Lane; but this, with other matters of detail, can be arranged on my return to Town.

You have drawn so largely on my gratitude, that it is almost impossible my motives can appear disinterested; I have therefore, only the generosity of your own nature to rely upon for belief in less selfish feelings, than may seem to actuate me.

12. MACREADY TO BULWER, *Elstree, Herts., March 29, 1836*

I would have waited your return to Town before troubling you further, but under the apprehension that you may perhaps be in correspondence with Mr.

---

[20] Frederick Vining (1790?-1871), a comic actor who made his London debut in 1813, later served as stage manager at the Haymarket and elsewhere, and was a member of Macready's Covent Garden companies, 1837-39. He was brother to James Vining and uncle to George Vining, who were better known actors than he. The part of King Louis was actually played by John Vandenhoff.

[21] Benjamin Nottingham Webster (1797-1882), a leading comedian and character actor who made his London debut in 1819, and later was dramatist and manager as well. During his management of the Haymarket Theatre (1837-53) he frequently employed Macready, and there he produced Bulwer's *The Sea-Captain* and *Money*. He did not play Lauzun, but the very minor role of de Montespan.

Morris on the subject of the cast of characters, I beg to say a few words (if unnecessary, you will excuse them) to put you on your guard in deciding upon this important measure.

You should stipulate for the aid of Farren,[22] who, I should suppose, would give his cooperation to a name like yours: — I have something of a horror of Webster in such a part as Lauzun, and think Vining, feeble as he may be, would be nearer to the resemblance: — he would, I think, be overweighed by the part of Louis, which some one like Ward or Cooper[23] (as our Muster roll of actors now stands) maugre your antipathy should perform.

My engagements are not yet fixed as to time, but I shall be careful to arrange them so as to give me, if needed, the month of July at least.

It is unnecessary to add that I am proud and happy in the estimate you put upon my humble endeavours to win you to the cause of our declining art, and earnestly wish they were more deserving of it.

Early in April, Macready and Morris disagreed over terms of engagement, and plans for *La Vallière* fell to the ground.

13. MORRIS TO BULWER, *Suffolk Street, Pall Mall East, April 4, 1836*[24]

Having just received a letter from Mr. Macready in reply to mine on the subject of his engagement at the Haymarket in which he states "that I must not count upon his Services beyond the end of July, or, perhaps, a week in August, and that he will not play in any other Piece" than yours,— I beg to apprize you, that I have written to Mr. Macready to acquaint him that I must decline such an engagement.

14. MACREADY TO BULWER, *Elstree, Herts., April 5, 1836*

You will very probably have received from Mr. Morris an intimation of the unsuccessful close of our negotiation before this can reach you; but lest he should have omitted to communicate to you his decision on this point, I think it right to put you in possession of it.— When I have the pleasure of seeing you, I shall, in a very few words, show you, that his expectations of advantage from

---

[22] William Farren (1786-1861), an extremely popular comic actor, especially of old men's parts (Sir Peter Teazle, Shallow, Malvolio, Polonius, and the like), made his London debut in 1818. He was tutor and promoter of Helen Faucit, whose mother was his mistress for many years before their marriage in 1856.

[23] Ward was an unimportant actor in Bunn's company this season, of whom Macready observes that he drank nearly a bottle of gin every night.

John Cooper (1790-1870), a second-rate actor who made his London debut in 1811, and who since the fall of 1833 had been Bunn's stage manager at Drury Lane, doing, as he once said, "Mr. Bunn's dirty work." In order to avoid contact with Bunn, Macready addressed his business affairs to Cooper but disliked him with increasing intensity. "Wooden-headed," "incompetent booby," "dull-brained clod" are typical of Macready's ephithets for him. Cooper retired in 1858, being then of Charles Kean's company at the Princess's Theatre.

[24] Original in the Knebworth Archives.

an engagement with me were founded on no principle of reciprocity, and were such as I could not for one instant think of submitting to.

I need not repeat that I regret the chance which deprives me of the pleasure I should feel in endeavoring to do justice to your conceptions; but I may assure you, that it is only in reference to yourself, I could desire to have made the proposed agreement at the Haymarket Theatre. I shall not take less interest in the event of the appearance of La Valliere, than if I had been a party in it, and with the warmest wishes for its success, even to the height of your own hopes, I am, my dear Sir. . . .

15. MACREADY TO BULWER, *Elstree, Herts., April 7, 1836*

The few remarks I made on Mr. Morris, when suggesting the Haymarket Theatre to your consideration, were intended to prepare you for a very capricious and unreasonable person: I regret that he should have borne out in this instance the general opinion entertained of him. I wrote to you at Knebworth, mentioning the receipt of his letter.— I have nothing to add (for I need not trouble you here with minute explanations) except that his expectations were really preposterous, and such as I could not have answered, even had I engaged to do so.

I grieve at and groan under the state in which our drama is — taken from the individuals, who alone ought to have voices in its direction, and committed to the tender mercies of fools, sharpers, and bankrupts.— Are its "wholesome days" never to return? — I will seize the first opportunity I may have in Town of endeavouring to find you at the Albany, & report to you the exact offer of Mr. Morris.

Meanwhile other events were shaping toward a strange catastrophe. Late in March, even before Macready returned from the country, Manager Bunn began a series of demands upon him which he construed as personal affronts, or even as calculated gestures to drive him out of his Drury Lane engagement. First came orders, received at Exeter, that on Easter Monday he was to play Richard III — a part he disliked and had long since abandoned. On April 16, to his own shame and the indignation of his friends, he was compelled to play *William Tell* cut down to an afterpiece. Then, on April 27, the bills announced that on the twenty-ninth he would play "The first three acts of *Richard III*." For two days Macready chewed his wrath, exacerbated not a little by the commiseration of his friends and acquaintances. The Garrick Club buzzed over this "scandalous and insulting proceeding." Somehow or other, when the night came, he went through the mutilated performance, though there boiled within him a "pent-up feeling of anger, shame, and desperate passion." As he was leaving the stage he passed Bunn's office, opened the door, saw Bunn sitting at his table: he leaped into the room, called him a "damned scoundrel," slapped his face, knocked him down and pummeled him, and was in turn knocked down and pummeled and got his finger bitten, until rescuers arrived.

Macready suffered untellable miseries over his dreadful behavior — including the shame of having the case heard in court and being fined £150 and costs. But the fact is that his disgrace was his making. Popular sympathy was on his side — the public and the profession rather rejoiced in the event. Offers of starring engagements poured in from everywhere, and on May 6 he concluded terms with Osbaldiston for fifteen nights in a month at Covent Garden, at £20 a night. Bulwer attempted to follow him with *La Vallière*, of course, but the new star rather than the new play was what the box-office required, and, besides, Macready had brought with him the novelty of T. N. Talfourd's *Ion*.[25]

16. MACREADY TO BULWER, *61 Lincolns Inn Fields, May 16*, [1836]

Your kind note made my visit to Town this morning much more agreeable than it otherwise would have been. Every friendly expression is felt with more than ordinary sensibility at this time.

In reply to your question as to the advisable course, I should say, it would be better, as you know something of Mr. Osbaldiston, that your communications should be direct.— I would therefore, having told him that you probably would address him on the subject, recommend you to go into the subject at once.— I beg you will consider yourself *secure* of my humble assistance in every way: — The terms I shall ask (in the excepted case of La Valliere) I am sure he will not refuse: — "or if" — as the O'Neil said — In one word you may rely on *me*.[26] He will keep open, if he can, through the summer — or as long as he can. I hope all will be settled to your perfect satisfaction.

On May 21, Macready heard from Bulwer that *La Vallière* had been rejected.

17. MACREADY TO BULWER, *Chambers, May 22*, [1836]

Your account of Mr. Osbaldiston's indifference on such an occasion only adds a proof, if any were needed, to the many that speak of our utterly fallen condition: — what hope is there for dramatic literature? — The elder Mr. Harris[27] would have promptly offered you a thousand pounds for your name:— Mr. H. Harris would have been liberal in his inducements to you to write.— Still, much as I deplore the present state of things, I cannot for your sake lament, that La Valliere has not been accepted at Covent Garden: it *could not* have been acted there with any chance of success: The company are quite unequal to such a play.— On the policy of publishing you must be the best judge; I would only suggest to you that you reduce the value of the work by publication both to the manager and to the audience in the Theatre; and some happy event may yet occur to place the direction of theatrical affairs in

---

[25] Thomas Noon Talfourd (1795-1854), an eminent lawyer (Serjeant-at-Law in 1833, Judge in 1849), literary executor and editor of the works of Charles Lamb, dramatic critic, and dramatist. Macready performed Talfourd's three plays: *Ion* at Covent Garden in May, 1836; *The Athenian Captive* at the Haymarket in August, 1838, and *Glencoe* at the Haymarket in May, 1840.

[26] Macready apparently intended to allude to the Irish hero of Bulwer's poem, *O'Neill; or, The Rebel* (London, 1827), in the third canto of which are numerous asseverations of secrecy and steadfastness.

[27] Thomas Harris (d. 1820), proprietor and manager of Covent Garden Theatre from 1767. His son, Henry Harris (d. 1839) became his assistant and deputy about 1810, and effectively managed the theatre until 1822 when he was forced out by a quarrel with Charles Kemble.

better hands, when, as a matter of course, your assistance must be eagerly sought for.

If however you think this a desperate chance,— if plays must be read and not acted, and if we, who are unfortunate enough to be players in these evil days, are driven from our country by the tyrannical monopoly, which our free state subjects us to, my regrets and wishes will attend its publication; and it will be in some respects a pleasing and a proud recollection, though a sad one, that you would not have thought me an unworthy agent in introducing a drama of yours to our stage, if any thing like taste or judgement had a voice in its direction.

We hear no more of *La Vallière* during the summer. Bulwer returned to the subject he had first mentioned in 1834, the death of Cromwell. Though he had then been quite off-hand about it ("great part of which was lost"), by now he had not only completed it but had committed at least three acts of it to the printers. Sometime, probably by the end of 1836, the whole of *Cromwell* was printed but it was never published. A single copy of it survives in the archives at Knebworth, where there is also a handsomely bound, carefully typewritten copy with an elaborate preface (perhaps by Bulwer's son), which mentions that its text was taken from a printed copy formerly in the possession of Macready. Bulwer let it be rumored that the play was "in the Press," and by somewhat irregular procedure it was reviewed (by William Johnson Fox)[28] in the April, 1837, *Westminster Review*. Fox described it as the third member of a mighty trilogy on the political struggles of the seventeenth century. The first part of the trilogy was to close with the death of Charles I. Cromwell was to appear in the first and rise to power in the second. In the third he was to be revealed at the height of his power, and then, through the noble opposition of Sir Harry Vane, in his final decline. Fox was a friend of Bulwer's, and much that he tells us was obviously inspired by conversations with the author, for parts I and II of the "trilogy" were never, so far as I know, any more than daydreams; and Sir Harry Vane, though under discussion at this time as the agent of opposition to Cromwell, does not appear in the printed text at all.

Fox's review caused considerable stir of interest, and other critics, tempted by the extracts he printed (mostly Cromwellian soliloquies, and indeed of high quality), were crying to see the whole play for a year or more afterward.[29] But Bulwer never released it. Time after time, as we shall see, he tried to rework it for the stage. It is very unlikely, under "the injurious restrictions of the foolish Lord Chamberlains," as Fox put it, that the play in any form could have been licensed for stage performance; but all in all it is too bad that even in its original form it was not made available to the reading public. In 1839 John Forster published his biography of Cromwell, and in 1845 Carlyle published Cromwell's letters and speeches; so that perhaps Bulwer no longer cared or dared to show his freely fictionized reading of an English history so important and so well known.

Bulwer's struggles with *Cromwell* in the summer of 1836 are recorded first in a note to John Forster.

---

[28] William Johnson Fox (1786-1864), a preacher, drama critic, and politician of high repute; friend of Bulwer, Forster, Dickens, *et al.;* Member of Parliament, 1847-63. In his reviews in the *Morning Chronicle* and elsewhere he praised Macready's work warmly; the editor at one time suspended his reviews at the instance of Alfred Bunn.

[29] Bulwer arranged for simultaneous American publication, and Saunders and Otley provided *The Southern Literary Messenger* with the manuscript of Act I, which was printed in that magazine "in anticipation" in September, 1836.

18. BULWER TO FORSTER, [*July 28, 1836*]

I am going to ask you to look over the sheets of my tragedy of Cromwell, ere the last 2 acts are finally printed off & to suggest any improvements your taste & experience can offer in those last portions — The first three acts are fixed, alas, by the Press. I wish also very much to entrust the sheets to Macready. Can you tell me where he is, & if within reach — of my persecution — I hope to send you the Play tomorrow night.

It is not so much meant for an acting play as La Vallière —. I have been obliged to work out the agency & catastrophe thro' a moral & preternatural channel for which I have to thank the superstition of Cromwell's fortunate day Since the actual & proper connexion between the events & catastrophe is forbidden by the History which assures us Cromwell, to the great perplexity of Dramatists thought proper to die a natural death. The Play is thus made rather a Dramatic representation of a life than a Drama.— And its interest must depend immeasurably more on a single character than an artful plot. Macready I think would find scope in Cromwell & properly dressed would look the character as well as act it.

Pray record your honest opinion as to my success or failure in the most difficult subject for tragedy that English History affords.

Forster spent Sunday, July 31, with other guests, at Elstree, and presumably he then deposited *Cromwell* with Macready, for the next day Macready read nearly the whole of it in the coach to London. He did not like it very well. "Though containing some passages happy in thought and strong in expression, I do not think, either in respect to character, arrangement, or poetical beauty, that this play will quite reach the level of his existing reputation." Before August 12 (a Friday), he had invited Bulwer and Forster to visit him at Elstree for dinner and the night in order to discuss it. The following pair of undated notes from Bulwer I take to belong to this occasion.

19. BULWER TO FORSTER

I have had a kind note from Macready asking us to go there Friday as he can't come to town.

Not seeing you (as to morrow would be late to send an answer) — I am obliged to decline —

But don't let me hinder you: pray send him the Play au plutôt

20. BULWER TO FORSTER

Mr. Macready I suppose has not come to town but perhaps you have had the kindness to send Cromwell to him & we shall meet on Friday.

As a minor alteration — I propose as a substitute for all the lines at the end — last page 183 — from "Put out the Lamps" — line 4 from top to insert what I now send. Omitting Whitelock's elegiac eulogium & giving Cromwell the last word.

What think you of it.

After dinner on August 12, Macready reports that "we discussed the subject of

Cromwell. Bulwer listened to the objections with great equanimity, and finally decided on delaying the publication, considering our respective suggestions as to the
alteration of the plot, and recasting it." Macready read considerably in Hume's *History
of England* to freshen his ideas, but by August 28 he still could not see what the play
needed, except total reworking. "On one point I am clear, that to make a play of
Cromwell he must begin *de novo,* and be content to lose all he has already done;
patch-work never is of value." Finally, on September 4, being then on tour at Bristol,
he spent a long Sunday composing a thorough analysis of what *Cromwell* required if
it was to become a stage play — complaining to himself the while that "this same
play has cost me much time and pains. I am not sure whether I ought to have undertaken it, but he has been kind in his expressions to me, and that has been my induce-
ment." His letter is a masterly and certainly conscientious critique. Act by act he
demonstrates the structural failure of the play as a succession of dramaticules, sometimes good within themselves, but wanting progressive continuity. Then, act by act, he
labors at a new framework, taking care to knit the whole together with definable lines
of motivation and result.

21. MACREADY TO BULWER, *Bristol, September 4, 1836*

After the trial I have made of your patience, I am ashamed to admit, as
I am bound to do, that I can promise no good result from it. My thoughts
have been continually dwelling on the Tragedy, and I have anxiously and
laboriously revolved the various modes of working the subject; but the very
earnestness of my desire to furnish some suggestion worthy your attention, and
an inconquerable diffidence in offering an opinion to you at all, seem to add
perplexity and difficulty to a task, which in ordinary cases is never one of the
easiest. — I find I cannot in so short a time fill up the outline of a plot with
the exact scenes, fitted to prepare and set off the leading events of the play.
I could only hope to do so by ruminating long in freedom upon it. Perhaps
my observations, made an article, on what seem to me the stage deficiencies
of the tragedy before me, may help to turn your thoughts towards the means
of making it more effective in representation. My apprehensions have strengthened into conviction, that it would not advance your fame to produce the
play upon the scene in its present form; and whether in the effect of their
publication the deep and noble thoughts, the nice touches of character, and
the stirring scenes contained in it would overweigh the advantages of a successful performance it is of course for you to judge. After what you have
already done, I should incline to doubt it. — You will excuse me if I overstep
the limits of my commission.

The principal objection to the play is want of action and continuity: there
is very little done upon the scene, and scarcely any succeeding action depends
on what goes before. Our memories must bring from history occurrences to
connect the story of the play and to explain the progressive change of character, which is not the case even in Shakespeare's rambling historical dramas.

In the first act, Cecil's renunciation of his allegiance to Cromwell is the
only action. The battle of Worcester is all that makes up the second, nothing
in the play represented as depending on it: indeed the play might end as the

curtain falls upon the words "The Lord hath fought for Cromwell", and no curiosity excited for coming events remain unsatisfied.

The third act is occupied by the conspiracy against Cromwell, which does not possess an interest sufficiently strong from the characters of the agents, and their seeming want of earnestness of purpose and of motive in their own natures, or the transactions, that are made prominent in the play — and yet this incident is in the very heart of the tragedy. — Cecil's interviews with Edith go to little beyond keeping alive their mutual passion in the auditor's mind, which is necessary for the effect of Edith's supplication for her lover's pardon to Cromwell. — The detection of the plot might, I think, be made more striking.

In Act fourth there is again little action, unless we may call so the manoeuvring with Whitelock — the narration of the weird woman is perhaps as good, and the reflections on "Killing no Murder," which influence Cromwell's conduct, equivalent to it, but the movement of the play is not in regular advance towards an object shown at an early period: there does not seem to me connection between the incidents. Cromwell is anxious to obtain the crown, but what great scenes, or workings of passion result from this anxiety? This act ends well with the abrupt intimation of Lady Claypole's danger.

In Act the fifth, the scenes of Cromwell, as the fearful and agonized father, only require a little more preparation through the preceding acts. — The three middle scenes are not essential to the plot, and could be omitted without disturbing its direct course. — Cromwell's death, I fancy, is capable of improved effect. In delirium character is lost, I think, very often, and it is seldom that it can be rendered pathetic.

— If the tragedy began on the field of Worcester, where Cromwell, having just succeeded to the command of the army, sees his way open to supreme power, Cecil's defection might make part of it, and help to retard the battle to its close. — The orders of the Parliament being delivered to Cromwell, and thwarting his views, might develope his designs on them and carry the interest forward.

In the Second Act, among other modes of hurrying the auditor into an acquaintance with the existing state of discontent, Cecil, as a proscribed royalist, might in a stolen interview with Edith speak of Cromwell's meditated usurpation and allude to a conspiracy on foot, by which he must fall.

Cromwell with Harrison or Martin, might have a powerful scene, as the messages are brought to him, introductory to that of the dissolution of the Parliament. — His daughter might also be introduced here in excellent contrast with him.

The Dissolution of the Long Parliament, — which might be followed by a grand scene of quarrel and final breaking off between himself and his friend — either Harrison or Martin, in this also his danger from conspiracy and the end of his ambitious views might be strongly urged, still pressing the interest onward.

The Third act might be given to the maturing of the conspiracy — with the interview between Lady Claypole and Cromwell, in which *she herself* might entreat him to resign his power etc.— not leaving to Edith to repeat to him her compunctious visitings — and much of his fine soliloquy over the body of Charles might be preserved over the picture of the King.

In the detection of the conspiracy if the pass-word were given from without, would not the consternation of the conspirators be very dramatic, as they reviewed their party and when made captive by the files of soldiers if the short altercation between them was silenced by the entrance of Cromwell?— And — as Harrison was pardoned, would it not give occasion for a strong & perhaps touching scene, if, after disposing of the other prisoners Harrison was left with Cromwell by his orders, and their mutual characters brought out in their altercation, Cromwell was to give him his pardon & leave him?— If the facts of history are adhered to, the exact time and place are at a poet's will.

Act the fourth might include Whitelocke's interview about the prisoners, Edith's supplication for Cecil, with Cromwell's anxiety for the crown.

In the Court might be introduced with much effect, I think, the intercession of the different ambassadors for the Portuguese nobleman, who was executed for murder, and Cromwell's constant determination to put him to death against their general remonstrances and implied menaces: — Then might follow the offer of the Crown to him and his reluctant refusal, which I should suppose might be full of interest — which the news of his child's illness would carry onward.

Act the fifth might well be filled up with the scenes of his daughter's death, one preparatory to his, and end with his own.

There is much which I cannot suggest precise place for — the death of Ireton might be brought to Cromwell, and his desolate state made a strong point of. I should think to give force to the incident of the conspiracy Syndercomb's fanaticism ought to be much more strongly marked — if you think it necessary to retain the outline of Harrison as sketched, I should suggest another of the Parliament to take his place in those scenes not strictly historical — for he appears, particularly in the conspiracy, quite harmless from his state of delusion.

But I am wandering on, and not considering how far I may uselessly have engaged your time already.—

It has occurred to me, that as Kemble[30] is engaged at Covent Garden — at least I am so informed — that with him, and Farren, and myself a strong cast of La Valliere might be obtained; but then there is the want of the heroine.— Would you like the experiment?— It would be a great gratification

---

[30] Charles Kemble (1775-1854), younger brother of John Philip Kemble and father of Fanny Kemble, made his London debut in 1794. A "first rate actor of second rate parts," as Macready once put it, he was accomplished in gentlemanly, poetic, and high comedic roles, but lacked the strength for tragedy. Macready quarreled with him bitterly in 1823, when Kemble was manager of Covent Garden Theatre, but eventually settled into a sort of grudging respect for him.

to me to endeavour to give a representation of Cromwell, and particularly from your pen; but I mention the other play in case you may be, as I expect you will, impatient of the extent of alteration for which I apply in this.

Bulwer was impressed by all this, but by no means discouraged. Having gone down to Devonshire for a few weeks' seclusion, he wrote to Forster for his opinions. Forster was full of the subject, being deep in his own biographical studies of seventeenth-century statesmen, and full of theory of dramatic writing too, all of which he let fly at Bulwer in a generous, impetuous (but not always quite intelligible) rush of advice.

22. BULWER TO FORSTER, *St. Mary Ottery, Devon,* [*September 6, 1836*]

I am so importuned to release the press of the proofs of Cromwell that I must entreat you to let me have the plan you suggested at your early leisure — it would be a great obligation.

23. FORSTER TO BULWER, *Saturday afternoon, September 17, 1836*

This, after all, will only be my *first* letter on the subject of Cromwell.

I go at once in medias res. Promising only that when I speak freely, it is with the consciousness that you well know how warm an admirer of your genius I have always been. Perfect admiration, as well as perfect love, can dispense with fear. . . .

The fault of the tragedy, as it now stands, seems to me to be that of having been originally cast in too statuesque a shape. The form of Cromwell is at the last, as it was at the first, calm, gigantic, and *stationary*. We have not lived a life of thoughts with him. We have not seen his passions as they rose, and took sudden, palpable, and present shape. We see him only after the various processes which fix his character are, as it were, complete; and the new complexion has, so to speak, lodged itself in the general mass. The emotion which we ourselves are really permitted to share, are, after *these* have taken shape and solidity with the rest, of comparatively little importance.

The alterations which I shall venture to suggest have for their object the showing the great character, you have as a whole so grandly felt, in actual and distinctive progress. I would have the high action and high passions of the man so vividly before the audience that one of the actors might — as the actors in some of the old mysteries used at times literally and honestly do — turn and appeal whether or no they were felt or done, with a "You SEE them!"

On consideration, too, I find that some cancellings of pages may be made so effectively in the first and second acts, that the treatment of the characters already there shall, by some suppression in one case, and bringing forward in one other instance, harmonize admirably with the changes I propose. I have not finished the marking of my copy of the tragedy with exact reference to all these points, but in a few days I shall have done so, and will then forward it to you, in a parcel, if you can send me instructions as to where I shall direct it.

The third and fourth acts (with the exception of some bits of writing which are too fine to be lost, and may be made available) I propose should be sacrificed altogether, and the fifth act, while I would have it in the main modelled as it is, I would alter materially in one or two points of the writing. I would bring forward Lady Claypole, put back Edith, and introduce two new and great characters, Sir Henry Vane and Ludlow, which should be great, with even little to say, all they have to say and do will most properly begin and end with the new acts of the tragedy.

Before encountering the details (which I mean to go through in these letters as minutely as possible) I should like to ask you to wait a few moments whilst I trouble you with one or two of my dogmatical definitions about dramatic writing,— or rather with an outline of one of them,— which will be something for me to start from, in many of the alterations I propose in the fifth act, and in some of the omissions in the first and second.

One thing, I think, should never be lost sight of in Dramatic Writing. All that is *material* is there actually present to the Eye. All that is *Ethereal,* therefore, should be absolutely discharged from the task of setting forth what is already visible, or ought to be visible. Now the passions of a scene, the progress of it, the results of it,— all these are visible and existing things, and should as little as possible be described with words. Words, in fact, flow at once from the existence of these things, and are never needed to assure us that they do exist. Virtually indeed they assure us of it, and in the highest degree, but (words as they are beside a passion!) they are there because of the passion, not the passion because of them. Now this *Effluence* of words, in my mind, as a pure effect of passion, constitutes the true dramatic writing; and it is, moreover,— disjoined from the material agents that produce it,— the action, the scenery, the place, the time,— comparatively unintelligible to all but to those who are capable of supplying from their own imagination those materials. In this, I have often felt, is the secret of the repugnance of the old dramatists to publishing their plays. And among some of those old dramatists are greater dramatic writers, on the principle I venture to lay down, than even Shakespeare himself.

But this, as I go on, I shall have occasion to enlarge on and illustrate. I have already said sufficient for the present purpose, and may open at once upon Act First, Scene First, of the tragedy itself —

Here, my dear Bulwer, I must come to a pause today. You will read what I have written in the spirit which prompts it I am sure. I have written it with the immediate care, currente calamo, as I should have spoken it to yourself — but some of the opinions have been paused over very much, and turned a variety of ways in my mind. I mean that, though I dare not now read them back as they are hastily put down here, they are not hastily formed.

I shall resume the subject, I hope, on Monday; and go on with it through, perhaps, two more letters, till it is completed.

24. BULWER TO FORSTER, *September 22, [1836]*

Many thanks for your most kind letter — containing the prelude to your Plan.— I like very much indeed — and am quite disposed to throw over acts ii & iii.— I have had an outline from Macready, sketched with a practiced & masterly hand very similar in much to yours. But getting rid of Act 1. altogether. I enclose his sketch which please to return.— If your plan preserve the two former acts it will certainly be preferable & save much time & expense. — I think it would be best to get rid of Cecil & Edith altogether or at least of their love. If Cecil be preserved — could he be made to have formed an early affection for Lady C.— & to represent a pure & lofty *sentiment* existing between them still, quite compatible with her marriage & religious character. — This might deepen & soften the interest especially about her deathbed.— I think Vane & Ludlow might be introduced, perhaps in the cancelled pages of Act 1.— Tho' their strength can be reserved for the middle acts. Would you propose to bring out the visionary & mystical parts of Vane's character in opposition to the sturdier vigour of Ludlow! — Just give a hint of the manner in which you would *heal* & contrast the characters — a sketch in your own profound manner — of the qualities and temperament of these two Intruders on the present plot.—

I am not living at Ottery but some miles off, incognito, to avoid the Lionism of a County Quarter. . . . Please to return Macready's letter. Your thoughtful expositions delight me.— & I await them eagerly.

25. FORSTER TO BULWER, *58 Lincolns Inn Fields, Thursday,*
    September 22, 1836

The only objection that I see to the first and Second Acts standing in the new plan almost exactly as they stand now, is the fact of there being so little immediate connection between them. For what was only fulfilling the conditions of the original design of the tragedy — (that of presenting in a succession of [scenes?] the results, as it were of the life and actions of Cromwell) — would be inconsistent with the new design — (that of giving in actual movement and progress the life and actions themselves)

This might be remedied, I would suggest, by throwing into the scene of Cecil and Edith (pp. 16-25) and also into the conclusion of the scene of Cecil and Cromwell (pp. 37-40) — some distinct and active mention of the fall of Charles the Second having been already proclaimed; and, more than this, of his having every immediate chance of bringing an army into the field. Time would be violated by this — but allowably, for the tragic writer's purpose. It might also be shadowed forth — though a certain general distinctness would be necessary — with just so much of uncertainty in respect to actual detail as would serve to connect, for every purpose of tragic interest in the minds of the audience, the magnificent Exit of Cromwell in the close of the first act (p. 43), actively and immediately with the stirring progress of events in the second act.

Reducing a few of the love passages of Cecil to admit of this and another purpose that might be served — I would have the Episode of Edith as it is in the first act, and connect it with the interest of Cromwell and Claypole at the opening of the fifth act, by having involved Cecil in the actual conspiracy (not against the life but against the government of Cromwell; the Overton and Bradshaw, not the Syndercombe, plot —) with a dramatic disclosure of which, and the flight of Ludlow into Switzerland, and the banishment of Vane to Carisbrook, the fourth act of the tragedy would have terminated.

Let me intimate here that one of the scenes of the fourth act will certainly be that which now stands between pp. 90 and 93 of the printed tragedy. I would have the Cecil part of it cut out (what is necessary to his connection with Sir Harry Vane's conspiracy must be differently arranged) and the exquisite speech of Cromwell spoken on the banks of the Thames (p. 87) might be used with great advantage in the Hampton Court Gardens Scene. I think you will find also that the course of the fourth act will leave some of those fine passages on the Killing no Murder book (115-118) free for adoption.

On Monday next, *at the very latest,* you shall have the book marked carefully with all these details. I am sure that I see my way, with very few alterations indeed in the matter already printed off — and with the continuing of very much of the fifth act — through a very noble tragedy. Your fifth act, as it now stands in purpose and effect, will be the grandest rounding off in the world for the peculiar action of the previous four acts.

The third act should open with Cromwell's return from Worcester. That great battle destroyed for the time both the Royalist and the Republican party. It was on its achievement, as you have well pictured, that the kingly ambition finally burst on Cromwell. Complete the picture by showing him in London on his return. As if to remove at once everything from his way, the second day after his return brought the news of the death of Ireton — the only man of whose personal influence over himself he really seems to have stood in awe. The mingled regret & triumph of this news is a dramatic effect. A series of dramatic scenes open after this. The more than kingly funeral of Ireton — the "drolling" dinner of Cromwell at Desborough's, which would be changed to Ludlow's or Vane's — the famous conference of the Republican & the army party, where Cromwell's disaster has wonderful scope — the schemes of Vane to get his reform act and settlement bill passed — and the final dissolution of the Long Parliament — these naturally make up the third act of the tragedy.— With much annoyance of the necessity I am under, I close this letter today. I WILL CERTAINLY WRITE AGAIN TOMORROW. I will then sketch the number and character of the Scenes, and refer you to some authorities for them.

26. FORSTER TO BULWER, *58 Lincolns Inn Fields, Saturday,*
   September 24, 1836

Illness had prevented my completion of the plan of Cromwell yesterday, and your delightful letter of this morning makes me not sorry for it.

I promise myself still a pleasant day tomorrow in another thorough revision of the subject, with the new lights you send. Look for a parcel on Tuesday (I will send it off by one of the Monday's coaches) containing the book, and everything still wanted to give proper expression & significance to the views I have hitherto expressed to you so imperfectly. . . .

27. BULWER TO FORSTER, *September 28, 1836*

I write a hasty line to thank you, for your letter, & to say how much struck I am by your views — Also to add, that, as I have not yet received the Parcel, containing Cromwell — I must beg you, if not already sent, *not* to forward it, as I leave Devonshire on Saturday early — for London. Direct it therefore to the Albany. . . .

To return to *La Vallière*. According to Macready's suggestion at the end of his *Cromwell* letter, negotiations with Osbaldiston were to be renewed, and on September 16, being still on tour, Macready heard from Bulwer of "his engagements with regard to *La Vallière.*" Apparently Bulwer empowered Macready to broach the subject to Osbaldiston, for soon after Macready returned to London the following curious letter was written.

28. OSBALDISTON TO BULWER, *Theatre Royal Covent Garden,*
   September 21, 1836[31]

I have this morning had some conversation with Mr. Macready on the subject of the same (I believe) Play respecting which I had the honour of an interview with you: & which if we can and without the assistance of Mr C Kemble (who, I fear, being ill, will not be able to study a new part) I shall be most happy to represent at Cov Garden — The favor of an early reply will much oblige. . . .

Thus Bulwer could boast in an "Advertisement" in the first edition of *La Vallière* that he had succeeded with Osbaldiston (as he had not with Bunn) in selling the play sight unseen.[32]

Toward the end of October the time of preparation drew near, and final alterations were in order.

29. BULWER TO FORSTER, [*Knebworth Park*], *October 20, 1836*

The more I consider, the more I have apprehensions about the Equivoque of the Marquis de Montespan in his use of the word "ravished." It would not do to risk any thing for such a trifle. Pray oblige me by consulting with Mac-

---

[31] Original in the Knebworth Archives.
[32] Edward Bulwer: *The Duchess de la Vallière, a play in five acts* (London, 1836).

ready about it. Unfortunately the whole humour of the character — if there
be any — rests upon this word. And the banishment of the word will I suppose banish the speaker himself. I know nothing of the Stage practically or
the temperament of the audience — But I have always heard they are more
prudish than the Censor. I am very anxious to know your opinions & fore-
bodings of the Play & also if anything be settled relative to the personification
of Lauzun.

Pray thank Macready for his kind note.

Bulwer called on Macready on October 31 to receive last minute suggestions, "to
which," says Macready, "he assented." On November 2 Macready read the play to
the actors in Osbaldiston's office: "the actors and actresses were, or seemed to be,
very much pleased with the play, but I cannot put much confidence in them."

Meanwhile a vexing problem arose concerning the casting, sweeping poor Bulwer
deep into the harassments of playhouse politics. Charles Kemble had been wanted for
the role of the smooth villain, Lauzun, but had declined it. This left it open, apparently, to the actor of next prestige in the theatre, the popular broad comedian, William
Farren. Macready wanted Farren's name in the bill, but he wanted to sink him in the
comic cuckold role of M. de Montespan. This role was extremely brief — so insignifi-
cant, in fact, that in later editions of the play (after 1841) it was omitted — and
Farren would not be so trapped. A flutter of warning is implicit in this note to Bulwer
from manager Osbaldiston.

30. Osbaldiston to Bulwer, *Theatre Royal Covent Garden,* October 26, 1836[33]

On a careful perusal of "La Valliere" I am inclined to think Mr. Farren
w^d do more for "Montespan" than for "Lauzun" if he would play that character — If however he sh^d think that too unimportant, still I sh^d prefer his
playing "Lauzun" than his name sh^d be omitted in the Drama. Pers: — I suggest this for your own consideration. . . .

31. Bulwer to Forster, *Albany, October 28, 1836*

Me voici in London, Mon cher —

Ten thousand thanks for your kind letters. — I should like much to see you.
Shall I call on you tomorrow about 3? — if I don't hear I will.

All I say about Farren is — that granting all you say, which I do, who is
there better? — if Kemble doesn't take it? — In that case I suppose Vandenhoff[34] must have it — & Bennett[35] take the King.

---

[33] Original in the Knebworth Archives.

[34] John Vandenhoff (1790-1861), a second-rate actor of leading roles (Hamlet, Lear,
Coriolanus, etc.); made his London debut in 1820 as Lear. He was much admired in the
provinces but could never attain first rank in London. He often played Iago to Macready's Othello, and in the early thirties Macready feared him (and privately denounced
him) as a rival. He was a member of Macready's Covent Garden company in 1838-39,
after which he withdrew to the provinces.

[35] George John Bennett (1800-79), a middling actor of supporting roles, whom Mac-
ready usually refers to as "bad," but whom he employed in his companies both at
Covent Garden and Drury Lane. He made his London debut in 1823 as an unsuccessful
Richard III. He was with Phelps at Sadler's Wells from 1844 to 1862.

Bulwer undertook to ingratiate Farren by assigning him to Montespan himself, but evidently he did so in such apologetic and open terms that Farren slipped the net, blissfully fixing upon the part of Lauzun. Neither blandishments nor halfhearted threats to withdraw the play could shake him.

32. MACREADY TO BULWER, *Chambers, Friday, [November 4, 1836]*

Forster had commission to tell you that the reading was attended with every demonstration of delight, that you could desire — If the laughter and tears in the manager's room may be taken as an augury of the effect upon an audience before the curtain, all will be as we wish.

I have not yet heard about Farren, but shall most likely this evening.— It is very unlucky, that you mentioned the part of Lauzun to him, which he talks of — but we must do our best with him.

I should think the subject excellent for the epilogue — political allusions are only dangerous, when they touch on questions that particularly excite the animosity of parties.

The rehearsals cannot well begin until after Monday 14th I will write to you at Knebworth what Farren says on Montespan — which he *must* act, or the success of the play is endangered. The part *told* remarkably well in the reading, but he was absent on the plea of illness.

I will write to you the instant anything is fixed. . . .

33. BULWER TO MACREADY, *Knebworth Park, Stevenage, Herts., November 6, 1836*

I enclose you the Epilogue I propose for Farren if he take Montespan. I think it has some points that may be successful on the stage.— There are two allusions of which I am doubtful: one the two lines in which Spring Rice[36] is mentioned by name, the other about the Duke of Brunswick & the Balloon.[37] I mean as to the taste of them.

Whenever you write about the rehearsals, you can let me know your opinion on these matters.

---

[36] Thomas Spring Rice (1790-1866), Secretary to the Treasury and Chancellor of the Exchequer in the 1830's; elevated to the peerage as Lord Monteagle in 1839. The allusion in the Epilogue was suppressed.

[37] The Epilogue contains these lines:
> "When I was young, were Dukes inclined to roam,—
> Six horses bore them half a mile from home;
> But now a Duke takes journeys to the moon,
> And steps his half a mile from a balloon!"

London was enjoying a ballooning craze in the autumn of 1836. Vauxhall Gardens had acquired a balloon and the services of the pioneer aeronaut Charles Green (1785-1870), who had made the first hydrogen-gas-filled balloon ascent as early as 1821, and made 526 ascents during his career. On September 9, Green took a party of nine passengers some two miles high and landed them at Cliffe in Kent. On November 7, he took two passengers on a projected trip to Paris; eighteen hours later they landed in the Duchy of Nassau in western Germany, and the balloon was thereafter famous as the Nassau Balloon. The Covent Garden Christmas pantomime of this season featured a balloon race between Green and his wife.

I hope the Epilogue may go toward strengthening the part of Montespan & therefore hasten to send it.

I have also written a prologue, but it is a very commonplace affair. I thought it might do well just to allude to the copyright Law, but I have not done it neatly in the prologue, & I shall keep the creature by me for a few days to see whether he will grow up any handsomer — which ugly babies sometimes do.

I heartily wish you could have given my Mother & myself the pleasure of your company here for a day or two. But I suppose just at this time it would be impossible.

I was extremely gratified by your kind note, which was most encouraging.

P.S. When you write please to return the Epilogue with any suggestions.

By the same post as this last, at the tag-end of a note to Forster, he mentioned that the Epilogue was in Macready's hands, and begged Forster's opinion of it.

34. BULWER TO MACREADY, *Knebworth, Stevenage, Herts., November 7, 1836*

I send you something which I propose as a substitute for the "horns." I think the idea is comic without the farce of the Scene as it now stands. But I am a little in doubt whether it may not be *un peu trop fort* to make Lauzun pay his envoy to Montespan's wife with her Husband's jewels — I mean not *trop fort* in itself, but *trop fort* for the starch of the audience. Pray consider and let me know: if it does — the Old Lady must be drest with due regard to the comic. Will you also see if there are any five or six lines that could be omitted, as it is a little too long to supply the place of the 2 pages to be cancelled in the printed copies. If nothing can be well omitted, it does not signify much, as in that case I must cancel 5 pages instead of 2, to gain the blank part of the last page of the Act.

Please when you have read, to return it — with any suggestions. I will then return you a copy for the Stage and have it printed in the meanwhile. Excuse all this trouble. — The idea is amusing enough, but I fear I have not done as much as I might with the Execution.

35. BULWER TO MACREADY, *Knebworth, November 8, 1836*

I have again to trouble you. Having received, today, a letter from Farren which seems likely to disconcert all our arrangements. — In it he says that on seeing the play he never could have had the *slightest hesitation* as to the part he should fix on — viz; de Lauzun. He then proceeds to dwell on what he conceives the spirit of the character, & concludes with saying: "it is the *only* part in the play I could act with justice to you — or your humble servant Wm Farren!" — I have only one consolation in thinking, from the bearing of his letter, that even without my most unlucky & rash note, he would have equally pitched upon Lauzun.

What is to be done? — can I be of any use writing, & in that case what shall I say, what points insist upon? — I hope it will be managed. But probably ere this you have heard Farren's choice, tho' I hasten to apprise you of the *contretemps.*

36. BULWER TO MACREADY, *Knebworth, Stevenage, Herts., November 9, 1836*

By the enclosed notes you will see I do all in my power to correct the first *faux pas* of writing to Farren, & I have as earnestly, yet as civilly, as I can, pressed on him the part of Montespan. I have adopted your hint as to the threat of withdrawing La Vallière. If you like the notes, please to seal & send them. You can give Osbaldiston the one for him when you see him. Farren's can go by the two penny Post. For the rest I leave a carte blanche entirely in your hands. Whatever you do — either in omitting Farren altogether, or even, if you judge right, withdrawing the Play (tho' that would be awkward) — will be entirely approved by me. — If my presence is necessary in town, I can come on two days' notice. But I think my note to Farren will do at least as much as seeing him would do. — Could the matter be compromised by Farren's taking the part of Montespan at first & Lauzun hereafter? This as you like. Or I would promise — if La Vallière succeed — to write him a thoroughly effective & prominent part in some future play. In that I will do all I can to smooth the obstacles. I agree with you that Farren could not fight with Bragelone, & thought that must be altered if he took that part. Fighting with Farren would be burlesque. The scene with La Vallière he might do better. — But we had better dismiss all thought of the possibility of his doing anything but Montespan, tho' without piquing his self love by considering him *unfit* for Lauzun, & putting him in as good humour as we can.

P.S. Thanks to your kindness in saving me already from all the annoyances I have been brought to consider ignominious with acting a play. I cannot — despite Farren — agree yet with Smollett or Le Sage.[38]

37. MACREADY TO BULWER, *Chambers, November 12, 1836*

I have delayed the acknowledgement of your last in the hope of being able to convey some certain intelligence to you, but uncertainty still exists upon the disposition of the characters. No effect has been produced upon Mr. Farren — I shall try the last experiment tonight by telling Miss Faucit[39] of the contem-

---

[38] Tobias Smollett (1721-71), the Scottish novelist, began his career as a rejected dramatist. Alain René Le Sage (1668-1747), the French novelist, was a very successful dramatist. In 1749 Smollett translated Le Sage's picaresque novel, *Gil Blas de Santillane,* which contains a long thread of satirical narrative of life among the actors. Bulwer is referring especially to a scene in Book III, Chapter xi, in which a poor fellow in a dirty shirt, being a poet whose tragedy has been accepted, calls on the company of actors at dinner to deliver their parts to them. The actors treat him with contemptuous indifference: "Keep your seats, gentlemen, it is only an author."

[39] Helena Saville Faucit, afterwards Lady Martin (1817-98), the finest of the early Victorian leading actresses; made her London debut at Covent Garden as Julia in Knowles's *The Hunchback* in January, 1836; was Macready's leading lady for several years; created the heroines in all five of Bulwer's plays that Macready performed. Macready occasionally entered cold or angry remarks about her in his diary, but he was

plated withdrawal of the play. In the meantime Mr. Osbaldiston has applied to Mr. C. Kemble to act Lauzun — but from what you told me, I conceive this to be a hopeless trial, unless the diva pecunia stand our friend in his calculations. I wanted Mr. Osbaldiston to say whether he would or would not give Lauzun to Mr. Farren in the event of C. Kemble's refusal: but he cannot make up his mind: — he must however on Monday or Tuesday at the latest for the play must be proceeded with.— I hope to have then some favourable news —

Forster sent a progress report as events appeared to him, on November 16. The second part of his letter reverts to the subject of *Cromwell* and develops a subject not again referred to — a historical comedy of court life in the days of William and Mary.

38. FORSTER TO BULWER, *November 16, 1836*

I have not been able to see Mr. Osbaldiston today, though I have called twice at the theatre. But I have seen and talked with Macready and I have engaged to meet Mr. O. tonight. The present decided intention is to produce the play on this day fortnight, and the first preparation rehearsal is "called" for tomorrow. You are not wanted to the first few rehearsals. I must see Mr. O., of course, before I can tell you of the final settlement of the cast, but Macready tells me that he thinks Farren will be placed in Lauzun and Webster in Montespan, and he is not disposed to make any personal stand against it. He is working very hard now, night and day, at Bragelone, and desires me, with his best remembrance, to tell you that his "whole heart is in it." I may add, by the way, that the scenery is "progressing," as the Yankees have it.

I have thought much of the Cromwell plot since, and cannot help thinking it "as good a plot as ever was laid,"—"a good plot, an excellent plot." The tender interest was just what was wanted, and its effect will be certain with the audience. Nor is there the slightest fear of offending the strictest truth of history. I am so much struck with the outline that was sketched out in our conversation the other day I shall not be easy till I have reduced it in every scene and dialogue to paper. I hope to have it for you on your arrival.

And the Comedy!!! Maynard must be Farren's part — Sergeant Maynard, the slyest and most dishonest fox of the whole herd — Maynard who had outlived all the revolution, and all lawyers, and, if his Dutch Highness had not come, must have outlived the law itself. Think of Farren, aged ninety, dressed up to this old Rogue! The last act must be the turning out of the old Court and the incoming of the new. Oh, what a satire! The grave gentleman, Evelyn, must be there. Then the bishops, and above all, that darling and foresworn Bishop Compton! Beautiful and grateful will be the contrast of James' well-

devoted to her, personally as well as professionally; it appears, indeed, that feelings developed between them which in less fastidious persons might have turned into an "affair." In 1851, Miss Faucit married Theodore Martin (1816-1909), a man of letters, who was chosen by Queen Victoria to write the life of the Prince Consort. Miss Faucit became an intimate of the Queen. Martin was knighted in 1880.

dressed sycophants, as they advance to embrace with passionate fervour William's ill-favoured and ill-accoutred Dutchmen! You must have the amusing attack of the mob on Judge Jeffries, too, and that venerable [*illegible*] mean unjust Judge — "in a sailor's jacket, with his eyebrows shaved," trying to escape. The base Halifax will be a fine opportunity and Marlborough and his Duchess, and the Princess Mary, who must be represented (must she not?) as the Duchess has described, indulging her gaiety on finding herself in her poor papa's rooms at Whitehall — "She ran about, looking into every closet and [*illegible*] and turning up the quilts upon the bed, as people do when they come to an inn, and with no other sort of concern to her appearance, &c &c. . . . laughing and jolly as to a wedding." The subject is splendid indeed. I am already getting up your materials, and you were born for the purpose of writing it. It is all over designed for your genius. No one else living could attempt it. We must have a long conversation about it on your arrival in town.

I see Osbaldiston to-night. I will write again to you by tomorrow's post stating the result. . . .

39. Bulwer to Forster, [*November 17, 1836*]

I am extremely obliged by your long & kind letter.— 1st as to Macready & the Play. I shall be very glad when the thing is settled one way or the other. — I shall omit the "ravished" or take "enraptured." . . .

The Comedy is superb — if we can mellow down its boldness — we must not startle — but insinuate the grand Satire in an undercurrent.

Cromwell shall be done.

40. Bulwer to Macready, [*November 22, 1836*]

I send you the prologue & epilogue.[40] The printers are waiting eagerly for them; & therefore if your better tact can suggest any verbal amendments, I will have them effect^d now; on hearing from you. Can you say whether I may depend on the play being produced Wednesday because of allowing the publishers to complete their arrangements? When are the rehearsals?

[P.S.] The copies for the stage will be sent to Mr Osbaldiston to-morrow Evening & I shall send you one also — the ravished of Montespan being altered for the raptured &c.[41] I have rewritten the Prologue & think it may do.

41. Bulwer to Forster, [*November 22, 1836*]

So sorry not arrived when you called. Want to know whether play positively fixed for tomorrow week. As the publishers must subscribe &c — must give them an answer tomorrow, Wednesday night.

---

[40] The Epilogue was never spoken, for the play proved too long for the audience's endurance. Besides, it was to have begun with a playful but dangerously overconfident plea against being "damned." In the course of time Bulwer regretted the Prologue, too (see Letter 211, Bulwer to Forster, November 5, 1840).

[41] For "ravished" and "raptured," Matthews printed "vanished" and "ruptured."

Just sent to Macready a brand new prologue. Look at it pray. I think it will do! — any *verbal* suggestions gratefully received — smaller the better. — Poets only hold out ½ penny begging [*word lost*] to Critics. . . . Want to know about rehearsals. — Suppose you are at Knowles's[42] — wish him all success —

42. MACREADY TO BULWER, *Chambers, November 22, 1836*

I looked into Forster's chambers yesterday with the hope of seeing you, wishing to thank you for your kind present, and to learn from yourself your intention respecting this postponement of La Valliere.

It ought in my mind to have the start of Mr. Knowles's play, for it is of great importance to pre-occupy the public interest. This may not strike you very forcibly, but I assure you it is a consideration of great moment in the success of a play.

There would be little delay, if we could once see it *on* the stage, which I fear we shall not do for some time unless you are urgent and peremptory.

43. MACREADY TO BULWER, *Chambers, Wednesday, [November 23, 1836]*

I have not time to offer an excuse for using the privilege you honor me by offering.

I like the prologue very much — but it must not *all* be spoken: there are one or two expressions which rather jar upon my ear — the *"glittering"* streams etc — [*illegible*] and the last line but two I could wish to see altered. It will be for you to choose what, for the sake of time, must be omitted in the recitation. Forster has acquainted you I understand with the hour of rehearsal today, and the wish expressed that you should be present. — The play has taken no form as yet — but one discovery is already made, that it much exceeds the *acting length.* — All this & all else we can talk of on the stage, where I hope to see you at twelve o'clock.

Mr. Osbaldiston is not taking any pains to expedite its production, as the play-bills may inform you, wherein I am announced to play every night this week: He does not understand the sort of attention necessary for a play of this kind. — You will however judge from what you see to day of what can & ought to be done.

Rehearsals of *La Vallière* were supposed to have begun on November 14, but they were long delayed. After a rehearsal on November 30, the day the play should have

---

[42] James Sheridan Knowles (1784-1862), Irish dramatist and actor. His *Virginius* provided Macready in 1820 one of his first decisive triumphs, and Macready kept the play in his repertory throughout his career. Other of his plays which Macready produced or starred in were *Caius Gracchus* (1823), *William Tell* (1825), *Alfred the Great* (1831), *Woman's Wit* (1838), and *The Secretary* (1843). In 1834 Macready and Knowles collaborated in an adaptation of Beaumont and Fletcher's *Maid's Tragedy*, called *The Bridal*, produced in Dublin in October of 1834 and in London in 1836. Knowles was extremely prolific. His best plays, besides *Virginius*, were *The Hunchback* (1832) and *The Love Chase* (1837). The present reference is to Knowles's *The Daughter* (or, *The Wrecker's Daughter*), due to open at Drury Lane on November 29.

opened, Macready records his anger against Farren, who "has, in my mind, seriously injured this play by his intrusion of himself into the part of Lauzun. He does not understand it. He is a very, *very ignorant* man." The next projected opening date was for mid-December, but as the time approached the play's unreadiness was desperately obvious, so a further postponement to Christmas week was agreed upon. On December 9 Macready tells the reasons. "Went much fatigued to an early rehearsal of *La Val-lière,* of which I begin to entertain strong and painful apprehensions. Mr. Farren does not convey to me the least tinge of resemblance to the character of Lauzun. Webster seems very unmeaning and inefficient in Montespan; Vandenhoff not very impassioned in the King, Miss Pelham[43] awfully bad in Madame Montespan, and Miss Faucit frequently feeble and monotonous in La Vallière. I do not feel that I can do anything worthy of myself in the part, but I will do my utmost. Bulwer and Count D'Orsay[44] were at rehearsal. The necessity of deferring the play until after Christmas was suggested, and upon reflection espoused by Bulwer."

Bulwer's arrangements for publication were now completed. The following letter is probably circa December 10, the "copy" referred to being proof-sheets. On December 13 we find Macready "making up a copy" to send to his brother Edward.[45]

44. BULWER TO MACREADY, *December* [*circa 10*], *1836*

I send you a copy of La Vallière. Is there any thing you would object to in the advertisement that follows the preface? I do not let it be printed till you have seen it. As Bunn gives out, I hear, that he refused the play, I thought something of the kind necessary. But I am not quite pleased with the thing I have drawn up. I have managed with the Publishers, to print La Vallière, & Cromwell when altered separately, & am thus enabled, without much loss, to keep back the Publication of La V. till the day of performance provided it be within 3 weeks or a month at farthest.

I have now only to repeat the thrice-told tale of my thanks for all your kindness. — I only wish I had been an Achilles that you had brought to the War.

[P.S.] I expect a stormy party agst me the first night.

P.S. If you could suggest any verbal alterations in the last scene, they can be done. I am just leaving town, but a line to the Albany will find me.

Shall any copies be sent to the reviews the week before performance, or shall all be kept back?

---

[43] Miss Pelham, a minor actress in Osbaldiston's company.

[44] Alfred, Count d'Orsay (1801-52), an intimate friend of Bulwer, Forster, and Macready. A French dandy and a clever artist, he visited England in the early 1820's and became attached to the family of the Earl of Blessington. In 1828 he married Harriet Gardiner, Blessington's daughter, though he was already involved in an affair with Lady Blessington. The marriage failed. After the Earl's death in 1829, d'Orsay and Lady Blessington set up an "irregular" household at Seamore Place and later at Gore House in Kensington, to which flocked a huge circle of the fashionable men of letters and the arts. They sold Gore House in 1849 and fled to Paris to escape their debts.

[45] Edward Neville Macready (1798-1848) was a military man. In his seventeenth year he distinguished himself at Waterloo by commanding a company whose officers had been killed, and was then made a lieutenant. Later he served in India and achieved his majority. After 1840 he was aide-de-campe to Stewart Mackenzie, Lord High Commissioner of the Ionian Islands. His wife, a Miss Rolls, published in 1839 a series of etchings of Macready in his principal characters.

The following quip from Bulwer to Forster is a tag to a long letter of indeterminate date, but apparently about the time of the publication and performance of *La Vallière*.

45. BULWER TO FORSTER

. . . A thousand thanks for all your & Macready's kindness about La Valliere — Had Colburn[46] been a manager he could have refused nothing to a Duchess. And I must say that a piece of that *rank* is not dear at 50£ for a night — considering *5 acts* are to be performed.

One more week's postponement brought on the opening night, January 4, 1837. Bulwer, accompanied by Forster, attended the final rehearsal. He "liked what I did," says Macready, but adds sourly that "authors are no judges of the performances of their own plays."

The Covent Garden playbill of Wednesday, January 4, announces "The New Original Play . . . which will be produced, with every attention to the elegance, correctness, and magnificence of the Scenery, Costume, &c. . . . under the direction of Mr. Henry Wallack," and gives the dramatis personae as follows:

> The Prologue to be spoken by MR. H. WALLACK
> Louis the Fourteenth...........................MR. VANDENHOFF
> The Duke de Lauzun..............................MR. W. FARREN
> Count de Grammont................................MR. PRITCHARD
> The Marquis de Bragelone.........................MR. MACREADY
> Marquis de Montespan.............................MR. WEBSTER
> Bertrand, *the Armourer*.........................MR. TILBURY
> *First Courtier*.................................MR. J. WEBSTER
> *Second Courtier*................................MR. BENDER
> *Third Courtier*.................................MR. COLLEIT [*sic*]
> Madame de Montespan..............................MISS PELHAM
> Madame de la Vallière............................MRS. W. WEST
> Mademoiselle de la Vallière......................MISS HELEN FAUCIT
> *The Queen of Louis the Fourteenth*..............MISS PARTRIDGE
> *Abbess*...MRS. GARRICK
> *First Lady*.....................................MISS LEE
> *Second Lady*....................................MISS BROOKES
> *Third Lady*.....................................MISS LAND
> *The Vocal Parts by* MISS TURPIN, MISS VINCENT, MISS LAND, MR. COLLINS, MR. RANSFORD, &C.
> *Courtiers, Gentlemen of the Chamber, Nuns, Ladies, Maids of Honour, &c.*

Marshall's scenery is described in flamboyant type, together with notice of the organ effect by the "New Grand Aeolophon." The performance began with Rossini's Overture to *Il Barbiere di Siviglia,* and concluded with H. Younge's Christmas Pantomime (ninth time) called *Harlequin and Georgey Barnwell;* or, *The London 'Prentice* — the usual potpourri of spectacular fun and nonsense, including an Abode of Idleness, a Home of Industry, a dioramic walk from Southwark to Camberwell, the new Houses of Parliament, an imitation of T. D. Rice singing "Jim Crow," a balloon race between Mr. and Mrs. Green, a tightrope ascent from the stage to the gallery, and a grand display of fireworks.

---

[46] Henry Colburn (d. 1855), founder of *The New Monthly Magazine, The Literary Gazette,* and other journals, was Bulwer's publisher at this time. Forster married Colburn's widow.

The house was full and fashionable that night, for the widespread publicity had drawn out great numbers of Bulwer's admirers. "The applause was fervent," Macready tells us, and Bulwer sought him alone afterwards to thank him "in the most energetic and ardent manner" for his performance. In his own opinion he had "acted Bragelone well, with earnestness and freshness; some passages were deficient in polish." Still the event was in doubt: "I fear it will not have any considerable success." The friends of the author, including Browning and Talfourd, thought that except in Macready's role the play was "much underacted"; Macready thought it was "shamefully performed." Moreover, it was much too long. On the last day of rehearsal Macready had persuaded Bulwer to cut out the first scene of the fifth act and the Epilogue was suppressed; but even so the performance did not end until eleven o'clock, and there was "considerable impatience manifested through the play." Lady Blessington and Count d'Orsay gave a celebrational supper party at midnight, but the author was a ghost at that feast — he "did not seem happy — his mind was 'away! away!' "

La Vallière was damned at once by the majority of the reviewers, and for a reason mainly unexpected by those closely concerned — for its immorality and profaneness. One critic found it "shockingly irreverent" because it contained such words as "Heaven," and "O Father, bless her." To another it was "the pathos of the stews," to another a "compound of German horrors with French libertinism." The Times of January 5 spewed black venom. "No man but one whose vanity has been flattered most extravagantly within the circle of his own little coterie . . . would have ventured to produce a drama, the subject of which is the heartless debaucheries of a profligate monarch and his equally profligate courtiers. It is in the worst taste of the worst school, the school of the modern French romance. We have all but an enforcement under the crucifix. . . . This may pass in Paris, where jaded roués and faded demireps require the stimulus of blasphemy to rouse their exhausted passions; but in England the public mind is, thank God, yet too healthy to demand such abominable incentives." We need not concern ourselves here with the pruriency of journalism in the year of Victoria's accession, nor even inquire how much of the opposition to the play was inspired by Bulwer's reputation as a political liberal. The simple result of the attacks was that Bulwer bowed to the inevitable, faced the facts, and cut.

The next several days' rehearsals were in fact a scramble of cut and patchwork, intensely harassing to Macready and in the long run productive of little good. On January 5 Macready arrived at the theatre to find Bulwer already there and in the process of cutting. Forster came too and "proposed his own rearrangement, which was acceded to." The next day the play was cut again, this time in accordance with Macready's suggestion, so as to reduce the third act (Macready had little to do in the third act) to less than ten minutes — "a desperate experiment." The audience objected to that arrangement. By the end of the second performance, Macready says, Bulwer and Forster had "concocted some plan for a new scene for me — to which I decidedly objected; indeed, as far as I can judge, it would destroy the character." Bulwer sent him this new scene on January 7, together with a note "couched in the strongest terms," asking as "a personal favour" that he act it. Unhappily, and very stiffly, Macready submitted: "wrote back by his servant to say that I could not resist the impulse of striving to show my appreciation of the honour he had done me, and that I would do it." During the day Forster called to urge him to do it "as another desperate stroke to retrieve the cast-down nature of Bulwer's fame." D'Orsay wrote to urge him to do it. Bulwer called to express himself "most deeply obliged." Thus, seeing how much it meant to Bulwer, Macready did not for the moment "repent having assented."

January 8 being Sunday, he took up the new scene to study it. He was shocked at what he read. "There is nothing in it, and no play can derive strength from a scene which is not missed when omitted, and which does not contain some new and striking effect with regard to the character. I think this has no power, and is merely to make time! — the worst motive for a scene." On Monday he again "returned to the new scene and went over the whole part of Bragelone — *who is now the play.*"

46. BULWER TO MACREADY, *Albany, Sunday, January 8, 1837*

There is one point in the last words you say in La Vallière which have been so generally mentioned to me, that I venture to name it to you. The two words — "Heaven bless her" — might be rendered more striking by the least alteration that might convey a moral or claptrap to the audience, & I suggest, therefore, that it should run thus:

Madame La Vallière as at Present: "Yes."

The action   ⎤ Bragelone: "Accept O
signifying the ⎬ Heaven Earth's worthiest offering — a
blessing   ⎦ repentant heart!"

This, which is only the addition of one line, will I think make a more complete and satisfactory impression on the whole audience and seem "to point the moral." Having made this suggestion, I leave its consideration to you.

In your new scene occur these words, "Heaven is less merciful" — suppose we get rid of the additional Heaven by substituting "Fate."

Forster tells me the Sunday papers were more favourable than could be expected — that the "Observer," commenting on the Saturday's performance, even augurs a long run.

Macready was impressed by Bulwer's "sanguine hope" and "indomitable resolution," and a few days later admired him even more when he learned how Osbaldiston — "the shabby fellow" — had tried to withdraw the production and alter the terms of royalty payment.

47. OSBALDISTON TO BULWER, *Theatre Royal Covent Garden, January 9, 1837*[47]

On mature consideration — seconded by the opinions of the Press — and still more influenced by the falling off in the receipts of the Houses — I do not see my way clear enough to run the risk of another representation of "La Valliere" which will involve me in so much additional expences — still if you can suggest anything on the subject shall be glad to hear from you before my Bill for tomorrow goes to press — I have no objection should *you* desire it, to play it tomorrow, (provided you do not demand any further payment) to try the experiment, otherwise with very great regret as also very great loss I must perforce withdraw it —

48. BULWER TO MACREADY, *Albany, January 10, 1837*

In the second Act instead of "Lord of Hosts" perhaps it will be better to say, "Merciful Heavens;" it makes the same metre & is more safe.

---

[47] Original in the Knebworth Archives.

To-night, I fancy & am given to understand, will decide whether La Vallière is to be withdrawn at once or not. In the former case allow me to say that my deepest regret will be that it did not do more justice both to your wonderful acting & to your most friendly services. For the rest I must say with the murdered Lauzun:

> "My future calls me back
> To rarer schemes" —

or content myself with parodying the lines of a greater man:

> "A *double* sorrow waits my luckless lot,
> My play is damned — and William Farren not."[48]
> *Tout à vous*

Macready was extremely nervous about the performance with the "new scene." He had made many alterations in it without consulting Bulwer, but on a hint from Forster decided to restore Bulwer's own writing, "which was very feeble." He was anxious to succeed that night, for Bulwer's sake and for his own, but "did not act the part to satisfy myself." He was surprised, therefore, at the end of the evening to find Bulwer "in very good spirits," and Osbaldiston and his lieutenant Wallack[49] agreeing that the play was much improved.

Nonetheless it was doomed. The Duchess herself, Helen Faucit, was so ill with influenza on the tenth as to be nearly inaudible, and the play was laid by for a week. William Farren, who in Macready's opinion "certainly was one of the causes of the play's ill-success," now was claiming he had undertaken the part only to oblige the theatre and Bulwer, and was asking to be released from the part of Lauzun.

49. BULWER TO FORSTER, *circa January 12, 1837*

. . . Miss Faucit's illness is one of the links of ill luck in which the poor Duchess has been thralled & spellbound. It must dull & damp the public. But what can't be cured must be endured —

I always had misgivings about the change in the 5th act. — I find, however, that it is a common impression that the play wants a catastrophe sufficiently xciting & wish I had killed Bragelone — But that now would be too violent a change and we must din it into the Public that there *is* a deep catastrophe tho' a Moral one. Which by degrees they will understand. Just ask Macready whether he can make use of the lines — after the [*illegible*] "Tis past we've

---

[48] The "greater man" was Lord Byron who, in the summer of 1821, after the Drury Lane failure of *Marino Faliero* and during the illness of his mother-in-law, circulated among his friends his "Elegy on the recovery of Lady Noel":

> "Behold the blessings of a lucky lot!
> My play is damned and Lady Noel *not*."

See Thomas Moore's *Life of Byron*, 2 vols. (London, 1829), II, 288; and *Lord Byron's Correspondence*, edited by John Murray, 2 vols. (New York, 1922), II, 177.

[49] Henry Wallack (1790-1870) and his brother James (1795?-1864), actors from childhood, divided their time between London and New York as actors and managers. In 1836-37 Henry Wallack was stage manager for Osbaldiston at Covent Garden Theatre. *La Vallière* was "produced under the direction of Mr. Henry Wallack."

conquered" which are in the rejected addition.[50] I should be greatly obliged if he could procure for me the prompt Book that I may have the Stage play [*words obliterated*] to the closet one by next Tuesday. I could if I have it tomorrow morning — I fear they would not give it to my asking.

After the sixth performance, on January 17, Macready took pains to reanalyze the causes of the failure: "Bulwer, has, I fear, added very little to the general effect of the play by the insertion of the new scene, and in my particular case he has done actual mischief. If he has not diminished the interest by lessening the probability (which, I think, he has) in the too sudden change of Bragelone from the warrior to the monk — yet he has so flurried me, so thrown me off my centre by the want of due preparation and proper harmonizing of the scene with the rest of the character, and so distressed me nightly by the hurry and fret into which I am thrown by the very brief allowance of time for my metamorphosis that I am confident he would have acted more judiciously in leaving the play as it stood on the third night — or of restoring some other person's scene. Acted Bragelone as well as I could, but not well. I am *spoiled* in it by Bulwer's injudicious amendments. There was disapprobation at the end of the play." It played but twice more, on January 18 and 20, to a total of eight nights. On the twenty-second Macready "was awoke with a very torturing pain" about his heart, so agonizing that he "thought that death was not far distant." His illness lasted a week or more, after which he went off to the provinces. He took *La Vallière* with him, and played it once, not very happily, in Dublin. Colonel D'Aguilar, the friend who had first brought Bulwer and Macready together, was enthusiastic over it, but his sanguine report was no grounds for hope of a renewal of the play at Covent Garden.

50. BULWER TO MACREADY, *March 25, 1837*

I trust that you are quite recovered from your long & severe indisposition. I heard yesterday from our friend d'Aguilar, who speaks in rapture of your acting in Bragelone & who was also pleased with the play. I wish to know whether there is any chance of its again appearing at Cov. Garden. I hear from Forster that there is some hitch as to Farren & Vandenhoff. Now that the neck of the run is broken, I do not think their loss very serious. I leave this, however, to your judgement. For my own part I am very little curious about it. I have written to M[r] Osbaldistone a short line merely to inquire his intention.

51. BULWER TO MACREADY, *Albany, April 7, 1837*

I am extremely obliged to you, my dear Sir, for your kind letter, which I delayed answering in the hope that I might hear from Mr Osbaldistone, announcing a definite decision respecting La Vallière. I have not yet done so, but

---

[50] A set of "Alterations for La Vallière, Act V, Scene last but one," in Bulwer's hand, is preserved in the Forster Library of the Victoria and Albert Museum. After Louise says "'Tis past! we've conquered!" Bragelone was supposed to add four lines of moral claptrap:
> "Oh! 'Conquered!' — Yes — poor Child — and Kings and Caesars
> Crown'd with the pomp of laurels, never knew
> A mightier victory than triumphant Virtue
> Wins from the weakness of the Struggling Soul."
Evidently Macready declined to speak them.

conclude he declines it. I need not say how much I have felt your kindness throughout — and my regret now is that I was unable to secure to your genius a *longer* triumph — greater for the time it could not be. I have heard many Opinions of La Vallière — I never heard but one of Mr Macready's Bragelone.

Bulwer's pride in *La Vallière* and his affection for it — his "first appeal to gods and galleries" as he called it — grew as the years went by, and in spite of its stage failure he came to look back upon it as his finest work. In the "Introductory Remarks" to his first collected *Dramatic Works* (London, 1841)[51] he claimed it to be "the most polished in point of diction" and to contain "the highest and the completest delineation of ideal character which I have yet accomplished, either in the drama or romance." He duly canvassed the reasons for its failure — its excessive length, the miscasting of Farren and Vandenhoff, the obscurity of the court intrigues, the lack of awesomeness of the catastrophe. Yet, he would have it, it did *not* fail positively, owing to the "extraordinary power which Mr. Macready threw into the part of Bragelone." Then — is this self-delusion or outright chicanery? — "It was performed nine nights," he wrote, "and the manager wished to have continued it for twenty. But the author thought it had already served its purpose, in affording him the experience of what to avoid in future." He hoped yet to alter it and have it staged again, so that it might achieve its proper theatrical good fortune. Of course he never did so.

---

[51] A somewhat abbreviated version of these Introductory Remarks was published by the Earl of Lytton, *Life of Edward Bulwer*, I, 554-62, under the mistaken notion that it had never been published.

chapter two

1837
1838

The Lady of Lyons; or,
Love and Pride

During the summer of 1837 Macready determined on a bold stroke — to take up the management of Covent Garden for the ensuing season and to restore that theatre to "legitimacy" — to provide a constantly varying bill of the standard classics in tasteful productions, of opera in judicious response to the current taste for it, and of new plays as they should become available. It seemed an admirable plan, and in the first month of the season, which was October, the public was offered eleven different bills, from Shakespeare to Sheridan Knowles. But the public was not much interested. By mid-November Macready was sunk in vexation, gloom, and arrears of nearly £1000. It appears that he told his woes to Bulwer, from whom, on November 15, he reports "a most delightful letter," agreeing to write a play for him. Bulwer, still smarting under the failure of *La Vallière*, enjoined Macready to absolute secrecy; and, amazingly, the secret of the authorship of the play that ensued was perfectly kept.

52. BULWER TO MACREADY, *8 Charles St., Berkeley Sq.,*
    [*circa November 15*], *1837*

Private and Confidential.

Tell me *frankly* — Do you really wish for the hazardous experiment of my assistance? I admire so much the stand you are making & I sympathize so much with your struggle, that if I really thought I could be of service, you might command me at once. I have been considering deeply the elements of Dramatic art, and I think I see the secret. But I may be mistaken — nothing more probable.

However, if you sincerely and thoroughly desire it, I will make the experiment. — And submit it to you — Act by Act — as it proceeds. I am aware that in this case, to be of use to you I ought to go to work soon. If you wish it,

I will name the time — as soon after Xmas as you like when you wish the Ms. and you shall have it. But before you answer let me impress this upon you. Waive all compliment — if you think the chances are that I should not succeed, it is better for you not to try and much better for me. I must suspend undertakings of moment and value — which I would delightedly do to serve you and the Drama — but not, I own, merely from restless curiosity, or the speculations of that tempting adventurer — Vanity. Secondly, are you sure that you shall continue your enterprise beyond Xmas? Is is not too severe a task? Were you not Manager, I would not be a second time Dramatist. If these questions should — as I predict — be not answered quite favourably — for I know I may trust to your candour — accept the will for the Deed. But if otherwise, tell me which you prefer, Comedy or Tragedy. I think the former in itself a safer speculation, but where are the Actors? — Whatever subject I select, you may depend on domestic interest and determined concentration up to the close. This letter, as the attempt to which it refers would be — is strictly confidential.

Wishing you all success. . . .

[P.S.] Don't answer this till you are quite at leisure.

53. MACREADY TO BULWER, *Covent Garden Theatre, December 4, 1837*

A fortnight since I was interrupted in the answer I was writing to your letter — a letter for which I assure you I have no words to thank you, — which quite overcame me — and which I shall treasure as one of the consolations which will be left me for all the sickness of heart I have endured in this laborious & dispiriting experiment. — I should very much wish to talk with you on the subject of your enquiry, for I am interrupted here, almost every moment, as I write; but this I may say, and in the most emphatic manner, that in my opinion there can be no doubt of the most triumphant and beneficial results from your assistance.

Can you not oblige me by looking in any evening here? — You are sure of finding me: — There are so many things on the subject that I should wish to say: but all that I could say would be weak in expressing the gratitude and sincere regard with which I must be, my dear Sir, Always Yours'

There is a legend (now partly confirmed by the following newly discovered letter) to the effect that Macready one day exclaimed to Bulwer, "Oh! that I could get a play like *The Honeymoon!*" and Bulwer thereupon saw his course so clearly that his comedy was completed within a fortnight.[1] The progress was not quite this swift, but Bulwer did indeed make haste. Macready records on December 20 a "note from Bulwer, informing me of his having begun a play and of his confidence in its success."

---

[1] *The Honey Moon: a comedy, in five acts* (London, 1805), in which Macready often played the Duke of Aranza, was one of several successful plays, all published posthumously, by John Tobin (1770-1804). *The Lady of Lyons* and *The Honey Moon* both show a vain and ambitious woman being shorn of her pride of place.

54. BULWER TO MACREADY, [*December 20, 1837*][2]

I have done half the play — & am more and more pleased with it as applied to what you wanted. You will be part comic — part tragic. The Honeymoon hero, with more, I think, of lightness & ease on one hand, & sentiment & high passion on the other. — What I now want to know, *by return of post*, if possible, is this — 1ˢᵗ In how short a time can you change a dress — (*no disguise of face requisite*) — from a loose dress of a smart young man of low rank (in France) to the demicourt dress of a supposed prince — could you wear one over the other? It would help me greatly if I could bring you in both in the same act — at an interval of 3 minutes —. Can this be managed. —

2ᵈˡʸ Did I ever understand you to say that you wanted to figure in a dance — or was it but a dream? —

3ᵈˡʸ My heroine (who by the by is charming tho' I say it) — ought to be played by a Lady light in hand — something like Vestris only with more feeling — Mrs. Nesbitt [*sic*] might conceive it — But who shall I have, a Huddart or a Faucit — or have you Miss Taylor[3] — This I wish to know in order not to overweight her more than I can help — I have done the 2 Acts of grave sentiment & passion viz: 3 & 4 —. Would you like to see them before I proceed. If so I will copy them out — but my inspiration (!!!) pushes me on so rapidly that I am afraid to cool in the vein —

---

[2] The original of this letter, not hitherto printed, is in the Library of the University of Illinois.

[3] Mme. Vestris, née Lucia Elizabeth Bartolozzi (1797-1856), married Auguste Vestris, a dancer, in 1813, and was deserted by him in 1816; married Charles James Mathews in 1838. She was the finest singing actress of her time, an excellent comedienne, and a skillful theatre manager. At the Olympic, in the early thirties, she produced Planché's extravaganzas, and later at Covent Garden, in such plays as Boucicault's *London Assurance,* she was responsible for innovations tending toward modern realism.

Mrs. Louisa Cranstoun Mordaunt Nisbett, later Lady Boothby (1812-58), a comedienne of much beauty and charm, and of unfortunate personal life. Two years after her successful London debut in 1829 she left the stage to marry a military man, John Nisbett, who was killed in a riding accident soon thereafter. She returned to the stage in 1832 and continued a popular favorite. She created Lady Gay Spanker in *London Assurance* in 1841, and was Macready's leading lady in his last Drury Lane company in 1842-43. Her marriage to Sir William Boothby in 1844 was terminated by his death in 1846. Again she returned to the stage, but retired in ill-health in 1851.

Marie Amelia Huddart, later Mrs. Warner (1804-54), an excellent tragic actress and one of Macready's favorites. In the early thirties Macready enjoyed her company as well as her stage work whenever he visited Dublin. In 1836 she established herself in London, the following year married Robert Warner, the proprietor of a popular tavern in Bow Street, and subsequently was a member of Macready's companies at Covent Garden and Drury Lane. After 1843 she assisted Phelps in the management of Sadler's Wells, and later managed the Marylebone Theatre. She supported Macready in his farewell performances. When she was dying of cancer in 1853, Macready solicited funds for her relief, and after her death he and Miss Burdett-Coutts assumed the care of her two children.

Harriette Deborah Taylor, later Mrs. Walter Lacy (1807-74), a leading actress in both comic and tragic lines. Her London debut was at Covent Garden in 1830. She starred as Helen in Knowles's *The Hunchback*. A member of Macready's first Covent Garden company, she played leading roles at Covent Garden for a dozen years. She retired in 1848.

My plot requires what I hate — viz an interval of 3 or 4 years between the 4th & 5th act   Is there any serious evil in this? if announced in the playbills? — So much for business — now for pleasure — I have some very fair Ladies to dine with me on Saturday next at 7 o'clock! Will you kindly join them —

A week and a day later Macready received four acts of the new play, under the title of *The Fraudulent Marriage,* and that night he read it.

55. MACREADY TO BULWER, *Covent Garden Theatre, December 29, [1837]*

I *devoured* your M. S. last night — am most anxious to lose no time in proceeding with it, if, as I have every reason to hope the strength & passion — the power, of the fifth act keeps pace with the four preceding ones. When shall I have the fifth? — I will keep these to note down what occurs to me on a second reading. I ought to see you on Sunday at latest to talk it all over. . . .

On December 30 he read it twice more, once to himself and once to his wife and sister. To his dismay, they had discovered the authorship. The next day, he called on Bulwer to discuss the play; "He has not settled his fifth act, and I cannot help him."

56. MACREADY TO BULWER, *Covent Garden Theatre, January 2, [1838]*

You will excuse my anxiety to know, if you have hit upon any termination yet. — I am quite an incapable: the necessity for despatch, and the number of other things to be thought upon so press me, that I am deprived of the little inventive knack, that has served me on similar occasions.

Let us hope that you have had some glimpse of a way out of the present difficulty.

57. BULWER TO MACREADY, *[circa January 2, 1838]*[4]

I have thought of the best plan for Act 5 & think I can keep up the interest tho' there will be no scene quite so striking as those in the 3rd. and 4th Act. I have set about it in earnest and you shall have the whole play by Sunday night. Write me a word where to send it. I stay in town on purpose to finish it. Now, however, for two preliminaries. In the first place I do not wish the play to be the property of the Theatre. As long as you are manager, heaven grant that be for 5 generations, the play is yours. The instant you cease it returns to me to prevent a litigation with your possible successor — this should be an author's arrangement. Secondly. May I again press upon your mind that my object in this attempt is to give you a popular and taking play. Now unless you feel thoroughly persuaded I will not say of its *certain* success, but of the great probability of its attraction, I entreat as a favour to both of

---

[4] The original of this letter and several following, identified as "typescript," is unknown. These typescripts are folded into a copy of Brander Matthews' *Letters of Bulwer-Lytton to Macready,* now in the Library of the University of Illinois. I have no doubt of the authenticity of these letters, though it is plain that the copyist has made numerous errors. Some I have tacitly corrected.

us, that you do not let any wish to compliment me, any delicate fear of wounding my amour propre, allow you to bring it on the stage. For you it would be detrimental to have your first new play either a failure or a luke-warm success, for me it would be permanent discouragement. Far rather would I, if you entertain a doubt, put aside this play and set to work at another, grudging no time, no thought, no trouble, to be really and effectively useful as an ally. I own that I have some apprehension from the want of an actress — Miss Faucit freezes me and I have some fear also that the 5th. act may be weaker than its predecessors. I wish all attention to be given to these and to all drawbacks. I know that your kindness to me might make you loth to avoid hazarding an attempt which you might think I wished to produce on the stage, but I have no desire of the kind. For both our sakes I repeat that I would avoid hazard, unless you yourself are sanguine. Having said this to you without one fear or scruple, I commit the decision, only remember that if you do shrink from responsibility of undertaking the play thus put to you, that I will cheerfully direct my labour to some new plot.

[*Enclosure*]

Programme of Act 5

Two years after act 4. The army has returned triumphantly from Italy. A regiment quartered at Lyons. Damas now a general — Melnotte who has changed his name till he has redeemed it, is Col. Morier, the hero of the day. Pauline's father has become a bankrupt. Pauline supports her parents (Morier ought to lose an arm if you don't object to that little operation.) She is persecuted by Beauseant the principal creditor of her father. Ultimately she is delivered from Beauseant by her lover (unknown), persuaded by Damas to go to a ball at the house that once belonged to the Deschappelles, just bought by Col. Morier, then the discovery is made, & "all goes merry as a marriage bell."

Macready records this last letter ("stipulating for a frank opinion" and "professing himself ready to begin another play, if I disapproved of this") on January 3. It is curious to note in his response to it his objection to "the clause of non-remuneration," for Bulwer had not exactly made such an offer. He may have done so in conversation, of course.

58. Macready to Bulwer, *Covent Garden Theatre, January 3, 1838*

You have taken from me long since all power of thanking you by the accumulated obligations you have laid upon me. — I have had a strong motive for wishing you to persevere in your task, — and I may truly say it is unmixed with any selfish consideration. — It has been my earnest desire to see you triumphantly vindicate your genius from the ungenerous treatment of the press, and I should glory in lending my humble assistance to the accomplish-ment of such an object. — You may therefore rely upon my caution with regard to its production: — you shall have my own frank opinion, & I will use the power I possess to obtain for you those, which may correct or confirm mine. — Rely upon me, that I will not commit you: — Nothing could recompense me for the pain it would cost me, should any but the most decisive success follow the experiment. You have bound me to sincerity, and even were I otherwise disposed, I must, at even a risk, be faithful to your injunctions.

There is only one point of your stipulation to which I object, & I hope — in the issue, if not at once — I may over-rule you: — you have already so drawn upon my gratitude that I WISH you would spare me the clause of non-remuneration. At all events, I *beg* that may stand over till our cause is tried.

I shall look anxiously to Sunday — and on Wednesday will send you my own opinion with an account of the impression made upon a limited audience by it.

P.S. I had forgot to request you to send to me on Sunday at 8. York Gate. Regent's Park.

59. BULWER TO MACREADY, [*January 4, 1838*][5]

I send you Act 5 in its rough copy. I may be able to polish the wording in transcribing it, but I hope that you will like the substance. I have thrown into it more passion & interest than I had dared to hope for & cannot but trust it will tell & sustain the others.

The only titles I can think of for the play are as follows:

1st. (Your own) Nobility.

2. How will it end.

3. Lost and won.

4. Love and pride.

I have received your most kind letter & will abide by Wednesday's decision. Send me back act 5 as soon as read, with any alterations you can suggest that I may copy it and return it with the rest.

Macready was not altogether pleased at such speed of delivery. "Read it, and have my apprehensions about it; he writes too hastily, he does not do himself justice." Immediately he reported his general dubiety, with one or two specific suggestions for revision.

60. MACREADY TO BULWER, *8 York Gate, Regent's Park, Thursday even,* [*January 4, 1838*]

I have read the fifth Act, and instantly report to you some objections. — In primis Melnotte should not enter with Damas — they left the stage together just before, and have to explain themselves, that two years have since elapsed. This will not be well. — Cannot some brother officers parting to their places of billet convey the fact of the time to the audience — then Damas's scene with Beauseant — Damas having told a friend, that Melnotte, or Morier has rushed to every person likely to give him information of Pauline. — Upon

---

[5] Typescript in the Library of the University of Illinois.

hearing Beauseant's news, he observes upon poor Melnotte's condition, who enters to him for the scene of despair, which now stands: — the minute details in the last scene are to be avoided — as dangerous.

I cannot judge of the quantity of effect in this act — taking it thus singly and hastily: — there is effect in it, but it is not easy to decide upon its chance with an audience without preparation.

The exit of Melnotte should be as to an object — not merely a description of his own condition. — I think you will find the suggested alteration of the opening of the act very much helps on the story. — I shall look most anxiously for Sunday. — Will you send it to me here?

[P.S.] We can pause upon the title.

Bulwer called to discuss the alterations, especially in the last act. These he executed overnight, and on January 6 he redelivered the whole manuscript.

61. BULWER TO MACREADY, *8 Charles St., Saturday, [January 6, 1838]*[6]

I now send you the play completed. I have done my part. I now confess I like Act 5 much. Perhaps in Act I it may be as well to omit the innkeeper's joke about the hare, but without it the dialogue is necessarily dull. I have left it therefore for you to omit or not. I wish the M.S. were fairer. But I hope it is intelligible, & I had no time.

Waiting your Wednesday report.

[*Enclosure*]

Alteration in commencement of act 5.

Scene 1st.

Enter Officers.

1st. Officer. Upon my word a very fine city (turning to second officer) your birthplace I think.

2nd. Officer. Yes, it is just two years and a half since I left it with gallant old Damas for the campaign in Italy, and now here we are again, Damas a general and I a Lieutenant!

3rd. Officer. Ah, we rise quick in the French Army. Now the war in Italy is over, I hope they will make work for our regiment elsewhere.

Enter Damas as General Damas.

Well met again gentlemen, I hope you will amuse yourselves tolerably during our short stay in Lyons. Dear Lyons, my native city, it is let me see, 2 years and a half since I beheld it last! How it is improved, a patriot does not regret growing older when the years that bring decay to himself only [ripen the prosperity?] of his country.

1st. Officer. And cover his own grey hairs with the laurel wreath, General! Ah, you made the best of your time in Italy, we had warm work there &c. (as written in the text).

On Sunday Macready gave it all a very careful reading (though apparently did

---

[6] Typescript in the Library of the University of Illinois.

not read it to a "limited audience" as promised), and concluded that it, "considering the time in which it has been planned and written, is really wonderful." Two days later he made his acceptance definite.

62. MACREADY TO BULWER, *8 York Gate, January 9, [1838]*

I write in my usual haste to say to you, that my impression of the play is fully confirmed by all the experiments I have made of it, — that the copy will be made out without delay — and that it will be read to the actors in the course of this week. — Please to remember, if you should hear anything of a New Play called (— — what?) that "it is the work of a young man, called Calvert — I fancy some relation to Sir Harry Calvert,[7] formerly Adjutant General". — It is as well to be provided, and if you will assume this as your nom de theatre you will oblige me: there is no other way to check inquisitiveness on the subject. Plays are pouring in upon us, but you will be first in the field.

P.S. You may conclude, should you hear nothing from me, that no news is good news, and that all is going smoothly forward.

63. BULWER TO MACREADY, *[circa January 10, 1838]*[8]

I am very glad to hear so good an account of our friend Melnotte. I hope he will turn out as well as we could wish. There is one thing by the bye that I have been taking for granted, a little too rashly perhaps, or rather I have forgotten that you are manager as well as actor, should now our friend have a run, have you time &c. to keep him company, as he will come to a stop very suddenly if he is not impelled by the superior energies of his impersonater.

2nd. Will you, in returning my M.S. let me run my eye over the copy, for my writing is so bad that some mistakes may have crept in. Also if the hare is to be omitted, ought I not to invent something humorous to put in the mouth of Glavis to end that scene.

3rd. About Melnotte's dress as Prince. Do you not think that one something like our Cabinet uniform, only dark green, instead of blue, would be suitable and appropriate.

Now as to Mr. Calvert. I think it would be a very good plan by and by, suppose the play have a run, but it is liable to some grave objections in the first instance. I fear the Town will be biassed against the thought of anything very good from an unknown author not heard of before in literature, whereas the anonymous at first might rouse curiosity & the name of Mr. Calvert might then become useful in turning it aside.

I am just returning to town thoroughly tired and knocked up

P.S. When do you expect it to be out?

---

[7] Sir Harry Calvert (1763-1826), fought in the American wars and the French wars, and in 1799 was made adjutant-general of the British forces; he was famous for his reforms of military schools and hospitals.

[8] Typescript in the Library of the University of Illinois.

64. MACREADY TO BULWER, *8 York Gate, Regent's Park, January 11, [1838]*

My hopes rise, as my intimacy with Melnotte grows. — I wish I was younger — and that my chere amie and myself had put our heads out of the window, when it was raining beauty — but as Falstaff says, "That's past praying for." Pray do not have any fear as to the *managing* of the play — I mean, as to using every means to sustain its course &c — Believe me, I shall be more tender of it, than if it were my own. My feelings (I hate to add the truth, my interests also) are all enlisted in its cause. — You shall have your own M. S. on Saturday morning, if not tomorrow; the fair copy is nearly finished. — I intend to read it to the actors, and distribute the parts on Tuesday next. —

The hare must be omitted, and if you give us a joke in its place, be kind enough to give a thought to the end of the second act. "Do you?" in italics would end the chapter of a novel and make the reader pause long, before he turned the leaf, to consider the state of mind and bring to his imagination the picture of Melnotte — but, I assure you, that on the stage the words would be ineffective to close an act. — After they are uttered, a resolution taken, or an impatient desire expressed to escape from his reflections, would perhaps carry it off — but you will no doubt supply the desideratum.

I had thought of the very kind of dress you mentioned — except that your suggestion of the changes of colour to green is an excellent amendment.

With respect to Mr. Calvert, — it is necessary to have a name to elude inquisitiveness — we are constantly liable to detection without some one to rest upon. — Curiosity is not awakened for an anonymous author, witness the first night of the Provost of Bruges! — It is not the *first night* that decides the attraction of a play — witness our new opera! — I think in all *the policy* of our proceeding you had better trust to my care and zeal.

I will use the means I possess to pique curiosity about it before it appears, but little can now be done in that way: — My confidence is in the originality of the play — its interest, poetry, and passion — added to which it is the first new play produced under my management — which will add something to the expectation of play-goers. — I hope to have it produced either on Thursday Feb. 1st — or Saturday Feb. 3rd — but I must work hard for this.

I cannot wonder at your fatigue — My astonishment is, that you keep your health and mind under the labours you impose upon yourself.

65. MACREADY TO BULWER, *8 York Gate, Regent's Park, January 14, [1838]*

I hope you will excuse my delay — I should have sent the accompanying packet on Saturday, but did not leave the Theatre until late in the afternoon, and today I have been incessantly employed.— Will you favour me with any communication addressed here — as I fear suspicions arising from your initials being seen at the Theatre.— I shall tell you the effect it produces at the reading on Tuesday.— Pray think of the end of the 2nd Act for me.— If you ever look at a playbill you will see the note of preparation sounded

66. BULWER TO MACREADY, *January 15, 1838*[9]

I send you a few words to supply the hare — not very witty but perhaps useful to point the distinction between Beauseant and Glavis. I send you also the best addition I could make to 'Do you'. I hope it will do. In the close of Act 4, after your speech and exit, strike out the line given to Damas. His going out explains without words. Strike out also Madame Deschappelle's last speech and leave nothing but Pauline "Claude, Claude, my husband."

    Mons.

You have a father still.

Indeed I would rather leave these out also, & drop the scene with your exit which is sure to be effective — Pauline merely rushing towards you and her father intercepting her. You can judge of this in the rehearsal.

I am still very unwell.

P.S. Have you thought of a title. I cannot. As a last resource we have the simple name "Melnotte."

I shall be glad to know who has Beauseant and who Glavis. Glavis should be a comic fellow.

67. MACREADY TO BULWER, *8 York Gate, Regent's Park, January 16, 1838*

I have delayed my reply to yours of yesterday, that I might give you fuller information on our proceedings. — The alterations you have sent me are, I think, improvements, and have been copied into the M.S. The title is still a puzzle to me — it is of consequence, and not hastily to be decided on — we have a week at least before it is necessary to publish it. — I hope you will approve the following disposition of the characters — Beauseant Elton — Glavis Meadows — Damas Bartley — Des Chappelles Waldron — Gaspar Diddear — Madame Deschappelles Mrs. Glover — Pauline Miss H. Faucit — Widow Melnotte Mrs. Clifford.[10]

---

[9] Typescript in the Library of the University of Illinois.

[10] Edward William Elton (1794-1843), a promising actor in the 1830's and early forties, a member of Macready's Covent Garden and Drury Lane companies. He was drowned in the Irish Sea in the wreck of the Pegasus.

Drinkwater Meadows (1799-1869), a comic actor, whose London debut was at Covent Garden in 1821, was a member of Macready's Covent Garden company. Macready expected to cast him as the Fool in *Lear* until he hit upon the strange notion that a woman (Priscilla Horton) should play the part (January 5, 1838). Meadows was later Secretary to the Covent Garden Theatrical Fund.

George Bartley (1782?-1858), a comic actor, was employed in Macready's Covent Garden company. He was loyal to Macready in resistance to Alfred Bunn's management in 1836, and conferred with Macready on plans to establish a new theatre. By the end of the Covent Garden engagement, however, Macready was accusing Bartley of conniving with the proprietors to oust him from management.

Waldron and Diddear were minor actors in Macready's Covent Garden company.

Julia Betterton Glover (1779-1850), a comic actress "of high talent," says Macready on the occasion of her death, but she had no "principle of honesty." He discounts her claim to be descended from Thomas Betterton, asserting that her family name was really Butterton. Her debut at Covent Garden was in 1797, and she played Andromache to

I read it this morning to the parties concerned and the impression was general. I am almost superstitious about uttering my thoughts and hopes on this subject — but you will not think on that account that I am cold in my appreciation of what you have done — both as to the work itself and in your consideration for my interest.

I will take the earliest opportunity of trying to find you at home to satisfy you on any points on which you may wish to be informed. I can also explain why I think it advisable that you should avoid the Theatre: — but if you at any time wish to see me, let me know, and I will come to you however embarrassed.

We *must*, I fear, use some *little* licence with the costume: — the cut of 1796 is so very ungraceful, that it will be impossible to "make up" decently with it. I must talk with you about the three dresses of Melnotte.

68. BULWER TO MACREADY, [*circa January 27, 1838*][11]

Additions and corrections to the part of Madame Deschappelles

Act 1st.   Scene 1st.   (Mrs Glover)

After the words "Do homage to the Beauty of Lyons" add "Ah, we live again in our children, especially when they have our eyes and complexion!"

After Beauseant's exit, Madame speaks, ending with "We kept up our dignity!" alter to the following "How forward these men are! I think we kept up our dignity! Every girl knows how to accept an offer, but it requires a vast deal of experience to refuse one with the proper air of disdainful affability & elegant self possession. I used to practice it at school with the dancing master."   In the same scene.

Damas says "You ought to be ashamed of such nonsense at your time of life" alter Madame's answer as follows, "My time of life! Sir, that is an expression never applied to any lady till she is sixty nine and three quarters, and only then by the clergyman of the Parish."

Ibid.

In Madame's last speech in this act and scene, after their words "Ah, you little coquette," omit what follows in the text and insert "When a young lady is always doing mischief, it is a sure sign that she takes after her mother!"

Act II.

Madame says "Ha, ha, how very severe, what wit!"
Add "Common people are rude, great people are only satirical."

Macready's Orestes on the occasion of his debut in London on September 16, 1816. As a member of Macready's Covent Garden company she was expected to play Madame Deschappelles in *The Lady of Lyons,* but on February 3 she absented herself from the theatre, claiming illness or injury, and the role was assigned to Mrs. W. Clifford, a minor actress in the company. Macready believed (March 21, 1838) that she had feigned illness in order to fill an engagement out of town.

[11] Typescript in the Library of the University of Illinois. Conjectural dating is based on Macready's diary note that he received alterations on this day.

Ibid.

Before exit of Madame she says "I don't like leaving girls alone with their lovers &c," instead of this speech insert "I don't like leaving girls alone with their lovers, but a Prince! Ah, that makes all the difference! Your great man never takes a liberty, except when he takes it away!"

Act 5th

Madame says to Pauline "Why Pauline, you are quite in dishabille &c" at the end of her speech add "Pedigree and jointure, you have them both in Mons. Beauseant, a young lady decorously brought up should only have two considerations in her choice of a husband. Ist, how was he born? 2nd. When will he die? All the rest are trifling details to be left to parental anxiety."

Ibid.

Instead of the line "He's wondrously informed, I wish you joy, sir" insert "She's wondrously improved, accept my blessing.

69. BULWER TO MACREADY, *Knebworth, January 31, 1838*[12]

How Lovelace[13] could have suspected, much less asserted such a thing I cannot fancy. I never breathed a syllable to him or to any human being — but one on whom I can faithfully depend. I begin to believe that the birds in the air are eavesdroppers. It might be as well, if rumours of our correspondence are afloat to hint that I was much interested in the play recommended you by Lady Blessington,[14] or the one which Lord Durham[15] tells me you recd. from Mr. Kennedy.[16] I think the sooner and more generally Mr. Calvert is made use of the better.

Ambition is too grand for our subject, but anything that uses the adjective, such as the Ambitious Lover or the Ambitious Suitor or Love and Pride would do pretty well. I sent you a list yesterday, but I really think the Ambitious Lover as good as any.

I perfectly concur with you on the necessity of preserving the incognito. Nothing pains me more than the thought of running the gauntlet barefaced as well as bare shouldered with La Vallière pinned to my back. I will use all caution & think your acuteness may yet put forth a wrong scent.

---

[12] Typescript in the Library of the University of Illinois.

[13] No one of this name appears in the Macready circle. The copyist has apparently misread "Wallace" — *vide* the Postscript and the following letter.

[14] Marguerite, Countess of Blessington (1789-1849) was the celebrated novelist, leader of fashion, and proprietress of Gore House, where with Count d'Orsay she received the male fashionable and artistic elite of London.

[15] John George Lambton, first Earl of Durham (1792-1840), a stormy liberal politician, known as Radical Jack, who helped draft and push through the Reform Bill of 1832. As Governor-General of Canada after 1838 he contributed to the union of Upper and Lower Canada.

[16] A Mr. W. Kennedy submitted a tragedy called the *Siege of Antwerp* on December 24, 1837 — "clever," says Macready, "but not, I think, sufficiently so for representation."

[P.S.] Wallace is malignant to me — abused me in the Foreign and British Quarterly.[17]

70. BULWER TO MACREADY, *Knebworth, February 2, 1838*[18]

Unless you like the ambitious lover or any of the titles in my last letter, let it be The Adventurer, or Love and Pride.

I am sure Mr. Wallace would not have repeated any report from unworthy motives. I only referred to a former attack to shew that no doubt very honestly, he was no great partizan of mine.

Pardon my query about Wednesday. It is so bad a day for our house that I looked askant on it for yours. I am fully assured of all your friendly zeal and generous exertions.

Macready records this proposal of the title of *The Adventurer* — "but when I saw it written down I would not consent to it." Had that title been adhered to it would have indicated that the emphasis of the play was on Macready's role of Claude Melnotte; but this was not true, as Macready suddenly realized. After reading the play over again the next day and conversing with Forster "on its degree of power, and more particularly of the quantity given to the character of Melnotte," he was induced "to give it a more scrutinizing examination" — out of which "to my surprise and regret, I find that it tapers off after the third act, and that the female character has the strength of the two last acts — *tant pis!*" On that very day, curiously, Bulwer was inventing the more fitting title, which was finally to obtain, *The Lady of Lyons; or, Love and Pride.*

71. BULWER TO MACREADY, *Knebworth, Sunday, [February 4, 1838]*[19]

I think titles are as much a plague to us as they were to Pauline & if we called it "No Title" it would hit off our own dilemma.

I agree with you that the adventurer is poor and bald. If you like "Ambition or the Village Prince" take it by all means. I fear it is rather vanity than ambition that urges the womankind of the play and rather love than ambition that inspires Claude. But it does not much matter.

I suggest two more. "The Lady of Lyons" — or Love and Pride."[20] False

---

[17] William Wallace (1786-1839), lawyer and writer, was one of Macready's oldest and best friends. His attack on Bulwer was a savage review of Bulwer's novels — "Mr. Bulwer and the Lady Novelists" — in *The British and Foreign Review; or, European Quarterly Journal* (December, 1836) III, vi, 477-510. On January 7, 1838, he had explained to Macready "his deep concern at having written that harsh article" and the steps he had taken to atone for it.

[18] Typescript in the Library of the University of Illinois.

[19] Typescript in the Library of the University of Illinois.

[20] Helen Faucit credited the naming of the play to George Bartley, the stage manager and the creator of Colonel Damas. One day at rehearsal, when the title was under discussion, he "turned to me, and taking off his hat, and bowing in the soldier-like manner of the colonel in the play, said, 'I think "my young cousin" should give the play a name. Shall it not be called *The Lady of Lyons?*'" See *On Some of Shakespeare's Female Characters* (London, 1904), p. 165. It is pleasant to restore the authority for the title to the author himself.

courtship and true love. Of these the first is not bad I think, at all events better than Pauline &c. Choose which you like without scruple. I shall be in town Tuesday evening if you want to see me the next day. Certainly you can wear the military undress — anything better than the heavy French hat &c.

72. BULWER TO MACREADY, *Charles St., February 6, [1838]*[21]

Seeing your most brilliant success in Lear,[22] I cannot but write a line to say that no consideration for any supposed impatience of mine, and no belief in the peculiar goodness of the [*words missing*] may interfere with the run of a play that has gained you such fame. If you should therefore at all think it advantageous for the theatre or ourself to postpone the "Adventurer" for a week or two longer, pray do not have any scruples as far as I am concerned.

P.S. I think the title looks very well.

Just arrived.

By the way, in the cottage scene, Act 3, there is a short speech of yours. (I quote from memory)

No lady — no not slave, this sad hour I do renounce all hope — despair is free!

Would it not be more effective to make one line of the thought —

No lady, no not slave. Despair is free!

I have originally so written it, but think it too epigrammatic for the slovenliness of passion expounded the thought.[23] You can see.

73. BULWER TO MACREADY, *Charles St., February 7, 1838*[24]

I am very sorry for Mrs. Glover's accident. People had no bones with La Vallière — it is hard they should be at all bones with your Lady of Lyons. Sub judice lis est. The matter is with you, either to postpone the play indefinitely till Mrs. Glover's recovery, or to put in some other person in her part. In the latter case would Mrs. Humby[25] do? You must consider and decide which course would be best.

The words "serious detriment to chances of success" are "words of fear. Unpleasing to an author's ear." And at the risk of seeming touchy and sensitive I must repeat what I before said. viz. That unless our hopes greatly exceed your doubts, I think we ought both to shrink from your experiment.

Bulwer's worries were apparently allayed on the evening of Friday, February 9, when he attended *King Lear* and visited Macready behind the scenes. They "talked about the play, with the arrangements for which he seemed well satisfied."

---

[21] Typescript in the Library of the University of Illinois.

[22] Macready's *King Lear* had opened on January 25 and played three times in the repertory by this date.

[23] Apparently an error in transcription.

[24] Typescript in the Library of the University of Illinois.

[25] Anne Ayre Humby (fl. 1817-49), a popular comedienne in servant roles since her London debut in 1817.

74. Bulwer to Macready, *February, [circa 13], 1838*

You will excuse my observing that it may be well to leave Mrs Clifford the lighter points I added to the part — unless she prove unequal to them in rehearsal. I do not think they require much skill in delivery & they round and polish the composition.

Another thing — can you give Miss Faucit any instructions to speak more clearly, to let her voice *travel* out of her throat? For she was perfectly inaudible in Cordelia. It is a great pity.

Pardon this.

P.S. I shall probably hear from you on Friday, the result of what I cannot see.

75. Macready to Bulwer, *8 York Gate, Tuesday, [February 13, 1838]*

I forgot to ask you, whether you wished any friends of yours, to be present on Thursday night — if so, let me know what private boxes you would like to have. I will send the cards to them in my own name, so that there will be no suspicion at the Theatre.

The first night success of *The Lady of Lyons* on Thursday, February 15, was indubitable. The pit rose to cheer it again and again at the conclusion, and as John Forster reported in the next *Examiner*, "It was a scene to raise, to revive, to give a new zest to play-going." Even Macready, never overly hopeful, was for once confident of victory. "Acted Claude Melnotte in Bulwer's play pretty well; the audience felt it very much, and were carried away by it; the play in the acting was completely successful. Was called for, and leading on Miss Faucit, was well received; gave out the play." The company that created *The Lady of Lyons*, as given in the Covent Garden playbill of the opening night, was as follows:

Beausent [*sic*]	MR. ELTON
Glavis	MR. MEADOWS
Colonel Damas	MR. BARTLEY
Mons. Deschappelles	MR. STRICKLAND
Captain Gervais	MR. HOWE
Captain Dupont	MR. PRITCHARD
Major Desmoulins	MR. ROBERTS
Landlord of the Golden Lion	MR. YARNOLD
Gaspar	MR. DIDDEAR
Claude Melnotte	MR. MACREADY
Servants	MR. COLLET, MR. BENDER
Notary	MR. HOLMES
Madame Deschappelles	MRS. W. CLIFFORD
Pauline Deschappelles	MISS HELEN FAUCIT
The Widow Melnotte	MRS. GRIFFITH
Janet	MRS. EAST
Marian	MISS GARRICK

The evening was concluded with the Christmas Pantomime (forty-second performance) called *Harlequin and Peeping Tom of Coventry; or, The Ladye Godiva and The Witch of Warwick*, plus Clarkson Stanfield's Diorama of *Scenes at Home and Abroad*. The playbill announces for the next night, replacing the pantomime, a new comic opera, called *The Black Domino*, for next Monday *King Lear*, for next Tuesday *Julius Caesar*, etc.

Macready's earlier misgivings about the hastiness and carelessness of Bulwer's workmanship were well founded, and perhaps in a less worried season he might have compelled the author to greater exertions. *The Lady of Lyons* is a charming and durable fable ruined by superficial writing. Bulwer took for subject a story by Helen Maria Williams, called *The History of Perourou; or, The Bellows Mender* (London, 1801). As he reshapes the story, the time is the Napoleonic era. Pauline Deschappelles, the proud daughter of a rich merchant of Lyons, aspires to marry into the nobility, and therefore snubs all suitors of common origin. One of these, a M. Beauséant, revenges himself by palming off on her as an Italian nobleman one Claude Melnotte, a gardener's son. When she discovers, after the marriage ceremony, that a trick has been played upon her, her chagrin is intense. But Claude, who is one of "nature's noblemen," and who genuinely loves her, offers to free her by divorce and runs away to Italy to join Napoleon's army. Two years later he returns, rich and celebrated, rescues Pauline from the financial clutches of the wicked Beauséant, and reclaims her affections. All ends happily. Simple as the story is, it was sturdy enough to hold the stage almost to the end of the century. If the author could have supplanted the dialogue verbiage with true verse or firm prose, and the banality with wit, we might enjoy it still today.

76. MACREADY TO BULWER, *York Gate, February 16, [1838]*

I hope you were satisfied with last night: — I heard nothing but expressions of delight — and was myself indeed delighted at the feeling of the audience.— I trust to be able to see you soon: — but would not have you come behind the scenes at present.

Bulwer was speaking in the House of Commons on the opening night, so he could not be present for most of the event. After his speech, according to legend, he hurried to the theatre to catch the last act. Meeting T. N. Talfourd, who was leaving the theatre, he asked diffidently how the play was going. "Oh, very well, for that sort of thing," Talfourd replied. Bulwer joined Lady Blessington in her box. At the end, when the applause was thundering, she turned toward him for his opinion. "Oh, very well," said Bulwer, "for that sort of thing," and hurried away.[26] The story is in most points likely enough, and especially interesting in view of the aftermath. Talfourd, who had a vulgarly high opinion of his own dramatic talents, let it be known that *The Lady* "perfectly disgusted him."[27] A week later the published volume revealed that Bulwer had dedicated it to him.

It is unlikely, however, that Lady Blessington was present on the opening night to play her little role in the legend. At any rate, in her note of congratulation to Bulwer she seems to date her enthusiasm for *The Lady* from reading Forster's review in the *Examiner,* which appeared three days later. Apparently she first saw the play during the week following.

77. LADY BLESSINGTON TO BULWER, *Gore House, Saturday,* *[February 24, 1838]*[28]

I confess, that I have rarely in my life, enjoyed so great a pleasure, as on finding that a play, which excited my feelings, and delighted my imagination,

---

[26] The Earl of Lytton, *The Life of Edward Bulwer,* I, 535.
[27] Macready's diary entry for February 27, 1838.
[28] This letter and Bulwer's response to it are in the Knebworth Archives.

more, than any other I had ever beheld, was from your pen — my proudest anticipations are fulfilled, for the success of the Lady of Lyons leaves all competitors behind, and this too without the *prestige* of its authorship being known — When I read the extracts in the Examiner last Sunday, I said that I thought there was only one man in England, or in the world, who *could* have written them. The thoughts, the language, struck me as being yours and yours only, but yet on reflection, I thought that you would have entrusted me with the secret, and knowing also your numerous other avocations I fancied it was impossible, that you could have found time, to have written this exquisite Play — Now shall I confess a weakness to you, I felt the charms of the high souled, and beautiful sentiments, and the eloquent words in which they are dressed, so strongly, that I was jealous for your fame, and pained, that *another could so write*. When I heard everyone I met proclaiming the Lady of Lyons to be perfection, nay some adding "Oh! if your friend Bulwer wrote a piece like this he might be as unrivalled in his theatrical, as in his novelist reputation," I have felt envious of the Author of this piece, which has now all praise, and wished that so dangerous a rival to you had not sprung forth. — And yet I never can give up, my honest and heartfelt admiration for La Valliere, which had it been brought out without your *name*, which served as the watch word for political animosity to take the field against it, and had it been properly cast, must have obtained a most brilliant success, for it richly merited it. The political attacks against the Lady of Lyons, *can do it no harm, every one feels the motives*. Heaven bless you, and preserve to your Country a *Genius* that ennobles it, prays your Affectionate and *proud* friend.

78. BULWER TO LADY BLESSINGTON

The moment you liked the Lady of Lyons, I was satisfied. — The wish to prove that your and Alfred's kind belief that I *could* hit off the Dramatic Knack impelled me to the attempt, as much as anything else. — But I should not like you to have known the pain of a second failure on my part — & therefore was silent till I thought you would be pleased — not pained.

Presumably Bulwer attended on the second night; and after the third, Saturday, February 17, he could not resist going to Macready's dressing room to express his gratitude and pleasure and to offer the use of his name whenever Macready wished it. He was disappointed to discover, as Macready had found out earlier, that Melnotte was not the dominant part.

By Sunday the reviews were nearly all in, and there was cause for fright. In spite of the generally favorable comment, the more reactionary of the Tory voices saw fit to denounce it for subversive politics! "He makes his peasant talk sad stuff," said the *Morning Post*, "such as a manly peasant would never talk, about his natural equality, and so on, with persons of family." The *Times* denounced "the republican claptraps" and the implied contempt for pride of ancestry. Macready was much alarmed, and doubted the play could overcome "the insidious imputation of disaffection." Bulwer himself called on Sunday to suggest that his name be not released until after the play was shown again on Wednesday.

79. BULWER TO MACREADY, [circa February 20, 1838][29]

It is not for me certainly to interfere with your arrangements, which I am sure are for the best. But I think it perhaps as well to say that I have met with 3 families who, balancing what play to go to, were decided by the Domino Noir — agst their first inclination towards Cov. Garden. 2 of these were for next Wednesday. — I cannot but think that despite the abridgement, the said Domino will be injurious.

I see you have a play of Talfourd's in preparation, & for this (whatever the success of mine — were I to give my name it would necessarily curtail and interfere with its run) I think the announcement would be now useless.

80. MACREADY TO BULWER, 8 York Gate, Wednesday, [February 21, 1838]

We are not, in a Theatre, always able to act as we would wish. — If the Domino had not had a chance given it by its repetition tonight, I shd have been assailed by complaints and accusations of injustice, which I would willingly make a sacrifice to avoid. — It is not my intention to do it after tonight, and I had made arrangements for the Diorama and two of Power's farces to follow the Lady of Lyons in future.

It is strange that I had intended to have written to you this morning, in consequence of the improved appearance of our Box Sheet for tonight, to ask your permission to use my own discretion about announcing your name from the Stage, if the house should be good and the play go, as it has hitherto done. The places taken yesterday for this evening were within eight of the total amount taken for last Monday. It is the universal opinion that the play *must* establish itself.

The announcement of Talfourd's play was inevitable, though it cannot be done for many weeks, and you may be quite sure, if I had not *known*, that it could not at all have affected what is now in course and in preparation — (viz: Coriolanus for our Monday nights) — that I would not have put it in the bill to injure any receipts for such a long period.

When I see you, you shall know more on this matter — only pray believe, that the interest of your play is with me a matter of much deeper moment than any other thing within that Theatre, and if it were my own, I could not think and act more for its success. — I wish you could be at the Theatre this evening.

On Wednesday, Macready addressed the house and boldly denied that the play contained any "political allusions that do not grow out of the piece, and are necessarily conducive to the working of the story." He reminded them that the licensor had

---

[29] Matthews misdated this letter "May, 1836" and thought it referred to *La Vallière*. The *Domino Noir*, which failed and was quickly withdrawn, was a comic opera by James Kenney and J. M. Morton, called *The Black Domino*, adapted from *Le Domino Noir* by Scribe, the music by Auber: it was played as an afterpiece to *The Lady of Lyons*. The "play of Talfourd's" was *The Athenian Captive*, which after many delays and difficulties was produced at the Haymarket the following August.

permitted the play, and declared that in his own conduct of the theatre, "art and literature have no politics." Bulwer then gave him *carte-blanche* for the time and manner of announcing his name.

81. MACREADY TO BULWER, *8 York Gate, February 23, [1838]*

I shall be most happy to accept your invitation on Sunday, if I can get free from one in which I am involved.— Will you let me take my chance of being able to do so.

I was about to write to you to say, that on resolving the matter of the announcement, I have come to the conclusion, that it cannot be done better than in tomorrow's bills, and in extra *separate* advertisements in all the papers, so that it would not creep out, but be sent all abroad at once.— The effect of surprise would be fully obtained, and all suspicion of clap-trap avoided, which by a second address to the audience might be incurred.— There would also be time for it to work its effect before Tuesday night, and we have the advantage next week of an intervening night between each performance.

The success of the play is so decided — the tone of those who speak of it so uniform, that I think there is no ground for further hesitation, and I further think that the mode of promulgating it should be by the simultaneous appearance of many different advertisements.

If I have your consent, it shall burst out tomorrow morning: — if it is to be done, which I think should, the loss of tomorrow would be the loss of Sunday also, and the blow ought to be struck for Tuesday. I do not think it could be better timed.— Pray let me have your immediate opinion — upon which I will instantly act.

The playbills and papers for Saturday, February 24, broke the news that Bulwer was the author, and the Tories screamed again. "We had no doubt," said the *Times,* "it was an issue from the mint of which that gentleman is deputy master, for the scribblers of the French Boulevard-Theatres are its real masters. No other school could or would produce such morbid sentimentality, such turbid sansculottism." The writer proceeds to speculate on the rise in the apothecaries' trade for cures for the nausea and bile engendered in the audience. The attack was too absurd to be effective. Macready described it as "vulgar, virulent, and impotent from its display of malice — such an article as I would *wish* my enemy to write against me."

82. MACREADY TO BULWER, *8 York Gate, February 25, [1838]*

The notice in the Times (which, I think, clearly beneficial to our cause) had at once determined me not to answer the M. Post. Your direction shall be faithfully attended to. I hope and believe, that our enemies have served us.— If we could but get the Queen to the Theatre, I think, it would determine our success.—

I very much regret that I cannot have the pleasure of dining with you today. — I will send the fifth act to you as soon as I can get it.

Macready's notion to get the Queen to attend came to pass. The first arrangement was for Saturday, March 3.

83. BULWER TO MACREADY, [*March 3*], *1838*

Lord Conyngham[30] suggests strongly, that if possible, the Omnibus[31] would be represented first — it might be said "By particular Desire" — without absolutely saying that it was by Royal Command

It is understood in the upper circles that the Queen is coming, therefore such a hint would be understood. I know not how far this is possible. The Queen will arrive at 8 — I hear from Serle[32] that he has disposed of all his boxes. Webster has written to me to ask me to write him a play for the Haymarket, so I hope we are getting up.

[P.S.] The Queen wants to read the Play. I have ordered a copy to be made up and sent to you at six — will *you see* it placed in Her M's Box.— Don't forget it.

84. MACREADY TO BULWER, *Covent Garden Theatre, Saturday,* [*March 3, 1838*]

I have been doing my utmost, as I will tell you: — I will *try* now to do what you wish.— The book, if it comes to me, shall be attended to.

I am almost dead, but to my best and last Your's

[P.S.] As I was about to close this note, the enclosed came from the Chamberlains's office, which forbids our altering the arrangement of the night's entertainments.

I was just on the point of sending for Bartley (to whom the enclosed is addressed) and giving him orders to apprise the people and prepare bills for the change, but now, you perceive, I am powerless.

It is vexatious — I wish Her Majesty would not encumber us with her help, as she has hitherto done.—

Her Majesty arrived only in time for the last act, but she sent word that she would return on Tuesday, March 6, for the whole performance. Macready noted on Tuesday that "the Queen came to see the play — no notice was taken of her." From the newspapers of the time, however, it would appear that everybody but Macready noticed her. With especial relish it was reported how, when there was reference in the play to the possibility of Pauline's marrying a foreign prince, the whole audience took it as applicable to Victoria's own pending marriage prospects, and when the character of Damas cried out "Foreign Prince! Foreign fiddlesticks!" the house broke into cheers and laughter, and Victoria smiled in enjoyment.[33]

---

[30] Francis Nathaniel Lord Conyngham, the second Marquis (1797-1876), holder of various posts at the court and in the government under George IV and William IV, and Victoria's Lord Chamberlain, 1835-39.

[31] *The Omnibus. A farce, in one act,* is attributed to the Irish actor and minor playwright Tyrone Power, then a member of Macready's company.

[32] Thomas James Serle was an actor, stage manager, and dramatist, for many years a trustworthy lieutenant, adviser, and friend to Macready. Macready created leading roles in two of his plays, *The Merchant of London* and *The House of Colberg* at Drury Lane in 1832, and *Master Clarke* at the Haymarket in 1840, and produced seven of his minor works during his seasons of management.

[33] From press clippings in the Lowne Collection of Macreadiana in the Garrick Club.

On March 8 Her Majesty sent messages of praise to Bulwer for the play and to Macready for his acting. Macready was annoyed to "see a man of Bulwer's great mind evidently so much delighted by the praise and compliments of a little girl — because a Queen!" But there could be no doubt of the box-office value of the royal approval.

The Lady continued to be presented regularly, alternating with *Coriolanus* after March 12 and taking its place in the repertory to the number of 33 performances during the season. On March 21, Macready sent the first royalty installment, a check for £210, which Bulwer generously refused to accept.

85. MACREADY TO BULWER, *8 York Gate, Regent's Park, March 21, 1838*

When you first proposed to lend the powerful assistance of your name and talent to my attempt, I reserved the subject of pecuniary compensation for a later consideration. Let me hope, that the first class, in my scale of payment to authors, though far below what I would wish to offer you, may not meet with objection from you. By this scale in a run of forty nights an author would receive the sum of six hundred pounds; and I have the pleasure of enclosing you a cheque for the amount with which I have credited you upon our first fourteen. I will not here repeat expressions of obligation, with which I must almost have wearied you, but merely assure you that I am and always must remain

86. BULWER TO MACREADY, *Charles St., March 22, 1838*

I am fully sensible of the generosity of your proposal. But our compact was not of an ordinary nature, and on consideration, you will see that it is impossible to lower it into a pecuniary arrangement. It was a compact based upon feelings worthy of the Art, which in our several lines we desired to serve — let me add that it was worthy of ourselves. On your side was a zeal for my reputation — on mine a sympathy with your cause. Can the feelings each of us experienced in success, ever be reduced into a matter of pounds & shillings?

I do not return this money to *you* — you, personally, have no concern with it — I return it as a Contribution toward the Expences of an attempt, in which as an English author and a lover of Art I have as deep an interest as yourself, & the risks of which never ought to have fallen upon one individual.

Do not imagine me guilty of the arrogant vanity of supposing that I confer a *favour*. I know that my effort has been of no pecuniary profit to yourself. The most it could do was, *perhaps*, to lighten losses at a period when luck ran strong against us. And fear not that you have not already overrequited me. The balance between us leaves the obligation on my side. I gave you but a fortnight, of time I should not have otherwise employed to advantage — you gave me a victory over enemies, and restored me to confidence in myself.— Neither money nor *any other kind of remuneration which money purchases*, can I accept — or you propose. My guerdon is the boast to have served, not as a Mercenary but a volunteer, in an enterprise that will long be memorable in the Literary History of my time. I will not sell my Waterloo Medal.

I trust & I believe that you will triumph eventually over all obstacles, &

that at the end of this Season, you will feel encouraged to a new Campaign in which the hazards may be less and the rewards greater. If *then,* either on your own part, or that of others, you ask me again to tempt Gods & Columns, I will not scruple to talk to you of Business. But *now* my confidence in the Nature of your own pride convinces me that you will sympathize with mine.

87. MACREADY TO BULWER, *8 York Gate, Regent's Park, March 23, 1838*

The favour you conferred upon me in your dedication of *La Vallière* impressed me with a sense of obligation, that will continue with life. In associating my name with your own you graced me with a lasting honour, & rendered me an important service. I was already sufficiently indebted to you to be conscious of my own inability ever to requite your kindness: — what then am I now to say to you? or how can I attempt to thank you for your letter of yesterday? After what I have already known of you, it would be an injustice to say it surprised me. I was quite overcome by it, & whatever may be the issue of the struggle I am engaged in, this one occurrence will prevent me from regretting the attempt I have made.

I accept this act of friendship from you, I hope, in its own spirit. I cannot dwell upon it: it is an event in my life, of which, I believe, my children will be proud.

Pray translate what you think should be my feelings into your own language, & let me, with the full credit of always retaining them, subscribe myself —

88. BULWER TO MACREADY, *March 28, 1838*

Many thanks to you, my dear Macready, for your most kind & generous letter — which pays me a thousandfold for all my good intentions, & small exertions.

May I ask you to direct & send by the earliest 2^d post the inclosed letter to Miss Martineau,[34] whose address I know not — it touches the Copyright Bill.

Thus Bulwer handsomely completed his gesture of assistance to Macready's cause. At the end of the month Macready arranged with William Jerdan to publish an account of Bulwer's "noble conduct" in the *Literary Gazette.*[35] Certain hostile journalists denounced this publishment as "puffing" and "humbug," but the general public was doubtless properly impressed by it. Bulwer's own sincerity in the matter is well expressed in part of a letter to Forster.

89. BULWER TO FORSTER, *Knebworth, Stevenage, Herts., April 10, 1838*

. . . I am sorry that the little affair between Macready & myself got into the Papers. — He was too generous in shewing the letter. — While touched & delighted by your kind expressions I must still express surprise that anyone

---

[34] Harriet Martineau (1802-76), the novelist, philosopher, and student of society.

[35] William Jerdan (1782-1869), journalist and editor, a personal friend and public champion of Macready. *The Literary Gazette* (March 31, 1838), XLIII, 203.

could suppose there was the least merit in what I did. — I should never have held up my head if I had done *otherwise;* & while boasting of my interest in Macready's self-sacrificing attempt to restore the Drama — cooly put my hand in the coffers barely adequate, I fear, to sustain the effort.

I was "desolate" as the Comical French say at being unable by a most singular combination of events — to attend the Theatre on Saturday. The success of Macready seems to have been brilliant — That of the play puzzles me — as accounts differ — [36]

When does the play of Talford (whose name his friends pronounce Ta*r*lford, Why, I wonder?) come out —

Now I am going to bore you. — I have no copy of Cromwell — could you peep into yours & extract those lines about England — beginning with "a beautiful land, this England, is it not?" — I don't remember them, & I want to quote them at Lincoln to try their effect — I am going thither to feast & speechify. . . .

The mystery behind this next note is explained in Macready's diary. He wanted to help Bulwer improve his elocution. On May 30 the proposal was made, and Bulwer "seemed very much obliged and pleased, and though doubtful of a good result, would be happy to receive my assistance." Probably nothing practical ever came of the suggestion.

90. MACREADY TO BULWER, *Covent Garden Theatre, May 26, 1838*

Herewith I return to you, after looking it over again, Marriage à la Mode with a note to its Author. — Vathek I will read before the close of our season, and Miss Landon I will take with me to Elstree; and "under the shade of melancholy boughs" do the best I can for her.[37]

Will you, any evening you may be lounging between the House of C. and Covent Garden, look into my room, that I may say a few words to you which are not worth pen and ink — indeed I do not know that they may be of the value of the breath that bears them, but I am sure you will not misunderstand them, and so I will say them when I see you.

---

[36] Byron's *The Two Foscari* had been produced on Saturday, April 7.

[37] *Marriage à la Mode,* and *Vathek* (from William Beckford's novel) were afterpieces written by a Miss Tallent (see Letter 118, Bulwer to Macready, December 12, 1838).

Letitia Elizabeth Landon (1802-38) was at that time an extremely popular poetess and novelist, known as "L.E.L." She had written, perhaps at Macready's suggestion, a tragedy called *Castruccio Castrucani.* She was at one time engaged to John Forster. When she married George Maclean, the Governor of Cape Coast Castle, in June of this year, Bulwer gave the bride away. Her early death at Cape Coast Castle posed a mystery that has never been solved, and greatly shocked her London friends.

chapter three

1838
1839

Richelieu; or, The Conspiracy

The quick, easy success of *The Lady of Lyons* stimulated Bulwer's theatrical ambitions anew. On March 8, 1838, just three weeks after the opening of *The Lady*, he told Macready that "though he had no wish to write for the stage, yet if I needed him, I had only to point out how he could assist my views." At the moment, however, there was no need for a new play. Not only was *The Lady* just beginning to return a profit, but Macready had on hand Talfourd's *Athenian Captive* and Knowles's *Woman's Wit,* besides some planned classical revivals, with which to finish the season.

Bulwer therefore tried the market with Benjamin Webster at the Haymarket, who (as he had reported to Macready on March 3) had asked him for a play. Nothing immediate was to come of this negotiation.

91. WEBSTER TO BULWER, *Theatre Royal Haymarket, February 28, 1838*[1]

I should be most happy to purchase the printing right of your admirable drama of "The Lady of Lyons" — to be published first in quo & afterwards in my edition of the "Modern Acting Drama."

Should you feel inclined to favour the above theatre with a drama the ensuing season, it would be my pride to produce it with every possible advantage.

92. WEBSTER TO BULWER, *Garrick Club, March 15, 1838*

I have delayed answering your polite note in order that I might furnish you with something like a list of my company which at present consists of Messers Power, Ranger, Strickland, Buckstone, Hunning, Glover (new), Wrench, Charles Mathews (a portion of the time), Perkins, Webster &c Mrs Glover,

---

[1] Original of this and the next in the Knebworth Archives.

Miss Taylor, Mrs Nesbitt, Miss Cooper (new), Mrs Humbey [*sic*], Mrs Fitz-williams, Mrs Waylett, Mad^me Sala, Miss Beresford, Madame Vestris (for a short period), etc.[2]

This is essentially a comedy company and therefore I beg respectfully to suggest, that, should you honour me so far as to write for the Haymarket, you did so without reference to any particular names and I will engage efficient persons, if I have them not, to give a proper effect to the characters imagined.

I confess I am most anxious to produce a drama from your pen at the Haymarket feeling it to be the only theatre from its size etc where the legitimate drama and the beauties of poetry can be duly appreciated; and I should be sadly grieved, if in this dearth of first rate talent the pitiful attempts of biased persons should prevent such an approved dramatist as yourself from lending your powerful aid towards restoring the taste of the Public for a healthy and sound state of the drama.

Mr. Sheridan Knowles has most certainly promised me a comedy but when I shall have it is exceedingly doubtful and I trust there will be field enough open for the production of more than one novelty of a high order recollecting that "The Bridal" and "The Love Chase" were both produced last season.

As Macready faced his second season of management, his search for new vehicles grew intense. As early as July 25 he talked with Bulwer about a play: "He wants a subject, and will go to work." During September, though the diary entries are meager, they record Macready's conferences with at least nine dramatic authors and the study of numerous old plays. Bulwer was still wanting a subject; on September 8 there was an exchange of notes, of which Bulwer's has been preserved.

---

[2] Tyrone Power (1795-1841), an extremely popular actor of comic Irish roles, which he commenced in London in 1826; was drowned in the sinking of the *S. S. President* on a return journey from America. Descendants of the same name have been on the stage to the present.

John Baldwin Buckstone (1802-79), a popular low comedian, whose London debut was in 1823; author of about 200 minor plays; manager of the Haymarket, 1853-76, where his ghost is said yet to walk.

Edmund Glover (1813-60), an actor and later a manager; son of Mrs. Julia Glover.

Benjamin Wrench (1778-1843), a comic actor of wide range of parts but secondary ability; made his London debut in 1809.

Charles James Mathews (1803-78), a skilled comic actor, especially in fashionable roles; made his London debut in 1835; in 1838 married Mme. Vestris, and engaged thereafter in numerous ventures in management, most of which failed financially; made successful world tours.

Ranger, Strickland, Hunning, and Perkins were minor performers.

Fanny Elizabeth Fitzwilliam, née Copeland (1801-54), a popular comic actress; made her London debut in 1817; was long identified with the Haymarket. Her husband Edward (1788-1852) was a comic singing actor, her son Edward Francis (1824-57) was a musical director at the Haymarket; her daughter-in-law Ellen (1822-80) played at the Haymarket for twenty-two years under Buckstone.

Harriet Waylett, née Cooke (1798-1851), a favorite actress of soubrette roles and a singer; made her London debut in 1820; in 1840 married George Alexander Lee, a theatrical musical director.

Miss Cooper, Mme. Sala, and Miss Beresford were minor performers.

93. BULWER TO MACREADY, *Rochford, Essex, [September 8, 1838]*[3]

Many thanks for the kind note. I return Love and Cabal.[4] The situations are powerful. But I dont see my way. The comic spirit of the subject should be court satire which ye English don't understand, and the Tragic has too much gloom for the kind of passion of moral or passion to be worked out. However it has suggested an idea of character tho' not of a story. viz. A Father, generous, high-spirited, able, who has a son that he doats on, but thinks that there is no happiness without worldly greatness & keeps pushing this idolised son on — blind to his real happiness, his feelings and his nature, till he sacrifices them to their perverted kind of affection. I see a moral very striking & intelligible to the worldly enterprising English to be worked out of this, character & the domestic interest might be strong. Everybody, loving and sympathising with the father in his ambition, & therefore going with him in the horror and remorse he has at the close. But I question whether a play has space to work the process of a suitable story out. The Honest Man's Fortune[5] has a splendid first act. I see nothing farther. I know the Historical life of La Ensenada but do not see how it is to be dramatized.[6] The character of an honest and great minister trying to revive the ancient grandeur of his country, and at last, frustrated by the Court, obtaining banishment for his pains — is very fine, but here comes again the too subtle spirit of Court intrigue, and the necessity for politics and the want of poetic justice, besides where is the domestic interest.

Forster will ask you to read my story of Calderon.[7] It would make a tragedy of progressive and intense interest, but it would not be too painful and gloomy. Nor could the situation admit comic admixture tho' a vein of comic irony might relieve the stormier passions of Calderon. You will let me know however if you think of that subject. The domestic English play would be the thing to work on if you cd hit on the story. The Simple Story[8] the lost, might do but perhaps we could get a stronger and newer situation.

After receipt of Bulwer's letter, Macready spent that whole same evening in his

---

[3] Typescript in the Library of the University of Illinois. The fifth sentence has probably been jumbled in transcription.

[4] *Love and Cabal* was a translation of Friedrich Schiller's *Kabale und Liebe, ein bürgerliches Trauerspiel in fünf aufzügen* (Mannheim, 1784). Various translations existed, such as Peter Colombine's *Cabal and Love* (London, 1795), and M. G. Lewis' *The Minister* (London, 1797).

[5] *The Honest Man's Fortune*, a comedy written about 1613, was included in the 1647 Folio of the plays of Beaumont and Fletcher, though modern scholars dispute the authorship.

[6] Zenón de Somodevilla, Marqués de la Ensenada (1702-81), a powerful and heroic Spanish statesman who effected much needed internal reforms in the Spanish government but was repeatedly banished by hostile monarchs.

[7] Bulwer's *Calderon, The Courtier. A Tale* was published together with *Leila; or, The Siege of Granada* in 1838.

[8] *A Simple Story* (London, 1791) is a novel by Elizabeth Inchbald (1753-1821), novelist, dramatist, and actress. The transcription of this sentence is obviously faulty.

library at Elstree trying to turn something up, and the next day he submitted his reflections, which are of special critical interest for they define Macready's needs and analyze Bulwer's best style with considerable clarity and penetration.

94. MACREADY TO BULWER, *Elstree, September 9, [1838]*

Your letter with Cabal and Love was delivered to me after I had despatched mine to Knebworth. I will not ask you to excuse me for thus troubling you with hurried and frequent letters, because I am secure of your indulgence, and I am anxious not to lose any time in laying before you any hint of either fable or character. That which you have framed out of Schiller's Miller must be very striking, but at the same time very tragic I should think.— I have been looking through an author, who has suggested framework for several successful dramas — most of the smaller kind,— but, if you would turn again to him (for I suppose you have almost forgotten him) I fancy something either of resemblance or contrast might present itself from some of his stories. — I mean Marmontel: — The Bad Mother — and the School for Fathers.[9] I see something dramatic in them.— Will you read a whimsical piece of Goldoni — L'avventuriere Onorato — ?[10] — It may point towards something. I have seen it acted, and been much amused with it — and have sometimes thought of adapting it to our stage. It affords great scope for touching on those unhealthy parts of our social system, which you have the power of taking advantage of for real good.— I mention all these different things, because out of several I have a dim and confused vision of a plot yielding opportunities for pathetic situations and also for humorous ones.— I trust you will persist in your adherence to the mixed plot — I may truly apply to your talent as a dramatic poet a character I find noted as "le veritable" — "il consiste à composer de manière qu'il y ait dans le même ouvrage, dans la même scène, ce qui fait pleurer ou rire même le peuple, et ce qui fournit aux penseurs un sujet inépuisable de réflexions."[11] It is therefore that I hope you will remain constant to the exercise of a power, which is possessed by no other living author — at least as far as we know.— Forster called yesterday afternoon and mentioned Calderon to me, which I will read without delay;— but if it is wholly tragic I should endeavour to dissuade you from it.— There is already a tragedy of high pretension in the Theatre, and there are others on the way — but our

---

[9] Jean François Marmontel (1723-99), dramatist, critic, and contributor to the *Encyclopédie*. His *Contes Moraux*, first printed in the *Mercure de France* from 1761 to 1786, were first collected in 1786 and widely translated. They were very popular in England. See George Saintsbury, *Marmontel's Moral Tales* (London, 1895), where the stories here referred to are Englished.

[10] Carlo Goldoni (1707-93), comic dramatist. *L'Avventuriere Onorato, commedia di tre atti in prosa,* was first presented in 1751. See *Tutte le Opere de Carlo Goldoni* (Milano, 1935), III, 863.

[11] Macready is probably quoting a recent letter from his friend M. de Fresne recommending to his attention Talma's preface to *Mémoires de Le Kain*. (See his diary of September 8.) The sentiment, a commonplace of contemporary French romanticists, echoes many a passage from Victor Hugo's Preface to *Cromwell* (1827).

tragic writers have not the art of mingling the lighter with their graver scenes. — I will let you know on Thursday my impression as to the fitness of Calderon for our great enterprise. I speak en monarque. — Are you likely to be passing through town soon again — if you are I would set aside business to see you, for the chances of eliciting something in conversation are so much greater than in correspondence!

P.S. I have opened my letter to request you will frank the enclosed one to Thomas Moore Esq.,[12] Sloperton Cottage n^r Devizes Wilts.

Bulwer was willing to devote himself to comedy, but not yet to the comedy of social criticism which Macready asked for. That was to come later, in *Money*. At the moment he could still see no variety but the romantic. He had just read a novel by Saintine, called *Une Maitresse de Louis XIII*,[13] and out of it he decocted a tentative plot. On September 9 (probably crossing Macready's last), he sent Macready an enormous *letter* describing the subject, and *in a separate envelope* a *programme* of the tentative plot. From this material the play *Richelieu* eventually grew. (For "de Marillac" of these sketches read "de Mauprat" of the play; for "Cinq Mars" read "Baradas" and for "Louise de la Porte" read "Julie de Montemar.")

95. BULWER TO MACREADY, *Rochford, September 9, 1838*[14]

In another envelope I send a programme of the proposed acts.

I have thought of a subject. The story full of incident — & interest. It is to

---

[12] Thomas Moore (1779-1852), the Irish poet, was a long-time friend of Macready's.

[13] Joseph Xavier Boniface Saintine (1798-1865), *Une Maitresse de Louis XIII*, second edition, 2 vols. (Paris, 1834). In the Preface to *Richelieu*, Bulwer acknowledges his indebtedness to this novel, as well as to de Vigny's *Cinq Mars* for the incident of the Secretaries. In his footnotes to the text of the play, and in the list of references submitted to Macready in Letter 110 (p. 94) we can see how widely he studied his subject in official histories and memoirs. Charles Qualia, in an article called "French Dramatic Sources of Bulwer-Lytton's *Richelieu*," *PMLA* (1927) XLII, 177-84, discovers the structural parallels between *Richelieu* and Victor Hugo's *Cromwell* and Casimir Delavigne's *Louis XI*. Stephen S. Stanton has made a detailed study of the parallels between *Richelieu* and Scribe's *Bertrand et Raton* ("English Drama and the French Well-Made Play, 1815-1915." Unpublished dissertation, Columbia University, 1955). Bulwer of course knew and admired those dramatists, and their "influence" may likely have operated. It must be noted, however, that nothing occurs in the present correspondence which would specifically support Mr. Qualia's or Mr. Stanton's thesis.

[14] The history of this letter and programme is vexed. The originals were presumably deposited intact in the Forster Library at the Victoria and Albert Museum. J. Fitzgerald Molloy printed the letter (but not the programme) in a book called *Famous Plays*, (London, 1886). He dated the letter September, 1839, omitting the specific date, September 9, which is discernible in the postmark on the cover. His treatment of spelling, punctuation, and paragraphing is quite irresponsible to the original. In 1913 Brander Matthews copied Molloy's text as Letter XXI in his collection. By this time, however, the ending of the original letter (all that follows the row of asterisks which I have inserted to mark the break) appears to have been removed from the Forster Library (at least it is not there now), and found its way into Matthews' collection. Matthews tacked this ending onto a very different letter, number XXXIV, which he dated, or rather misdated, December 24, 1838 (see *Bulwer to Macready*, c. January 1, 1839). Thus in Matthews' book the ending is printed twice, once as copied from Molloy, and once as

this effect — "In the time of Louis 13. The Chevalier de Marillac is the wittiest & bravest gentleman — celebrated for his extravagant valour & his enthusiasm for enjoyment — but in his most mirthful moments — a dark cloud comes over him at one name — the name of *Richelieu!* — He confides to his friend *Cinq Mars* the reason — viz: He had once entered into a conspiracy agst Richelieu — Richelieu discovered & sent for him — "Chevalier de Marillac," said he — "I do not desire to shed your blood on the scaffold, but you must die. Here is a command on the frontier — fall in battle." — He went to the Post, but met glory & not death. Richelieu reviewing troops found him still living — & said — "Remember the Sword is over your head — I take your parole — to appear before me once a quarter. You can still find Death. I will give you time for it" — Hence his xtravagant valour — hence his desire to make the most of life.— While making this confidence to Cinq Mars — he is sent for by Richelieu. He goes as to death — Richelieu receives him sternly — reminds him of his long delay — upbraids him for his profligate life &c. Marillac answers with mingled wit & nobleness & at last instead of sentencing him to death Richelieu tells him that he has qualities that make him wish to attach him to himself — & that he will marry him to a girl with great dowry & give him high office at Court — He must marry directly. Marillac goes out enchanted.

— Now Richelieu's motive is this. Louis 13 has fallen in love with this girl — Louise de La Porte & wishes to make her his mistress — All the King's mistresses have hitherto opposed Richelieu. He is resolved that the King shall have no more — He will have no rival with the King — He therefore resolves to marry her to Marillac — whose life is in his power — whom he can hold in command — whom he believes to be too noble to suffer the adulterous connection.— Marillac is then introduced just married with high appointments & large dowry the girl beautiful — when, on his wedding day Cinq Mars tells him that the King loves his wife. His rage & despair — conceives himself duped. Scene with the girl in which he recoils from her — Suddenly three knocks at the door. He is sent for by the King — & despatched to a distance — the bride — not wived — is summoned to court —

Marillac — all pride & wrath & casting all upon Richelieu, agrees to conspire against the Cardinal's life — The fortress where Richelieu lodges is garrisoned with the friends of the conspirators — just as he has agreed — he receives an anonymous letter telling him that his wife is at Chantilly that she will sleep in the chamber of the Montmorencies — that Louis means to enter the room that night — that if he wishes to guard his honour he can enter the palace by a secret passage which opens in a picture of Hugo de Montmorency

---

copied from the stray manuscript. I have corrected the text of the letter (down to the asterisks) according to the Forster Library original, added the ending as Matthews printed it at the end of Letter XXXIV, and added the programme, which has not heretofore been printed at all.

the last Duke who had been beheaded by Louis (an act for which the King always felt remorse)   This Montmorency had been the most intimate friend of Marillac — & who had left him his armour as a present. — A thought strikes Marillac — & he goes off the stage.

— Louise alone in this vast room — the picture of Montmorenci in complete armour — a bed at the end — She complains of her Husband's want of love & laments her hard fate — dismisses her women — The King enters & locks the doors — after supplication & resistance on her part, he advances to seize her. When from Montmorenci's pictures comes a cry of "Hold." — & the form descends from the panell — & interposes — The King horror-struck — & superstitious — flies Louise faints — the form is Marillac — While she is still insensible, the clock strikes. It is the hour he is to meet the conspirators — He summons her women, & leaves her —

Richelieu alone at night when Marillac enters to him — tells him his life is in his power — upbraids him for his disgrace &c. — Richelieu informs him that he has married him to Louise *to prevent* her dishonour — that he had sent the anonymous letter &c — & converts Marillac into gratitude — But what is to be done The conspirators have filled the Fortress? — They (viz Richelieu & Marillac) retire into another room — & presently the conspirators enter the one they have left, & Marillac joins them & tells them the Cardinal is dead — that he will see to the funeral &c. & they had better go at once & announce it to the King. That there are no marks of violence, that it seems like a fit (being suffocation). —

Scene in the Streets of Paris

The King who had always feared & hated Richelieu hears the news & is at first rejoiced — the courtiers delighted — Paris in a jubilee. — But suddenly comes news of commotion, riot, — messengers announce the defeat of the armies The Spaniards have crossed the frontiers. His general, de Feuguieres, is slain — Hubbub & uproar without with cries of "Hurrah — The old Cardinal is dead —" &c — when there is a counter cry of the Cardinal, the Cardinal — & a band of soldiers appears followed by Richelieu himself in complete armour — at this sight — the confusion — the amaze — &c — The mob changes humours, & there is a cry of "Long live the *Great* Cardinal!"

Scene, the King's Chamber

— The King enraged at the trick played on him — & at his having committed himself to joy at the Cardinal's Death — hears that de Marillac had announced the false report — orders him to the Bastille — tells the Count de Charost — to forbid Richelieu the Louvre, & declares henceforth he will reign alone. Joy of the Anti-cardinalists — when the great doors are thrown open, & Richelieu pale, suffering, sick — in his Cardinal's robes leaning on his pages — enters — & calls on Charost (the very man who is to forbid his entrance) to give him his arm — which Charost tremblingly does before the eyes of the King. Richelieu & the King alone. — Richelieu says he has come to tender his resignation. The King accepts it — & Richelieu summons 6 Secretaries groaning beneath sacks of public papers — all demanding immediate attention — Richelieu retires to a distance — & appears almost dying — The King desperately betakes himself to the papers — his perplexity bewilderment & horror at the dangers round him — at last he summons the Cardinal to his side & implores him to resume the Office. The Cardinal with great seeming reluctance — says he only will on one condition — complete power — over foes & friends — Louis must never again interfere with public business — He then makes him sign various papers — & when all is done — the old man throws off the dying state — rises with Lion like energy. "France is again France — to the frontiers — *I* lead the armies &c." (a splendid burst) Louis — half enfeebled — half ashamed — retires. Richelieu alone — gives various papers to the Secretaries; & summons Marillac & his Wife. He asks her if she has been happy — she says "No" thinking her Husband hates her — put the same question to Marillac — who thinking she wishes to be separated — says the same. He then tells them as the marriage has not been fulfilled they can be divorced. — They wofully agree — when turning to Marillac he shows him the King's order that he should go to the Bastille — & then adds that in favour of his service in saving *his* (R's) life, — he has the power to soften his sentence — But he must lose his offices at Court & go into xile — On hearing this Louise turns around — her love breaks out — she will go with him into banishment &c. & the reconciliation is complete. Richelieu regarding them then adds — "Your sentence remains the same — we banish you still — Ambassador to Austria."

* *

As they are in each other's arms, happy, Richelieu looks coldly at them & mutters, "After all our pains as Ministers, Kings & Courtiers, Human happiness still goes on."

END.

Now look well at this story; you will see incident & position are good. But then there is one great objection. Who is to do Richelieu? Marillac has the principal part & requires you. But a bad Richelieu would spoil all. On the other hand, if you took Richelieu, there would be two acts without you, which will never do, & the principal intent of the plot would not fall on you. Tell me what is to be done. Must we give up this idea?

[P.S.] The incidents are all Historical

Don't let me begin the thing if you don't think it will do — & decide about Marillac & Richelieu. Send me back the papers.

You can consult Forster, of course.

You will find much of this story in "Une Maitresse de Louis 13," by Saintine.

96. BULWER TO MACREADY, *Rochford, Essex,* [*September 9, 1839*]

Direct me P. O. Rochford Essex

To be all in verse

Not to be read till
after the letter.

Act 1ˢᵗ

Scene 1ˢᵗ

A room in Marillac's House — A table with wine & dice round which are Marillac Cinq Mars & other young Nobles. Marillac the gayest of all, save when the word Richelieu is named. — The others withdraw —

Scene II.

Cinq Mars & Marillac — The latter relates the terrible conditions of the Cardinal — when suddenly an officer enters & summons Marillac to Richelieu. He goes in despair.   Scene III.

Richelieu in his room with his creature Jacques Sirois. — talks of the King's love for Louise La Porte. & his resolution that the King shall have neither friend nor mistress — Then gliding off to his *Black Book* — he speaks of Marillac & tells Sirois he has sent for him — (leaving the audience to suppose for Execution Enter Marillac — in which scene after terrifying Marillac, Richelieu proposes to marry him   Exit Marillac. Richelieu's soliloquy.

End of Act 1ˢᵗ

N.B. Marillac, noble, impassioned — very witty & careless. Richelieu dry — subtle — flashes of genius — with the latent foibles, now & then visible — such as fancying he is a great Poet.   Act II.

Scene 1ˢᵗ

A sumptuous Hotel

Marillac spendidly dressed — He is just married — friends congratulating — He rejoiced   fallen in love with his bride — enter Cinq Mars —

Scene II

Cinq Mars & Marillac — The latter learns that the King loves his wife Louise — & fears she loves him — His soldier like rage & shame — Enter his bride whom he treats with irony & bitterness — Enter a Gentleman of the King's to send him to Fontainebleau. — He goes — & the Gentleman orders Louise to go to Chantilly to attend the Queen — A few words between Cinq Mars & the Gentleman to let the audience know how the King discovered the marriage &c.

Act III

Marillac at Fontainebleau — his rage &c — The same nobles as in the first scene — now conspirators agst Richelieu — the King's brother favours it — Marillac agrees to join — time fixed. — Conspirators go out — The anonymous letter given to him — (see the paper sent with this) — He rushes out —

Scene II

The Room at Chantilly. Night — Louise — the scene with the King & the seeming apparition of the picture — The Clock strikes — Marillac repairs to the Conspiracy

Act IV.

Richelieu alone — the entrance of Marillac — See the paper — Act to end with the resuscitation of Richelieu

Act V.

The interview between the King & Cardinal to the close as in the paper.

The next day, at the end of a long letter to Forster mainly concerned with some publishing problems, Bulwer adds a few lines about the proposed play.

97. BULWER TO FORSTER, *Rochford, September 10, 1838*

. . . I have written to Macready the programme of a play. Pray see & study it. — The difficulty is that there are two great characters — Richelieu & Marillac — the hero. The former appears rarely & will have only one splendid Scene. Act 5. but that will require a great actor. — Who can do it? Ward is too dull & fat & everyone knows the thin face of Richelieu. — his haughty air — his sardonic smile. Marillac would have a splendid scene in every act — but in the 5th would unluckily be subordinate to the grand historical scene of the Mighty Cardinal — a puppet in his hands. — These are the objections — But the subject itself is full of life. — Let me hear your suggestions. The novel I refer to — see letter to Macready — makes its plot like Fletcher's "Wife for a Month."[15] A glorious subject but w^d be coarse on the Stage. —

I have said my say.

Thus the character of Richelieu was first conceived as a secondary figure in a romantic comedy who embarrassed the project by threatening to steal the interest from the hero.

Macready's response is lost, but he evidently rejected the idea at once as too confusing. Apparently, too, he urged Bulwer not to confide in Forster, who had lately been making rather a nuisance of himself around the theatre, and could not, Macready thought, be trusted to keep secrets. He was evidently not aware that Bulwer was already in communication with Forster on the subject. Of this a woeful sequel would unfold.

98. BULWER TO MACREADY, *Rochford, September 16, 1838*

Many thanks for your letter. You are right about the Plot — it is too crowded & the interest too divided. — But Richelieu would be a splendid fellow for the Stage, if we could hit on a good plot to bring him out — connected with some domestic interest. His wit — his lightness — his address — relieve so admirably his profound sagacity — his Churchman's pride — his relentless vindictiveness & the sublime passion for the glory of France that elevated all. He would be

---

[15] John Fletcher (1579-1625), the dramatist. *A Wife for a Month* was written in 1624.

a new addition to the Historical portraits of the Stage; but then he must be connected with a plot in which he would have all the stage to himself, & in which some Home interest might link itself with the Historical. Alas, I've no such story yet & he must stand over, tho' I will not wholly give him up.— I know Volpone well & have been often struck with the force of the very situation you point out.

I wish if you could lay your hands on *L'aventuriere oubliato* —[16] & the stories in Marmontel you allude to — that you w^d send them down directed to be left at the P. O. Rochford.— Depend on it, I don't cease racking my brains, & something must come at last. I see many subjects, but not *the* one which ought to be popular. You are quite right that we ought to have lightness & comedy, unless indeed — A second "Venice preserved" should ever be sent by the miraculous interposition of Apollo —

It shall be as you like about Forster.

But I think on talking it over when the play is done you will see the impossibility of concealment from him.— Is there not some collection of Italian nouvelettes by Roscoe[17] which might suggest a plot?

The same day, in a long letter to Forster, Bulwer briefly renews the subject of Richelieu.

99. BULWER TO FORSTER, [*September 16, 1838*]

. . . I have heard from Macready today & agree with him on the main. I shall write to him on Sunday. The thing would be to get some grand Historical interest, but treat it lightly. Richelieu has never been brought on the Stage, but his character is most dramatic — And he has always what Macready wishes for — one leg in Comedy the other in Tragedy. . . .

For a week Bulwer ruminated — then, oddly, he came up with the heaviest of all possible tragic subjects, an Englished arrangement of the Orestes story. Being in London for the opening night of Covent Garden (September 24), he proposed it to Macready in his dressing room. When Macready told him the next day that he "did not think it *possible* to make the *Murder of Clytemnestra* palatable to an English audience," he "seemed stiff and not pleased at my want of enthusiasm."

Weeks passed with no apparent progress. On October 3 Bulwer told Forster, "The play stands dead still — Not a subject to be found — tho' I have read for it like a tiger —."

100. MACREADY TO BULWER, *13 Cumberland Terrace, Regent's Park,* *October 7, 1838*

Has nothing yet occurred to you? — We cry to you like the spirits to their deity — "We want but you — we want but you." The prospect looks promise

---

[16] The title was *L'Avventuriere Onorato*. Bulwer's memory, or Matthews' transcription, is at fault.

[17] Thomas Roscoe (1791-1871), translator: *The Italian Novelists*, second edition, 4 vols. (London, 1836).

[*sic*]. The popularity of "the Ladye" continues undiminished. Did you look at Macklin's Man of the World?[18] — Such a keen hunter after the prizes of ambition, power & wealth, turned from his pursuit by the discovery of better things existing in the heart's indulgences. — I am so immersed in action, that I have no time to think beyond the object immediately in hand. But I look out to you as a mariner perilled on the ocean does to land. I scratch these lines in a stolen interval.

Bulwer urged Forster on October 19 to keep mum on the subject: "You recollect my proposed play of Richelieu. Do not mention the idea to anyone. Perhaps as I had dropped it, you may have done so already — let me know if you have." He was at work on it again. Macready records on October 24 that Bulwer "had made out the rough sketch of a play, an historical comedy, on the subject of Richelieu. I answered him, delighted at the news."

101. BULWER TO MACREADY, *Knebworth, Stevenage, October 23, 1838*

You will be pleased to hear that I completed the rough Sketch of a Play in 5 acts — & I hope you will like it. I have taken the subject of Richelieu. Not being able to find any other so original & effective, & have employed somewhat of the story I before communicated to you, but simplified and connected. — *You* are Richelieu, & Richelieu is brought out, accordingly, as the prominent light round which the other satellites move. It is written on the plan of a great Historical Comedy, & I have endeavoured to concentrate a striking picture of the passions & events — the intrigue & ambition of that era — in a familiar point of view. At present it is all in prose, & for my own part I should prefer leaving it so as being better suited to the careless strokes — the rapid effects — & above all the easy & natural light which I desire & design to cast upon the large passion & dark characters brought upon the stage. But as I suppose blank verse will be more likely to ensure solid & permanent success, I fear I must recast several portions into that form. — Let me know your opinion. The comic vein in Richelieu himself is produced by the irony that he really loved, his easy confidence & the brilliant charlatanism of his resources. I cannot say there is much wit anywhere, but there are some situations of Humour — & much I think that somehow or other will get a laugh, & keep the audience in constant play.

Now, for the rest, I am obliged to bring in *many* characters (I am putting a *reign* upon the stage — tho' condensed into the usual unity of time — & I cannot help it). 2^{ndly} I shall put you to the xpence of a mob — a mob — & a large one too, I must have! Do you mind this? — I have avoided, however, overweighting any part except that of the Lover, which I suppose will fall to Anderson.[19] And here I want the brilliant Frenchman witty, but passionate —

---

[18] Charles Macklin (c. 1700-97), Irish-born actor and dramatist. *The Man of the World,* his masterpiece, was produced at Covent Garden Theatre in 1781, with the octogenarian author in the leading role of Sir Pertinax MacSycophant.

[19] James Robertson Anderson (1811-95), an excellent young leading actor in Macready's Covent Garden company and sharer with T. J. Serle in managerial capacities in Macready's Drury Lane company. His London debut was with Macready in 1837.

irregular, yet noble — with one foot on crime, the other on virtue. Mr. Anderson will spoil my conception. But I cannot help that — However, I am running on as if I were sure you would like & take it after all — which, after my false conjectures as to my beloved Orestes — is sheer credulity. — As I am beginning to copy out and retouch, let me know — *au plutôt* — if you have any general hints or suggestions to offer, and what you think about the blank verse.

P.S. Do what I will, & I avoid all long speeches, Richelieu will be, I fear, half an hour longer than the Lady. Does that signify? The Lady is very short.

I see you have turned the Happy Family into the Foresters.[20]

As Forster knew of the Richelieu plot, I suppose he must now be taken into confidence. If so, send for him & enjoin all caution.

Bulwer had written his *Richelieu* in prose, but Macready with an eye on "literature" must have insisted on its being poetized. The task took nearly three weeks. On November 4 Bulwer announced to Forster that the end was in sight, and a week later that it was reached.

102. BULWER TO FORSTER, [*November 4, 1838*]

. . . Richelieu will be given up to Macready next week — bound hand & foot! — Of his crimes or deserts I can say nothing —. . . . Io triumphe for Cromwell.[21] I long to see him — If you *do* come — bring him to see his Contemporary Richelieu. The same age produced both *twice*. Humph. Curious coincidence!

103. BULWER TO FORSTER, *Knebworth, Sunday, November 11,* [*1838*]

This morning I put the last strokes to Richelieu. What further mutilations he may receive rests with Fell Cibber![22] — I shall be delighted to dine with you on Tuesday ¼ past 6 — But as I am only in town a day or two, & wish to know what Macready decides, I shall leave the MS. *chez lui* on Monday on my way to Charles St. Perhaps by Tuesday Even^g he will glance over it & then consign it to your care — & criticism. The mere diction will probably want a few more flowers. — But the general form & construction is what I am most anxious about.

Thanks for your kind xpressions — Believe me I pay back with interest your friendly esteem. I long to take off my hat to Mr. P. Protector

Tout à vous

---

[20] *Die Silberne Hochzeit,* by the popular German dramatist, August von Kotzebue (1761-1819), had been made a popular English play by Benjamin Thompson as *The Happy Family* (London, 1799). T. J. Serle now adapted it into a musical drama called *The Foresters; or, Twenty Five Years Since,* which Macready produced in October, 1838.

[21] This and following references to Cromwell indicate release from the press of first copies of Forster's *Oliver Cromwell,* which are volumes 6 and 7 of his *Lives of Eminent British Statesmen,* 7 vols. (London, 1831-39).

[22] "Fell Cibber" — i.e., "play mutilator" — is an oddly disparaging way for Bulwer to refer to Macready. He does so twice in notes to Forster. I take it to be not ill-humored. Elsewhere he applies the phrase to Charles Kean.

104. BULWER TO MACREADY, *Charles St., November [12], 1838*

I hope you will be able to read my scrawl. I send you the Play complete. Acts I & III may require a little shortening, but you are a master at that. The rest average the length of Acts in the Lady of Lyons.

I hope the story is clear. And if the Domestic interest is not so strong as in the Lady, I trust the acting of Richelieu's part may counterbalance the defect. For the rest, I say of this as of the Lady — if at all hazardous or uncertain, it must not be acted, & I must try again. Let me know your opinion as soon as you can form it.

Macready stayed up till half-past two that night to read it, and rose next morning, "weary and brain-tired," to fear that after all it was by no means ready.

105. MACREADY TO BULWER, *13 Cumberland Terrace, November 13, [1838]*

I read Richelieu last night, or rather this morning. — I write now in great haste, being late for my rehearsal. My impression is that you have over-tasked me — but I must read it again & again and thoroughly master it, before I can offer any precise observations on it.

At present I have an idea, that the interest of Mauprat & Julie wants still greater prominence: You must let me keep the M.S. for these two or three days to come, for I shall think of nothing else, till I see my way clearly in it. Meantime I have strong hopes that it will take its high place.

Excuse my haste, which is unwilling. . . .

On receipt of this, Bulwer called at the theatre and "seemed disappointed" at Macready's lack of enthusiasm. To Forster the next day he sent a suggestion for an improvement in the fourth act. He also enclosed a note from Charles Kean asking him for a play.

106. BULWER TO FORSTER, *[November 14, 1838]*

. . . Tell Macready when you see him — that if in the 4th act — he can see a way for a closing & pathetic scene between Mauprat, Richelieu & Julie — the interest will be clenched —

Read the enclosed letter. Is it not handsomely expressed? — It warrants me, if Richelieu came out at Drury Lane, we should have little to fear from the "Times", — I need not say I have declined with all the kindliness I really feel for the manner & tone of the letter — the request

[P.S.] To Night I shall feast on Cromwell

107. CHARLES KEAN TO BULWER, *Liverpool, Adelphi Hotel,*
November 12, 1838

The flattering success that has attended my attempts in the Provinces to do justice to the character of Claude Melnotte, and the debt of gratitude I owe you for the means thus afforded of advancing my professional career, must be my apology for addressing you, if a better excuse did not exist in your character as an author, and the deserved influence you possess over our dramatic literature.

I am most anxious to appear in London in a new part, & feel that your assistance would be invaluable in the promotion of this purpose, & of my desire to carry out all the objects of the Legitimate Drama in a spirit of honorable competition.— If it should suit y^r views to give me the benefit of your great talents on this occasion, I shall be sincerely grateful, & though pecuniary considerations can be no object with you, I think it right to add — as a matter of business — that I place myself and a carte blanche at your disposal — I trust there is no indelicacy in saying this, when I reflect I should still remain your debtor, by the honor I might hope to derive from the representations of any character from the pen of Sir Lytton Bulwer

Forster showed the Kean letter to Macready, who was infuriated by it, for Kean was then starring at Drury Lane under the management of the perfidious Bunn, and apparently hurting Macready's business noticeably. Forster too was annoyed, for as a critic he was dedicated to cutting Kean down to size. He would not allow Bulwer a moment of "kindliness" toward the upstart.

108. FORSTER TO BULWER, *58 Lincolns Inn Fields, Thursday,*
    [November 15, 1838]

I enclose Mr. Kean's letter, which, crawling as it is, assured me not a little as a proof of his complete break up. The Hamlets and Macbeths are over now — and it is *now* to be "honourable competition"! How are the violent fallen. This is the modest person who a few months back, when he fancied the ball at his feet, embraced the friendship and lent himself to the violent practices of a scoundrel who had in former days (as he had often complained to me) covered him with all manner of ignominy & insult — betraying the confidence and attempting to defame the character of old friends of his own whose only fault was the disposition to treat his execrable acting too gently. *All this is fact within my knowledge.* No one knew this Kean better than I in old times, no one knows him better still. . . .

Macready met me as I entered his room last night, and before I had time to say a word, with an emphatic ejaculation of praise and glory to Richelieu. The scene proposed hits his view. But he will write to you speedily. Meanwhile he entreats me to ask you for *the list of authorities* you promised touching the manners of the Great Cardinal. He will have him out, he says, before Xmas. . . .

[P.S.] A very fine house to the Lady of Lyons last night — & it went, Macready said, as on "a first night."

I could not help telling him of Charles Kean — privately of course.

On November 15, Macready read *Richelieu* again, only to dislike it more explicitly. He thought that it, "though excellent in parts, is deficient in the important point of continuity of interest. I should say that the character is not *servatus ad imum*. At home read some scenes in the latter part of *Richelieu*, which are not effective. I fear the play will not do — cannot be made effective." The next day before going to the theatre he read it to his wife and sister, making notes for alterations.

109. MACREADY TO BULWER, *Covent Garden Theatre, November* [*circa 16, 1838*]

My head has been at work — turning over and over the plot — until it almost aches. — Tomorrow I hope to have the book in my hand, which I cannot today. — Have you the outline of Marillac, that you sent to me? — I feel more strongly the urgent necessity for hanging the domestic interest upon Richelieu's fortunes.

On November 17 we find Bulwer remarking in a postscript to Forster, "I have not yet heard from Fell Cibber," and sending Macready the promised list of "authorities."

110. BULWER TO MACREADY, *November* [*17*], *1838*

> Anquetil. *Les Intrigues du Cabinet:* Vol. on
>   Louis XIII.
> Voltaire. *Hist. Gén.:* Vol. containing *Admin-
>   istration de Richelieu.*
> *Testament politique,* by Richelieu (Apochry-
>   phal!).
> *Mémoires de Richelieu.*
> ———————— *de Brienne.*
> *Journal de Richelieu* (I have never seen it).
> *Histoire du Père Joseph.*
> *Mémoires du Montglat.*
> *Hist. de France.*[23]

Above I send you a list of Books relative to Richelieu. Eno' to consult if you were going to write his History. But I do not think you will obtain from them much insight into his *manner,* at least very few details on it. Scattered anecdotes that may seem trivial, when collected, furnish a notion of his raillery — his address — his terrible good humour. His vindictiveness — his daring — his wisdom — his genius are in the broad events of his history. In France there is a kind of traditional Notion of his Personnel much the same as we have of Henry 8th or Queen Mary — or almost of Cromwell, viz: a Notion not to be found in books, but as it were, orally handed down. And this seems general as to his familiarity with his friends — his stateliness to the world — the high physical spirits that successful men nearly always have & which, as in Crom-

[23] Louis Pierre Anquetil (1723-1806), *L'Intrigue du cabinet, sous Henri IV et Louis XIII,* 4 vols. (Paris, 1780); François Maris Arouet de Voltaire (1694-1778), *Essai sur l'histoire générale et sur les moeurs et l'esprit des nations,* 7 vols. (Paris, 1756); Armand Jean du Plessis, Cardinal, Duc de Richelieu (1585-1642), *Testament politique,* Édition critique par Louis André (Paris, 1947); *Mémoires de Cardinal de Richelieu,* Société de l'histoire de France, 10 vols. (1907-31); Louis Henri de Loménie, Comte de Brienne (1636-98), *Mémoires . . .* Société de l'histoire de France, 3 vols. (1916-19); François de Paule de Clermont, Marquis de Montglat, *Mémoires . . . ,* 3 vols. (Paris, 1825-26).

well, can almost approach the buffoon, when most the Butcher. For the mere trick of the Manner, I fear you will have to draw on your own genius almost entirely.

Your note has just arrived. I shall be in (here) from eleven to two. If inconvenient to call here, I will call on you, wherever you like, after three o'clock. But as I rather wish to leave town, *if* you *can* call here, it would be a little more convenient to me. In that case you had best bring his Eminence with you.

The interview at Bulwer's chambers on November 17 was an extremely significant one, and may well mark the turning point in the play's fortunes. Macready appears to have brought to it some fundamental plan for repairing the deficiencies. "Called on Bulwer, and talked over the play *Richelieu*. He combatted my objections, and acceded to them, as his judgment swayed him; but when I developed the whole plan of alterations he was in ecstasies. I never saw him so excited, several times exclaiming he was 'enchanted' with the plan, and observed, in high spirits, 'what a fellow you are!' He was indeed delighted.[24] I left him the play and he promised to let me have it in a week! He is a wonderful man." Bulwer was so excited by Macready's plan that the very next day he brought around "two scenes, good ones, that he had already written," and they "settled the plot of the remainder." The week required for reworking was reduced to four days. The completed play was again in Macready's hands on November 21.

It is impossible to know what Macready's plan of revision was, but from detailed comparison of Bulwer's original sketch with the play as finally published — by subtracting one from the other — I conclude that it had to do with strengthening the story of the conspiracy against Richelieu and the King. Bulwer had originally set this going only in the second act, and dropped it in the middle of the fourth, thus being "deficient in the important point of continuity of interest." It would be like Macready to think of starting the conspiracy in the very first scene, and sustaining its suspense to the denouement — just as in the last act of *La Vallière* he had insisted on the King's second pursuit of Louise to the nunnery. If this be so, we must probably credit (or blame) Macready too for hatching the "packet" sequence by which the rise and fall of the conspiracy is charted. This is melodrama mechanics at its shoddiest, but it is also the paper chain by which the flimsy action is held together.

During the four days that Bulwer worked at revision, Macready read assiduously in Alfred de Vigny's *Cinq Mars*[25] (which Bulwer loaned him, though it was not on Bulwer's list of recommended books), in order to acclimate himself to the times and the character. And, at Forster's suggestion, he arranged that on the following Sunday the three of them should go through the play together.

He read it again as soon as Bulwer delivered it on November 21, but, alas, he did not like it much better than before. "I begin to be deadened to the interest of its story; it seems to be occasionally lengthy. I fear it has not the clinging interest of his present successful play, but hope & trust are good supporters." The next day he read it and thought about it and cut two acts for the Sunday reading, and complained of being "very much fatigued:" "do not yet see my way into it." On the twenty-third and twenty-fourth he gave it all the time he could spare, and cut the remainder.

The events of Sunday, November 25, were painful and disheartening to all concerned. "Sir Edward Bulwer and Forster came to dinner; after which I read the play

---

[24] So Pollock. Toynbee prints "delightful."

[25] Alfred Victor, Comte de Vigny (1797-1863), poet, dramatist, and novelist. His novel *Cinq Mars* was published in Paris in 1826.

of *Richelieu* to them and Catherine and Letitia; its effect was not what I had hoped, and in the fifth act Forster was asleep. This evidently hurt Bulwer, and we talked long after it. Forster, when Bulwer had gone, sat long talking over it, and admitted (what he never would have done but for this accident) that the interest of the play was not sufficient. I deeply feel the disappointment on Bulwer's account, to whom I am *so much indebted.*" Bulwer was hurt by Forster's behavior; even more important, he was deeply chagrined by the ineffectiveness of his work as it now stood "cut for the stage." At once he withdrew the play, with a resolution to re-examine his whole esthetic of verse-drama. His letter of November 26, with its blast at Forster, was delivered to Macready in his box at Covent Garden, where Forster was sitting beside him. Forster was "importunate on its purport, which I was obliged to tell him I could not (according to Bulwer's expressed wish) communicate." Macready "went home very ill, and hastened to bed."

111. BULWER TO MACREADY, *November* [*26*], *1838*

On hearing the play read last night, one thing struck & surprised me more than anything else, viz., the prosaic and almost bald cast of the general Diction. This I say surprised, because I knew I had written a Poem, and yet by some alchemy — the poetry was subtracted.

On consideration I find it is to be accounted for thus: (As in the Preface I stated,) the business part was purposely left plain and simple, prosaic in words — in order to throw the whole vividness of contrast and light upon those passages, where thought or passion, as in real life, burst spontaneously into poetry. The consequence of this adherence to the Grandeur of Nature has become a melancholy defect on the Stage (owing of course, to some error in treatment) — for every one almost of these passages is struck out, as not essential to the business, and the *rari nantes* that remain will undergo the same process by the further condensation requisite. So that at last there will remain a stripped & gaunt skeleton of prose robbed of all the bloom & *purpureum lumen* of the Poetry that it once possessed.

And the Play as I wrote it & as you first read it will no longer appear on the Stage. This bareness of dialogue is much more destructive to the effect than you would imagine. And I observed that the parts most effective in reading were (as in the 4th act) where the mutilation had not yet reached.— Now, to obviate this — when the Play is once condensed — the Dialogue of the retained parts should be rewritten and the business part rendered poetical. A fearful vice in composition (according to my conceptions of Art), but which I suppose is nevertheless essential — since I now see why more experienced Dramatists — Knowles and Talfourd — have studiously sought it — I say, when a Door is to be shut, "Shut the Door." Knowles would say, as I think he has said somewhere, "Let the room be airless." Probably he is right. — Now, this change in style will be tedious work — *invitâ Minervâ.* I doubt if I can do it at all. At the same time, far from complaining of the omission of the poetical passages, I see the necessity of their still more ruthless suppression & I begin at length to despair both of the play & of myself.— Unless, therefore, on consideration, you see — what at present you deem doubtful —

the triumphant effect of the Portraiture & action of Richelieu himself, you had better return me the Play, & if I can form myself on a New School of art — & unlearn all that toil & thought have hitherto taught me — I will attempt another.

But for this year you must do without me.

Meanwhile I will beg you not to consult Forster farther. Nor to listen to his suggestions. The disposition, certainly not that of partial respect, with which he came to the reading — broke out in spite of himself very early in the first scenes of the Play, & the [*page torn here*] *Manqué d'égards* at the close, altho' I do not suppose it intended as an affront, & tho' Heaven knows I have as little over-susceptibility on such points as most men, was only of a piece with a certain spirit of disparagement — which I have of late observed in him towards myself. Of course I can blame no one for measuring me according to the standard he honestly forms, nor would it disturb my regard for him generally. But I must be permitted to dispute the accuracy of the measurement, tho' I have all respect for the integrity of the Gauger.

Believe me, my dear Macready, fully sensible of your consideration for my own credit — & confident of the soundness of your ultimate judgement.

112. MACREADY TO BULWER, *Covent Garden Theatre, November 27, [1838]*

Mrs Macready brought me your note here last night — it found me ill, and made me something worse — for it was not possible I could read it without pain. — I must make time to offer you a few remarks upon it — In the first place I apprehend you do not fully perceive the relation in which I hold myself to you. You have laid me under obligations, which I cannot hope to repay: — of course you will believe that the substantial part of my debt is the least in my account — you have made it compulsory upon me to consider everything connected with your reputation of paramount importance, and the testimony I give of my estimate of your fame inevitably makes the standard by which I measure your success much higher than that which I apply to others. — Victory to another author would be little more than defeat to you. Nothing short of a spendid triumph ought to follow what you have done. — You do not enter the lists of dramatic authorship on equal terms with your competitors. This is my view of your position — in regard to what you have already achieved in literature — to your station, and your political interests.

I therefore, although endangering the prospect of the most powerful name there is to champion my cause and foregoing the *best hope* of my season, would hesitate upon every manifestation of doubt — every hint of uncertainty as to the result of a work of yours. — The hazard I would run in my own case, I shall not hold myself justified in doing in yours. — A portrait however finely touched (and what could be more beautiful than La Vallière!) without a strong course of action is not dramatic. You told me, that you had relied on the *acting* of the two last acts, from which the interest broke off, to carry on the play. You have trusted too much to what is weak, where action, that is strongly interesting, does not advance.— The play would succeed. I do not doubt; but the success would, I fear, be not what *your success* ought to be. I have been carried away by the character, and have not, until the examination has brought it before me, seen the effect of the ensemble.— If, as in the former programme, the fates of the two could palpably appear to depend on Richelieu, it would quite, I think, alter the case.— That want of cause in the mob's rising — the non-appearance of any object in Richelieu's entrance are detractions from the effect of the splendid scene that follows. If Mauprat had been beloved by the people & had been lodged in the Bastille & the mob rose to rescue him — or anything of that sort, all would be linked together; which at present is not the case — herein I think, and only here is the mistake of the play.— I need not say — perhaps I ought not — what an irreparable loss is that of your name from the honour of my season. But I can only say, your will is absolute here. No selfish consideration can make me waiver in my devotion to the interests of your fame.— If the play, as it is, came from a common writer it would be a prize — but I would not be contented with its chance of success, as it is, from you or rather for you.— There is a mistake, and I am disposed to dispute the correctness of your view of it — but I have not time, nor would you care, that I should argue on it.

Forster, with all his faults, is so warm-hearted, and I think so thoroughly enwrapt in an ardent admiration of you, that I apprehend you misjudge the intent of anything he may have said.

I will do whatever you wish — if I am to return the M.S.— shall I send with it the copy, which has been partly made?

I say little about my regret, & disappointment — but I could suffer none so severe — you have been in truth to me grande decus, columna rerum.

Bulwer was so touched by Macready's concern that he decided not to give up after all. He wrote to this effect, and carried the letter himself to Macready's dressing room that night, and they sat and talked long about *Richelieu*.

113. Bulwer to Macready, *Charles St., November 27, 1838*

I am very sorry you have been unwell, & hope you are restored. You are right, indeed, in supposing that I do not perceive the existence of any relation between us in which any little service I may ever have rendered to you has not been most amply repaid. But even were some figures on my side the Balance, not rubbed out, your present letter would indeed be "the moistened sponge" of Aeschylus,[26] blotting all the record.— I fully appreciate the manly & generous friendship you express so well. I have only one way to answer it — I had intended to turn to some other work before me. But I will now lay all by, & neither think nor labour at anything else until something or other be done, to realize our common object. Send back Richelieu, with any remarks that may occur to you. If it seem to you possible — either by alterations or by

---

[26] Aeschylus, *Agamemnon,* 1. 1329, "One touch of a moistened sponge wipes it all away."

throwing the latter acts overboard altogether — to produce such situations as may be triumphant — the Historical character of Richelieu is not to be replaced, & therefore is worth preserving. But if neither of us can think of such situations, we must lay his Eminence on the shelf & try for something else. You may still count on me — Health serving & God willing — no less as "a lance at need" than as, my dear Macready,

Y^r sincere & obliged friend

P.S. Forster has just written me a very kind and handsome note, which entirely exonerates him from anything worse than the *mauvais goût de n'être pas charmé de moi-même*. Who can complain of being in the same Boat with Richelieu himself? But I acquit him even of the *mauvais goût*, if he wish it. And after all, you and I know that it is only Tyrants & Cardinals who never sleep.

I would make the alterations you hint at in Richelieu — But I fear they would not suffice after all — The mob might be done away with altogether — & in Act 5, the bell a deep ringing for De Mauprat's execution. But even then I fear the mysterious *something* will be wanting.

Forster had suffered agonies of shame, and the incident on Monday — the letter from Bulwer that he was not allowed to see — was too much for him.

114. FORSTER TO BULWER, *58 Lincolns Inn Fields, Tuesday, November 27, 1838*

Private

I have to apologize for not having prepared the enclosed memoranda before; but I had some difficulty in finding the letters they are founded upon.

I have to apologize more deeply for what occurred on Sunday night. Is it necessary for me to say that any act of apparent rudeness from me to you was most unintentional, and has ever since its occurrence been deeply regretted. I will not trust myself to describe, indeed, the pain I have suffered since.

I offer no extenuation of this unfortunate matter — most unfortunate for me. I merely ask you to forgive it and to forgive me — and with this confidence I ask it, that during the many years I have known and admired your writings and been honored by your friendship — this is the first occasion in which I have seemed indifferent to what interested you. God knows with how little truth I *seemed* so then, or with how much sincere sorrow I write this note to you.

115. BULWER TO FORSTER, *8 Charles St., November 27, 1838*

I am very much obliged by your kind & friendly letter. I do not deny that I felt pain — But it was rather that of a friendly feeling hurt than a vain one wounded. . . . Your letter has done more than remove the impression — it has substituted another of unalloyed pleasure & satisfaction. — Many thanks for your kind memorandum & the trouble & pains it has cost you. — I heard loud praises of Cromwell yesterday from D'Orsay who compares you to

Mignet[27] (one of his gods) & Lady B.— I have sent the Book to Lord Lansdowne[28] who is a good judge — & whom I wish you to know —. . . . Pray
think no more of the main subject of your letter —. Unless as a new lease of
esteem & regard between yourself &

My dear Forster
Y[rs] truly

Thus the peace was made. Bulwer always treasured Forster's apology, for it epit-
omized Forster's rough but devoted friendship. Some thirty years later, when assembling the correspondence in a letterpress, he took this letter out of sequence and
pasted it at the front. Above it are penned these words: "What faults he has lie on
the surface. He may be irritated, sometimes bluff to rudeness — But these are trifling
irregularities in a nature solid & valuable as a block of gold. 1869."

For a few days Bulwer prodded about half-heartedly in search of another subject.
Macready loaned him an old play to think about, but he could not keep Richelieu out
of his mind.

116. BULWER TO MACREADY, *November 30 and December 1, 1838*

I will send you back your play. I can make nothing of it. It seems to me
that no improvement could give the outline stuff & volume eno' for a 5 act
play — tho' it would make a very pretty 3 act piece.— I see nothing else at
present, but shall continue to think and read for it. It is no use beginning
with a plot that does not both catch my fancy or suit *your* notion. Only I
warn you that the former object will not be effected without it be grounded on
some conception that may satisfy me as an author as well as a Dramatist.

I propose meanwhile to complete Richelieu. You can then read it, as we
settled, to a select few & abide by the issue. I have very little heart for it, I
own, but I see nothing else to be done & for anything else I have still less
heart. Let me know what you mean about omitting altogether the scene at
Marion de Lorme's.

Do you mean to have no substitute for it?

What think you of merely the outside of the House? François coming out
with the packet and making brief use of Huguet and Mauprat. Remember
you wanted to have the packet absolutely given to François.

I propose to end Act IV by bringing on Baradas at close — & a stormy
struggle in Richelieu — between his rage — his craft & secret design — his
tenderness for Julie, &c.— & at last so to overpower him with all these rapid
emotions that he shall fall back in their arms.

I will answer for the effect of this to close the act, & besides it will prepare
for his illness in act 5.— But if you don't fancy it, let me know, as it will
save me much labour.

---

[27] François Auguste Marie Mignet (1796-1884), historian and journalist, author of
Histoire de la révolution française (Paris, 1824).

[28] Lord Henry Petty, third Marquis of Lansdowne (1780-1863), a prominent Whig
politician and liberal patron of literature and the arts. Bulwer enlisted Lansdowne's interest in Macready's affairs, and Macready, who "did not love a lord," actually came to be
on comfortable social terms with Lansdowne.

[P.S.] If you or Forster have any scattered & desultory remarks to make, let me have them for consideration, as I shall go over the whole play.

I have thought that one reason why the conspiracy & plot seem arrested at Act 3 is that Richelieu *has* the packet — & even subsequently the audience feel that having the packet, he can save himself at last. The interest might be greatly heightened by delaying the receipt of the packet till Act V. Thus — Scene before Marion's House, Act 2 or 3 — Mauprat about to enter when he sees François coming out with Marion — & hears her telling him to give it to the Cardinal. He, not knowing what it is, but suspecting it to be a betrayal of the plot, wrests it from François, who does not recognize him in the dark — in his subsequent scene with the Cardinal he is too agitated to recur to it. He is arrested next day — & it is only in Act V — when in Prison with Joseph — that he remembers it. Still unaware of its importance — he gives it to Joseph, who opens & rushes out with it. — This it is that recovers the Cardinal, & the loss of this packet in Act 4 will greatly increase the apparent desperation of the situation.

The only objections I see to this are — 1st, Is it natural that Mauprat should have delayed so long giving it? 2ndly, will it not entail the loss of some fine passages in act between François & Richelieu? (The sword may be kept in, however.)

If this plan be adopted — & the actual importance of the packet kept in view throughout — the suspense may be very great. I tell more perhaps — if, without giving the scene before Marion de Lorme's, François may return to Richelieu to say that it has been reft from him — he knows not by whom — & leave the audience uncertain till Mauprat produces it saying how he came by it. Another effect of this will be tightening the connection between Mauprat & Richelieu. — Another thing I should like would be to keep Julie on the stage during Act 5 — Scene with Richelieu & the king — she would augment the interest. But would this be possible? Think over what I have written & give me your thoughts. If you like what I suggest, I'll talk it over with you — I fear Richelieu must be settled one way or other (even if for delayed representation) before I can go with free mind to anything else. In fact, in Act V Joseph may visit Mauprat to ask him what he knew about Beringhen's person as discovery of that is the last hope. Mauprat replies that he is quite ignorant of it. Joseph gives him up for lost when he mentions the word packet — this reminds Mauprat that he had overheard Marion & François — had seized the packet, which had no address — imagining it solely the exposure of the plot ags^t Richelieu's life. I fancy I see great strength in all this, but it is too long to enter into minutiae — by letter.

Among the Bulwer manuscripts preserved in the Forster Library at the Victoria and Albert Museum are three pages in Bulwer's hand which perhaps represent his ruminations on the play at this critical time. Not all the points made herein were actually realized in the play as we now read it, but many of them seem to reflect the recent correspondence.

117. BULWER MEMORANDUM

Proposed alterations in Richelieu

2nd Act —

To bring on Julie with Courtier

— After Richelieu & Joseph, a short & rapid scene at Marion de Lorme's —

3^d Act

Scene at the Castle — *after which,* a Scene with Louis & Baradas — to shew the anger of Louis ags^t Richelieu — to obtain the writ to send Mauprat to Bastille whether Cardinal be alive or dead — to leave audience in anxious uncertainty as to result & so carry on the action —

4th Act — Mob omitted —

The Gardens of the Louvre — Belief in Richelieu's Death — Louis & Baradas, & Courtiers — when enter — Mauprat — to announce Richelieu's safety — seeing Baradas his rage overcomes him — He draws — the King highly incensed. The writ given to guard — Mauprat seized — Baradas fearing that he wishes to announce his share in M's murder — stops & interrupts all he says — he is being hurried off when 3 knocks at the garden gates

Enter Richelieu & guards — Rest of Scene much the same as now — But if possible — a less quiet & more bustly end — more between Baradas & Richelieu — Stake agst the Headsman — encreased terror.

When Joseph tells him to resign — he shows Bouillon's Despatch — but Joseph says — if you present this they will say you forged it — your only witnesses De Mauprat & Francois poor creature — Richelieu startled —

Act 5 — Abandon the intellectual for the terrific interest generally

De Mauprat in Dungeon with Joseph. Enter Baradas to persuade him to give up Julie — on refusal — orders the Headsman — bids him toll the Bell — & execute him in 40 minutes. Scene rapid & vehement — Joseph saying at close — that only hope is in Richelieu's success in last experiment at power

Scene 2nd Louis — when enter Julie — then Baradas — as from the Bastille — much as now — Bell tolling at intervals. Enter Richelieu *with* his 4 Secretaries who sleep while he speaks to King — shortly telling him that before he decides on giving power to Orleans & Baradas to hear the Sec^s — retires to the [*illegible*] as before (all this not 12 lines) — Secretaries compressed — Last Secretary gives the King Despatch to Bouillon — Louis in despair trusting to Cardinal — begging him to reign — Richelieu says simply "on the condition of absolute power! — Richelieu thinks on Despatch as now — writes a line to Gov. of Bastille — His order to be obeyed to the letter — Enter Julie — then De Mauprat followed by a figure in a black mantle & hood — no part of face visible who remains motionless in a corner. — When Baradas enters thro' a line of courtiers — they all bow when Richelieu seizes him by the hand before he recognizes Julie & Mauprat — leads him suddenly to black figure — Behold your Bride — unveil her — mantle falls & shows the headsman with the hideous mask and the axe over his shoulder

"You have lost your stake
Richelieu makes him pass out side by side with headsman thro the same line
of courtiers — saying "Take warning my Lords" — Then rapid end

---

Dialogue of the whole play when compressed to be rendered more spirited,
close, & poetical —

Orleans to be omitted altogether

Query — instead — the introduction of one comic character — often on —
but saying little

Query whether Richelieu's Fool — (He kept them — so did Louis) — or
Query Orleans character in a qualified measure given to a courtier confidant
to Baradas — who shall be a thoro' french Wit — & appear from the first
scene.— not cowardly but *selfish* & can be a part for Bartley — a *relief* character —

NB — no act except Act 5 — to exceed 380 lines —

On December 2 he called on Macready to read him the plot of a new comedy, but
mainly to discuss "at great length" the plot of *Richelieu.* A week later he sent Macready a complete revision — which Macready thought "greatly improved, but still
not quite to the point of success"— and he persuaded Macready to read it to a
selected audience on the following Sunday. To Forster, on the eighth, he wrote,
"Richelieu returns to Macready today. I hope he'll ask me to the reading. His hints
have improved it WONDERFULLY."

118. BULWER TO MACREADY, *Charles St., Wednesday, December [12], 1838*

I sent you last year an afterpiece taken from Vathek and another called, I
think, Marriage à la Mode. They were by a Miss Tallent, a Constituent of
mine.— Could you lay your hands on them, & return them if among the
rejected addresses? You said they were kept in order to be looked over in the
recess.

When you inform me on Monday of the fate of our old friend The Clergyman, could you oblige me by sending your note *here before* 2 o'clock — as at
that hour a person will be going down to me at Knebworth and I shall have
the ultimatum a day sooner. I am perfectly prepared for stern truths, and the
more I think of it, the more I feel convinced of the advisability of not making
the experiment — unless opinions sh^d be decidedly in favour of the success —
the more so, as very considerable portions of the play are carried on in the
absence of the Clergyman, & may therefore be yet more doubtful on the stage
than the closet.

In Act 5 there sh^d be a little alteration. R. says to the Sec^y, "Free pardon
to the Prisoner Huguet." — This interrupts the grander order — let him say
it to the officer at the time he snatches away Mauprat's death-writ — as the
officer is following Baradas out.

If Richelieu gives the Despatch to the King instead of the Secretary, he
must be seated so near Louis that by a little "mutual stretching" it can be
done without rising; in that case, when the Sec^y says, "Designs against your
life," alter to "Designs ags^t yourself."

Louis

Myself most urgent.

Richelieu *(giving the Despatch)*

Sire, in this department
There is one matter. Here — *most urgent* — Take
The Count's advice in't.

If you think Joseph's advice about resigning, Act 4, not effective, you have but to omit it & follow up the Exit of Courtier with lines to the following effect:

Exit Courtier

Richelieu

God help thee, child — she hears not! look upon her —
The storm that rends the rock — uproots the flower —
Her father loved me so! — & and in that age
When friends are broken. — She has been to me
Soother, Nurse, plaything — daughter — Are these tears?
O shame — shame — dotage —

Joseph

Tears are not for eyes

That rather need the lightning which can pierce
Thro' barred gates & triple walls — to smite
Crime where it cowers in secret.

The Despatch!

Set every spy to work! The morrow's sun
Must see that written treason in your hands
Or rise upon your ruin.

Richelieu

Ay, — & Close

Upon my Death! . . . I am not made to live.
Friends, glory, France, all reft from me — my star
Like some vain holy day mimickry of fire
Piercing th' imperial Heaven, & falling down
Rayless and blackened to the Dust, — a thing
For all Men's feet to trample! yea — to-morrow
France or a grave — Look up, child — Lead on, Joseph —

Julie

Baradas & De Beringhen, Etc.

The effect of this is to confine, consolidate the intent on the Packet & on Richelieu's Death as the consequence of its probable loss.

I leave town to-morrow at 2, if you have any suggestions to make before.

119. MACREADY TO BULWER, *13 Cumberland Terrace, Thursday morn,*
  [*December 13, 1838*]

I think the alterations, in your letter, most valuable — & will attend to them. I am strongly of opinion that the suggestion of resigning should not be pressed by Joseph & I had not intended to retain the dialogue upon it at the reading. — The only important recommendation I have to make is to heighten the close of the scene between François & Huguet (I am not quite easy about it altogether — the monk's disguise, &c. — Qu. Could not François be introduced then in his own person — entering upon a conversation between De Beringhen & Huguet — his attempts to speak to Huguet interrupted by both during the negotiation that is going on — when the packet is produced he seizes it & the scene ends with a struggle for it — the audience uncertain of the issue?)

I do not know what exactly to recommend, but I think the beginning of the 5th act rather doubtful. — For the rest, I am almost afraid to say how much I think of what you have done. — The play seems to me to wear quite a different face. — The interest is greatly increased, and the movement accelerated, whilst a direct continuity is maintained throughout. — But I may judge comparatively, and therefore cannot build much upon my own opinion. On Sunday we will try the fresher ones, and you should have the result before two on Monday.

Will you think over François' scene? *Who is to do* François? I do not coincide with the introduction of the speech on the past & present of France, which I think will check the passion of the scene — but I think the loneliness of heart and want of object to attach itself to may be retained. I shall try it. — You have raised *me* to high hope — but I shall report the verdict faithfully. — Caesaris fortunam.

120. BULWER TO MACREADY, *December 14, 1838*

I enclose you a new Design for the early Part of Act 5, by which we heighten the suspense and avoid — the going from — to return to the Louvre — making François (as you once seemed to wish) come with the packet at the critical moment. Should you prefer the scenes first written, François, if you think it advisable, can still come in with the Despatch by a little alteration. As I have not the copy of the Play — & go by memory — one or two little points for alteration in the last scenes, if my proposed alteration please you, I may have forgotten. But I think I have guarded agst most. If you take the New Scenes, you will dispense with Baradas being led thro' the file of Courtiers & the words, "My Lords take warning." In this ½ sheet I enclose a few general amendments. In the other envelope — the principal one — Let me know how you like it — I was anxious you should have the option before Sunday's reading.

P.S. You do right to omit the speech about France, Act 4 — any cuts that don't interfere with the natural development in the only 2 long Acts, viz: Act 1 — Act 2, would be seasonable, especially where you are not on.

Alterations *(passim)*

In act 5 — when Julie comes to the King and says anxiously, "Be his Bride?" Louis answers, "A form, a mere *Decorum*. Thou knowest *I* love thee." I fear the effect of this open avowal of adultery and connivance on an English audience. What say you? — it would be softened by his merely saying "Yes" — if you think the Audience will sufficiently understand by that — the consistency of his loving her & yet wishing her to marry another.

In Act **V** — when Joseph says, "Fall back, *Count*," he should say, "Fall back, Son!"

In act 4 — in my last alteration, when Richelieu is pitying Julie — says, "I could weep to see her thus — But" — the effect would, I think, be better if he felt the tears with indignation at his own weakness — thus:

"Are these tears?

O shame — shame, Dotage" —

At the end of that Dialogue before Baradas enters he says, "France or a grave — the Purple or the shroud," which is tautology; more action in the following words, "France or a grave — Look up, Child — Lead us, Joseph." In Act 2 — towards the close when Richelieu says all forsake him save the indomitable heart of Armand Richelieu — it would be well to allude to Julie as she now plays so prominent a part also to Mauprat — thus:

"Of Armand Richelieu.

Joseph

Naught beside —

Richelieu

Why, Julie,

My own dear foster Child, forgive me! yes,
This morning, shining thro' their happy tears
Thy soft eyes blest me! & thy Lord; in danger
He would forsake me not!

Joseph

And Joseph —

Richelieu

You

Well, I believe it — you like me — are lonely
And the world loves you not: & I, my Joseph,
I am the only man who cared," &c.

The last alteration in words to Joseph is to soften the coarse words not discerned in the play of "All who do hate & fear you!"

The group which gathered at Macready's on December 16 was an interestingly assorted one: the poet-dramatist, Robert Browning; the actor-dramatist, T. J. Serle; Henry Smith, an old friend of Macready's, who combined playwriting with selling insurance; the portrait painter, John Bryant Lane; and two journalists, W. J. Fox and Samuel Blanchard. Two other journalists, Rintoul of the *Spectator* and William

Wallace, though invited, were unable to come.[29] When the guests arrived, about noon, Macready gave them each pencil and paper, asked that no one speak during the process, and read them the entire play. The experiment was immediately and immensely successful. Browning passed judgment first (he used afterwards to boast of it), putting down simply, "The plays — *the thing* —" Blanchard and Fox were enthusiastic. Serle noticed by way of warning that the third act was stronger than those which followed. Smith alone took noticeable exception. Macready interviewed them severally, received his further guests for dinner and music, and ended the day by making his report to Bulwer.

121. MACREADY TO BULWER, *13 Cumberland Terrace, December 16, [1838]*

At a very late hour (Sunday night) to ensure your receipt of this tomorrow, I give you a brief account of what passed. My audience were Messrs — Blanchard — Fox — Serle — Smith — Browning — Lane — M^{rs} & Miss Macready. — I would not allow a word to be *spoken,* that no effect of sympathy should be produced except by the play itself — I read it throughout in perfect silence, and had provided the jury with paper and pencils to write down their opinions, before I would unchain their tongues. — I enclose you the verdict. — Mrs. Macready and my sister were quite surprised at the great increase of interest, and thought, from the rapidity of the action and its pathos, that it read like *another play.* — The effect here was *decided success* — I endeavoured afterwards to extract the precise opinions of each separately — whether the play should be acted? — "CERTAINLY": — whether I ought to advise the author to have it acted from its apparent chance of success? "YES": — "that its literary merit in any case must justify its production, and satisfy any author": — the deepest interest was excited among my auditors; partial and *minor* exceptions were taken (besides those of occasional length) which I can discuss with you. You would have been more delighted — *much more* — with its effect today, than you were annoyed by its result on the previous Sunday. — Pray — excuse the brevity of this account — and understand from it that to you the experiment was *MOST GRATIFYING.* It is *very late,* and as I fear I shall be late tomorrow — I write tonight to ensure its arrival at Knebworth in due time.

[*Enclosures*]

"The plays — *the thing* —"
                    RB
(in Macready's hand): Mr. Browning

---

[29] Henry Smith once "published a tragedy." (*Diaries,* February 6, 1834.)

John Bryant Lane (1788-1868), an artist, spent ten years in Rome painting a gigantic *Vision of Joseph,* and was expelled by the papal authorities because of it; thereafter (1828-64) became a fashionable portrait painter.

W. J. Fox was now dramatic critic for the *Morning Chronicle.*

Samuel Laman Blanchard (1804-45), an editor and miscellaneous writer, was now editor of the *Courier,* a liberal evening newspaper.

Robert Stephen Rintoul (1787-1858), a journalist, founded *The Spectator* in 1828, and was an ardent advocate of the Reform Bill and champion of the working classes.

WILL SUCCEED — better at the beginning than the end — Cardinal
rather too self-descriptive & vain — *talks* too continually of France

TJS

(in Macready's hand): Mr. Serle.

It does not want interest as a literary production — it does as a dramatic
work — it omits the main fault of the Duchesse de la Valliere & substitutes
the fall of a minister — or a mistress — for the great human questions which
alone agitate a mixed audience —
(in Macready's hand): Mr. Smith — a man of no *common* mind — divided
between scientific and literary pursuits.

For Macready the issue was decided, but not so for Bulwer. He expressed his
apprehensions in a letter which Macready notes as "an honour to the writer."

122. BULWER TO MACREADY, *Knebworth, December 18, 1838*

Many thanks for your kind consideration in writing so late at night & collect-
ing so many written opinions. The result of them is encouraging, but at the
risk of seeming over-fearful I must add also — that it is not *decisive*. Fox's is
the most enthusiastic. But he is an enthusiastic person, & kindhearted — I
doubt his judgement. Serle's assurance that it will succeed better at the beginning than the end occasions some misgivings — for after the first night or two,
the end is much more important and excites more attention than the beginning.
Browning's short line of "the play is the thing" is a laconism that may mean
much or little — besides he wants xperience. Mr. Smith's is altogether chilling,
the more so that he has repeated a criticism of your own. I doubt whether he
hits the right nail in saying that the fate of a mistress of [or?] a minister was
the *real* interest of La Vallière or Richelieu, or that great human Questions
are not involved in both plays. But the fact of his opinion that the latter wants
interest as a Dramatic work is startling and clear — & we need not inquire if
he be right or wrong in guessing *why* it wants it. It may be said that the
interest of Richard III^d is only the fate of a bloody tyrant — not greater in
itself or results than the fate of a mighty statesman. But Richard III certainly
does not want interest; and in Richelieu — it is the fate of France, of the
heart of Europe, as embodied in the Packet and the success of Baradas, which
makes the grander interest. But if that interest is not perceived, there is a
want somewhere in the execution. To my mind the real defects in the play
are two-fold — 1st, that the tender interest as in Mauprat and Julie is weakened
and swallowed up in the fortunes of Richelieu; & 2^{ndly}, and I think this graver
— that the final triumph is not wrought out by the pure intellect of Richelieu,
but depends on the accidental success of François — a conception which wants
grandeur, & if the play were unmixed tragedy, would be very much worse
than it is now. I wish this could be obviated. But I don't well see how.
For if I were to create a new agency for the recovery of the Despatch & make
that discovery the result from the beginning of the unerring machinations of

the Cardinal, he would retain from first to last — that calm certainty of success which would be fatal to the struggle, the uncertainty & the passion which at present create the pathos of the play & the suspense of the audience.

I would not go the least upon the mere literary merits of the play — 1st, because they don't depend upon poetical wording of which everyone can judge, but upon somewhat naked intellect of which few are capable of judging & upon the variety and individualization of the characters, the effect of which must depend upon the actors. What I feel is this — that if I myself were certain of the Dramatic strength of the play, which I was in the Lady of Lyons, I should at once decide upon the xperiment from the opinions we have collected. But I own I am doubtful tho' hopeful of the degree of Dramatic strength, & remain just as irresolute now as I was before. I fancy that the effect on the stage of scenes cannot be conveyed by reading. Thus in the 5th act the grouping of all the characters round Richelieu — the effect of his sudden recovery, &c., no reading, I think, can accurately gauge — & in the 4th act the clinging of Julie to Richelieu, the protection he gives her, will have, I imagine, the physical effect of making the audience forget whether he is her father or not. There they are before you, flesh & blood — the old man and the young Bride involved in the same fate & creating the sympathy of a Domestic relation. More than all my dependence on the stage is in the acting of Richelieu — the embodiment of the portraiture, the work, the gesture, the personation which reading cannot give. But still I may certainly overrate all this, for if the play do fail in interest, the character may reward the actor but not suffice to carry off any tediousness in the play, especially as he is not always on the stage. On the whole, therefore, I am unable to give a casting vote — and leave it to you, with this assurance that if it be withdrawn, you shall have another by the end of February.

I hope you received my alterations for Act V, &c., which you ought to have done Saturday morning — If so, pray tell me whether they are adopted or not — or if you can think of any plan to make the seizure of the Packet arise more from Richelieu's intellect and yet not disturb the previous passion and suspense. I think, too, that the effect of Richelieu's relation to Julie wd be infinitely increased if we could introduce, however briefly, more fondness between them. Either in Act 1 when she is introduced, or 3 when she escapes the King — something more to put into action what he says in Act 4 when he calls her "Nurse, Soother, Plaything, Daughter," &c. Tell me also what omissions and minor alterations are suggested. If we *should* decide "on inducting the Clergyman," I must have the Play again before it is copied out — with such cuts as you may think needful. So as to weave up and repolish the whole.

You say a Mr Lane was present, you have not sent his opinion. I shall be here for ten days longer, if you like to send it down — in that case I will subjoin the Direction.

What I much want to know is whether the jury knew or guessed whom I was. I fancy it from the wording of their criticisms.

And there is eno' in the mannerism to betray me. I don't feel very sanguine in Blanchard's judgement — as he thought both Miss Landon's & Hunt's[30] plays were of brilliant success. To tell you the truth, it is rather your letter and what you say of the opinion of M^rs and Miss Macready that encourage me than the pencil notices.

P.S. Have you ferreted out Miss Tallent's play yet?

Direction if the Play be sent down:

To go by the Bedford coach (no other) leaves Holborn George & Blue Boar at 2 precisely. Directed to me at Knebworth Park, near Codicote (*Not* Stevenage) Herts to be left at the Lodge by the 28 milestone.

As there is no hurry it need not be sent till you have had leisure to decide on the cuts and reconsider the whole matter — perhaps it may keep till I return.

Was Act III felt weak?

123. MACREADY TO BULWER, *13 Cumberland Terrace, Regent's Park, December 21, 1838*

You bind me down to the single care of your reputation; interest; — and my extreme anxiety on that one consideration, in making me unusually timid, perhaps in some degree affects the clearness and steadiness of my judgement. Nothing would be gained to me, if your expectations and hopes were not to the height fulfilled. The object attained of course comprises all besides; but success to me might not be perfect satisfaction to you, and then I am utterly bankrupted in feeling — I had rather — much rather end my season. — I am therefore nervous, and hesitate in offering opinion. I really cannot trust myself: but must try to help your decision by the judgements of others. — I ought to tell you, that it was confidently stated among them (not in my hearing, but reported to me afterwards by Mrs Macready) that the play was yours, and the next day, Serle said to me, "I think I ought in honesty to say to you, that I am sure I know who the author is." — I have endeavoured to get from him more particularly his opinion — He thinks the 3^d Act so very strong, that it is possible the two following may have seemed weaker from its great strength. — The 4th Act he seemed on re-consideration to think might have a power, that he had over-looked — but the coup of the Cardinal in the 5th he, as all the rest, looked on as a great effect. — It is his opinion, whatever the degree of success may be, that the result must be honorable to ANY author (I do not mention your name) that the conception & portrait of Richelieu alone would sustain any previous reputation. — He objects to the too frequently recurring egotism of the Cardinal, and thinks it would be a mark for hostility in criticism. — Very much would depend upon the filling out of your conception in the performance, as

---

[30] James Henry Leigh Hunt (1784-1859), poet, essayist, and critic. His play, *A Legend of Florence*, which Macready had read at Forster's insistence and disliked, was finally produced at Covent Garden in February, 1840.

Miss Landon's tragedy, *Castruccio Castrucani*, was published by Blanchard in *Life and Literary Remains of L. E. L.*, 2 vols. (London, 1841).

he says — and to that I can say nothing. I may fail where most I strive for, and desire success.— I should say Serle is warmer upon this than on most subjects, on which I have conversed with him.— Browning meant much — very much.— Smith's was dictated by a spirit of exception — he rarely approves without discovering something to alter — he has written plays, and in almost every instance I have known, the dramatist peeps out in his criticisms: he thought *very highly* of the play, and was moved by it.— He wrote me a long note the next day — telling me that it had kept him awake for hours,— endeavouring to devise some means to make Julie the retriever of the packet, and sent me his sketch, but I did not see its availability.— With regard to the general question of the play's interest, I never read before a more deeply attentive — I think I may say — enwrapt auditory — several were moved to tears — and upon the various questions "Will it succeed? — Ought I to advise the author to produce it?"— the answers were unanimously in the affirmative. —I quite agree with you in what would be gained on one side and lost on the other by Richelieu's intellect working out the final triumph, but the loss would be far greater than the gain.— There is no doubt very much, which the movement and the picture on the stage will add — and I myself should *delight* in hearing cheers to this play — but I cannot decide for the reasons I have, in beginning my letter, alluded to.— If all were not exactly as we wished I should be almost disposed to throw down the thirty pieces of silver and like the arch-traitor go and hang myself.— Lane, who is an artist — was in a state of entrancement. Shall I try it before the jury of actors (it is not a special one, but sometimes hits upon the truth) and if I feel coldness, or hear a discouraging report (for like Richard I can "play the eaves-dropper," by others ears) shall we then reserve it for the Haymarket, where I am confident of it? — You must decide: — I would in any other case. Mrs Macready and my sister were certainly delighted with it, and quite carried away by the interest.— I send you the M.S.— in which you will perceive some pencilled brackets — on queries for omission: — one or two words here and there are merely hints to myself in the reading, which I had little time to prepare for.

In act 1st — The repetition of the allusion to his poetry — addressed to Joseph — was universally disapproved of: — The introduction very much liked, but the objection to its recurrence was strong and unanimous.

Act 2nd The "curse thou" at Baradas' exit was mentioned: — the recurrence of the paté after the 2nd Act was also the subject of a general protest.

Act 3rd Was thought a great act by all: — but the concluding scene was felt to be a declination.— I am strongly of opinion, that the matter in that scene, necessary to the action, might, with augmentation of effect, be introduced at the opening of Act 4th.— The enquiry of the effect of the news upon the King might stand — & lead to the displaying the writ for Mauprat — Huguet, who had brought the news the preceding night and desired to call on the morrow — Baradas being unprepared for him — might be announced as importunate to see B. — might come to claim his reward & be disposed of by the archers, now at hand as in 3rd Act — the King enters, and all proceeds.

In Act 4th — There was also general exception taken to the very frequent allusion to apostrophising of "France" by Richelieu — I in the reading, changed the word once or twice — but still I felt it came too often before me.

In Act 5th — Would it not strengthen the 1st Scene — if Joseph were to make the audience know his object in seeking Huguet — viz. — that he has learned he has the packet — if he were more violent in his endeavour to obtain an interview and rush away, almost in despair, as if to find some means to effect his purpose? this would give interest to his importunity — if he even begged the Governor to tell Huguet he was there & to send him the paper to transfer to the Cardinal — this would also arouse the interest of De Beringhen's visit — François must not let Beringhen go, when once he clutches him, but they must exeunt in the struggle, and their voices die away in the distance.—

Let me know at your earliest convenience your opinion on what I have reported: — if you decide on passing the Rubicon, pray let me have the M.S. as soon as possible — not to hurry it out, but that I may employ every leisure minute in identifying myself with Richelieu.— I will not act it till I feel I can — and until I am told I do.

I enclose in this parcel your constituents' piece.— I should have written more collectedly but for an event in my family this evening — a boy added to my little flock.

P.S. Will you oblige me by franking the enclosed letter?

On December 24, "A letter from Bulwer — the noble-hearted fellow! — wishing to try the play before the green-room. I wrote assenting."

124. BULWER TO MACREADY, [*December 24, 1838*][31]

I congratulate you heartily on the safe footing of your offspring[32] (taking an unfair advantage of my less material child) has established in the world. Long life and happiness to him! In my earlier days, in that old language of the affections over which time or the devil draws red hot ploughshares, the advent of these shrill-tongued strangers was always a very nervous event to me. Never myself having been in the family way (which is odd!) I have a most terrific notion of what ladies go through, and shall feel happy when I get a good account from you of Mrs. Macready. I now approach my own creation, which, if it die immediately, will certainly not have to complain of want of nursing.

Do you recollect that passage in the "Confessions," when Rousseau, haunted by vague fear that he was destined to be damned, resolved to convince himself

---

[31] The text of this fragment of a letter is taken from an article called "The Stage in Relation to Literature," by Robert Lytton, Bulwer's son, printed in the *Fortnightly Review* (August, 1883), XL, 222.

[32] Henry Frederick Bulwer Macready was born December 21, 1838; died August 12, 1857.

one way or the other; and taking up a stone shied it at a tree? If the stone hit, he was to be saved; if it missed, he was to be damned. Luckily it hit the tree, and Rousseau walked away with his mind perfectly at ease.[33] Let us follow this notable example. Our tree shall be in the Green-room. You shall shy at the actors. If it hit the mark well and good. If not we shall know our fate. To speak literally, I accept your proposal to abide by the issue of a reading to the actors; though I remember that jury anticipated great things from *La Vallière,* and I think they generally judge according as they like their parts. The general tone of your friendly and generous letter induces me, indeed, to release you at once from the responsibility of the decision, and to say boldly that I am prepared to have the play acted. It can therefore be read with that impression to the Green-room, and if it does not take there, why it will not be too late to retreat. If it does, I can only say *Make-ready!* Present! Fire! All I could doubt was the theatrical interest of the story. Your account reassured me on that point, and therefore you will have fair play for your own art and genius in the predominant character. I must leave it to you to determine what steps should be taken to preserve the incognito as well as we can. I have been thinking that you are not strong in afterpieces. Shall I try to do you in two or three Acts? I don't know that I shall have time, but if I have I can try. Of course this must be the most profound secret, successful or not. I don't wish to be known as an author of afterpieces. But all things are in themselves worthy if they worthily serve the Republic.

125. MACREADY TO BULWER, *13 Cumberland Terrace, Monday night,*
    [*December 24, 1838*]

Most earnestly do I thank you for the expression of your kind wishes for Mrs Macready's and her babe's welfare. All goes on as well as we could expect, but it is as yet too soon to say that we have dismissed our anxiety.— The newcomer is however to all appearance a stout gentleman, and therefore encourages our hopes, that we shall all soon feel at ease.— I shall some day ask you how far you think sensibility a blessing or a curse; but now I must engage all your attention on one subject.— There seems to me no better course than that you have decided on — viz: to make an experiment on the green-room: I will add to the regular audience other ears, that may be of assistance to us in forming a correct judgment of the event. I will take good aim, and endeavour not only to hit, but to hit hard.

From the positive tone in which the authorship was assigned here, I should much doubt the success of any attempt at actual concealment — the most we can do, I apprehend, is not to acknowledge, and that is not much.

I perceive the strength of your objections to my desire of terminating the 3^d Act with the departure of Huguet &c — they are most just: — but then, as

---

[33] Jean Jacques Rousseau (1712-78), the philosopher. The anecdote referred to is told in Book VI of the *Confessions.*

the next best means of sustaining a weak part, would it not be possible to make François rush in to Baradas in that scene — of course after Huguet's arrest — tell him of the seizure of the pacquet, and learning from him that Mauprat has it, would not the hope presented to François of recovering it, and the disappointment and fear, whetting Baradas' resolution to make himself master of Mauprat's fate, lend an additional interest to the close of that act, and the beginning of the 4th? — I think something, and in the continuity of interest, not a little, might be gained — if this be possible. We may *try* the recurrence of the play in Act 1st — either partially or entirely — I am always for experiment: — perhaps the mean may prove a golden one.

How am I to thank you for your too generous offer of an after-piece? You go beyond my power to do my feelings common justice.— I have but one answer, in thanking you from my very soul, and that is, there are cogent reasons why your name should not be associated with an inferior subject — accident might betray you, and I should never forgive myself for having consented to profit by what might in the least degree compromise you.— What would *motive* be to such men as Barnes or Bacon of the Times[34] — or to a person, who knowing nothing of you, has expressed his hatred of you — a hate, that of envy, which too many writers for the press feel with him? It is a hazard, which you *ought not* to incur — and which I feel I ought not for an instant to think of assenting to.— I am quite sure, my dear Bulwer, that you have a pleasure in knowing from me, that your friendly aid has far, far outstripped, in the benefit it has yielded, all, that all my other friends have done to assist me in my undertaking. How then can I entertain a thought, that in possible service to me may bring a moment's annoyance to you? Let me request you, thanking you fervently and gratefully as I do, to dismiss any such idea from your mind.

Fox has, since I wrote, seen Forster, and expressed himself very enthusiastically on the subject of the Cardinal.— I have more hope than I dare to avow:– but the test will be the next reading.— As soon as you can let me have it, I will put it in train.

After a long conference on December 31, Bulwer returned the manuscript corrected for the greenroom, and with numerous notes for further revision and suggestions anticipatory of costumes, properties, and stage decor.

126. BULWER TO MACREADY, [*January 1, 1839*]

I send the play as you wished. I make the following suggestions:

In Act 1st — about the Play. I think the effect of his grave kindness to Mauprat and Julie is heightened by the comic contrast of reading his play to himself. This may be as follows:

---

[34] Thomas Barnes (1785-1841), editor of the *Times* from 1817, and Bacon, of his staff, were in Macready's eyes among his worst enemies. "Vermin," he called them; "active agents in mischief and wanton inflicters of mental torture." When Barnes died, in 1841, Macready was glad that both were "gone where we all must soon follow."

Richelieu

Go!

When you return I have a feast for you —
The last great act of my great play.

Joseph (*going out hastily*)

Worse than

The Scourge!

Richelieu (*taking up his play*)

These verses. Gone! Poor Man!

(*Seats himself with his play*)

Sublime:

Enter Mauprat & Julie
& as follows.

Act III

In the scene after Huguet is sent to Bastile — I have put some lines into DeBer's mouth — as an excuse to go out. As he must not see François, otherwise he would recognize him at the Bastile. I mention this, for the lines are no great things & you might otherwise cut them out as superfluous.

Act II

You have cut out about the Pigmies & Hercules, but better retain. Bah! in policy we foil gigantic danger.

By giants, not dwarfs — the statues of our stately fortune are sculptured by the chisel not the axe. Because they connect themselves with his employment of Marion & François.

In Act V — when François and DeBer go out struggling for the packet, DeBeringhen must not cry out loud, lest it should seem odd that they are not overheard — the struggle should be rapid, intense — but not noisy. If any blades used, Daggers not swords — as more commodious for close struggle.

Act 3 — still ends weakly. But I have done all I can.

In the play as printed, I shall add more Elaborate analysis of Richelieu's character & Louis's so as to remove ground for the criticisms I referred to last night. And if on the stage he stand out too amiably, it will be seen that he does so from the omission of touches too minute & subtle or scenes too lengthened for the action of a Play. — I shall long to know how it comes out in the green room. I feel very sure of Act V & think better of the interest for our time and labour. Fortunately I had done my corrections to-day before the news of poor L. E. L.'s death, which I have just seen in the paper. It has quite overcome me. And I cannot write now many little things that occur to me. So young, so gifted & I found a letter from her yesterday in high spirits. I have not been so shocked for years. — I hope I shall hear a good acct. of M^{rs} M.

[P.S.] Since writing the enclosed — it occurs to me that if you adopt my suggestion, Act 3 & show the Bed &c. — it would add to the suspense & surprise by omitting Richelieu's words, "You have slain me — I am dead," &c., & leave the audience in expectation till Mauprat returns, as to what his device really is.

There are unfortunately so many papers used by way of writs, despatches &c., that we must distinguish broadly between them; the Writs of banishment & Death for Mauprat should be short scraps of Parchment & Richelieu's conditions of power which the King signs should be in a small portfolio or pocketbook with clasps. If I remember the History rightly, the Document containing these & other articles of Richelieu's power was absolutely found (after R's death) in a red & gold morocco book. The Despatch must be distinguished from the writs, but I hardly know how.

I should add about Dress. That I think in the pictures of Richelieu, he wears the colour & order of the Saint Esprit — that Louis never wore any colors but black & orange ribbons — that Mauprat must wear black for his first dress as Julie alludes to that colour, & that the general costume is very like Bragelone's, with trowsers to the knee, bows & a mantle. You will see, Act 5, that I have made the King say he promised to hold Baradas' life sacred — 1st, because that will account for the Vindictive and ruthless Cardinal not killing him; 2nd, because at the Commencement Richelieu saying he had another bride, the Grave for Baradas — unless some such obstacle arise at the close, there would be no reason in Baradas' subsequent conduct for the Cardinal's changing his mind. By the way, Richelieu lived more splendidly than the King. Can the scene of their respective rooms convey this idea?

On January 2, Macready sought Bulwer's advice on a problem which had been vexing him for the last two weeks — whether he should dare to produce a play that had come to him from Fanny Kemble Butler — "one of the most powerful of the modern plays I have ever seen — most painful, almost shocking, but full of power, poetry, and pathos."[35] Forster, with typical bravado, insisted that he must bring it out. But with Bulwer's advice (backed later by Henry Hart Milman[36] and Harriet Martineau) Macready chose discretion over valor and declined it.

127. BULWER TO MACREADY, [*January 3, 1839*]

I am very sorry I could not return the play this Eveng. Not having received it till late in the Noon & not being able to work at it till 11 at Night.— Of its talent I say Nothing.— It has some xquisite touches — & some great power. But I agree more with Serle than Forster & for your sake & hers I say, "Pause — Reflect," before you make a very dangerous xperiment. Try the ordeal of

---

[35] Frances Anne Kemble (1809-93), actress and writer, was the daughter of Charles Kemble; in 1834 she married Pierce Butler, an American, and divorced him fourteen years later. Her play, *An English Tragedy,* was based on the life of Lord de Ros, a notorious roué and cardsharp, and it contained a "powerful" seduction scene. It was published in her volume of *Plays* (London, 1863) and produced in New York in 1864.

[36] Henry Hart Milman (1791-1868), English clergyman, historian, and dramatist. His *Fazio,* produced in 1815, became a nineteenth-century stock piece. After 1849 he was Dean of St. Paul's.

reading it to women, & a few plain (not literary) men. Honestly I think that without great alteration — the 3rd Act would close with hisses. At all events, the Pathos depends on the Judge not Anne — and if Vandenhoff does the Judge — why —

P.S. I should not have said so much about the play — if you were not Manager. I fear the result might be a shock upon your *management* among a widish class. Moreover, I fear that as Acts 2 & 3 end with the strongest (viz: most indelicate) positions, & yet with the feeblest agents; there will be no respect for the actors to stifle the revolt at the situations.

January 5 was the fateful and happy day of the greenroom reading. "Read Bulwer's play to the actors, and was most agreeably surprised to find it excite them in a very extraordinary manner. Besides our company, Brydone, Marshall, and a Mr. Clarke, Serle's brother-in-law, were present.[37] The expression of delight was universal and enthusiastic." He reported the success to Bulwer with unrestrained enthusiasm, and that night Bulwer came to his box to express his pleasure at the news.

128. MACREADY TO BULWER, *Covent Garden Theatre, Saturday 20 m.p.*
    3 o'clock, [January 5, 1839]

Triumph! the enthusiasm which accompanied the reading and followed the conclusion of the Play was beyond any I have *ever* witnessed in a green-room — It was, I may say, acclamation rather than expression of opinion.— Now this will be a test of the correctness of green-room judgements.— We had some lay-brothers — not of our order.— Every hit told. If I were to hesitate one minute upon it now, I should expect the proprietors and players would unite in taking out a commission of lunacy against me. You could not have DESIRED anything (of its kind) more gratifying.

But — (who invented that word?) — as to the author! — it was ludicrous to hear the confident assertion of all, that they knew him directly.— Your name was not mentioned *of course* in my hearing — but they have said it could be no other person than the *one*, "and no mistake".

You must digest this as you best can: — Salvator Rosa cannot help us any longer here.[38]

We shall read Jerrold's play, I hope, on Tuesday, and bring it out at once,[39] whilst yours will be under a long course of preparation.

[37] Mr. Brydone was business manager for Macready at Covent Garden in 1838-39, and after serving with Mme. Vestris, returned to Macready for the Drury Lane season of 1841-42. Early in 1842 Macready dismissed him for incompetence.

Charles Marshall (1806-90) was a distinguished scene painter. Trained under Marinari at Drury Lane, he developed his art at the Surrey and other minor theatres. At Covent Garden he achieved great success in staging Shakespeare, *The Lady of Lyons, Richelieu*, etc. (1837-39). In 1844 he succeeded William Grieve as scene painter to the opera at Her Majesty's Theatre.

[38] Salvator Rosa (1615-73), the Italian landscape and historical painter. The sentence must depend upon some private meaning between Macready and Bulwer.

[39] Douglas William Jerrold (1803-57), dramatist and wit, was a contributor to *Punch* from its founding in 1841. We are not told the name of the play in question. In No-

Thank you very much for your kind and excellent counsel about Mrs. Butler's play: — I have acted on it. –

COMPLETE VICTORY.

Macready turned in his resignation of the management of Covent Garden on January 8, to be effective at the end of the current season, and the next day he and his lieutenants decided to recoup recent losses by bringing out *Richelieu* without delay. As a matter of fact, however, owing to difficulties with the actors, Macready's problems in grappling with his own part, and other intricacies of production, two months were to elapse before *Richelieu*'s opening night.

129. BULWER TO MACREADY, [*January 10*], 1839[40]

Many thanks for the tickets. I cannot find any substitute for François, tho' I have been hunting thro' all the memoirs of the next reign for some Son of Fortune brought up by the Cardinal, whose character would correspond.

He must therefore stay as he is at present. Let me have back my MSS., as soon as they are copied. They ought to bear the motto, *"Cut & Come again."*

If there are any lines to be altered or strengthened, let me know. We will fight up every inch of our way.

Don't give Louis to Serle without mature thought. He would look it well — & walk it well. But would he do the passage where he discovers the treason & reads the scroll with sufficient fire and strength? for the Cardinal's effect would be much impaired if Louis's agony & dismay were not forcible — also is he distinctly audible?

There are so many allusions to the youth of François & so much of the interest of the character depends on his being young, that I have very great doubts of the Audience being sufficiently conscious of the great youth of Elton! Wig him as you will.

When does Jerrold's play come out?

P.S. I am in a deadly rage Having just rec'd the accounts for The Lady in the Provinces 17£ 3s!!! — the Agency at the Dramatic Authors must be shamefully done. I should like to remodel the whole thing. I am the only man of Business of my whole tribe.

130. MACREADY TO BULWER, *Covent Garden Theatre, January 12,* [1839]

I hope to be able to send your M. S. tomorrow or Monday: — I have to revise the acts of it, as I deliver them to the copyist, that your handwriting may

---

vember Macready had liked it enough to pay £50 advance on it, but on January 9 he rejected it as "a very heavy and . . . hopeless affair . . . its want of action and purpose." On February 8, 1842, he produced Jerrold's *The Prisoner of War,* which was successful; but this is probably not the same piece.

[40] Matthews dated this letter "February," but the concern over casting problems marks it as obviously of earlier date. The postscript gives the clue: in the Knebworth Archives there is a note from Bulwer to Forster, dated January 10, enclosing the provincial account of *The Lady of Lyons,* dated January 9.

not appear — Though your name, "albeit I hear it not" is blazoned on the title-page by the general will.

I have tried Mrs Warner for François — she will not show her legs, though they are worth looking at. I am afraid Medea herself could not invent a cosmetic that should give youth to Elton — and I agree with you, that he is required in the King: — under these circumstances I see nothing for it, but to take Mr. Howe[41] under regular *drill,* and work him into the part.

Will you oblige me by franking the enclosed to

Miss Twiss[42]

Holbrook Rectory

near Ipswich

Jerrold's play is for the present (which I fear includes a long future) withdrawn. — Richelieu is the flag under which we fight — & "Honor's thought reigns solely in the breast of any man." —[43]

I shall see you, I hope, next week, and give you a fresh account of our proceedings. —

Macready had infinite difficulty in comprehending — or rather in accepting — the character of Richelieu as Bulwer wanted it shown. I doubt indeed that he ever played the role as the author intended it. As early as November Bulwer had sent him a list of books to read, but had warned him that the truth about Richelieu's personality lay rather in the French traditional notion, "not to be found in books, but as it were orally handed down," of his "familiarity with his friends," and his "high physical spirits . . . which, as in Cromwell, can almost approach the buffoon." But Macready had even then turned for enlightenment to de Vigny's *Cinq Mars,* in which Richelieu's aspects of dryness, dignity, wily intellectuality, cruelty, and despotism are underscored. It happened that de Vigny was visiting England in the early months of 1839, and Macready arranged through Alfred d'Orsay to consult him on the role. On February 1 he was flattered to read (and transcribe) de Vigny's prophecy and promise: "Il sera bien beau dans Richelieu, et j'aurai beaucoup à lui dire de cet homme, dont j'ai été *l'ennemi intime* pendant tout le terme que j'ai écrit *Cinq Mars." L'ennemi intime:* that was precisely the attitude Macready was looking for. He met de Vigny at Lady Blessington's on February 16 and "had a most interesting conversation on *Richelieu."* By the twentieth he could hardly see his way into the role, "which Bulwer had made particularly difficult by its inconsistency; he has made him resort to low jest, which outrages one's notions of the ideal Cardinal Richelieu, with all his vanity, and suppleness and craft." The next day he called on de Vigny; "sat with him very long, and was amply repaid for the time I gave. He related to me a variety of anecdotes illustrative of the characters of Louis XIII, Richelieu, of *Cinq Mars,* etc. . . . I was very much pleased with him." A day later he was far gone indeed: "Gave my attention to

---

[41] Henry Howe (real name Hutchinson; 1812-96), actor, made his London debut in 1834; belonged to Macready's Covent Garden companies, and thereafter played continuously at the Haymarket for 40 years. After 1881 he was a member of Henry Irving's Lyceum company, and affectionately known as "Daddy" Howe.

[42] Macready was a lifelong friend of the Twiss family since meeting them in Bath in 1815. This is presumably Fanny Twiss, sister to the famous Horace Twiss (1787-1849), lawyer, M.P., journalist, and wit; nephew of Mrs. Siddons; celebrated for his dinner parties.

[43] Shakespeare's *Henry V,* II. Chorus, 3-4.

the inquiry as to the possibility of reconciling the character which Bulwer has drawn under the name of Cardinal Richelieu with the original, from which it so entirely differs. Was not much cheered by the result of my investigation and experiment." After a session of educating the actor Elton in "the weak and nervous character of Louis, of which he knew nothing" (for Bulwer's lines tell little of what de Vigny told so much), he resumed study of his own part, which, he declared, he "must *fabricate.*"

At the same time, it appears, Bulwer was worrying about the characterization, too.

131. BULWER TO MACREADY, [*February 22, 1839*][44]

Voltaire, who was the Richelieu of letters, once sent to knock up Le Kain[45] (who was to act a tyrant in one of his plays) at two o'clock in the morning. "But, sir," said the messenger, "Monsieur Le Kain will be asleep." "Go, sir," answered the author, "tyrants never sleep." Though I am not Voltaire, I give to my Cardinals as little rest as he vouchsafed to his tyrants. I have three suggestions to make. 1st. I know not if you conceive Richlieu's illness (Act V.) as I do? I do not mean it for a show illness. He is really ill, though he may exaggerate *a little*. When they are going to tear France from him, they do really tug at his heart-strings. He is really near fainting at the prospect of his experiment with the Secretaries; and it is the mind invigorating the body — it is the might of France passing into him, which effects the cure. If there be delusion, it is all sublimed and exalted by the high-hearted truth at the bottom of it. This is *my* conception. Is it yours also? Or would you really have him all vulpine? 2nd. I think it natural to anticipate the probability of some of the conspirators wishing to see Richelieu dead, in Act III. It would also give a higher notion of the Cardinal's self-possession, if, when De Mauprat returns and says, "Live the King! Cardinal Richelieu is no more," he were to throw open the folding-doors, and you saw a bed in the recess (which, of course, would be obscure and dim) with the distinct outline of Richelieu's form. Huguet might advance half way to gaze upon the body, and De Mauprat follow him, grasping his dagger with the byplay of fear and resolve, when Huguet would say, "Are his eyes open?" "Wide," answers De Mauprat. Huguet, "Then I will not look on him," and turns away. This would not delay the action, and I think it would be more natural and more effective. 3rdly. When Richelieu addresses the mob, I think you snub them a little too much in the old play way, and don't enough see his address in managing them. I think that in the middle of his third speech one or two timid voices should cry out, "Meat a farthing a pound!" and he, stopping for a moment, rejoins, "Bah! would that be fair to the butchers?" This would create a laugh with the mob; and he would then go on, with increased effect, to ordering them to disperse. That single touch would, in my opinion, add much to the indicated genius of the man, and do away with the mere bullying of the crowd. *Apropos* of the crowd, however, how the devil do you mean to manage that the King and Richelieu should address them through the palisades? Unless they can be elevated some-

---

[44] The text of this letter is taken from Robert Lytton, *Fortnightly Review,* XL, 222.
[45] Lekain (Henri Louis Cain; 1728-78), Voltaire's favorite tragic actor, famous for his "natural" diction and costuming.

how by steps or platforms the effect will be ludicrous, like talking to so many monkeys in a large cage. Properly, they would show themselves at a balcony, but this is impossible. Will you have the kindness to turn to the end of Act IV.? Julie, in her last speech, says, "You shall not go! You will not!" Put in a stage direction to Julie (*caressingly*), for otherwise, if Miss Faucit delivers the words "shall not" in the tone of a command, she will destroy all the interest of her part. After she sees that the old man is ill, she must not appear to bully him. Her very agony must be made expressive by being subdued. Tell me if I hit off your idea at the end of Act IV., and if my alterations generally meet your suggestion, which was a masterpiece in conception. Why the deuce were you not author as well as actor? I am now going to retaliate, and (mark my modesty) suggest how I meant a line to be said by you. In Act IV., when you say, "And sheltered by the wings of sacred Rome," I want you *actually* to shelter her with the priestly robe, and to cower over her like an old eagle. When I wrote this I had in my mind a dim recollection of an action of yours, somewhere, I think, as Lear with Cordelia. I *think* it was Lear; but I remember that, wherever it was, it was thoroughly grand and tender in its *protectiveness*.

> Now my weary lips I close
> And leave the Cardinal to repose.

132. MACREADY TO BULWER, *Covent Garden Theatre, February 23,* [*1839*]

Opiates are quite in as much request with Cardinals as with tyrants — I wake to work myself into the mind of Richelieu — or rather to re-create his and transfuse it into myself, which rumples one's pillow not a little.

I like very much indeed what you have done & think the interest & effect greatly heightened. — I had expressed my intention of endeavouring to make the dying scene as impressive as my sick King Henry's which is one of my capi d'opera: I will try and realise your notion of the "dove-like brooding over"— Miss Faucit.— The omission of the lines "I am dead" I had decided on to mention to you — & the others of Huguet I have inserted. Richelieu's joke to the mob is too great a hazard.— Your directions I have attended to. The play shall be done to a *point of* costume.

I am thinking all of it.

133. MACREADY TO BULWER, *13 Cumberland Terrace, February 24,* [*1839*]

There are one or two things, about which I wished to speak with you.— 1st I wish to advertise the title of the Play — what is it to be? —"Richelieu; or the Conspiracy": — I do not think we should be without the second: — 2d — We are under the necessity of producing it on a Thursday — Thursday March 7th — Again, will the allusion of De Beringhen in the last act to the "Paté" of the 2nd be effective — will the "Paté" be remembered? — The few lines with Baradas also, after the departure of Louis, asking for his hand, interrupt the feeling in its progress toward the climax, which we must try to make it reach.— I am not quite at ease also about the "scourge".

Count de Vigny gave me more than two hours on Thursday, and brought the man Richelieu directly before me.— Can you give me the additional lines you have for me, as time is now of great importance.

Bulwer, Forster, and de Vigny were all in his room on February 25 after a performance of *Lear,* and "Bulwer spoke to me about Richelieu, and satisfied me on the justice of his draught of the character from the evidence that history has given us." In the context of the events this can only be read as a mild sarcasm, as well as the words that follow: *"Allons donc à la gloire!"*

134. MACREADY TO BULWER, *Covent Garden Theatre, February 26,* [*1839*]

I have taken the first two passages you have marked, which I can best use and have also copied in the tag, which I think will answer all the purposes required. I return you both the pieces of M. S.— I thank you very much for the additional information about Richelieu, it sets me so much more at my ease— I earnestly hope I may be able to do you justice but I am too nervous to have an opinion on the subject.

There is one matter, an important one, upon which I have not yet touched: but I have not done so, because I could ask the question even at a later hour than the present, which I take the opportunity of doing. What are the terms of the play of Richelieu? I need not, I trust, add, they are for you to fix.

135. BULWER TO MACREADY, *February 27, 1839*

I am glad the tag does. With regard to the Business part of your letter I can only say that it seems to me that the terms had better be regulated by the success. And that all I shall expect is that they may not be so estimated as to defeat my primary object— that of being of service to your enterprise.

Will you kindly have copied out & sent to me tomorrow, the 4 first lines said by Baradas— Act 1st, Scene 1st, immediately following Orleans: "Well, Marion, see how the Play prospers yonder."

These 4 lines have been lost by the Printer and I have no other copy. Pray let me have them Wednesday— tomorrow.

136. MACREADY TO BULWER, *Cumberland Terrace, Wednesday,* [*February 27, 1839*]

————————— *Garden*

> *Baradas* (taking out a parchment)
>   I have now
> All the conditions drawn: it only needs
> Our signatures.— Upon receipt of this
> Bouillon will join his army with the Spaniard —
> March on to Paris — there dethrone the King: —
> You will be Regent: I, and ye, My Lords
> Form the new Council. So much for the care
> Of our great scheme.—

The person who has brought me your note is waiting, therefore I hastily send you the speech of Baradas after Orleans's direction to Marion.

You have already been such a benefactor to my undertaking, that I must insist on this most valued assistance of yours being treated by you only as a thing of business.— I never can repay what you have done for me. Therefore it is idle to say more. . . .

137. MACREADY TO BULWER, *Cumberland Terrace, Wednesday Night,* [*February 27, 1839*]

With much to think of, you will forgive some forgetfulness.— Cte de Vigny informs me that there *is still* a castle of Richelieu's in existence at Ruelle exactly the distance you have fixed from Paris — where still the "oubliettes" are to be seen.— Will you object if I substitute this (the verse will not suffer) for St. Denis? — I hope I am not too late in this communication which I shd have made to you for the Press.

138. BULWER TO MACREADY, *March* [*4*], *1839*

I cannot devise any change for the metaphorical line act III, & must leave it to your own abrupt inspiration. May I beg you to guard me the first night from a race who have previously declared themselves my most bitter persecutors.— They are always found in the shilling gallery the first night of my plays & carry on their malignant discords under the innocent but delusive appellation of "BABIES"!

Pray ordain that all such implike armfuls may be interdicted to the youthful matrons — who sit amongst the gods.

May I beg you to give the enclosed to Warde, whose address I don't know — it requires the alteration of one word in Act V, his dialogue with Julie: instead of "dark — dreaming eyes," let him say, "inspiring eyes."

139. BULWER TO MACREADY, *March* [*4*], *1839*

If de Beringhen must have another jest, I can think of no better than

> "St. Denis travelled without his head.
> I'm luckier than St. Denis."
>
> *Exit.*

In Act II, when Mauprat rushes out for the first time thro' the gardens saying, "I loathe the face of Man," Baradas exclaims, "I have him!" This must be allowed for in the very next scene between you & Joseph — you use the same xpression, "I have them now — I have them." Let Baradas say instead:

> "Go where thou wilt — the hell hounds of Revenge
> Pant in thy track, & dog thee down."

Baradas ought to be longer & more florid expressing his exultation than Richelieu, whose simplicity of phrase comes from the ease of superior power & uniform success — with whom in fact what raises all the Devils in Baradas' heart is mere Child's play.

Ward will, I trust, understand that the characteristics of Baradas are prodigious energy, restlessness — with youth — love — jealousy — hate put in contest with the vast & dark movement of the old Statesman's intellect — & concealed vindictiveness.— Much will depend on his forcing out this contrast. Let me have a list of the *Dramatis personae* — the names of the actors for all — to print with the play tonight or tomorrow morning as early as convenient. Let me know exactly what part in the Soliloquy, Act III, you speak, that they may be referred to in the printed play.

How do you spell Ruelle? The old way was Ruel — I find it was the place where Richelieu entertained the poet.

Of the other final preparations there is little to note. Marshall's scenery was ready by February 25, and the costumes, by Head, were available for the final rehearsals. Bulwer's name was kept out of the advertisements for weeks, but his authorship was an open secret, and when it was blazoned in the bills of March 5, the play that night being the ever-popular *Lady of Lyons,* the audience that gathered was jubilant with expectancy. The irritations of rehearsal, rather than the accomplishments, are scattered through Macready's diary entries. On February 27 he was cross at Bulwer for inviting Lady Blessington and d'Orsay to be present. On the twenty-eighth Helen Faucit asked for a day's leave of absence — impossible to grant. On March 2, one of the actors, Mr. ———, absented himself because of gout, brought on by excessive drinking. On the sixth of March the Lord Chamberlain sent word that the Queen would attend opening night — an honor Macready found onerous. She wanted a book of the play — the responsibility for this Macready passed on to Forster.

140. FORSTER TO BULWER, *Thursday morning,* [*March 7, 1839*][46]

A note of mine followed you all over London last night, but unsuccessfully.

It was written in consequence of a "haste, post haste" dispatch which arrived here between 5 and 6 yesterday evening from our friend Macready.

The Queen is going to see *Richelieu,* and had sent the Lord Chamberlain's Deputy to Macready to ask him for a copy of the play. Her message was to the effect, that *in any state* she was to have it — if practicable, in any way that night. A second messenger arrived to tell me that proofs would do. Meanwhile, I had dispatched my Mercury to Hertford Street, and after an unsuccessful search for you, he brought back my note. I then (a little before 8) started off myself to Saunders and Otley, where I gave instructions from you of a very peremptory kind, which they told me should be faithfully attended to. I hope they have been. My boy is going to call as he takes this missive to you — to ascertain — so that by asking him, you will know . . . D'Orsay, by the way, in writing to me yesterday, asked if I could oblige him with the sight of a copy from you. May this be? and will you send it, or shall I?

Lastly!! *I have the box here for to-night — the lower stage box —* I herewith enclose it. At 5 you will be here?

---

[46] The text of this letter is taken from Richard Renton, *John Forster and His Friendships* (London, 1912), pp. 101-102.

141. BULWER TO FORSTER, [*March 7, 1839*]

I trust you will have the copies — I have enjoined it strictly on Saunders & Otley for the Queen also — I will be with you — Deo volente — at 5.

Yours nervousishly

On the afternoon of March 7, Bulwer disturbed Macready's rest to deliver him the Queen's book, and immediately thereafter word arrived that she would not come.

It is curious to notice that Macready paid the first royalty installment, as for fifteen nights, on the very day of opening.

142. MACREADY TO BULWER, *13 Cumberland Terrace, March 7, 1839*

I must beg to write to you "en marchand".— Remembering, though not repeating, my obligation to you, I will endeavour to satisfy you, that I enter upon this bargain, as I should do, if it were our *first* transaction of business.

Imprimis, I certainly think you are entitled to, and ought to demand, some certainty for your name, and I should willingly give it, if I were a stranger to all but it: — ergo, I enclose you this cheque for £300; which, with your consent, I will count against the first fifteen nights in the event of success — for the next fifteen I propose an additional £200 — and for the next ten another £100.

If you think these terms fair to yourself, (of course the property of the play's representation reverting to yourself from the period of my secession from the Theatre) I shall be most happy to act upon them: — if you have any exception to take on the score of underpayment, I shall readily receive it: but *only* on *that score*.

The original company of *Richelieu,* as announced in advance of the opening night by the Covent Garden playbills, was as follows:

Louis XIII, *King of France*............................MR. ELTON
Gaston, Duke of Orleans............................MR. DIDDEAR
Cardinal Richelieu...................................MR. MACREADY
Count de Baradas....................................MR. WARDE
The Chevalier de Mauprat..........................MR. ANDERSON
Count de Clermont...................................MR. ROBERTS
The Sieur de Beringhen..............................MR. VINING
Father Joseph..MR. PHELPS
Huguet...MR. G. BENNETT
François..MR. HOWE
Page to Baradas...................................MISS E. PHILLIPS
Secretaries of State........MR. TILBURY, MR. YARNOLD, MR. W. H. PAYNE
Courtiers...........................MESSRS. C. J. SMITH, BENDER,
PAULO, GOUGH, THORNE, BRADY,
BURDET, SMITH, KIRKE, and HOLLINGSWORTH
Governor of the Bastile...........................MR. WALDRON
Gaoler..MR. AYLIFFE
Turnkey..MR. ANDREWS
Captain of the King's Archer Guard................MR. T. MATHEWS
Pages to the King........MESDAMES REED, CORDER, LEE, and VALANDUKE

Pages to the Cardinal..........MESDAMES MATHEWS, MEW, and MORGAN
Gentlemen, Priests, Sub-Secretaries, Arquebussiers, Halberdiers
Julie de Mortemar...............................MISS HELEN FAUCIT
Marion de Lorme..................................MISS CHARLES

Musical arrangements, under the direction of Mr. T. Cooke, included an Overture from Gluck and entre-acts from Martini, Grétry, and Gluck. *Richelieu* was followed by an "Operatic Entertainment of *The Invincibles*."

Something of the excitement of the opening night is still held for us in a few lines of description by Westland Marston: "In March, 1839, I fought my way with another young enthusiast to the pit door of old Covent Garden on the first night of Bulwer's 'Richelieu.' What a human sea it was, and how lit up by expectation, that surged and roared for two hours against that grim, all-ignoring barrier. . . . The interest connected with a new play was increased by the fact that Bulwer was the author, for with us young critics his epigrams, his rhetorical flashes, . . . had made him a favorite."[47] "The house overflowed in every part," wrote William Jerdan; "and even what are called the slips, were fully tenanted by a respectable audience."[48] At the end of the performance Macready was greeted by the entire audience which "rose *en masse* and cheered him for some moments." Bulwer himself rose and bowed repeatedly from his box.

Macready was not pleased with his own work. "Acted Cardinal Richelieu very nervously; lost my self-possession, and was obliged to use too much effort; it did not satisfy me at all, there were no artist-like touches through the play. How can a person get up such a play and do justice at the same time to such a character? It is not possible. Was called for and very enthusiastically received. . . . The success of the play seemed to be unequivocal. What will the papers say?" The papers spoke very kindly, especially of Macready, praising his acting and his mise-en-scène with little reserve. Toward Bulwer, of course, his traditional enemies exerted what hostility they could muster, denouncing his claptrap plot-making, his falsification of history, his melodrama, his bad verse. But the burden of the report was victory for play and players both.[49]

It is painful to note something like a rift in the friendship about the time of the production. Bulwer himself, I fancy, was never much aware of the tension, but with Macready the crosspatch entries in his diaries reveal that it came nearly to the snapping point. On March 8 Macready met his company to cut and alter the play for the second night. "When we had separated, Bulwer came and altered all we had arranged — annoying and disconcerting me very much. I struggled for the omission of several passages, but he was triumphant, and therefore no longer *so docile* as I had hithertofore found him." Two notes of niggling, though practical, suggestion came from Bulwer this same day.

143. BULWER TO MACREADY, *March [8], 1839*

Several persons have told me they did not understand how Huguet got the packet, & in the bustle of the scene (the guards being between the audience & Mauprat in going out) the words "to Huguet" & the previous question to Huguet were not heard distinctly. I hope this will find you at Rehearsal and that you will make this as distinct & emphatic as possible. So much depends on it.

---

[47] Westland Marston, *Our Recent Actors*, 2 vols. (London, 1888), I, 37-38.
[48] *Literary Gazette* (March 9, 1839), XLV, 157.
[49] For a report of some distinctive details of Macready's production, see Bulwer's letter to Calcraft, footnote 19 (p. 145) in Chapter 4.

144. BULWER TO MACREADY, *March [8], 1839*

There was a little point I forgot to mention today. In Act II^d, Scene with
Beringhen & Mauprat (the part that's left after Julie's exit), DeBeringhen in
going out also says — "Don't stir — no form," &c.; the effect of this was destroyed by Mauprat's remaining *seated!* whereas he ought to be bustling about
in angry agitation. When DeBeringhen says, "Don't stir," he ought to seem as
if making at DeBer.— So with "no form"— it is Mauprat's action here that
should give point to the other parts. Please just to cast your Universal Eye —
Richelieu-like — over this, as tho' a trifle, it is an important one & worth the
postage of this — from our House.

[P.S.] I hear at the House nothing but admiration of your acting.

On March 10 and 11 Bulwer was still making alterations, and finally on the
thirteenth sent two letters more, one of which unstoppered all Macready's pent-up annoyance. "Two long notes from Bulwer — with more last words — and a lengthy
criticism on some points of my performance, in which he wishes me to substitute
coarse and vulgar attempt at low farcical point in one instance, and melodramatic
rant in another for the more delicate shadings of character that I endeavour to give.
I have long had surmises about Bulwer's taste from several things in the comedy of
La Vallière — in the original of *The Lady of Lyons* and in the original copy of this
play. I am *sure* that his taste is not to be depended on. . . . Difficulty in answering
Bulwer's notes without giving offense — at last dismissed his worrying prosings with
brief generalities."

145. BULWER TO MACREADY, *House of Commons, Tuesday Night,*
       [March 12, 1839][50]

I saw a good deal of the play last night, which went off better than on
Monday — The restitution of the 2nd Scene Act III^d was quite right — I wish
time could allow a little of the Comic part Act II. It is *missed — & has been*
complained of to me in *many* quarters. But perhaps, at all events it is too late
to re-alter even if time could be spared. —

I write to say I was much more struck with your acting in the 3 last acts
tonight than even heretofore.— And so, I think, was the house generally —
Forgive me if I say that the *more* you come out from subdued dryness into
power (which you did tonight) the more brilliant your success will be, & the
more you will realize the Cardinal — *colere* et *orgueilleux* — dont chaque
pensée avait tout le *chaleur* d'un *passion* — De Vigney [*sic*] is wrong in thinking him so *sec* There was plenty of animal spirits in him — In the grave part
of your performance I see only one sentence in which I could wish another
conception — it is the End of the Act — "Thoust lost — the stake — away
with him" Now you speak "away with him —" with contemptuous Sport —
like a man brushing away a trifle! — After the Electric rise — the audience
are prepared for something more vehement — & the thought of your concep-

---

[50] The text of this letter, printed by Toynbee, *The Diaries*, I, 501-502, has been
corrected from the original in the Library of Princeton University.

tion is almost too subtle for the gigantic audience you have — But, I think It would be more like the Cardinal who was accustomed to come & feast over the Executions of his foes — to throw more of the deadly force of malignant & Exalting vindictiveness into the words — Something more to correspond with his laugh in baffling the murderers at the castle — I would have him release the Devil of his rage upon his victim — . I would make him follow with Eyes that threaten savage victory the retreating form of Baradas — In fact here I would have the effect that of POWER — the closing power of the speech. In the Comic part — (You must pardon my presumption in this) I much still fancy that greater breadth of humour — more of what the french call "Malice" would illustrate the character more vividly, & be infinitely more effective — I fancy the Cardinal with a CHUCKLE — "le rire presque gai — mai toujours insultant" — which is ascribed to him — Thus — in "Colonel & Nobleman my bashful Huguet that can never be" — If it could be said with a more jovial laugh — & then with a pointed slyness (no *pause* — but fronting the audience) & almost a wink of the Eye to Joseph — "*We'll* promise it! — &c — This I think w^d be more effective — So after he has told Huguet he may be Noble — Why not let him exchange a broad humorous glance with Joseph whom he passes at the moment — as much as to say — There now is not that cleverly done." At "Joseph Bishop Joseph" — I think it will be much more effective if you don't repeat *Joseph* twice — but make the point more sudden & hearty "Ah Joseph — Bishop Joseph — & absolutely touch his ribs with the forefinger — there should be, I am sure, no pause & no reiteration between Joseph — & Bishop Joseph. —

Now I have said Eno' to make you think me the most presuming dog — you have ever seen thrusting his paws into other people's paniers — But — Mon Cher — you have been as frank with me — so tit for tat.

May I further beg you to IMPLORE Miss Faucit — to say I love AND I am Woman — & with much majestic swelling as she can — Tonight she says "I love *but* I am Woman" which is nonsense — & she whined it into the bargain. —

Think as leniently as you can of my suggestions

146. BULWER TO MACREADY, *March 13, 1839*

Pardon one more 2 penny post, to suggest 3 small cuts, — which seem to me important. After Miss Faucit, act III, exclaims:

> "More royalty in Woman's honest heart
> Than dwells within the crowned majesty
> And sceptered anger of a hundred Kings,"

she now adds, "Yielded — Heavens yielded." Omit that "yielded Heavens yielded." It comes weak after her effect & interferes with the suddenness of your "To my breast, close, close!"

Act 5. When Julie rushes to Mauprat & says "Do with me as you will," omit Mauprat's "Once more! why this is mercy, Count!" & let him come at once to "Think, my Julie, life at the best is short — but love immortal."

In the same act, when Baradas sees the paper in the King's hand — and rushes forward, crying, "Hold," & is put back by Joseph. Omit "Death the Despatch"— the audience know what it is — & the familiar & hackneyed word becomes almost ludicrous & hurt the effect tonight. His action suffices to paint his despair & let the King run on. I had forgot to say that several persons round me thought that Richelieu should say more to François — something in reward — & declared themselves disappointed that he did not. If you don't object, you might say, *"Your fortune's made,* brave boy; never say fail again."

I am very glad you kept in the lines, Act III, "Strange while I laughed"— they were effective & wanted for the after line, "My omens lied not."

As *Richelieu* grew in success, perhaps Macready's temper cooled. On March 14 he at last felt that he had "acted the part very fairly," and de Vigny came round after the play and "expressed himself delighted." (De Vigny wrote him from Paris later on that if the portrait of Richelieu were ever lost in France, one would have to cross the sea to see Macready's performance, so perfect was the resemblance.)[51] On this day he received a note from Bulwer "proposing another subject for a play this season, if I wished it." His only comment was, "What an indefatigable man."

147. BULWER TO MACREADY, *Hertford, [circa March 23, 1839]*

I enclose my note for 5£ Haynes Bayley [*sic*][52] of whose distress and illness I am truly sorry to learn. I should rejoice to aid in extending the subscription but I really hardly know whom to apply to — having once before vainly suggested relief for the same person. Lady Blessington might.

The season ran on in seeming prosperity to the middle of July, with *Richelieu* playing a total of 37 nights. Under the surface, however, Macready's managerial problems were most painful. Early in April he discovered that owing to a technicality in his contract he was not in effect manager of Covent Garden at all, but only a sort of salaried master of ceremonies. His trusted treasurer, Robertson, was revealed to be only a tool of the proprietors, and had been turning over the theatre's income to them in secret. Even before this shocking revelation, Bulwer had been concerned about Macready's managerial future. On March 31, writing to excuse his absence from a banquet in Macready's honor given by the Shakespeare Club the day before, he proposed a subscription company under Macready's supervision.

148. BULWER TO MACREADY, *March 31, [1839]*

I came to town purposely to attend the dinner yesterday — but was so poorly with the disabling complaint in my head, that I was quite unequal to going.

I postponed sending an excuse thinking to the last moment, I might get better, which I sometimes do suddenly.

But all in vain & I am at last reluctantly obliged to remain at home.

---

[51] Lady (Juliet) Pollock, *Macready as I Knew Him* (London, 1885), pp. 128-30.
[52] Thomas Haynes Bayly (1797-1839), a minor lyric poet, novelist and playwright; often in financial difficulties and at this time in his last illness.

I am very sorry to hear you, too, have been unwell, but trust you are now recovered, & that your dinner went off well.

I shall be happy whenever it suits you, to consult as to the best mode of meeting the present dramatic difficulties.

I have long been of opinion that a subscription Company might be got up to start a Theatre & elect you Manager — & if you think this, should be glad to coöperate in starting it — or if there is anything else in which I can practically assist in restoring your career, pray command me.

In accepting his second royalty payment, on April 24, Bulwer alluded to the treachery of the proprietors, and invited Macready to a dinner to meet Lord Lansdowne, who might support his project politically.

149. BULWER TO MACREADY, *April 24, 1839*

I delayed answering your note in the hope of calling. But have been prevented. I really feel many scruples & much reluctance touching the Enclosure, since I hear that these Goths — the proprietors — have seized on the Surplus, & that after all your success, you may be defrauded of its just gains. Under these circumstances I feel as if I were swelling the tribe of Barabbas, in appropriating to myself any farther portion of profits inadequate to your own just demands & claims. Nor should I prevail on myself to do so had I had not an equal scruple with regard to your pride & a feeling that, were it not so, you might be deterred from applying for any assistance I could give you at some future period — the experience of one season at Cov^t Garden will place that Theatre at your own terms — the next — and I feel convinced that you will live to complete what you have so nobly begun. I met Young[53] last night, who spoke with enthusiasm of your exertions, &c.

Will you dine with me on Sunday May 12th, to meet Lords Lansdowne & Durham,[54] ½ past 7.

150. MACREADY TO BULWER, *13 Cumberland Terrace, April 25, [1839]*[55]

Your too generous scruples would not have been entertained by me one moment, except to draw forth, what I now return you, my warmest thanks for your most kind and friendly consideration of me. — Let it at once silence every question in your mind to know. . . .

of Honor, and to be utterly regardless of truth or even decency: — but the

---

[53] Charles Mayne Young (1777-1856), leading actor of the "Kemble school" when Macready began his London career in 1817, excelling in both tragedy and comedy; made his London debut in 1807 and retired in 1832; Macready maintained toward him an unusually cordial attitude.

[54] For Durham, Matthews printed "Wrexham." Macready's diary entry of May 12 supplies the guest list.

[55] This letter was written on two sides of a single sheet. The bottom of the sheet has been cut off, apparently by an autograph-seeker. Thus a few lines are missing from the bottom of the first side.

amount, to which they can wrong me in a pecuniary point of view, is not worth thinking of in the sweeping sacrifice, that I have made. They have signally failed in an attempt to misrepresent me to the public and the performers: and all I now care about in their proceedings is a certain quantity of inconvenience and annoyance. . . .

Bulwer's promised dinner to meet Lord Lansdowne occurred on May 12, but Macready's congenital distaste for aristocracy rather put him off from hope of any aid from Lansdowne. On June 12 Macready and his lieutenant Serle drew up a petition to the Lord Chamberlain, "asking for a personal license," and through the early summer Bulwer continued to encourage Macready and to pull strings in his behalf. But nothing came of it. In mid-October the Lord Chamberlain tardily replied, "regretting that he was obliged to refuse."

chapter four

1839

The Sea-Captain; or,
The Birthright

Bulwer's next play, *The Sea-Captain; or, The Birthright* — or, as it was first called, *Norman* — was written speedily. On March 28, 1839, just three weeks after the opening of *Richelieu,* Forster reported to Macready that Bulwer "had nearly finished" it, and that it was "most powerful." Macready could not concern himself with it at the moment, busy as he was with *Richelieu,* the plans for his forthcoming elaborate production of *Henry V,* and his lethal quarrel with the Covent Garden proprietors. On April 6 he signed an agreement with Benjamin Webster to play the next season (mid-August to mid-January) at the Haymarket. Bulwer, though still hopeful of establishing Macready in a theatre of his own, took the cue to offer *Norman* to Webster.

151. BULWER TO WEBSTER, *36 Hertford St., May 28, 1839*[1]

In reply to your letter I beg now to say that you may, if you like, act the Lady of Lyons — from the 1st of January next for the sum of fifty guineas — paid in advance.—

With regard to Richelieu — I should advise you to consider well whether you would find it answer to get up so xpensive a play —. I fear that the xperiment wd disappoint you — The splendour of detail at Covent Garden — would throw into shade less elaborate preparations — & yet for a play that has lost the gloss of novelty you would find equal expense a hazardous adventure. This, however, it is for you to weigh & determine — If you shd ultimately decide on the hazard — you may act it for the same period as the Lady of Lyons for the same sum — viz: 50 guineas till Jany *[illegible].*

I have written a play of very strong domestic interest that I think will suit

---

[1] Original in the Houghton Library at Harvard University.

the Haymarket well — It was written with that view — But before I say more
of it — or propose the terms, I shall wait for Mr Macready's opinion — And
till Henry 5th is out — he is not at leisure to read it criticaly [*sic*] — It is an
English subject — cast about the time of Elizabeth & would not require much
cost in getting up —. The principal parts by Macready, Mrs Warner &
O. Smith —[2]

152. WEBSTER TO BULWER, *Theatre Royal Haymarket, May 28, 1839*[3]

I beg to enclose you the Fifty guineas for the permission to perform "The
Lady of Lyons" at the above theatre until the 1st January next — With regard
to "Richelieu" I will follow your kind advice & consider whether it will be
worth my while to play it.

I am delighted at the prospect of producing a play of yours originally at the
Haymarket and assure you nothing shall be wanted as regards getting up.

The *Henry V* production, which was to be the staple of the Covent Garden program
during its last five weeks, opened on Monday, June 10. In an undated note a few days
before this event, Bulwer explained to Forster that affairs of Parliament would prevent his attendance on the opening night, and — "Perhaps you had better send me
Norman with any short suggestions for alteration." Immediately after the opening,
probably the next day, we find Bulwer acknowledging Macready's third royalty payment for *Richelieu*, asking for a quick opinion on *Norman* (which evidently he was
then first showing to Macready), and describing his progress into yet another play.

153. BULWER TO MACREADY, [*circa June 11*], 1839

I beg to acknowledge your draft for £100. I can only express my reluctance
to be the cause of any diminution from your inadequate profits, but I feel that
you would not listen to a bashfulness of this kind — & that any scruples from
me might only be an obstacle to any future assistance I can have it in my
power to afford you as a "Professional Author."

I have the fullest reliance on the intention & good wishes of L^{ds} Lansdowne
& Normanby[4] — I am just returned from dining with the former, where you &
your xcellencies & talents were the subject of general conversation & sympathy.
—Whenever your request is drawn out, will you suffer me to see it? — & whenever it goes before the P. Council, will you apprise me, that I may have an
interview with any influential persons.

I sh^d be very much obliged if you would read Norman even hastily, at your
early leisure, as I shall soon go abroad — & there may be much to alter —
supposing you like it as a whole. Time therefore w^d be a great object to me.

---

[2] O. Smith, a minor actor in the 1830's and 1840's.

[3] Original in the Knebworth Archives.

[4] Constantine Henry Phipps (1797-1863), Lord Mulgrave (1831) and Marquis of
Normanby (1838), a novelist and political writer, holder of various cabinet posts under
Whig administrations before 1841; later ambassador to France and minister to the court
of Tuscany.

I am in the middle of a sentimental Modern Comedy — a good subject — in case Norman does not do. But I find Comedy xceedingly difficult & get on very slowly — I dare say I shall write it over 3 or 4 times. — There is a great deal of dramatic pathos & passion in the part designed for you, & a very good low Comedy, old gentleman part, for Farren. I am most sorry to hear the fiends are still at you. I hope to see the [Henry] V^th next week when we will talk of these matters — I am enraptured at its brilliant success. I hear nothing can equal the splendour of the pageant xcept the greatness of the acting.

Macready gave *Norman* a first reading on a Sunday morning, June 16, while driving into town with his wife and sister. His response to it was brief and firm: *"I do not like it."* The next Thursday he went over it again: "Was much struck with the *effect* of the two last acts, though I do not altogether like the play, it is far too melodramatic. Wrote to Bulwer upon it." Presumably his letter was tantamount to rejection: the following response from Bulwer (if it really belongs to this sequence) sounds so.

154. BULWER TO MACREADY, *Fulham, Monday morning, [June 24?], 1839*

I am extremely obliged to you for your frank communication. I can say unaffectedly, my only wish was to bring you some aid, in a struggle with which I heartily sympathize, & my only regret is now not to have succeeded in that object.

Will you have the goodness to send the Ms sealed up to 36 (a) Hertford St.

Still Bulwer was not to be dissuaded. While Macready struggled toward the end of his season Bulwer and Forster labored over the play — though whether it was *Norman* or the "sentimental Modern Comedy" mentioned on June 11 we cannot tell.

155. BULWER TO FORSTER, *[July 11, 1839]*

I think now that Henry 5th is out of Macready's head & I hope — migrated towards his pocket — that he may kindly have time to look at the Play. For, I may as well have all the suggestions at once — yours & his — The alterations may take time and I shall soon go abroad. . . .

Pray therefore if Macready will spare the time, send him the Play.

156. BULWER TO MACREADY, *Hertford St., Tuesday [really Monday],*
July 15, 1839

I was extremely vexed not to be able to come to you yesterday Evening, having been unavoidably & long engaged to dinner. But I have taken a box for tomorrow[5] — an occasion which inspires me with the most melancholy interest & the deepest regret that my wish and effort to assist your struggle were so unavailing. I hope yet that some happy event may consistently with prudence & profit, retain you at the head of our suffering Drama.

---

[5] On July 16, Macready ended his management at Covent Garden. The play was *Henry V.*

157. BULWER TO MACREADY, *Hertford St., Tuesday, 1839*[6]

A foreign Lady of distinction, known to a most intimate friend of mine, has written the accompanying play. She makes it a particular request, that you w^d glance over it & accord her 2 minutes interview. It is probable (I have not seen the play myself) that it may *not* suit the English stage, but I should feel peculiarly obliged, in that case, by such an intimation as may most soothe disappointment, & if moreover you could spare the time to receive her visit it would be an additional favour; should the latter be possible — will you be kind eno' to fix the day & hour, & as I am leaving town will you send your reply to me, to the R^t Honble C. D'Eyncourt,[7] 5 Albemarle S^t who will be good eno' to communicate its purport to the Lady.

An enormous testimonial dinner for Macready, which Bulwer helped to arrange, was held at the Freemasons' Tavern on July 20. Sometime during the following week, it appears, Bulwer sent him *Norman* revised, for a "second reading," again hoping for a speedy decision. In a note to Forster on July 27 he mentioned that "Macready has the play."

158. BULWER TO MACREADY, *Hertford St., [circa July 24], 1839*

I send you Norman — the only parts of consequence between Mother & son omitted are in the 5th act on his second surrender of his birthright — which the present Plot — that will be far more popular & safe — does not permit.— I feel certain of your own effects as the most powerful & empassioned you have had yet in any play of mine — during the first four acts [*words missing*] think to strengthen your 5th act if possible — Tho' I think you will grant that your joining the hands of the parents over Violet's form as if over an altar will produce a much greater effect on the stage than you might suppose in the Closet. I hope certainly, that you will not entertain doubts as to the Play generally — for if this won't do, I can do no other & Mr Webster must look elsewhere — It is literally, *"Aut Caesar aut nihil."*

But I hope on second reading you will think better of it.

Any suggestions towards brightening up Gain's [Gaussen's?] part & others — of course I should be most happy to receive. I am going on to Herts on Saturday & hope something will be decided ere then.

Macready makes no mention in his diary of this second receipt of *Norman,* nor of his reaction to it, though he reports at length on certain social exchanges with Bulwer about this time. On July 29 he and Catherine spent a cheerful day, though cold and rainy, at a party at Bulwer's villa at Fulham. On August 7 and 8, Bulwer, along with Dickens and Forster, visited the Macreadys at Elstree for the christening of the infant Henry. On both these last days Macready "talked much with Bulwer about a new play."

---

[6] The specific date of this letter, the "foreign Lady," and the "accompanying play" are not identifiable.

[7] Charles Tennyson (1784-1861), a relative of Tennyson the poet, was a Whig M.P. from 1818 to 1852. He added the name D'Eyncourt (from his mother's line) in 1835.

After Macready began his Haymarket engagement, on August 19, his need for a play became pressing. Webster was depending on him to provide one to offset the forthcoming production of Knowles's *Love* at Covent Garden; and for his own sake he needed one to bolster his reputation against that of Ellen Tree and other starring actors whom Webster was featuring on Macready's off-nights. He read, and gave up as hopeless, new pieces by Leigh Hunt and Robert Browning, and turned back to Bulwer for help.

Bulwer had gone to Cheltenham for the waters, leaving Forster to serve as his agent. On August 30 and on September 4 Forster wrote him that Webster was ready to pay £600 in advance for any piece, success or failure, and that haste was necessary, for Knowles was in the field. Bulwer responded gloomily that he was getting nowhere with the writing.

159. BULWER TO FORSTER, *Cheltenham, September 1, 1839*

. . . To save you trouble, you had better send the sheet I have written above to Mr. Webster.— only get it back again. As to Norman — I see that all attempts to throw comedy into his part — mar his character completely — & I rather think, if I were to work out that play — the best plan w^d be to increase the tragic instead of relieve the comic part — to also alter the agency now trusted to Gaussen — & to paint the suspense of *terror* in the darkest colours possible — . . . . I am now, then, so wholly at a loss for a subject, that I look in despair to the paper before me — I have thought once or twice of taking the character of The Troubadour for a subject — the poetical not real character — The half soldier half poet — gay — joyous — fond of Wine & Women — with the grave & noble sentiment of chivalrous poetry — running beneath the character. — The times are picturesque — the courts of Toulouse or Navarre full of romantic incident & the costumes good.— But then the Troubadour should sing — which Macready MIGHT not fancy! — I have also once or twice thought of adapting Faust for the stage but that is a hit or miss sort of speculation — In short I am just where I have been all the year. . . .

160. WEBSTER TO FORSTER, *Theatre Royal Haymarket, September 3, 1839*[8]

I agree entirely with the terms and conditions proposed in Sir E. L. Bulwer's letter to you dated Cheltenham Sept 1st 1839 concerning the new Play for the Haymarket and beg you will return him my grateful acknowledgements for the friendly feeling with which he views the whole business. As Sir Edward means to break new ground it may be as well that he should know who he has at command in the female department — Mrs Warner, Miss Taylor, Mrs Glover, Miss Horton,[9] Mrs W. Clifford and Miss *Helen Faucit* are with me for the

---

[8] Original in the Knebworth Archives.

[9] Priscilla Horton (1818-95), an actress and singer of much charm; made her debut at the Surrey as a child actress; was a member of Macready's Covent Garden and Drury Lane companies; played the Fool in *Lear* when Macready restored that character in 1838; in 1844 married Thomas German Reed, who had been associated with Macready as musical director; retired in 1877.

whole season — The Gentlemen I need not mention — with regard to "Richelieu" we are at a standstill with the cast, therefore must pass that over for the present though I am decidedly of Sir Edward's opinion as to its effect —

I hardly know how sufficiently to express my thanks to you for the disinterested kindness with which you have acted towards me in this business. . . .

P.S. The letter shall be taken every care of —

Back in London on September 6, Bulwer called on Macready, "and talked a good deal about his projected play." To Forster, on the twenty-first, he reported he has been "very busy about the play." He delivered it four days later, once more completed, to Macready. No longer was it *Norman,* but by manipulation of the materials of *Norman,* a play about the Spanish Inquisition!

161. BULWER TO MACREADY, *Craven Lodge, Fulham, September 25, 1839*

I send you the play founded on Norman, but entirely changed, & I think so much of it that I regret it is not at your own theatre it is to be produced. You will find your part greatly strengthened — & also the comic relief you wanted — Elvira (that Woman), tho' still strong, is toned down. But there are 2 other characters, Gaspar & the Inquisitor — whom I fear we shall be put to for suitable actors. I can't do better than this — I am sure. I should be greatly obliged by your opinion as soon as possible. If you can suggest no alterations, *tant mieux.* — It will want my last verbal revision.

Perhaps too in the last Act — you may suggest means for an earlier entrance for Don Caesar. Pray write me a line as soon as you can. I stay in Town or at Fulham for your judgement.

Macready recorded that he did not like it so well as the original, and to Bulwer he proposed a compromise.

162. MACREADY TO BULWER, *Suffolk Place, Wednesday,* [*September 25, 1839*]

I have gone through the plots of the two pieces collaterally, and see no just cause or impediment why the best of both should not be joined together in a happy union. — But it would save time & make matters much much clearer, if I could see you and with the two *M. S. S.* in hand, go over the whole. I see a *most effective* play out of them.

Can I see you tonight at the Theatre? or if requisite, I would come up again tomorrow — but if you are a free agent, perhaps all could be done tonight.

One result of their conference that night appears to have been an understanding that Macready should read *The Inquisition,* as it was then called, to a select group of friends to get their fresh judgments. This he did at Elstree on Tuesday, October 1.

163. BULWER TO MACREADY, *September 30, 1839*

As I am prevented going to Knebworth, write about the play to Hertford St. I shall trim up your first act with a little more poetry. I think that Act 2 should end with something comic — even if you object to the veil — it gives more buoyancy & life to Caesar & contrasts the later acts.

[P.S.] I hope to see you in Shylock. As I happen to be a peculiar Miser in paper, I have been very unhappy at the loss of the ½ quire I sent you by mistake & humbly request to see it once more.

"I'm very poor — a very poor hidalgo!"[10]

164. MACREADY TO BULWER, *1 Suffolk Place, Haymarket, October 2, 1839*

I would not answer your note till I could speak with the confidence, that experiment gives me. I prepared myself for *"the reading"* of "The Inquisition" yesterday by a whole morning's consideration, — and at night I read it to what I regard as a very good audience — four persons, and all of different dispositions and habits of thought. — The conclusion was unanimous — the effect of the third act was triumphant — I should say overwhelming: — the 4th act very considerably less. The 5th act was felt heavy and deficient in interest. I deferred to your judgement, and *did my best* to bring out the effect of the reconciliation in the blessing — but *here is the fact* — the éclaircissement is made — the guilty one disposed of — the parties, that *must be* happy, are placed together before the audience — when that is done the sooner the curtain falls on them, the better for every play. — The general feeling was that the climax of the play's effect was the 3rd Act. — I then read the last act of *Norman* — and the ENTHUSIASM was completely rekindled — in FULL BLAZE AGAIN. I think I see how, with little difficulty & not a great deal of trouble, the objectionable part of Norman may be replaced by the more effective introduction of Gaspar — I will go directly at it and send you the notes of what seems to me practicable. — I do not doubt that in placing the great interview, as originally, in 4th act, & retaining the great scene of Norman's 5th act, we shall [have] another triumphant Play — Vivat! —

I must not lose time — and therefore will break off. — As to the stray or waif, in the form of a half quire, which came to me, I will account for it in my next parcel.

Bulwer sent in the next revision (or three acts of it) about October 7. It was now presumably restored in scene to Elizabethan England, and rechristened *The Birthright*. Two days later Macready summoned Webster and his lieutenant Willmott to his chambers and "read to them the three acts of Bulwer's play. Bulwer came in while we were thus engaged and was gratified in hearing that the acts made so favourable an impression. He left with me the other two acts, which I read to them. They approved, and I observed that my hands were now washed of the business; if Webster chose to accept it he had only to signify as much to Sir Edward Bulwer and arrange all the rest with him. They left me." Later Bulwer returned and they went over the play to make notes of alterations. "I told him the half-quire of paper, which he had before him, was that which he had sent me by mistake. When he had done his notes he went

----

[10] This is the "Spanish" version of Sir Maurice Beevor's refrain in *The Sea Captain:* "I'm very poor — a very poor old knight."

on talking, evidently to divert my attention, as he folded up the half-quire and put it in his pocket! How very whimsical!" Webster moved swiftly to close the deal, paying £600 in full for the London rights for three years.

165. WEBSTER TO BULWER, *Theatre Royal Haymarket, October 9, 1839*[11]

Upon hearing the play I am so satisfied that if you will be kind enough to write me particulars of the terms upon which I am to have it, I will forward you a check for the sum agreed on.

I also wish to purchase the right of representation of "The Lady of Lyons" & "Richelieu" for my next season and if you have no objection will settle that matter at the same time as the other.

166. WEBSTER TO BULWER, *Theatre Royal Haymarket, October 9, 1839*

I herewith send you a check for six hundred pounds for your new play and another check of one hundred pounds for the exclusive town rights of the representation of your plays of "The Lady of Lyons" & "Richelieu" the ensuing season of the above theatre commencing in 1840.

My reason for asking a letter of particulars as to terms was because I have no document to file showing the nature of our agreement, the arrangement with Mr. Forster being verbal and I thought it might save having recourse to a more formal proceeding.

167. BULWER-WEBSTER CONTRACT FOR PERFORMANCE RIGHTS, *London, October 11, 1839*[12]

Mr Webster Lessee of the Theatre Royal Haymarket, has purchased of Sir E L Bulwer B^t for the sum of 600 the right to represent the new play called "The Birthright for the sum of 600£ on the following conditions. Mr Webster is to possess for 3 years dating from the first night of performance the xclusive right of the Dramatic representation in London — (the Literary Copyright & the profits of performances in the provinces remaining with Sir E L Bulwer) At the end of the said term of 3 years Mr Webster may perform or cause to be performed the said play — for the whole or any part of a further term of 3 Years — provided solely that he be then the Lessee of the Theatre Royal Haymarket — But should he have ceased to be Lessee during any part of the said further term of 3 years — this additional privilege of representation is forfeited & reverts to Sir E L Bulwer. At the Expiration of the first term of 3 years — Sir E L Bulwer has the right & privilege to cause the said play to be acted in any theatre, in London & Westminster if he so please. — And at the expiration of the entire term of six years dating from the Night of the first representation of the Play in 1839 — the entire theatrical copyright returns to Sir E L Bulwer & remains vested solely in him, his Heirs, or Executors — And the Parties,

---

[11] Original of this letter and the next in the Knebworth Archives.

[12] A copy of this "letter of particulars," in Bulwer's hand, is in the Houghton Library of Harvard University.

herein contracting — agree to execute at the request of either — a legal instrument — to the above purpose & effect.

E. L. Bulwer

October 11ᵗʰ
1839

Mr Webster has also purchased of Sir E L Bulwer the exclusive right to represent the two plays of "Richelieu" & the "Lady of Lyons" — for the season of 1840 — in his theatre in the Haymarket without detriment to Sir E L Bulwer's privilege or profits as to the performance of the said plays in the provinces — And the receipt of the 2 several sums of 600£ & 100£—is hereby acknowledged

by me

E L Bulwer

We find Macready on October 15 referring to the play by its final title, *The Sea-Captain*. He conferred with Webster that day about the dresses and scenery. The casting was nearly completed by then, and partial rehearsals had already begun.

168. WEBSTER TO BULWER, *Theatre Royal Haymarket, October 17, 1839*[13]

Your play will be produced on the 30ᵗʰ or 31ˢᵗ inst.

Mr Macready & Mr Forster deem your presence immediately amongst us of the greatest consequence — Indeed we cannot proceed well without you. Mr M. expected you tomorrow. The play reads admirably and seems to come out stronger with every rehearsal. I shall be sadly deceived if it is not a great hit.

With regard to the receipt it is perfectly unnecessary and not at all desired on my part from the first.

Miss Faucit has not heard the play read or seen the part yet in consequence of her severe illness and Mr M. does not intend her to know what it is until he has spoken to her on the subject. Last night we were obliged to substitute "The Stranger" for "The Lady of Lyons" on this account. I mean of Miss F's illness, so that that point is as yet undecided.

It is ironic that Bulwer should have been paid so much and so quickly for what is his worst play. *The Sea-Captain* is a cheap and easy melodrama derived from a minor novel of the elder Dumas about John Paul Jones, called *Le Capitaine Paul* — or from Dumas' own stage version of it, produced in October, 1838, called *Paul Jones*.[14] Supposedly set in Elizabethan England, its hero the type of "the wild and gallant contemporaries of Sir Walter Raleigh," the play is actually no more than a pretentious version of the nautical melodrama so beloved in the minor theatres of Victorian days, and spoofed in *The Pirates of Penzance*. Norman, the sea captain, is an orphan brought up by pirates but later become respectable. He returns to England to claim the hand of a young lady named Violet (also an orphan) whom he had sometime lately rescued from the Moors; and to claim, too, as it develops, his "birthright," for he is the eldest son of a noble family and heir to vast estates. One scene in the fourth act, when the noble son confronts the guilty mother, Lady Arundel, who, Jocasta-like, had so many years ago put him out to die, is moving and excellent —

---

[13] Original in the Knebworth Archives.
[14] Alexandre Dumas, *Le Capitaine Paul*, 2 vols. (Paris, 1838); and *Paul Jones,* drame en cinq actes (Paris, 1838).

or rather could be so except for the absurdities of the context in which it stands. Though it was to run for forty performances it was generally regarded a failure. The critics slated it, and Thackeray wrote a special *Yellowplush Paper*[15] to shatter it with ridicule. Bulwer suppressed it from his collected works. Thirty years later he caused to be staged a revision of it called *The Rightful Heir*,[16] considerably improved but still a failure.

Faced with the cold reality of performing the play, Macready began to take its problems seriously. On October 15, for instance, he "devoted the whole day, without intermission" to it, and had Forster come to dinner to hear it read aloud in the evening. It "seemed to interest, but the employment of the pirates, and the violence in the fifth act was unanimously disapproved. Forster took the book home to consider it." Forster sent Bulwer a sheaf of criticism (lost), but Bulwer could not understand some of his points and resisted others.

169. BULWER TO FORSTER, *Knebworth, Stevenage, Herts.,* [*October 18, 1839*]

Many thanks for your most kind & critical letter.— The first alteration you propose in Act 5 — is the same as Macready proposed before — viz. a scene in the castle between Lady A. & Sir M — & to dispose of Sir M. thereby. I tried this — but in vain — It is impossible for her to execute him & he must die — otherwise a witness to blow up the whole is left. If he could not prove the birthright — without the papers, he c^d reveal the scoundrel & that would be the true poison to Lady A — He must die — & I strongly contend for the necessity of his dying by his own agent. The cunning knave sh^d fall into his own Pit — If in your alteration you can compass this — I will willingly try to do it in the way you like best.—

You leave me so in the dark as to your other alterations that I know not what to say.— But I would not for a great deal lose the short dialogue between Violet & Lady A. when the former rushes from the chapel — & describes the two Normans. This seems to me to contain real terror in reading at least — & to be quite of the Classical, nay Greek Drama — not melodrama.— Moreover Lady A could not be in the Chapel while Norman & Ashdale are engaged with Gaussen there — And if you omit that intrigue with Gaussen's plan & Death you omit the whole external plot.— In fact to say truth, your letter is not quite intelligible to me — & I do not think you have thoroughly seen all the difficulties of the alterations you w^d propose. I don't think the letter clumsy — but there I may be wrong.

I will come up to town if you require it certainly; that is if you do not think a written outline will do — But I cannot manage it before Saturday. Now can you make any engagement for me to see you & Macready on that day — any time after 4 — . If Macready acts I can see him after the play — hearing in the meanwhile your proposed alterations.— I will then go to the Cottage Sunday to make them — as I must return on Monday.— You can perhaps make an early appointment not later than 12 with Macready to glance over the said

---

[15] "Epistles to the Literati" XIII, *Fraser's Magazine* (January, 1840), XXI, 71-80.
[16] *The Rightful Heir, A Drama in five acts.* (London, 1868.)

corrections — But think well, in the interim, over what I have said above — Sir M. must die — & ought to do so thro' Gaussen —

Many thanks for your troubles & pains with Colburn — Will you give me a line by return of Post — fixing the hour for my calling on you — & also if you can fix the necessary interview with Macready. How did the play go off in the green room.

[P.S.] If you will give me a chop at 6 — or ½ past 6 I shall be charmed to dine with you — I wish you w^d make Macready send Saunders the play for printing.

P.S. I shall get your letter Saturday before I start.

Macready's study of the play on October 20 was interrupted by Bulwer, who "talked over the required alterations with me. What he had done in them was very bad." The next day Bulwer brought more alterations: "in good spirits, thinking he had done them well, in which opinion I agreed." They went over the play together and Macready transmitted the alterations to the actors.

170. BULWER TO FORSTER, [*October 22, 1839*]

I was sorry to miss you when you called on Sunday but hope you were not much inconvenienced by the visit — I had gone to Macready's in despair. But you will be happy to hear that at last all is settled to Macready's satisfaction. Will you go with me to the Play. In that case will you ask Webster for a Box for us 2 — or rather for me. We can be alone.

More alterations came in on October 23, but after this not much could be done, for the play was committed to the printers.

171. BULWER TO MACREADY, *Knebworth, Wednesday, October 23, 1839*

I have made some alterations in the diction of the earlier acts, & to save time I enclose you the proofs — which when you have read, please to send to Saunders & Otley. The principal are as follows:

Act I.

1.

It seems a little too abrupt. Norman's entering to Violet so immediately after Prudence goes out. I have given her therefore a few pretty lines which strengthen her part, p. 18.

2.

Your comedy with Prudence is improved by being put into blank verse — it makes the change less abrupt — the words are very little altered, pages 20-21.

3.

I have altered your final exit at close of Act. But don't know whether it will do.

Scattered throughout this act, there are a few verbal alterations which you can attend to or not, as you glance over them.

Act II.

By a very trifling alteration in words, Sir Maurice's Dialogues with Lady A. & Percy are put in blank verse. It will not give them any more trouble. But some actors do not act blank verse so well & easily as they do prose. If this be the case with Strickland, better perhaps not disturb him. I leave this to you.

One or 2 verbal alterations in this act which you will see in the margin. Act III, page 59.

I have given a very happy point to Sir Maurice which I should like inserted, if you see no objection. Give me a line to say if you like these corrections, and if your closing lines, Act I, will do.

[P.S.] Pray let Saunders have the proofs as soon as possible.

172. MACREADY TO BULWER, *1 York Gate, Regent's Park, October 24, 1839*

I have only time to say, that your alterations have been received and transferred to the parts of the actors (a work of some time) and have been forwarded to Messrs Sanders & Otley — I think they are all emendations.— What a character Sir Maurice has grown to! — I will do my best with the closing lines of Act 1st

In greatest haste. . . .

The three days immediately preceding the opening were fraught with worry. On Monday, October 28, the rehearsal was in such bad shape that Bulwer wanted to withdraw the play, and only Forster's blustering optimism prevented him. On Tuesday Bulwer begged Macready to give him an opinion. "I really *could not*. I could not see the play's chances, having so little to *do* myself and not knowing — as no one ever can, *without action* or rather agency — the value of what I have to say. I would speak out at once if I knew which course to take for his interest — his interest is mine and that of the theatre." Again Macready had discovered during rehearsals that his role was not dominant, and the fate of the play lay rather with Mrs. Warner, whom he thought not adequate to her role. By Wednesday Bulwer was more confident but Macready less so. Thursday was the opening: "Went in great anxiety, and uncomfortably to the theatre. Rehearsed the new play. . . . Returned home very, very uncomfortably. My mind depressed, and my spirits suffering much from misgiving and apprehension. Read the play over. Went to the theatre. Acted Norman in Bulwer's play with some energy and occasional inspiration. Was received very warmly, and called for at the end, greeted with much enthusiasm. . . . There were wreaths thrown upon the stage. I am most thankful to God for what I feel a great escape."

The Haymarket playbill of Thursday, October 31, emphasizes (as Macready's own bills were not wont to do) the work of the scenic artists, crediting the scenery to Mr. Phillips, Mr. Morris, and Assistants; the dresses to Mr. Barnett and Miss Smith; the "appointments" to Mr. T. Ireland. The acting company was as follows:

Percy, Lord Ashdale		MR. J. WEBSTER
Sir Maurice Beevor		MR. STRICKLAND
Norman, *Captain of a ship of war*		MR. MACREADY
Falkner, *his Lieutenant*		MR. HOWE
Giles Gaussen		MR. O. SMITH
Luke	*Pirates*	MR. GALLOT
Michael		MR. GREEN
Onslow, *a Priest*		MR. PHELPS
Landlord		MR. T. F. MATHEWS
Walters		MR. WORRELL

Sailors, Servants, &c.
Lady Arundel.....................................MRS. WARNER
Violet..MISS HELEN FAUCIT
Mistress Prudence.............................MRS. W. CLIFFORD

The Sea-Captain was followed by a farce of John Bernard's called *His Last Legs,* starring Tyrone Power, and a second farce by T. E. Wilks called *My Wife's Dentist.*

In spite of the wreaths thrown (how the critics enjoyed this carefully prepared "vegetable homage"), and the cries for Author! at which Bulwer "responded by putting his head out of the box and bowing genteely to the audience" as the reporters tell us,[17] Bulwer knew the play was below his proper mark. The tag of a note to Forster on November 1 indicates the worst.

173. BULWER TO FORSTER, [*November 1, 1839*]

. . . All my private acquaintance shake their heads dolefully at the play — & all find out reasons for not liking it at all —. Some say it is quite beneath me — others that it is so unKimmon heavy — I shall judge for myself tonight. . . .

The day of November 1 was largely occupied with cuts and alterations, performed mainly by Macready and acceded to by Bulwer. It is difficult to see how Bulwer could have given much thought to the matter, for on that day his insane wife had released one of her attacks on him in a letter to the *Times,* and, his mind in a turmoil, he could hardly wait for the rehearsal to end so that he could consult Macready on whether to answer it. Macready was unhappy in his performance that night and more doubtful of the play: "I fear it has not *substance* to sustain it." Helen Faucit was begging to be released from her part, and Macready had to persuade her to continue. November 2 brought more curtailments, and a note on a technical problem.

174. BULWER TO MACREADY, *November* [2], *1839*

Pray have the papers dipp'd in spirits of wine. The delay in burning marred the effects yesterday. I think I shall propose a few more cuts Act 5. But shall try and see that last scene again to-night.

175. BULWER TO MACREADY, *Herne Bay, Sunday night, November 4, 1839*

It seems to me that if it were possible you would tear the proofs instead of burning them, you would greatly heighten the effect. Each time I have seen this, I have felt the effect destroyed by the comparative tameness of the physical agency — the delay in taking fire & the awkward struggle & *no* struggle of Ashdale. In my earliest sketch of the play I had introduced a watchfire, which would have had a very different effect, but which I omitted as too evident for the purpose. The action of tearing the paper is far more forcible — it is in fact making the actor the agent; whereas when fire does it, he is only passive — the Fire is the agent. I don't know whether you will like to venture this experiment one night. I must leave it in your hands.

I should like much to hear if Knowles[18] swamps us — a single word on that subject sent to Craven Cottage will be forwarded to me.

---

[17] *Morning Post,* November 1, 1839; *The Spectator,* November 9, 1839.
[18] Knowles's *Love* was the current novelty of the Vestris management at Covent Garden. It opened on November 4, 1829, and ran for nearly 50 nights.

176. MACREADY TO BULWER, *1 York Gate, November 11, 1839*

Thinking you may wish to know something of the progress of the Sea Captain, I send you a few lines reporting our condition. Our houses have improved evidently since Saturday week — the three last still increasing on the former, and as far as I could judge — which was only of the scenes where I was concerned — I should say that the effect upon the audience, and the interest of the play had grown with the audiences.—I hear no high accounts of Love as an acting play, except at secondhand from Covent Garden sources.— It certainly has excited no enthusiasm.— I hear the Sunday press is not frantic about its composition but lauds the acting, which I learn from report is very bad.— I have read the best scenes, in which there is eloquence, some passion, and poetry, but I do not think unless the press aid it very materially, that it is calculated to depress us — The audiences *weep well*,— and there is not a tear in the five acts of Love — though I think there should be. My family have been twice since the first night to The Sea Captain and they think it improves on repetition — but they, and others, wish the burning to replace the tearing of the papers.— Webster is in very good spirits, and observed to me on Friday night — "Well, sir, you see they have not hurt us at Covent Garden" — which all looks well.— Sincerely hoping that your rustication may give you both health and spirits, I am always

and sincerely Yours,

177. BULWER TO MACREADY, *Dublin, November 30, 1839*

I shall be glad to hear how the Sea Captain gets on tho' judging from the House I last saw & from the newspaper accounts of the crowds at Cov. Garden, I am fearful that I shall not have a very favourable answer.— It wants 6 weeks to the 15th January. I can hardly imagine that Webster can find it answer to run it on every night till then.— Do you think during the recess it would be advisable or safe to alter the play — substitute in the 3^d act some other agency for Onslow's death — get rid of Gaussen — and study some new strength for Act 5? To do so would unfortunately in some measure justify the Hostile critics.

Richelieu has been brought out here with great success. Calcraft[19] plays it

---

[19] John William Calcraft (real name Cole), actor and theatre manager in Dublin, to whom Macready was often engaged. A letter from Bulwer to Calcraft on this occasion (November 29, 1839) is preserved in the British Museum (Add. MSS. 33964). Bulwer speaks of his gratification in Calcraft's performance of Richelieu, and his surprise at "the splendour & correctness of your decoration & arrangements." Then he enters some caveats, interesting because they reflect vivid moments of Macready's original production. In Act III, Richelieu's revelation of Julie, which always produced a great effect at Covent Garden, was not effective at Dublin because Mauprat failed to show sufficient consternation: "He ought in fact to be startled to the other end of the stage.— His sword should fall from his grasp — & above all full room should be left for the Cardinal to stand in plain view between the 2 parties as he pronounces the words 'Lo, my Witness.' " In Act IV, when Richelieu appears, "Your courtiers ought again to express much more dismay & astonishment — I don't know if your scene admits of your coming down the middle of the stage — But you were a little too long in coming last night & were in the midst of the courtiers before they perceived what all the audience did — Their alarm

better than you w^d suppose and the *mise en scène* is xcellent. Calcraft copies your Cardinal of course — and to those who have not seen the original it is effective.

Toward the end of November Bulwer released the fourth edition of the play, with a special preface in which he lashed his enemies, the critics, in a dozen pages of splenetic and self-sick maundering. Forster was furious, all Bulwer's friends were ashamed, and Thackeray's Yellowplush was inspired to compare Bulwer to the boy at school who when he "rord and wep because the knotty boys called him nicknames, was nicknamed wuss and wuss."

178. MACREADY TO BULWER, *1 York Gate, Regent's Park, December 3, 1839*

My report of our progress is not so satisfactory as I could wish: — our houses have trained off considerably.— Webster showed me the last week's receipts last night — we averaged £95 per night (which is not a winning game) through the last week.— This week he has put up the Lady of Lyons for the Monday (last night — when the house was very good) and the Merchant of Venice for Thursday: — The Sea-Captain on the other four nights.— I asked him last night what he anticipated, and he informed me, that he expected The Sea-Captain to carry us on to the end of the season, but not without intervening plays.— It is very difficult to get at the truth about Covent Garden receipts, but I believe them, from the individual reports made to me, to be greatly exaggerated. As to the question of the policy of altering The Sea-Captain, I know no instance of the success of such an experiment.— Mr. Webster (of whose judgement and penetration I have no opinion whatever) would be well pleased to have it altered for the next season — but until you can alter Mrs Warner, Mr. Strickland, and Mr. J. Webster,[20] I can see little real benefit to be derived from altering their parts: — The Mother must be the person, whose passions are moved the most strongly, and there must be agony employed *on* Norman, and not through him.— Therefore whatever may be added to his words, his actions must still be subservient to stronger persons — I therefore cannot see that the result would recompense the labour.— I read your preface to the 4th Edition — and my impression was that you had left a record of the ignorance and spite of your assailants — I thought too, that it was argumentatively put, and without temper: — but I hear angry observations on it: — and

---

& astonishment at his resuscitation make the effect of that situation —. . . . At your swoon at the close of the act — I think you will find it more effective to omit Heaven love my country." In Act V, Richelieu should lean on Joseph. There should be more astonishment from the group, Beringhen should be softened: "He is not meant as a fop or buffoon — but a lighthearted unprincipled careless Frenchman." Mauprat should wear black, since Julie refers to his "sable" — or else her word should be changed to "crimson." He speaks further on "an effect Macready makes which you either softened or abridged. . . . while the lovers are kneeling to the King you turn to receive the felicitations of the Courtiers.— But at Cov^t Garden they formed themselves into a Lane & Richelieu passes haughtily down it with the consciousness & enjoyment of recovered power, as they bow obsequiously to right & left."

[20] John Webster, a minor actor, not to be confused with Webster, the manager.

a pretty general opinion among your friends, that it was not worth your while, though they sympathise entirely with you: — I shall look at it again, — though I scarcely expect to change my opinion, for I read it with great attention.

Webster asked me, if I would speak to you about another play, which he is anxious about for the next season. — Have you any thought of one? — I think that if you could light upon a promising subject, it would be by far the better policy than an alteration of The Sea-Captain.

179. MACREADY TO BULWER, *1 York Gate, December 10, [1839]*

There is no doubt that the Press has done much — very much — and our own weakness — in Lady Arundel, and Sir Maurice — has not enabled us to offer sufficient resistance: — There is another most important consideration — which is this, our afterpiece was reduced to mere average, when they (C. Gn) with a striking novelty, The Beggars' Opera, took up their play at its point of declension. — They could not have stood it out — press — and the other friends to boot, if they had been as we — single-handed. — It is la fortune de la guerre — but it is too true, much, very much personal animosity has been with all the energy of spite at work against us. — You have been too successful to be easily forgiven, and you have a tone of thought and impulses in conduct, which the great majority of the world & the literary world, I grieve to say, in particular cannot understand, and will be revenged upon. — With regard to the matter you give me to think upon, I can only reason as I would for myself, and I cannot recommend a course to another, that I should not adopt myself. —

I certainly would prefer a wider field than that in which I am doomed to labour, but great effects have been produced there, and in Theatres as small; and Archylus would not have disdained a shed at Salamis when driven out of Athens — Remember too, he returned. — Look at the Lady of Lyons at the Haymarket after the season at Covent Garden! — I am urging Webster to reinforce & remodel his company, and we must endeavour to fix the drama at the Haymarket, if only that it may be invited and supplicated to return to its proper temple. — If you could find a good historical subject — a character with action — you would trample on this opposition of spite & envy — *Who* are your critics? — I read of you in Dublin with much pleasure.

At the end of December Helen Faucit retired from the part of Violet because of illness.[21] Up to that time there had been thirty-five performances. Three more were added before the season ended on January 15, and two more in March when the new season began, thus making forty performances in all.

In October, 1839, the Lord Chamberlain, Uxbridge, had refused Macready's request for a personal license, which Bulwer had supported. In December the report was abroad that Charles Kemble, who held the post of dramatic censor, was dying, and

[21] Miss Faucit was genuinely ill, but her condition was probably exacerbated by the current greenroom and scandal-sheet gossip about her personal relations with Macready. Throughout the year 1840 Macready alludes to the matter in his diary (with Miss Faucit's name suppressed).

Bulwer sought to obtain the post for Macready. Kemble did not die, as a matter of fact, until 1854, but he did resign the post, which was given to his son John Mitchell Kemble.[22] Nonetheless Bulwer's efforts were warmly appreciated by Macready and served to cement their friendship.

180. BULWER TO MACREADY, *Hertford St., December 20, 1839*

W[d] the office of censor (Dramatic) be one either agreeable to yourself or which as being still on the Boards you could with propriety accept? I say this, for in consequence of C. Kemble's health, applications are already being made for the post. J. Kemble jun. has applied. Now I have learned to-day that there w[d] be every disposition to give you the preference sh[d] you wish to apply — and that being the case hasten to tell you so.

Yours in hurry

[P.S.] The subscription to the testimonial is very good.[23] At all events keep this secret.

181. MACREADY TO BULWER, *1 York Gate, Regent's Park, December 20, 1839*

I am too much obliged to you to endeavour to say how much. — Most cordially and earnestly do I thank you for your kind and friendly thought for me.

The office would be most acceptable to me, ensuring what I have not, independence. If I could hold it — retaining my place in the Theatre for four years longer — I could fulfil all my wishes with regard to my children's education without more restraint on my own expenses than I should be happy to impose on myself.— If the condition of obtaining it were my retirement from the stage at the end of the ensuing year — 1840 — (up to which period my engagements are signed) I should be compelled to think a good deal — but *that* I should prefer with a certain income to the hazard, in which illness and accident place my present position.

I cannot understand why my calling should affect my judgment or integrity in such an office, the duties of which I could very easily discharge with it.— It was given to Kemble, a proprietor of the Theatre, whose interest might often (proof existing) tend to sway an opinion.— An actor of any note would scarcely incur censure for the liberty to utter a sentiment, or act a play, which would either offend public morals, or reflect upon a government.— Cibber[24] was poet-laureate and actor at the same time — C. Kemble was proprietor and censor.— Would it be more unreasonable or derogatory for me to hold the two occupations for four years longer? If it should be thought so, I would resign my uncertain profession for the security it would afford me, supposing I could obtain it.—

---

[22] John Mitchell Kemble (1807-57), philologist and historian; succeeded his father to the post of Examiner of Stage-Plays on February 25, 1840.

[23] This testimonial (to Macready?) is nowhere explained.

[24] Colley Cibber (1671-1757), actor, playwright, and manager; poet laureate from 1730.

You will I know advise me as to the best methods to be pursued in my application (I presume I should be at the worst permitted to play out my next year's engagement) and [I] will instantly act upon your suggestions.—

If I could thank you to satisfy myself, I would make the effort: — I cannot, and therefore shall merely say that I am

Gratefully and sincerely Yours

182. BULWER TO MACREADY, *December [21], 1839*

I am very glad I wrote to you. But do you not overrate the salary of the censor? Is it more than 2 or 3 hundred a year? I cannot see the least necessity for your implying any pledge as to leaving the stage, and since you see no objection to being censor while you act, I am sure no one else ought. Nor could any voice be raised against your appointment.— Since you ask my suggestion, I earnestly entreat you to write *at once* to the Lord Chamberlain (Uxbridge).[25] Don't lose a moment — ask for the vacancy — should it occur. Kemble's health the natural excuse — others are applying. I should state the reasons you suggest in y^r note to me why actor and censor are not incompatible, but you might also add that rather than lose the appointment, you w^d resign altogether.

This they w^d never dream of wishing — quite the reverse. But still the offer might be made.

Send me at the same time & as soon as possible a duplicate of your Memorial that I may make proper use of it. I have secured Lord Uxbridge's brother-in-Law, the vice-Chamberlain George Byng, your great admirer a friend — & I am now going to write to him to say you will accept the appointment.

In dreadful haste — but in the sincerest delight to serve your views in every way.

[P.S.] My haste is to catch Byng before he leaves town.

183. MACREADY TO BULWER, *1 York Gate, December 23, 1839*

I have despatched this afternoon a letter to Lord Normanby enclosing a copy of that to the Chamberlain, and merely alluding to the sacrifice of the two last years, pecuniary and other, having been very heavy.

Whatever be the results my gratitude to you is the same.

---

[25] Sir Henry William Paget, first Marquis of Anglesey and second Earl of Uxbridge (1768-1854), commanded cavalry with distinction in Spain and at Waterloo; served as lord lieutenant of Ireland in 1828; favored Catholic emancipation; field marshal, 1846.

chapter five

1840

Money

It had become Bulwer's habit to begin a new play for Macready as soon as the last was produced, but after *The Sea-Captain* he did not respond as usual. For some while in late 1839, into December, he was absent in Ireland, licking his wounds over the critical disaster of *The Sea-Captain* and deeply in trouble because of his wife's attacks on him, which were coming to a vicious climax; his health was bad, too. At the moment Macready did not need a new vehicle. After his season at the Haymarket he was engaged for a while at Drury Lane, where he brought out a new tragedy by James Haynes, called *Mary Stuart.*[1] He returned to the Haymarket in mid-March. The box-receipts dwindled. "Our houses are falling," he recorded on April 3, "and the want of something to draw attention to our theatre makes me apprehensive as I always am, nervous and uneasy." On May 23 he introduced Talfourd's *Glencoe.*[2] When this failed to draw, he turned again to Bulwer for help.

184. BULWER TO MACREADY, *May 24, 1840*

I was summoned to Kneb Saturday, return this evening & find by mistake all my letters have been forwarded to me; if therefore you have written to me, I have not had your note. Did you, then, make any appointment with me tomorrow evening, if so, when and where?

185. MACREADY TO BULWER, *5 Clarence Terrace, Regent's Park, June 15, 1840*

For the last three weeks I have been looking from day to day for the power of calling on you, but I have been so confined by influenza and violent rheu-

---

[1] James Haynes had long been a dramatist, although one of minor stature. *Mary Stuart* opened on January 22 and achieved a moderate success of twenty nights.

[2] *Glencoe* played twenty-two nights, and was accounted the least successful of Talfourd's three plays.

matism, that my house has been my prison with occasional night-rules to undergo the torture of acting at the Haymarket.

Forster has told me what I have been most concerned to hear, that you have been ill — the object of my enquiry needed the best health, for it was to ask, if we had any hope of anything from your pen this summer. We are panting for it like the hart for the springs — Have you seen Glencoe?

Will you, if you can, give me your interest for a very worthy person, whom I found in every way deserving, — and for whom I retain the kindest feelings — I mean Bryden.[3]

There is it appears, a new Board to be appointed in connection with the Board of Trade, whose duties will be to guard the public interests in the construction of new Railways, and in the working of those that already exist. Mr. French[4] has already asked from Mr. Labouchere[5] (who has the appointment) the place of Secretary for Bryden, and his application has been backed, as I understand: If you could give him the weight of your interest, it might be the means of securing the appointment to him, and I should feel myself a large sharer in the obligation.

I received the Committee's message through him respecting the choice between the two designs but I preferred leaving it to the artist's hand.

Toward the end of June came the welcome news that Bulwer was at work again, and moreover that his play was to be a contemporary comedy, perhaps even "touching on those unhealthy parts of our social system," as Macready had urged him to do nearly two years before.

186. BULWER TO MACREADY, *June 27, 1840*

I have thought of a comedy & will show you the first two acts when in a state for it before I proceed further. But what I wish to know is — whether it would be possible to get Farren at the Haymarket, also Anderson. I hardly know how I could in any way get on in my present plan without them.

I have an old gentleman whom Strickland c[d] not make effective, but who w[d] suit Farren . . . & I have a young Lord with a dash of wit & sentiment about him whom Webster or Lacy[6] w[d] ruin.

W[d] Buckstone & Elton be at the Haymarket?

In short, tho' my Comedy may not do at all — which I can soon see — it won't do at all events without quiet force — the characters, yours excepted,

---

[3] A Mr. Bryden is mentioned in Macready's *Diaries,* but Toynbee, the editor, seems to confuse him with Brydone, Macready's sometime business manager.

[4] Mr. French was an M.P.

[5] Henry Labouchere (1798-1869), Whig M.P. from 1826; President of the Board of Trade, 1840-41 and 1847-51; Colonial Secretary under Palmerston, 1855-58; created Baron Taunton, 1859.

[6] Walter Lacy (real name, Williams; 1809-98), an actor; made his London debut in 1838; worked in Charles Kean's company in the 1850's and later with Irving; married Harriette Taylor; was a respectable light comedian and an amusing personality.

are very equal. My proposed title is "Appearances", the idea a genteel Comedy of the present day — the Moral, a satire on the way appearances of all kinds impose on the public, you a rogue playing the respectable man — & the Intellect of the play. I repeat that as yet it is very uncertain whether it will do. But if I can achieve the first acts, I think I see my way thro' the rest.—

Lastly. When w^d it most be wanted & best come out?

Pray get me minute & faithful answers touching Farren, Anderson etc. [P. S.] I still continue in a very bad way. Hope to get over to Carlsbad.

187. MACREADY TO BULWER, *5 Clarence Terrace, Regent's Park, June 28, 1840*

Your intelligence filled up the measure of yesterday's good news, and it was a day of unmixed good.— Among the best was the well-doing of Mrs Macready after giving me another boy[7] — and the promise of your comedy came at night to crown the good fortune of the day.— If bidding can bring Farren and Anderson, Webster will not stint his offers, and I should think with the prospect of acting in a play of yours, they would come within his means.— He, Webster, does not hesitate in saying *he would engage them.*— Buckstone will sail for America next week.— If you mean that there is a part for Elton, which he would like to do, I think he might be had — but he is very restive about parts.— The title I think excellent.— The sooner it is in hand, the better: — we are ready for it, — that is, to prepare for it *now* — and from hence onward, there is no bad time.—

I am very sorry to learn so unsatisfactory an account of yourself. I am afraid you do not give yourself a fair chance here by all that reaches me of you. You are too much worth to be either fretted or thrown away. I wish you would think so.

Bulwer was too ailing, however, to proceed at his usual rate. It is curious to read in Macready's diary entry of July 13 that Forster "told me of the plot of Bulwer's projected comedy, which pleased me": for that very day Forster received the following gloomy lines in a letter from Bulwer, who had gone to Cheltenham to take the waters.

188. BULWER TO FORSTER, *Cheltenham, [July 12, 1840]*

. . . Tho' somewhat better generally my peculiar complaints remain stationary — & with them the Play.— The Cheltenham Waters are no Hippocrene to the Comic Muse. And a serious perusal of Sheridan's Plays — incites less of inspiration than despair — . . . .

Benjamin Webster was pressing Bulwer for a new play also, as well as bargaining for the rights to the previous successful pieces. Bulwer asked Macready to advise and represent him in these negotiations.

---

[7] Walter Francis Sheil Macready, born June 27, 1840; died February 3, 1853.

189. WEBSTER TO BULWER, *Theatre Royal Haymarket, July 18, 1840*[8]

Will you be kind enough to inform me on what terms I am to have the exclusive right of acting in London next year "The Lady of Lyons" — "Richelieu" did not do anything for me, but I should still wish to retain the acting right of it, if within my means — M[r] Macready informs me you are writing a Comedy I trust and hope that we shall speedily see it produced at the Haymarket. Such a work from your pen would, I am sure, be a rare treat —

190. MACREADY TO BULWER, *5 Clarence Terrace, Regent's Park, July 25, 1840*

I wish you had added to your account of Harry Martin a word about your own health, which I should have been happy in believing improved by your wandering.— I have done my best for you in the way of bargain with Webster.— The fact is that the Lady of Lyons is a positive attraction and the best play he has.— I mentioned to him that the Covent Garden people were wishing to have it — he urged that Richelieu had not done much service — to which I rejoined, that it was not acted in a way to attract — some words were thrown in about the Sea Captain also, but the end was, that he will be glad to purchase the exclusive rights of acting the two plays of Lady of Lyons & Richelieu for the two next seasons — viz: — 1841-2, and 1842-3, — either paying you down at once (— i.e. now) £200 — for the whole two seasons: — or paying you £120 *now* for the first season, 1841-2 — and £100 at the beginning of the second season 1842-3.— I hope you will be satisfied with what I have done — which of course is subject to your acceptance.

The real truth is, that Webster will never be able to do Richelieu in a way that can do it justice, and therefore it will not be so valuable to him as it ought to be. —

I hope that you have not given up the Comedy, with which, as Forster described the story to me, I was very much struck. Leave Henry Martin in Chepstow till the Comedy is out.— A successful Comedy would quite make a sensation.— Pray, make one.

I return you Webster's letter — of course you will not let him know, but that I have asked — upon *your* valuation, not on *my own.*

191. MACREADY TO BULWER, *5 Clarence Terrace, Regent's Park, July 27, 1840*

You have set down the terms exactly as they are understood between Mr. Webster & myself, and I wish either tomorrow morning or evening, according to his time of visiting the Theatre, [to] arrange with him to pay the amount, £200, into your bankers — or to you — you will send him a letter acknowledging the same and investing him with the exclusive right of acting the two plays in London for the period stipulated.

---

[8] Original in the Knebworth Archives. A note from Bulwer dated August 3, 1840 (in the Houghton Library at Harvard University), confirms Webster's rights to *The Lady of Lyons* and *Richelieu,* for the sum of £200, until January 15, 1843.

I sincerely hope the change of air will restore you, and that the Respectable Man will be your avaunt-courier [*sic*] on your return. — I should not apprehend the deficiency you fear, — and fancy that where a situation can be obtained, comic passion, which is very effective, is not very difficult.

I hope I shall see you, if you are not very much hurried before your departure, and I further hope you will not give yourself more to do in the business of getting well, whilst you remain in England.

By the beginning of August Bulwer had returned to London, still in bad health, to prepare for his journey to the spas of the continent. Macready and Forster called on him on August 2 at Craven Cottage, Fulham: "Found Bulwer not well — looking weak and shaken; he was cheerful. . . . We talked about his comedy, of which he read some scenes, and I agreed to think them over." But evidently Macready thought poorly of them. The manuscript of *Appearances* gathers dust in the archives at Knebworth. It was never published or produced, and was never in the years of correspondence that lay ahead referred to again.

On August 7 Macready entertained Bulwer and Forster at dinner. In anticipation of their coming he read all day "for a subject to suggest to Bulwer." He read through Voltaire's *Nanine*[9] and Goldoni's *Pamela*,[10] and "deliberated long and made notes upon a subject for Bulwer to write upon." After dinner the three of them "discussed at great length the subject I had thought upon; indeed, we gave the whole evening to it." Unfortunately Macready gives us no clue here as to what his idea was, but there is no doubt that it gave Bulwer the substance of his next (and probably best) play, to be called *Money*. Some three or four days later, writing from Margate the day before sailing to Brussels, Bulwer reported to Forster the extent of his progress.

192. BULWER TO FORSTER, *Margate*, [*circa August 11, 1840*]

I expect to sail tomorrow. My address for some days will be Poste restante Bruxelles. . . .

I have begun the Comedy — Done Act I & Part of Act V. I find the subject gives scope for plenty of character — sufficient brightness & some interest. In fact I could make a very good light Comedy of it. — But I fear that Macready's part will (as I suspected) — work out without sufficient idiosyncracy [*sic*] & intellectual force — too much of the mere young Bellvilles & Belmours. — If I find such the inevitable case I shall abandon that part to Wallack — & try to furnish forth another character in the same play for Macready. A Mr Doleful, who at present is really good & individualized —. . . tho' belonging rather to the broad Comic —. He is a man always complaining of his luck — a widower — lamenting his sainted Maria — who was the plague of his life! every piece of good fortune he thinks is unlucky — Sees everything *en noir* — but withal is Kind-feeling — & says very sensible wholesome truths. — He is the man who is to sing & dance — as in the *Proverbs* — How would Macready like *that*! — Mr Stout the Political Economist comes out well — also a humbug worldly Sir John "The Girl's Father"

---

[9] Voltaire's *Nanine, ou, Le préjugé vaincu, comédie* was first performed in 1749.

[10] Goldoni's *La Pamela* was first performed in 1750. See *Tutte le Opere de Carlo Goldoni* (Milano, 1935), III, 327-409.

— I have a good idea for a Modern Dandy — a man who never thinks of anyone but himself — but have not yet wrought it up.— The heroine is insipid I fear as yet — But you will hear more from Brussells.

On August 12 Forster read this to Macready, who noted delightedly, "His expedition is wonderful!" On the seventeenth Bulwer reported to Forster that Brussels was dull and full and himself weak and suffering much and ready to move on to Aix-la-Chapelle for the waters. "The Play I am sorry to say — doesn't promise as I had xpected —. Macready's character fails in saliency & individuality." Forster reported this to Macready on August 26, and both were so alarmed for Bulwer's health as to expect an early grave for him. But on that very day, at Aix, Bulwer was writing in cheerier tone, and reporting genuine progress with the play and especially with the vexing problem of Macready's character of Alfred Evelyn. The reports now came thick and fast.

193. BULWER TO FORSTER, *Aix-la-Chapelle, Thursday,* [*August 26, 1840*]

. . . I have at last succeeded in fixing a character on the young man (Macready) and the comedy is at least cast at present in the proper mould. Whether it will go on well I can't say yet — But the first Act & a half are really, I hope, good. The character is that of a half misanthrope, soured by past poverty & despising the world that rallies round his new fortune —. The surface irony & a half careless wit: beneath a strong & passionate temperament.

194. BULWER TO FORSTER, *Aix-la-Chapelle, Saturday,* [*August 29, 1840*]

. . . Aix la Chapelle is detestable. But I continue to improve tho' gradually.— All literary labour is sternly interdicted — But I creep on 2 or 3 pages a day with the Play.— I fancy it is comedy & so far in a new genre that it certainly admits stronger & more real grave passions than the comedy of the last century. But is not that true to the time. All we act more in earnest than our grandfathers. I want *most especially Mrs Glover.* I have a Widow — always gay & goodhumoured — in love with Mr Doleful always cynical & wretched — Mrs. Clifford could not do it. For there must be some comeliness — or something to [*word missing*] instead — Is Mrs Orger available[11] — But nothing like Mrs Glover.— Macready's [*word missing*] Inamorata — is in an interesting position. But as yet has not eno' to say.— Macready's part is individualized — but difficult to act at present — alternations too quick from gaiety to Passion — I shall oil him all over before I've done. I am now in Act 3.— which I intend to end with Crockfords or some Club — I must have an exact picture of a real Club [*words missing*]. I have admitted many allusions to present manners &c throughout. . . . But whether the whole will do, I can't say till I come to Act 5. Where I see great difficulty is the want of a sudden catastrophe. As yet I content myself with thinking that it is the first of my attempts at Comedy which appears to me to have at all hit on the right vein.— . . . .

---

[11] Mary Ann Orger (1788-1849), a popular comic actress; after a career as a child actress, she made her adult debut as Lydia Languish in 1808.

195. BULWER TO FORSTER, [*September 1 or 2, 1840*]

. . . I am in Act 5 of the Comedy — and but for this new Annoyance which has made me ill again it would have been finished & I, I think, nearly convalescent

But! ——

To return to the Comedy — It is, I hope, quite comic eno — rather too much so — Acts 3 & 4 must I should fancy produce great laughter — During this time Macready or Evelyn is playing off the apparently ruined man.— There are unfortunately a great many characters & all PARTS.— But what I most fear is not having an Actress for a gay, laughing, witty, warmhearted Widow of about 28 who ought to be pretty in love with Doleful the melancholy man — & comic from the contrast.— It is a part for Vestris or Mrs Nesbitt — who can do it? — Who's Mrs Fitzwilliam. Miss Faucit will I hope have a very fine 5. Act. But not quite eno' in the others — she has no comedy. But very interesting position & a character of some power — & great earnestness.

I give you a programme of the Characters.

Sir John Vesey — a cunning — worldly — old Humbug
 a part for Farren — But I suppose him Strickland. He plays off against Macready. This is the second best part.

Lord Glossmore — a Tory — ci devant jeune homme
 a sort of Lord Allen

Sir Fred. Blount — Dandy & Egotist —

Mr Stout.   Political Economist & Philosopher

Captain Smooth   a character requiring great finesse.
 capital part — finest Card player in Europe — particularly ruinous, deadly bland, caressing & well bred! — He is accomplice with Evelyn in his trick — appears to have ruined him
  I suppose Phelps —[12]

Macfinch —   A Scotch silversmith — Broad Comedy & Broad Scotch
other tradesmen

Toke.   Butler to Evelyn. Broad High Life below Stairs Comedy

Evelyn. Has been a sizar & scholar — elevated to sudden & enormous wealth — He equaly [*sic*] despises Mankind in both. Generous in act — misanthropical in word — But not so much the dry cold comedy — as the comedy of a man of wit — still young & enjoying the effect of what he does — a mixture of Pride Passion & Whim — in love with Clara — having been refused by her when Poor — proposes to Georgina from pique —

Doleful — a capital part — Friend to Evelyn — always gloomy — a widower mourning for a Wife who had plagued him to death — goodhearted —

---

[12] Samuel Phelps (1804-78), actor and manager; made his London debut in 1837 and served in Macready's Covent Garden and Drury Lane companies; in 1844 undertook management of Sadler's Wells Theatre and for nearly twenty years made it the home of Shakespeare and classical repertory; not a great tragic actor, but an extraordinarily gifted comedian.

witty — in love with Lady Beevor — the Widow — suppose Webster the Manager takes this.

Women.

Clara — a poor dependant in love with Evelyn — H. Faucit

Georgina — Daughter to Sir John Vesey — who has entangled Evelyn.— a part that may be disagreeable if the actress is not fashionable young light in heart & pretty.— I suppose Miss Taylor might do it — But she is very essential to the dignity of Evelyn's part.

Lady Beevor — The Widow in question. . . .

196. FORSTER TO BULWER, *Thursday, September 10, 1840*

I wrote to you at Frankfort, but suppose you have not had the letter. It matters little. There were some crude notions about the comedy in it, which these ripe results of your own, that you describe, render of no earthly value. I am greatly taken with the programme of the characters, and incidents, too, as far as you have hinted them to me. The Crockford will be capital, and so Macready thought. I have not seen him since your last letter, but shall this Evening; and report his opinion in my next.— Mrs Glover of course you have — but there is an actress now playing at the Haymarket for whom that widow you describe is exquisitely suited. She will play it better than either Mrs. Nesbitt or Madame Vestris, or indeed anyone I could name, or, in my time, I recollect. Her name is Stirling[13]— and she continues with Webster. Could not Priscilla Horton, the most docile and delicate of the living actresses, be admirably taught for Georgina? Wrench, too, who has surprised everyone in his part in Mrs Inchbalds comedy,[14] will, I think, be strong in one of your men.— So don't fear about the company, but push on the comedy to its happy close. I wait for it with eager expectation — yet nothing like that Macready seems to have. . . .

197. BULWER TO MACREADY, *Aix-la-Chapelle, September 13, 1840*

I sent you 3 Acts of the Comedy by the Bag — from Brussells I send now 2 by the Post. A thousand pardons for taxing you so heavily. But I have no choice of any other conveyance — & am just leaving Aix. I know, however, that you will not grudge it if the thing is good. As I have little time to write now — I come at once to my critical remarks.

1st. The Scotch of Macfinch &c had better be looked over by one more learned than I am in that Athenian tongue.

2nd. The reading of the will — & the serving the execution & arrest. Dramatic Vraisemblance of this I am not an adequate judge.

---

[13] Fanny Stirling (born Mary Anne Kehl; 1815-95), comic actress; made her debut in 1832 as Fanny Clifton; married Edward Stirling, actor and dramatist; retired in 1870 to teach elocution; in 1894 married again, becoming Lady Gregory.

[14] Mrs. Inchbald's *To Marry, or Not to Marry* (1805), in which Macready played Sir Oswin Mortland, had been revived at the Haymarket on August 15.

3d. Is Doleful too much the name of a Farce — if so, change it.

4. I think in the first 3 acts you will find little to alter. But in Act 4 — the 2 scenes with Lady B. & Clara — & Toke & the Tradesmen don't help on the Plot much — they were wanted, however, especially the last to give time for change of dress & smooth the lapse of the theme from money to dinner; you will see if this part requires any amendment. Would it be possible to introduce another Scene of Passion here with Clara & Evelyn? I fear not.

5. Are the Acts too long! They are shorter than in the Jealous Wife.[15]

6. And principally with regard to Act 5 I don't feel too easy. The first idea suggested by you & worked on by me was of course to carry on Evelyn's trick to the last — & bring in the creditors &c when it is discovered that he is as rich as ever. I so made Act 5 at first. But I found these great objections:

1st. The trick was so palpable to the audience that having been carried thro' Acts 3 & 4, it became stale in Act 5 — & the final discovery was much less comic than you w^d suppose.

2ndly. From the conviction of the audience that Georgina supposing him poor w^d decline his hand, all the interest in the strong scene between Evelyn & Clara was weakened — whereas Sir John having discovered — & his having got a supposed letter from Georgina after that discovery — the audience might think him again deceived & entangled & therefore take a deeper interest in the position with Clara.

3dly. After Georgina (whom I then brought on the stage still supposing him ruined) declined him for Frederic, he of course rushes to Clara. But his burst is spoilt by the presence of the crowd of vulgar creditors, Glossmore, Kite, &c. waiting for their money — & somehow or other in short I found that in this conception the grave & the gay spoilt each other. My present idea of Sir John discovering the trick has given much more interest to the act. Yet I am not pleased with it still altogether. I think it wants coup & completeness. But you are the best judge. I am sure on the whole that we have ample stuff for a better comedy than I ever thought I should write, thanks to your suggestion to which I have but given a form. I have only got a rough copy of bits & scraps. Therefore Pray let me know very early at Frankfort that you have received the 5 parcels. They will probably arrive the same day or within a day of each other.

[P.S.] I propose "Money;" a Comedy for the title. I had thought of Money makes the Man or Men & Money. But I think Money the best & prettiest.

198. BULWER TO FORSTER, *Aix-la-Chapelle, September 14, [1840]*

. . . Now — to the Play — I have this morning finished it — & I think it is much better than I had ever hoped to make it. I shall send it to Macready — by today or tomorrow thro' the Brussells Bag — at least 4 Acts in 4 letters —

---

[15] *The Jealous Wife* (1761), by George Colman the Elder (1732-94) provided Macready one of his best comic roles, Mr. Oakley.

Act 5. I fear must go by Post! — not having it yet copied & not being able to get a bag when I leave this. It will be directed Theatre Royal Haymarket — so pray tell him to order to take them in — & to let me know of their safe arrival to Frankfort. I shall hope also to hear from you as to your opinion &c — My health has fallen back lately — . . . .

199. BULWER TO FORSTER, *Aix-la-Chapelle, Monday, [September 15, 1840]*

. . . I have sent off the Play to Macready Haymarket   Acts 1.2.3 — by the Brusselles Bag
Acts 4 & 5 by Post from Aix. . . .

200. BULWER TO MACREADY, *Nonnewërth, The Rhine, September 15, 1840*

"*This address till I reach Coblentz, Frankfort on Maine.*"

I write to tell you — from Nonnewërth — the Gem of the Rhine — the Isle on which Roland's mistress lived, a Nun — the isle on which when I was younger I wasted a world of enthusiasm in the Pilgrims of the Rhine[16] — before me the Drachenfels — beside me Rolandseck — and such a Devil of a cold room as I am in!!! No fireplace — no curtains, & my beast of a servant has lost my Nightcap! And yet it *is* Nonnewërth — I ought to feel romantic — I'm sure I'm freezing. And *Mon Dieu, Mon Dieu qu'oi faire* — for a Nightcap! Out of my window, the prospect is enchanting, except that there is a great deal of dirty linen hanging up to dry. Schiller wrote his finest ballad on the legend of this spot (I wonder whether he generally slept with a Nightcap). *Revenons à nos moutons.* Last Night as I was travelling — between Aix-la-Chapelle & Boulogne — much too cold to sleep (tho' then I had a Nightcap!) — & smoking a cigar of more than ordinary merit — the moon & stars bright in Heaven & myself considering how many Thalers de Prusse I had thrown away in the vain search for health — my mind by a natural diversion settled itself on the Comedy of Money (you've no notion how cold I am!), and I was more & more persuaded that Act 5 wanted shortening — tho' I find it difficult to suggest the precise alteration.

I take it for granted that two objects are necessary — 1st, to keep the audience in some suspense; 2ndly, to give as much interest as possible to the scene between Evelyn & Clara. Hence I imagine that Sir John ought to discover the trick (that discovery effecting these objects). But on the other hand, this a little lowers the intellectual dignity of Evelyn, whose excuse for this trick ought to be its success, & makes the catastrophe turn not on his successful skill in outhumbugging Sir John, but on the accident of Sir John's punishment in the deceit of the dower. What think you of that objection? — I think also that the Audience will want to see reintroduced & shamed that Chorus of Worldly

---

[16] Bulwer mentions the romance of Roland the Crusader and the nun of Nonnewërth, together with the building of Rolandseck, in Chapter X of *The Pilgrims of the Rhine* (London, 1834). The ballad referred to is Schiller's *The Knight of Toggenburg*.

Characters who have moved round the principals — thro the Play. This last I could effect with encreased comedy. Suppose Sir John knows that Evelyn is not ruined — but the rest imagine he is. Bring in Glossmore — tradesmen — several members of the Club, &c., whom he may be supposed to have borrowed of. And while they are insisting on their money, Sir John hugging himself in his superior cleverness & saying to Evelyn, "I'll stand by you, my dear fellow." But in this Comedy *Evelyn can have no share*. It must succeed his Interview with Clara and his conviction that Georgina had lent him the 10,000£. He therefore can have no spirits for any kind of joke — otherwise the time to introduce them is when Sir John has dismissed Lady Beevor for Georgina — then they come in — to them Sharp announcing not only the boro', but a vomit of things, showing Evelyn's opulence — the astonishment of the Dupes who are dismissed by Evelyn's merely saying to Sharp as he is running on, "Pay these gentlemen, will you?" — Sir John's rapture & then the coup of Georgina's departure. But in all this, as I before said, what can Evelyn do? His part is not strong as it ought to be — already in Act 5. In short, you must well consider this act. — I think it w^d be desirable, if possible, to reintroduce the crowd of characters. But if the 4 acts do, we may consider the Play as settled, for we shall be sure to shape out the 5th which has some very good things in its position. — After your last speech in Act 5 as sent to you, I propose to add something to take away from its didactic tone & bring back both the comic spirit & the picture subject of the Play. It will run thus

Doleful

But for the truth & the Love when found, to make us tolerably happy — we should not be without —

Lady Beevor

Good health.

Doleful

Good spirits

Clara

A good heart.

Evelyn (*shaking his head at Clara & half gaily, half sadly*)
And enough *Money!*

I write this taking it for granted you have ere now received the 5 acts & hoping to hear to that effect at Frankfort. I continue very poorly. The climate is dreadfully cold & I am now just going to retire to rest — without A Nightcap!

If the play does generally, send me a detail of all the corrections you would suggest, & if I don't return to England, I will send it you thus amended & with its best polish. With regard to the terms — I take it for granted that Webster will agree to the same as for the Sea Captain — 600£ down for 2 years — provided he continues the Haymarket. — But I must not count on the chickens, unless I hear from you that they will bear hatching. — Whoever does Blount must not haw-haw, but be perfectly simple & young & good looking & smooth. Doleful & Sir John require very good actors.

On September 18 Macready "received by post a letter and two acts, fourth and fifth, of a comedy by Bulwer; the others are sent by the Ambassador's bag — it is completed!" The next day — in cabs, at home, and at the theatre — he completed his first reading of it. After that night's performance Forster came to him from Covent Garden bearing the cheering news that Knowles's new piece, *The Bride of Messina*,[17] looked unlikely to prove a strong rival to future Haymarket programs. They turned their attention to the new hope that lay before them. "I began to read the comedy to Forster, and was led on to read it through, to our mutual amusement. Went to bed at half-past three o'clock." Macready's reports to Bulwer are lost, but their enthusiasm is reflected in some of Bulwer's responses.

201. BULWER TO MACREADY, *Frankfort, September 26, 1840*

Your letter of the 21st reached me this morning (not the other — the Lost Unpaid). I am truly enchanted that the comedy seems to you good, & likely to succeed, & your congratulations are so warm & friendly that they make me insensible to the cold of this Barbarous Climate. I continue ill & am indeed worse than ever as to my principal malady. I shall return to England in a few days — and if you will then return me my copy or another — with all your suggestions — I will see to them during the few days I shall stay in Town; & leaving the Play & its fate in your hands, set out either to Italy or Cadiz. All the Doctors here concurring in the advice of a warm climate for the Winter.

With regard to the Characters — would the interest of the Play be heightened by making Georgina more interesting & Blount more witty — more of the gay blood of the old Comedy. His & her parts both are at present disagreeable & will require great skill in indifferent actors to carry off.— So indeed will Sir John — for I recollect how Sir Maurice in the Sea Captain was spoilt because the audience will not sympathize in Humour when unconvinced unless the actor has great subtlety. Consider all this well. Consider also Act 5, thro' which I do not yet see my way to improvement. W^d it prolong the interest to make Blount & Georgina return with Lady Beevor — Georgina having declined to run off but refusing Evelyn before Sir John can interfere & generally expressing her regret at her deception? — So thro' their consistency Blount & Georgina must be elevated throughout from their present selfish insignificance.

Does not the ending of Act 2 leave rather a painful impression & displease one with Evelyn — all the sympathy being for the girl? Can what Evelyn says in that 5 Scene with Clara be embellished & heightened? Her part beats his there.

Will you agst I come to town have the Law points as to the vraisemblance of the will & the technicalities of serving the Execution & the Arrest looked

---

[17] *John of Procida; or, The Bridals of Messina,* by Knowles, opened at Covent Garden on September 19, 1840, and ran for seventeen nights.

up — one w^d not fail on these points. The Stage allows a certain looseness — but sufficient accuracy to satisfy a miscellaneous audience must be kept up. See also, I entreat, to the Scotch of our friend Macfinch.

I will have a little programme of the Scenes — of the Actors agst we meet.

As for you, my dear Macready, whenever you can find me a Man with more thoroughly the air, breeding & person of a gentleman, I will allow that you may be diffident as to acting the man of fashion — not till then.

Recollect — that Evelyn is always simple — I should suggest his first dress — a black frock buttoned up, black stock & no collar (which always looks rather seedy), trowsers without straps & shoes; in his second dress — exactly your usual costume. Sir John should wear a blue coat with velvet collar, buttoned up — the *King's button*. In the Evening — his order of the Guelph — breeches & silk stockings. Blount must be perfectly dressed — also Smooth. D'Orsay may be consulted here. Stout, with a little brown coat, blotting-paper trowsers, coloured cravat & thick stick. Glossmore is a ci devant jeune homme about 45, wears studs & plenty of shirt. Doleful ought to be handsome, to account for Lady B — liking him.

The Butler's pantry was meant, partly to give time to the others to dress, & partly to carry on the time from morning till dinner — otherwise it is superfluous.

I conclude the parts to be cast as follows:

Lady Beevor:	Mrs. Stirling, whom Forster recommends
Clara:	Miss Faucit
Georgina:	Miss Taylor *i.e.* Mrs. Lacy
Glossmore:	Who?
Smooth:	Phelps — who better? His part seems to me excellent. I sh^d like to act it
Blount:	Lacy
Stout:	Wrench
Sir John:	Strickland
Macfinch:	Who?
Doleful:	The Manager Webster

The old Member with the snuff-box pray don't omit — even to his last word. He is the Philosophy of the whole scene. The perfect indifference of the ordinary world to the emotions of its principal actors. No matter who is ruined, all he cares about is his snuff-box. You must enter the man who performs this. I hope the Play is not much too long. What I most fear are some long speeches of Sir John's at the beginning; but they seemed necessary for the full development of his character afterwards.

You see, my dear Fellow, that you must always suggest my plots & situations. Till you gave me the outline I was all abroad — I only return to your lips your own chalice. I have thought of another capital subject for a Comedy if this succeeds, viz.: *"The Public."* That is the various humbug carried on on behalf & under name of the Public — together with the absurd inconsistencies of that precious Fallacy called Public Opinion. The distinction between the grave eternal *People* & the noisy frivolous false likeness called the Public. I see great fun & a high moral out of this — if when the time comes we can think of a story. The Principal Character should be a Minister or a Patriot, & what a satire one might make on the Press!

By the way, I hope the Politics in the Comedy — being all general & not at all Party — viz. between that [*sic* by Matthews: that between?] Glossmore & Evelyn — will not lay us open to unfair charges or censors notice hisses [*sic* by Matthews: censorious hisses?]. Think of this.

[P.S.] I shall expect here y^r promised & dictated letter sent after you receive this. My address will be The Cottage, Fulham.

202. BULWER TO FORSTER, *Frankfort, [September 26, 1840]*

I am delighted to hear from Macready the good news, that you & he like the Play.— I fancied it good — but could not rely on my own judgement — yours & his are very cheering.—

I shall now be in town very shortly — for a few days — during which time I shall correct the Disowned & Devereux[18] for Press & give the 3 prefaces — after which I shall start for a Warmer climate. For the rash is worse than ever — & as it extends its inflammation to the interior it becomes dangerous. . . .

203. FORSTER TO BULWER, *Monday, September 28, [1840]*

I received your letter of the 14th last Saturday (the 19th I mean) and but for that villainous Colburn should have answered it at once. As it is, I lose not a moment. I knew of course that Macready had written both on that Saturday & the next Monday of the Comedy — or I should have said my say to you of that alone. — Well — you know what we think of it! It is a great success! I expected very much, but not *so* much. The characters characters, the incidents capital, the passion first carried to the high natural common-life point, the humour fit to be its neighbour, the satire easy, pleasant, and quite unstrained. You really have made a hit. [*Marginal insertion:* I heard it read first by Macready after seeing Knowles new play — an unprofitable and tedious night — and though the reading kept us together till ½ past 3 in the morning, nothing could be so lively & enjoying as we. This is a good test. Again he read it last night — Effect encreased — and his "old women" enchanted as Moliere's in their best of humours.] If to read a good comedy is to keep the best company in the world, as somebody said, where the best things are spoken and the most amusing happen — and where there is throughout, too, sufficient natural and earnest feeling to tie together all that is said and done in a light yet lasting

---

[18] These novels had been published in the twenties — *The Disowned,* 3 vols. (1828), and *Devereux: A Tale,* 2 vols. (1829). Bulwer was preparing them for his first *Collected Works* (1840).

bond — then Money (an admirable title!) is an admirable Comedy. The first and third acts are splendid — nor could such effects be better placed. The second and fourth are admirable in relief and progress, and the effects of the fifth will be strong and natural. Be under no apprehension of this. Don't think — either without night-cap or with too strong a one — it may be advisable to have in all the characters, rank & file, at the last. It is better as it is. I felt at first a slight objection as to Old Vesey's apparent discomfiture of Evelyn's scheme — but this vanishes on consideration. But for the scheme, Georgy is not [at] all likely to have eloped with Blunt [sic]. A word or two, at the same time, might be introduced to make this clearer; and such alterations are all that seem to me to be called for. Some pruning must take place as a matter of course; and the scene of the Butler's pantry seems scarcely called for. I will report to you faithfully, however, when the rehearsals begin. That will be the time for decisions on these points. One thing additional you will be prepared to hear. You have, with the exception of Macready to whom I think Evelyn well-suited, overtasked the actors. That worldly old humbug should have been played by King or Munden — that Deadly Smooth by plausible Jack Palmer — that Doleful by Dowton, through whose genial eyes would have flashed the lie to his groans.[19] I console myself yet with thinking that these characters are so much beyond the strength of the people that must play them as to make the danger less. The extra quantity of strength in these cases some-times goes to the support of the actor! It has often been found so.— I impress Macready with the necessity of making the exertion to get Wallack into Smooth. Your Lady Beevor will be good, your Georgiana [sic] by no means bad. Clara will be better played by Miss Faucit than any one else could do it, and on the whole the arrangements may not be so bad as we fear.— . . . .

204. BULWER TO FORSTER, *Frankfort, Saturday, October 3, 1840*

. . . I am charmed that you like the play. But still things come out so differently in acting. Poor La Valliere read promisingly. . . .

About this time (the letter is undated) Bulwer named his terms to Webster. The interesting (and later significant) feature of his proposals is his firm statement of conditions under which he reserved the right to withdraw the play before performance.

205. BULWER TO WEBSTER[20]

I have now made the final corrections in the Comedy — & as you are naturally anxious to save time — & as I understand that there are hopes of securing

---

[19] These were comedians of the preceding generation. Tom King (1730-1804) was the original Sir Peter Teazle and Sir Anthony Absolute.

Joseph Shepherd Munden (1758-1832), one of Lamb's favorite actors, created Old Dornton in Holcroft's *The Road to Ruin.*

John Palmer (1742-98) was the original Joseph Surface.

William Dowton (1764-1851) was praised by Hunt and Hazlitt for his Absolute, Hardcastle, Dornton, and Falstaff.

[20] Original in the Houghton Library of Harvard University.

the talents of Mr Wallack for the part of Smooth, which I have carefully retouched, or that — failing him — it is arranged to secure Mr Vining — I am willing to conclude the agreement at your earliest convenience.

The terms, with w^h I believe, you are already acquainted, being identical with those on which we treated for the Sea Captain. If you will do me the favour to send me a copy of the agreement so based, I will sign & return it to you — & as I am leaving Town I beg to state that my Bankers are Sir Claude Scott & Co Cavendish Square.

There is one point however, on which my anxiety for the success of this Comedy makes it necessary that I should reserve a right which can only indeed be exercised for the credit & advantage of both — It is this, if at any time during the rehearsals, or prior to the actual representation of the Comedy — I should feel convinced, that, whether from my own not having sufficiently consulted the peculiar talents of the more important actors or from any other cause the play would not be likely to have that success which could alone answer to either of us — I reserve the absolute right to withdraw it,— of course on repaying the Money —. Included in this right — is naturally the lesser one to defer the representation should it seem to me imperatively desirable from any unforeseen circumstances. Perhaps for instance had the Sea Captain last year been so delayed as to avoid interference with Mr Knowles's play it might have been more successful — And farther — to save all misunderstanding — will you allow me to say — that as on such matters I should not go alone by my own judgement — but by the more practical advice of Mr Macready & my friend Mr Forster who have been kind eno' to make themselves thoroghly acquainted with the nature of the play — so in my absence from Town, during the earlier rehearsals — you will consider them as the representatives of my opinions —

You will pardon, I hope, this reserve which as I before said — can only be exercised for your benefit as well as mine —

206. Bulwer to Forster

I have written to Mr. Webster —, as since we may hope for Wallack & faute de mieux are assured of Vining — the matter may as well be settled: — Always indeed, as I have distinctly expressed in my letter — reserving the right to withdraw the play should the rehearsals prove that I have not sufficiently suited the parts to the actors.— Your kindness, my dear Forster, & my confidence in your & Macready's judgement, have made me impose on you two the not very pleasant task of being, with regard to this, the representatives of my opinions to Mr. Webster. You know — & you two only can eno' understand the importance I attach to the success of the Comedy — which if a hit at all — & that must depend on the Ensemble & the actors — may be of long & real service not only to myself but the Stage —. . . . & restore to the Haymarket (what with the example it will set to other writers) — its old realm of genteel Comedy.— And therefore I shall leave the Interests of the Experiment so far as I am concerned with confidence to your & Macready's representation thereof at the Friendly Court of the Manager

P.S.

Perhaps — as Hammersly's affair[21] has put me to some little inconvenience, you will see that Mr. Webster pays the 600£ to Sir C. Scott & Co. Cavendish Sq — as soon as it may be agreeable to him — in fact that is really the agreement on receiving the Play —

As early as September 26 Macready told Webster, who had been badgering him about his responsibility for bringing new plays to the theatre, that *Money* existed, but until he had got it properly marked and cut (and on September 28 had tried out again on Forster, his wife, and his sister), he would not show it. At last on September 29, "Messrs. Webster and Willmott[22] called at three o'clock to hear the comedy read. I read it to them, and Mr. Webster accepted it, expressing his wish to have it produced as soon as possible."

But a long and troubled chapter of events would ensue before *Money* finally appeared. Webster himself originated the first stumbling block by assuming to himself, against Macready's wishes, the role of Doleful (later called Graves). On September 30 Macready "spoke to Willmott, telling him that I had thought of Webster for Lord Glossmore — he told me that Mr. Webster himself wished to act Doleful!" During the performance that night Macready put it to Webster himself that "he would be the best we could have for Lord Glossmore." This brought on a flood of complaint. "He began a long desultory harangue about his talent, and what he had been and done, of which I have lived in total ignorance; and though I told him I had nothing to do with this, that Glossmore was a very good part, and was particularized by Sir E. Bulwer as requiring a good actor, he ran on wearying me — quoting his performance of Louis XIII, which I was much averse to. I hear a storm ringing! God direct and speed me right." But Macready does not tell all. Apparently in his annoyance at Webster he threatened to withdraw the play and take it to the Covent Garden; for the next day he received a woeful and probably well-justified bill of Webster's complaints, reading in part as follows:

207. WEBSTER TO MACREADY, *September 30, 1840*[23]

. . . Every man is more or less an egotist, especially in the profession we have adopted. . . . The pieces introduced by you are always attended with great expense, and in five act matters I have not had an attractive novelty since the first season. As regards the authors, no allowance is ever made to me for previous failures and you always appear . . . to encourage a contrary feeling. Secondly an increase of actors, witness Mr. George Bennet's engagement . . . then there are extra scene painters, drapes &c. I know you will say you do not compel me to this. but you also say you will not act with such & such actors, and unless such effects are produced by such scenery, and such drapes,

---

[21] On Monday, September 21, 1840, the Bank of Hammersly and Co. stopped payments in consequence of the death of the proprietor.

[22] Mr. Willmott, an assistant in numerous theatre managements of the time, including Macready's, where he was titled Stage Director.

[23] The text of this fragment is taken from Catalog 94 of the Argosy Book Stores, Inc., N.Y.C.

it is no use to attempt to bring out such & such pieces. Now all these points as far as my success will allow and even beyond I have always cheerfully acceded to . . . till at last my patience is exhausted as my pocket will soon be, if I do not make a stand against these continued unproductive outlays. Last evening you thought proper upon my merely making an observation upon the cast of Sir E. L. Bulwer's new comedy, to threaten to send it to Covent Garden Theatre — a Theatre directly opposed to the one in which you are receiving one hundred pounds per week at the least for ten months in the year. But if you feel justified in so doing, I beg to repeat what I then said, that you are at perfect liberty to act as you please; for however I might regret such decision, no threats shall scare me from delivering an opinion where my own interests are vitally concerned . . . Unless we work amicably and zealously together . . . it would be far better for me to jog on comfortably in my old and humble but profitable way, than to endure the continued scene of splendid misery which will probably end in loss . . . Perfectly free to act either for or against me. . . .

October 1 was a banquet of crow for Macready. Not only did Webster thus firmly rebuke him for his impetuous threat, but he also learned from one of his spies that there was no likelihood that the Mme. Vestris management at Covent Garden could or would engage him or take on the play. And further, on this day arrived Bulwer's letter of September 26 (No. 202 above) which cast Webster in the part Webster wanted. Macready was driven into more generous attitudes. To Forster he acknowledged that he could have "no further objection" to Webster as Doleful; and he proposed also "that in case Mr. Wallack should not wish to take Smooth, that I would give five extra nights to Mr. Webster to make up a salary to Vining, if he would engage him." To Webster he claims to have "answered him very mildly," and "gave him full leave" to break off their contract, "if too onerous for his establishment." Webster assured Forster that he would not dismiss Macready, and sent Macready "a rude note . . . considering my engagement conclusive." Macready ended the day perching uncomfortably on his diginity, offering again to have his contract broken — and spent the next several days in stewing wonderment that Webster would not answer his letters. All this was but the climax of a long series of hostilities between manager and man, brought on partly by Webster's rather slovenly approach to problems but even more, I fear, by Macready's haughty usurpation of managerial prerogatives. A week later, on October 8, Webster appears to have humbled himself sufficiently to appease Macready, and a sort of peace was patched up between them, solid enough for the production of *Money* to proceed.

Bulwer got home from the Continent on October 13. Macready had spent many days by now in marking and emending the play: at least three of his letters of suggestions to Bulwer (September 30, October 5, and October 13) have been lost.

On October 15 another problem arose. The part of Smooth, which Bulwer had been so particular about, was to have been played by Henry Wallack. But now Macready noticed that Smooth had only three lines in the first scene and seven in the second, so that he "could not, with any respect to his pretensions, propose such a part to Mr. Wallack." Wallack called to hear the part described, and, as anticipated, he declined it. Once more, then, Macready offered to play without salary for a few nights to offset the expense of hiring Vining for the role. Webster himself tried to talk Wallack into it, but without success. In the long run, Smooth was played by Benjamin Wrench, and Vining was engaged for Lord Glossmore.

Almost daily during the latter part of October Macready was busy over the book of the play, cutting, correcting, inserting Bulwer's alterations, and learning the play director-wise. On October 24 he at last "read it to the company, who were much excited by it. It was quite successful with them." The triumph of that day was marred only by the idle tongue of the wretched Wallack, who, after Macready had taken such pains to excuse him from the part of Smooth, went about the greenroom letting it be known he had refused it. October 28 was the first day of rehearsal: it left Macready exhausted.

208. BULWER TO FORSTER, [*October 27, 1840*]

. . . In leaving town tomorrow for K — I shall call on Macready & will leave with him my ideas about the Dresses — .

. . . Don't forget that the address of the Tailor if he & Webster can agree as to clothing the Club &c. is Jackson — Ryder St St James's — At all events he should make for Smooth & Blount. . . .

After the second rehearsal, on October 29, Macready sought to define and limit his responsibility to the production. He passed on to Webster Bulwer's notes about costume and "Spoke to Mr. Webster about the scenery and dresses of the play of *Money,* observing to him most emphatically that I did not wish to have anything whatever to do with them — that I would aid the acting as much as I could, but that I had rather he arranged the other matters in his own way." But the canny Webster seems to have elected to take the cash and let the credit go. Macready alone was more than he could cope with, and now the author (and friend Forster, too) were to be watching his every move. He made plain that it "was not his wish" to assume final authority on matters of staging.

209. MACREADY TO BULWER, *5 Clarence Terrace, Regent's Park, November 1, 1840*

I would have written you yesterday, but I wanted two important things — health & time. I am now driven up to a few minutes — Imprimis — about the Club-room — it is needful the scene *Act 3rd Scene last* — & *Act 5th Scene 1st* should be the same — that *the Club* — the locus in quo should be ascertained. *What room is it* to be? — the drawing-room — or the Coffee-room — Qu. — *Drawing-room.* — Say definitively for the working of the scene stops, till I know. It will be important to *discover the Club-scene,* that the drawing-room — Act 3rd Scene 1st — should change to a room as if of Lady Franklin's — nearer to the proscenium. — This can very well be done, by the Servant — entering after — "approach of the Honeymoon is to the Human Race" & saying "My Lady will see you now, Sir:" — Will you give Graves a few lines to take him off with the servant — *change scene.* — *Enter Servant & Graves* — *Servant* — "I thought My Lady was here, Sir: — I'll tell her you're waiting" — exit. *Graves.* "My heart beats," &c &c. — to the End. *We get much by this.* — Will you do it? —

Is Evelyn to be pronounced Ē-velyn or Ĕv-e-lyn? What Bank will you substitute for Hammersleys? Ransom's? Will you have the play announced (I SUPPOSE SO) with *your name?* It is of course advisable. — Will you give a hint of your wish as to *Toke's dress?* — and as to the women's dresses? — We are progressing, but slowly on the stage — it is too much for some of the actors. —

What do you think of a *Prologue?* — It is so long since a Comedy was produced. —

Will you re-consider the speech on *"Battledore"?* which *ought* to be an effect, but does not seem to me up to the mark — in its close — of effect — Forster thinks it is a coup manqué. —

Qu.? — Should Evelyn say — is it not ungenerous in his situation —"Ah Madam you would accept me now!"—

Can you give me — (I have not the old copy) — a line or two for Tabouret in *Act 2nd Sc. 1st* —

Mr. Wrench wishes, but I do not see the need, to have a line more in his first scene. — Are you aware that Forster has transferred Smooth to him? — He also proposes a white coat & light blue trowsers for his first dress — but *I do not see that.* — I like your sketch of the dresses very much. — Voici tout! — I hope you are better and with that earnest hope remain always —

210. BULWER TO MACREADY, [*November 3*], *1840*

Yours is rec[d] to-day. Regarding the Prologue & Epilogue. I have a superstitious horror of such things. I shall never forget the cold damp thrown over the Theater when M[r] H. Wallack in black shorts stepp[d] forward to freeze the Audience with the prologue to La Vallière. Besides — the Play is already long & the 10 minutes occupied by Prologue & Epilogue it's to be spared. I will think over it, but not with a good heart. Meanwhile tell me who you propose to speak them. There are no persons to whom such things could be trusted except yourself — and out of the rest, perhaps Miss Faucit? Eh! Give me your idea on this — as of course the kind of composition depends on who is to be the Oracle.

With regard to Smooth's white coat (I suppose great-coat), there is one objection. It is the London Season that is Summer — & besides it is a very dangerous article of dress unless the figure carries it off well. If he likes to wear it, Jackson must make it — in the present fashion — no buttons behind.

I will see if another line can be added to his part in his first scene, when I get the proofs thereof, having no copy here. —Toke should have black shorts & silks — powder — smart showy waistcoat & his butler's jacket on (when he has his scene) — to shew what he is. When he comes on to you — a blue coat & gilt buttons. — You did not tell me how to smooth over the difficulty that Clara, knowing Evelyn had been led to suppose Georgina wrote to the Nurse, w[d] of course have foreseen that he must suspect Georgina to have paid him the money. There is another difficulty. Evelyn bribes Sharp to say the Codicil contained 20,000£. Now all such evidence w[d] have to be filed at Doctors' Commons. I fear it could be hardly settled legally in the off-hand manner Evelyn does it on the Stage. Let me know these 2 points — what could be s^d to smooth them. I think it better to let Mrs. Glover, who I hope takes the part, say the line about Sir Fred to prepare for his *dwopping* the R.

I see great difficulties in the way of changing the Scene for Graves & Lady F — it would make the joke still more dangerous by appearing more brought in on purpose, & I don't think a Scene should change without it practically & absolutely forwards the Plot. But would it not solve all difficulties to let the whole scene from the commencement of the Act to the place in Sir John's Study — & throw in a word to signify that it is his study? & make it natural for Graves to be shewn there. The scene itself might be a good humbug scene — Parliamentary blue Books — Great Tin Boxes as if holding Title Deeds inscribed "the Vesey Property" — Huge sort of Bureau, &c. This seems to me to smooth all difficulties. Let me know.

With regard to the Club-room. Since they must both, Act 3 & Act 5, be the same, it must be a drawing-room — in that case Smooth in Act 5 can't breakfast there, but he may be munching a biscuit with a glass of sherry — omit the egg. But as we may as well be as accurate as we can, c^d you quietly find out thro' D'Orsay or any member of Crockford's[24] without saying for what purpose, whether whist & piquet would be *ever* played in the great Drawing-room at Crockford's — or in some other room set apart for the purpose. If it s^hd turn out to be ags^t the Fundamental rules of the Club to play in the great drawing-room why we must have the legitimate card-room for the scene. But if it s^hd happen that — tho' not frequent or customary — yet that it does occasionally happen that a Table is made up in the great Draw^g-room, that is all we want.

I would write to some member — but I think it better that they sh^d not guess what the inquiry is for. Besides I sh^d not like to seem as if I had made the Manager put Crockford's on the Stage. There is no objection for him to do so, but it might seem a clap-trap for me to dictate it.

You surprise me about the Battledore. Merely cork & feather is a good point. Is that the part you object to? Will you try it again in Rehearsal — & let me have an inkling how you w^d have the Point turn? if you still find it don't tell.

Macready's suggestion that there be a prologue was evidently seconded by Forster. Bulwer was implacable in his veto.

211. BULWER TO FORSTER, *Knebworth, Stevenage, Herts., November 5, 1840*

> Guy Fawkes Day
> Suited to Thee
> O Forster Fawkes!

Miserable man — What insane [*illegible*] what gloomy & sinister frenzy —

---

[24] Crockford's Club, a luxurious gambling house at 50 St. James's Street, was built in 1827 by William Crockford (1775-1844). Crockford retired from the management in 1840, having "won the whole of the ready money of the then existing generation."

inspired thee with the thought of a prologue — Prologue. I would as lief thou wouldst talk to me of rat's bane! — Hast thou no remembrance — Unfortunate Being that thou art — of the fatal apparition of Mr H. Wallack — with his hat under his arm — (would his head had been under it) — stepping forward to pronounce the Funeral Oration upon La Valliere! Dost thou not remember how from his ominous jowls slowly circled the ineffable & Stygian vapour which grew stiller & colder as it welled from Pit to Gallery & finally left the wretched listeners — numbed & lifeless on their dewy seats? — Prologue! — And who, O inspired one of Nox & Erebus, — who was to better that solemn & mortiferous Exordium — who was to ring that ghastly knell — ushering in the burial of the living! — Hang thyself O Infamous Forster — Sexton Webster or Sexton Phelps!!! — Never recur to that black & horrible suggestion — at which I vow that my hair bristled & my knees knocked and the damps of death gathered on my brow —. Prologue — why not a Sermon — a long — a grave — a funereal Sermon — Go to — Go to — I see the blush of shame already mounting over thy ingenuous face. I spare all aggravation of the remorse which — if thou *hast* a conscience, if thou dost acknowledge reverence of the gods — must already be busy at thy heart — Return thanks to the Powers that watch over human Destinies — that thy friend's innocent nursling has escaped thy murderous propositions — that the crime of deliberate Infanticide is not added to thy sins — Repent — Amend — Redeem! —

Having thus discharged on thee some of the vials of my pious indignation — I first ask thee if thou hast any thoughts of repairing thine iniquities — by a visit here — where despite thy guilt thou shalt be warmly welcomed — yea as if Nothing had happened! — I shall abide here yet several days — finding the air agreeable with me — Next hast thou seen the rehearsals — Strickland Wrench Lacy — Webster — what are they? Have they a glimmering — Is there hope.—. . . .

212. BULWER TO MACREADY, *Knebworth, November [5?], 1840*

Do you like the following emendation for the battledore — after the words "everywhere, nowhere. How grave are the players, how anxious the bystanders — how noisy the battledores. Does it signify 3 straws what's the worth of the Shuttlecock?" — omitting perhaps "Go & play by yourselves," &c., or "How grave are the players, how anxious the bystanders — how noisy the battledores. A delightful game! What's the worth of the Shuttlecock!" Would you give me one word to say if you like either of these two & if so which, that I may copy it into the printed Play. I'm ashamed to worry you so much.

I remain stolidly unconvinced about the change of Scene for Graves. I think it really very dangerous & awkward, & you must remember, that if this scene with the dancing & the sudden entrance of Sir John &c. is too near the Proscenium, all the effect must be ruined. However, tho' most reluctantly, if you continue to insist on its necessity, I must try & do what you want. But really the stage is deep eno' both for that & the Club. Directly I get the proofs of the 4th Act, probably tomorrow or next day, I will see about the alteration with Sharp & the Tradesmen. Tho' I had fancied that Scene more effective for Evelyn than the one with Glossmore & Blount, you won't save much time by it.— Abandon the Prologue as a thought of our Evil Genius — Phelps & Webster settle that point.

I tremble for Strickland & for Lacy. How do Rees[25] & Wrench get on?

[P.S.] I am better, thank you. And how is my little godson? better I hope, too — sympathetically.

213. MACREADY TO BULWER, *5 Clarence Terrace, Regent's Park, November 5, [1840]*

Your letter greets me on my return home.— I have been from 10 to half past 12, rehearsing nothing but the Club scene — and we have only reached the point of Blount &c. sitting down to Whist.— I tell you this to make your mind as easy as I can upon the score of due pains being taken. Yesterday morning I had Mr. Strickland here from half past ten to three; and I dismissed him perfectly satisfied that Sir John was one of the greatest comic parts on the stage — "if he could but do it." — He is sincere in his wish to try, and anxious to put himself completely under tuition, therefore I have more hope of him: — if it can be driven into him, I will ply hard and often enough.— Forster shall report to you when it begins to take form — but this Club-scene will occupy us long before we can make advance.— Everyone is so high in hope about the play, that I almost yield to the current, and am disposed to go beyond my customary limit of "it ought to succeed"— but superstition will not let me venture to say more.

You must not find fault with the trouble I give you, nor with my change of mind — I revolve passages, till I find or fancy I find a chance of giving effect to them — I should like the Battledore speech to stand as at first — only inserting the lines —"Everywhere — nowhere! — How grave the players! how anxious the bystanders — how noisy the battledores — and when this something John &c."—

Let us *try* the change of scene,— if it does not work well — rely on it, we will not hazard it.— Wrench begins to open his eyes, and to see what was before evident enough — he is *very* docile — & Rees I can dragoon — alias, Cardigan.

I wish to make another cut — i.e. (*Act 3rd* Sc. 1st) — to omit the imparting to Clara by Sir John, that he has conveyed the idea that Georgy "wrote the letter", I do not see its necessity, and the omission lightens the scene & *relieves Strickland* – an important consideration.— Away then with the thought of the Prologue.— Next week I trust Forster will be able to report progress to

---

[25] David Rees, a minor comic actor. Matthews printed "Rice."

you.— My little Henry is slowly advancing — I am truly happy to know that you are better and with thanks for your enquiries

P.S. The cut I propose is from —"I pity you — I do indeed — after that omit to "My dear Clara, don't take on"— &c.—

After the rehearsal of November 5, "where I spent two hours in the rehearsal of one page of the club scene," Macready began for the first time to mutter against his own part of Alfred Evelyn. "As I write, doubt and misgivings arise in my mind. I have nothing great or striking in situation, character, humour, or passion to develop. The power of all this is thrown on Mr. Strickland and partially on Mr. Webster." On this very point Bulwer himself had been fearful from the beginning. Later on Macready's dislike of the part was to crystallize into positive detestation. He is said to have called Evelyn "a damned walking gentleman," and he once told Westland Marston that he "would never have performed Evelyn had it not been written by Bulwer."[26] To Bulwer, however, he did not, at least at the moment, communicate his dissatisfaction.

214. MACREADY TO BULWER, 5 Clarence Terrace, Regent's Park, November 7, 1840

We are creeping: — advancing as miners through a porphyry dyke — but we *are* advancing.— I am earnestly requested to obtain your opinion as to Wrench's (Smooth's) dress coat — which you have not mentioned. Roth[27] says, that velvet collars are very rarely worn in dress — shall I adhere to mine? — and — pray consider this — what am I to do with regard to the Club? — There is not time to change my dress from the 1st scene 3rd Act — to the Club scene: — if I change my coat & waistcoat and hat &c.— will it be enough? The change of the entire dress will not be possible — tell me then, what you would have me do? — Do you mean Evelyn's first coat to be a light or dark iron grey — approaching a black? — I wish to know, that I may be forward.—

215. BULWER TO MACREADY, November 8, 1840

I cannot say how much I feel your kindness in all the Labour & zeal you bestow upon the Play. I am sure it owes it to you rather than me to succeed. — I have only just got the proofs of Act 4. But hope to-morrow to send you the alterations you wish in that & Act 3, viz.: relative to Graves — and Sharp versus tradesmen. 3 Additions to your part have occurred to me. Do you like them?

Act 2. Instead of "Ay, here as easy where money versus men:" "Right. Down with those who take the liberty to admire any liberty except our liberty! — That *is* liberty!" and instead of "Both sides alike poor men"— in rejoinder to Glossmore —"Right as without Law there w^{d} be no property. So to be a Law for Property is the only proper property of Law! That is Law!"

---

[26] William Archer, *William Charles Macready* (London, 1890), p. 127; Westland Marston, *Our Recent Actors,* 2 vols. (London, 1888), I, 85.

[27] On April 18, 1842, Macready recorded that "Mr. Roth came to ask about the arrangement of a dress for Prince Albert for a fancy ball."

Again, when Sir John, speaking of Smooth, Act 2, says, "An uncommonly clever fellow," Evelyn may say — "Clever, yes! when a man steals a loaf we cry down the knavery; when a man diverts his neighbor's millstream to grind his own corn, we cry up the cleverness. And every one courts Captain Dudley Smooth?" You need not answer on these points till you answer my next letter with the other corrections. You wanted something to say to Tabouret, Act 2. It can come thus: "A levée as usual, good day. Ah Tabouret, your designs for the Draperies (Tab shewing Draw^g) very good, and what do you want, Mr. Crimson?"

Add then afterwards, "as celebrated for vis-à-vis, salvers, furniture & coats," &c. Every time Stout enters he ought to be wiping his forehead. When Georgina, Act 1, removes her arm from Blount's chair, it ought to be because Sir John frowns significantly & nudges her.

Wrench's dress coat may be a brown one. With regard to clothes one must remember that one must be always a little more dressy on the stage than in real life. And velvet . . . a dress. But as you fancy it. Certainly the mere change of a coat will do for a club. I have some little doubts of your wearing tights at your dinner. It is certainly not usual in real life — but a Bachelor receiving Ladies may pay them that mark of civility. They love tights as Dandies love flesh-coloured drawers in opera Dances. Besides, it impresses & lightens a good figure. The dark grey as you were for having it, not too merry will do for the first dress.

216. BULWER TO MACREADY, *Knebworth, Monday, November 10, 1840*

I enclose the alteration you require, & now will you let me know, as well as you can, what you adopt, because of the Printed Copies. Especially for the proofs for America, which ought to go instantly. You observe that this alteration, Act IV, strengthens Sharp's part and makes a goodish Actor necessary. Who acts it? However pressed you may be for Servants, pray let Sharp speak to the *two* — two doubles the comedy & bustle of this short scene.— And it will come to the same thing, since *Toke* may usher in Glossmore & Blount.

May I ask you when you write to send me the cast of the Dramatis Personae as acted — as I don't know who act Sharp, the Tradesmen, &c. I hope Macfinch's representative speaks Scotch decently. Furthermore, when do you think the play will be out?

I am delighted to hear such good accounts thanks to your indomitable inspirations. I'm very sorry to inflict on your opprest time the new burthen of an answer to these details.

[P.S.] I highly approve of your cut in the dialogue between Sir John & Clara.

I still greatly dread the change of scene for Graves & Lady F. But you will judge in the rehearsal.

In the Forster Library at the Victoria and Albert Museum are preserved two sheets of alterations for the last acts — quite probably not those referred to in the last two letters, but included here as representative of the author's minute care to the smallest details.

217. Bulwer, Memorandum of Alterations

Act 3. Scene ii
Sir John
For "my dear Clara don't take on —" read
my dear Clara *don't cry* —

Act IV

Scene iv. Toke & other Servants
instead of "I vill arrest him dis very day"
read, "I will put what you call an
Execution in de gutes & de cattles".

Act IV
Scene v

Sir John

For yes the picture may be fine
read yes the painting may be fine

Same scene farther on

Evelyn

For "Sir John I am arrested"
read Sir John the bailiffs are in the House."
Stout instead of He's arrested &c
Read
The Bailiffs in the House, &c —

Next page

Evelyn

instead of or bail me or something
read   or see that my people pack out the bailiff
or do it yourself or something &c

Sir John

instead of   Pay — bail
read
Pay, kick —
Smooth (next page
instead of
But my dear John — theyve no right to arrest the dinner
read
But my dear John — it is for us at least
to put an Execution — on the dinner

Act V. Scene

3rd page of the scene

Sir John

    instead of Deadly Smooth — the arrest

read   Deadly Smooth, the Execution —

Act V Scene 3ᵈ

Dole for *reports wrong* me there —

Sir John

    instead of to humbug your

own father, read

    to bubble your own father

& on the next page

omit in Sir John's Speech

    "Don't humbug me."

The next crisis to arise, from November 9 through 12, was from a problem as old as the theatre is old — the case of the drunken actor. Forster assumed the generalship in this emergency, and his reports to Bulwer are full.

218. FORSTER TO BULWER, *58 Lincolns Inn Fields, Tuesday,*
    [*November 10, 1840*]

P.S. I should say that Webster is not at all unwilling to do what is best — only he is for the most ignorant of what it is. He is going to great expense in *furnishing.*

My dear Bulwer

    Again another delay!

    Mr. Strickland has been suddenly ill, but is better, and expected to be at rehearsal tomorrow. There has been no rehearsal today in consequence.

    But a more annoying circumstance threatens difficulty to us. Mr. David Rees — who is the man for Stout; I know no other half so good anywhere — played last night in Werner on the emergency of Mr. Stricklands illness, and exhibited decided drunkenness.

    I am so alarmed about this that I say he ought not to be put into Stout. At any rate, another person must study it, and rehearse it, to be ready in case of any filthy incapability on the part of Mr. Rees. Mr Webster pleads for him — I am disposed to be obdurate — and so, I think, is Macready. We have a consultation at rehearsal tomorrow. I will write you the result immediately afterwards.

    Macready's drilling in the Club scene has been first rate, and promises a glorious result.

    I am dissatisfied with some of the scenes — and Webster has promised to have another & *much better* painter at once employed. He consented to this last night & I shall enforce it tomorrow.

Macready being reluctant to take all the responsibility of objection on himself — I am afraid — unless you pass another week at Knebworth — that I may not see it even for a day. For the difficulties at rehearsals will chiefly occur within the next 7 days. But I'll write again tomorrow.

219. FORSTER TO BULWER, *Thursday, November 12, 1840*

. . . We have had a long conference about Stout.— Pity me for what I went thro in the cause of that staunch vestryman and Great Economist last night! Let it stand as some part of my atonement for the ghostly figure of Mr. H. Wallack's [*illegible*] tights which I so unthinkingly raised — to torture your quiet pillow with. I saw Mr. Roxby[28] — the substitute proposed. Let the recollection sleep.

Mr Webster has just brought me piteous letters of penitence from Mr. Rees with solemn protestations of amendment.— After discussion of the matter last night Macready & myself had already come to a conclusion which nothing but the desperate state of the case would warrant, but which, in the hopelessness of any other alternative but the instant withdrawal of the Comedy to your probable inconvenience many ways, we hope you will approve.

This it is. Mr. Webster has just solemnly engaged himself to me — & is to send me an agreement to that effect, formally signed — that if Mr Rees, *at any time* between the present date and the production of the Comedy, *or at any time on the night of its production* before the whole five acts are over, should present himself *to the audience* in such a condition as to warrant the suspicion of the least drunkenness — the Comedy is to be at once withdrawn — Mr Webster leaving the money in your hands, and incurring all the expenses at present gone to, and consenting to continue to do so — until he finds a person we can all approve for the part of Stout. Suppose for example Mr Rees were quite sober in the first act of the Comedy, and appears in the third with a dash of drunkenness — Macready will have the right (and never fear that he would sternly exercise it) of refusing again to go upon the stage, except to explain the cause of the instant withdrawal. So if on any night now before the Comedy is produced, the thing occurs again (the occurrence of this other night is attributed to a three months periodical visitation which always occupies more than one day!) we will at once compel Webster to these conditions, and withdraw the Comedy till next season.

With these precautions Macready thinks we are safe — and he feels no danger after the Comedy has once been acted. That he will explain to you himself. . . .

. . . the rehearsal was again delayed today — until tomorrow. The new painter is at work on the Scenes, & all proceeding as it ought.—. . . .

---

[28] Robert Roxby (1809?-66), a comic actor then playing at the Olympic; afterwards stage manager of Drury Lane for eleven years and supporting actor with Mathews and Mme. Vestris at the Lyceum.

Though Macready was dubious —"a drunkard's vow of sobriety!" — David Rees appears to have kept his pledge and brought off Stout creditably and without further hindrance. It is only sad to report that within three years he came to the expected end, being found dead one morning in his lodgings in Cork, "with his head on the floor and his legs in the bed. His head and face were swollen to an enormous size, and were quite black. Mr. Rees, we regret to state had long devoted himself to habits of intemperance, by which, there is no doubt, his death was caused."[29]

220. BULWER TO MACREADY, *November 13, 1840*

A thousand thanks for all that has been done, touching that Vitious Rees. I think it settled the best way — if no other person can be found! But still one's eye sh^d be directed to that object. *Could* Oxberry[30] do it? I send you some more additions for your part, the first two I think you may like — I am in doubt about the others — in which my object was this. That as Blount, Glossmore & Stout all press their bets on Evelyn, he sh^d strike out the moral — of every man eager after money — & the additions I propose in this strengthen your part perhaps, but I have great fear whether they do not in the first place mar the rapidity of the whole scene. Secondly whether by forcing *any reflection* whatever upon the Audience one does not stop the current of the careless laughter that ought to flow thro' the Scene. You will consider this well & try it carefully, if you think them worth trying at all. I am very anxious for an answer on one point by next post if possible.

You will substitute Sharp with the Tradesmen — Act 4 — for the scene as it stood before. As that is an alteration that will unsettle the types, & I must send the proofs to America & no time to lose. Don't trouble yourself to answer the rest, unless you like to say Yes or No to the enclosed.

[P.S.] I shall be in Town Monday for a few days.

221. MACREADY TO BULWER, *5 Clarence Terrace, Regent's Park, November 14, 1840*

I would have written to you before but indeed I have not had time.— *All* the alterations I have received, and most thankfully made use of, therefore you may arrange them for the press as sent to me.— I like the Club introductions very much.—"More last words"— Will you give me half a line to round the period in my last speech to Clara, Act 3rd — after — "robs your earth for ever of its summer"— *to the effect* of "smiles complacently upon you"—"and says let us part friends".— Again — a line of more determined purpose in the dialogue with Graves — Act 3rd — "Sir John is alarmed, is he?" — *to the effect of* — "Duped by this over-reaching charlatan — He shall find I can perhaps match him at his own weapons." — I think it needs more clearness of purpose.—

---

[29] Unidentified newspaper clipping in the Lowne Collection of Macreadiana at the Garrick Club.

[30] William Henry Oxberry (1808-52), comic actor and dramatist; son of the more famous William Oxberry (1784-1824), the actor, editor, and publisher.

If the play could be ACTED, its success would be great: — it grows upon me. I have only to try to make your meaning clear — if I can help to do that, it is a pleasure to me: but I need not observe that all the effort in the world will not make a meaning, where the author has not given it.— It certainly OUGHT to succeed.

I am glad you will be in Town on Monday — With Webster any difficulty is increased ten fold.— I am glad to hear you will be here on Monday.—

222. BULWER TO FORSTER, *Knebworth, Sunday, [November 15, 1840]*

> Could you get me the list of
> the Dramatis Personae

I shall be in Town tomorrow & shall hope to see you the next day — when I will call — & thank you for all your kindness touching Money — Is it possible that it can be acted next Saturday. I see it announced for that day.

Will you give Macready the enclosed paper.—

Few letters passed after mid-November, but Bulwer and Forster were often present at rehearsals. The play was going badly. On the sixteenth Forster was there, and so critical of what he saw that he was, Macready says, "nearly becoming disagreeable to the actors." Later in the day, as if soothing one set of frayed nerves, Macready "spoke to Strickland about his part in the new play, and gave him all the encouragement I could." On the seventeenth both "Bulwer and Forster came in; the play is in a seriously backward and ineffective state." On November 21 it "went so heavily and unsatisfactorily that Bulwer became very nervous — quite ill-tempered, and spoke harshly to the actors — haughtily, I should say, certainly unphilosophically; but how much has he to excuse the manifestation of his suffering! I quite feel for him. I did and said all I could. . . . Spoke to Miss Helen Faucit wishing her to *act* at the rehearsal on Monday morning." On Monday the twenty-third things were so bad that, as Macready reports, Bulwer wanted to throw in the sponge. "Went to theatre, and rehearsed the three last acts of Money, which certainly appeared to me, through the whole of Mr. Strickland's part and much of Mr. Wrench's, dull and dangerous. Bulwer and Forster were so impressed with this that they decided on withdrawing the play. I pointed out to Bulwer the consideration due to Webster, and suggested its retention till the summer, when Farren might be engaged to act the part — the only chance for it! He entered with Webster and Forster, and, when I went up to ascertain if it was to be withdrawn or not, I found them in debate — Mr. Webster declaring that he should be bankrupted if it was (but it was the *agreement* that Sir. E. L. B — should withdraw it at the last moment if not satisfied with the acting) and Bulwer proposing either to withdraw it till the summer, or postpone its performance a few days till a new scene could be substituted to end the fourth act; Mr. Webster adverse to both, and insisting on his confidence of the play's *success!* — which he has not seen rehearsed!! It was left for a final trial at tomorrow's rehearsal."

It is curious that Webster "had not seen it rehearsed" when he was playing the important role of Graves. He appears to have absented himself rather often on managerial business, as on the fourteenth "to go to a sale and make a bargain of some card-tables!" On November 19 Macready notes that he "came in after haggling about his broker's bargains. He will spoil the play yet. *He will!*"

The overnight postponement of decision to withdraw the play paid handsomely, for the events of the twenty-fourth were all positive. The rehearsal of the three first acts "looked with golden promise." Bulwer brought in his revision of the ending of the fourth act, which "was a great improvement." He apologized to Miss Faucit for having spoken to her sharply: "he is a gentlemanly-minded man." Forster confided to Macready that the play was to be dedicated to him: "he has merited it." On this day Macready even settled part of his own quarrel with Webster by renewing his engagement for the next season.

The rehearsal of November 25 was largely devoted to installing the new scene of the fourth act and all looked well for an early opening night.

But just then an unforeseeable tragedy struck. For nearly two months Macready's infant son Henry had been extremely ill and fast growing worse. Then, during the night of November 25, his little girl Joan,[31] who had sickened only a day or two before, suddenly died. Preparations for the play were halted, of course. Macready wrote out his grief, day after day, for hours at a time, in his diary. Meanwhile Forster appears to have managed the professional negotiations for both his friends.

223. FORSTER TO BULWER, *Lincolns Inn Fields, Friday morning,* [*November 27, 1840*]

I sought you at Fenton's yesterday. Poor Macready had had a dreadful blow. Little Henry continues very ill, and he has suddenly lost darling little Joan — my god daughter — who died yesterday morning. She had had an attack of jaundice, but was recovering and in good spirits, and none of us dreamt of danger. I do not know the final particulars of the sudden change. Though I was at the house the whole of yesterday I could not ask them. I loved her more than I can express — and am suffering deeply — but poor Macready & Mrs Macready and all the house — You can guess their state, with the life of another child hanging on so frail a thread. God help us all, & grant that that may be saved — since it would in some sort comfort Macready in his affliction. I will write again tonight, and tell you how he is.

Webster was with me yesterday in the highest sorrow, as may be well supposed, on his own account. He was quite sensible however of all the proprieties of the case, and at once adopted my suggestion & issued a placard — stating that a severe affliction in Macready's family would prevent his appearance that night, and that the Comedy was necessarily deferred till "Mr Macready can resume his professional duties." This will not be, of course, till after the funeral. (It is also in papers today.)

Meanwhile the poor dear Comedy can afford to wait so long. I have [entreated] Mr Webster to keep his actors to their duty, and shall instruct Wilmott tonight to have two or three strict rehearsals to keep up the knowledge of Macready's business. Pray send me a line to Saunders & Otley, as authority to go to them and restrain the publication. . . .

224. BULWER TO FORSTER, [*November 27, 1840*]

How shocked I am at the news you give me — It is impossible for me to say — It is a blow so dreadful that it is impossible to offer him any consolation. I

---

[31] Harriet Joanna Macready, born July 13, 1837; died November 25, 1840.

know not what to write to him on the subject.— As for the Play — I cannot bear the thought of the pain it must give him at anytime to appear, in a Comedy with his heart full of grief — Poor Fellow — & poor Mrs Macready — My heart bleeds for them — I shall go up to Town to enquire after them. . . .

225. BULWER TO FORSTER, *Monday,* [*November 30, 1840*]

> Please let me know where
> the Macreadys are

I was stupid eno' in the distress I felt in writing to Macready to direct Cambridge instead of Clarence Terrace & as I sent the letter by my Mother's servant — the house was not found out — & the letter written on Friday not delivered till yesterday when I called. I was much grieved by the answer I received as to poor M^rs M's health. I do hope they have Locock[32] for the Baby. He is so *very* clever. I was speaking on the subject yesterday to a person most skilled in Children who s^d infantine fever was best cured by a change of air & who seemed to think the Regents Park too low and damp for one suffering from that complaint.

I shall go to Knebworth Wednesday. W^d you like to dine here tomorrow. Let me know in the morning if you can. If not — I leave the Play in your hands. Whenever it is acted pray see my dear fellow — to some previous rehearsal —. The actors will run down like clockweights into all their bad first habits. I don't have any heart to see the Play the first night — When I know how poor Macready will be suffering.

226. MACREADY TO BULWER, *5 Clarence Terrace, Regent's Park, November 30, 1840*

From my heart of hearts I thank you for your cordial expressions of condolence with sufferings, which amid all the probable misfortunes of my life I had not prepared myself for.— I have lost what cannot be replaced: — the want of what I have loved as so sweet and precious will only end with life itself. But under this grievous infliction I have had much to be grateful for in the warm sympathy of dear and valued friends, and in the devotion of my most amiable and admirable wife, who has been a pattern of fortitude and affection beyond all praise. I thank God, her health has not yet suffered under what she has so beautifully borne, and if, as we now begin more confidently to hope, our dear little boy should be mercifully spared to us, I trust she will pass through her trials without the injury to her health, that might have been feared.

I could never satisfy myself, my dear Bulwer — my most kind and excellent friend, with any words, in which I might try to convey my acknowledgments for your letter.— My heart has thanked you, and will ever thank you for it.

With a lasting recollection of this most valued instance of your regard I am always your most grateful and attached friend.

---

[32] Sir Charles Locock (1799-1875), physician, first accoucheur to Queen Victoria in 1840.

By December 3, though the infant Henry was still in grave danger, rehearsals were resumed, and plans were laid, subject to revision on the doctor's advice, to open *Money* on Tuesday, December 8.

227. BULWER TO FORSTER, *Knebworth, [December 5, 1840]*

I am very much obliged by your note.— But you say nothing of poor little Henry's health — If better or no — I earnestly trust that your silence on this head & the reappointment of the Play prove that he is better. I find my Mother is coming to town, so that I have fixed to leave here the very day the Play is acted — in that case may look in — you will therefore be good eno' to secure at all events for yourself the Box Webster was to give me — in case I join you — I enclose some hint for the rehearsal,— one of which I made to you before — But the late disastrous events must have put it out of our heads

If poor Henry is really *still* in danger or gets worse — I should be strong agst the production of the Play on Tuesday.— It must be a new drain on Macready's mind, when it must require relaxation. And you might urge on Webster this plain truth — that if (w^h God forbid) any new affliction sh^d befall — the withdrawal of the Play after a few nights must be a necessary consequence & an irrecoverable blow to it. I do not, Heavens witness think of this selfish view of the Case myself — But it might have strength with Webster — in case he wishes any indelicate or inconsiderate hurry with the Play. I want Macready's feelings to be consulted above all things.

228. BULWER TO FORSTER, *Knebworth, Sunday, [December 6, 1840]*

Much as your letter pained & dismayed me, I cannot say that I was unprepared for it. An Illness so long in one so young — is always most seriously alarming & I rather share your melancholy opinion than that of the D^{rs}

With regard to the play. My anxious wish is to defer it at all events, unless (which I cannot expect) — the poor Infant sh^d be actually out of danger —. It must be a terrible drag to Macready — it must destroy all pleasure of success in myself — & Webster must see that if after 4 or 5 nights the play is withdrawn from whatever cause, an irremediable damp is thrown upon it —

Unless I hear from you on Tuesday Morning, not only that the play is to be acted, but that the Child is greatly better, I shall stay here a day or two longer. — Pray therefore write on Monday or as you are now in so good an understanding with Webster, & know my wishes I feel confident you will not let the play be acted unless under the most favorable change.

I have settled all about the publication with Saunders to whom if postponed you need only send a line to say "Put off the Publication."

I have sent some days back, Devereux to Mr Whiting.

God bless & strengthen this poor family — & may it after all turn out better than we dare to hope.

229. FORSTER TO BULWER, *Monday, December 7, [1840]*

The Comedy *is* to be produced tomorrow. So *pray do not fail to be in town.* It is very important every way. I shall expect you in the box (which is still reserved for you, & which I shall occupy alone in the Course of the Evening.

Dear little Henry has had a great change for the better. . . .

I have had a long interview with Elliotson[33] this afternoon (his physician — who has done more good to him than all the rest) and put the whole case to him as a matter of business as strongly as I could. His answer was decisive — that the comedy should be produced by all means. Macready is convinced of the expediency of doing it too, and if you had seen him at the rehearsal today you would have no fear of his doing it all justice. The very necessity of Exertion seems to give him greater means of responding to it — & his performance was never finer than this morning. I distrust Webster in Graves, but have no serious fear of any kind. The Comedy is sure to be a great success. The scenery & appointments are really first rate. We had the carpets down this morning.

Macready returned to the public in *Werner* on Monday the seventh, and after a final rehearsal on Tuesday the run of *Money* began. Macready was of course "depressed and low-spirited," and though determined to do his best, he felt that he "wanted lightness, self-possession, and, in the serious scenes, truth. I was not good — I feel it." He noticed that in the last scene Miss Faucit "had quite the advantage over me. This was natural."

The Haymarket playbill of Tuesday, October 8, gives star billing to Macready and Helen Faucit, and calls attention to the "entirely new Scenery, Dresses, Furniture, and Appurtenances." The scenery is credited to the house artists, Mr. G. Morris and Assistants, but especially to "Mr. Charles Marshall (*of the Theatres Royal Covent Garden and Drury Lane*)," Marshall being the "much better painter" whom Forster had referred to in his letter (218) of November 10. The dramatis personae was as follows:

Lord Glossmore	MR. F. VINING
Sir John Vesey, Bart.	MR. STRICKLAND
Sir Frederick Blount	MR. W. LACY
Mr. Benjamin Stout, M. P.	MR. DAVID REES
Evelyn	MR. MACREADY
Graves	MR. WEBSTER
Captain Dudley Smooth	MR. WRENCH
Sharpe, *the Lawyer*	MR. WALDRON
Toke, *the Butler*	MR. OXBERRY
Flat	MR. WORRELL
Green	MR. T. F. MATHEWS
Tabouret, *Upholsterer*	MR. HOWE
Frantz, *Tailor*	MR. O. SMITH
Mc'Finch, *Silversmith*	MR. GOUGH
Grub, *Publisher*	MR. CAULFIELD
Patent, *Coachmaker*	MR. CLARK

---

[33] Dr. John Elliotson (1791-1868), eminent physician who regularly attended the Macready family; was compelled in 1838 to give up his position as professor of medicine at University College for practising mesmerism.

Crimson, *Portrait Painter*..............................MR. GALLOT
Mc'Stucco, *Architect*................................MR. MORGUE
Kite, *Horse dealer*..................................MR. SANTER
Page to Sir John....................................MISS GROVE
Footmen......................MESSRS. BISHOP, GREEN, ENNIS, &c.
Members of the Club, Waiters, Servants, &c.
Lady Franklin......................................MRS. GLOVER
Georgina Vesey..................................MISS P. HORTON
Clara Douglas................................MISS HELEN FAUCIT

The Music of the evening consisted of Weber's Overture to *Preciosa* and Strauss's waltz, *Hommage à la Reine de la Grande Britagne.* The evening concluded with Mark Lemon's new farce called *Bob Short.*

Money was an instantaneous and immense success, and ran some eighty performances to the end of the Haymarket season. It deserved to succeed. Together with Boucicault's *London Assurance,* produced at Covent Garden only a few months later,[34] it is a rarely successful effort of its generation to rouse the Comic Muse from her long slumber. The basic idea of the play is that social success and for most men happiness depend upon "plenty of money." The story by which the idea is illustrated is that of a young man named Alfred Evelyn, who was a nobody when poor, but suddenly finds himself the center of a horde of friends and parasites when he accedes to an enormous fortune. In order to sift the true friends from the false, and also to determine which of two young ladies he had better marry, he pretends to have lost all his money by gambling. Such scenes as the reading of the will in the first act, the splendor of Evelyn's daily living in the second, the club life and the climactic gambling bout at Crockford's in the third, in the fourth act the ganging-up of tradesmen clamoring to have their accounts settled as Evelyn pretends to be bankrupt, and finally the revelation of the true heroine, Clara Douglas, who offers Evelyn her private fortune, and the unmasking of the false one, Georgina Vesey, who bolts and marries a fool — these scenes are firmly contrived, peopled with amusing contemporary types, and embedded in a sound comic structure. It should, perhaps alone of Bulwer's plays, have validity on the stage today.

During the long run of *Money* Macready has little to say about it, save to mention now and then that he had played it "well" or played it "feebly," or to label it "an ineffective, inferior part." Bulwer continued to tinker at it throughout December, submitting some principal alterations on December 23. At the instance of manager Webster, Macready applied to the Lord Chamberlain for a two months' extension of the Haymarket season, down to March 15.

230. BULWER TO FORSTER, [*December 10, 1840*]

After feasting with you, I have received 2 or 3 opinions touching the play — & as in Macready's state of mind I cannot intrude upon him — so easily as you — I communicate with you —

These opinions are unanimous in favour of the first *two* Acts — unanimous in finding fault with the last scene of Act 4.— They say (they all sat in the front of the House) — that there was something discordant in the bustle of the dinner scene — that the Actors generally were too noisy & not "genteel" eno'

---

[34] Dionysius Lardner Boucicault (1822-90), an actor and prolific dramatist. *London Assurance,* his first play in London, produced by Madame Vestris in March, 1841, was a great success.

about it — that they contrived to throw Evelyn (This is probably Stout) into too great a hurry & bustle — & that the effect of his Last — "Lend me 10£ &c was thereby lost.— They also say that that Scene seemed to them the most protracted. Their gathered opinion is that the Play wanted oil & glibness — & that even the Club Scene was too jerky & wanted the decorum of a fashionable Club — I suspect this to arise from the manner that Stout says Hush — he is to marry Sir John's Daughter & from the swaggering indignation of the Members at Sir John's saying a Perfect gang of them — Now I don't know how all this will go off tonight —. But with regard to the Club — if this is too violent — it is easily omitted —. Sir John saying as now to Glossmore & Blount — Arnt [sic] you ashamed of yourselves — His own Cousins — & they merely expostulating in dumb shew — omitting — "in a conspiracy a perfect gang of them — Indignation of Members & Stout's Hush he's to marry Sir John's daughter —

They all say Act. 5. was very good & their chief objections really seem to the 2 strongest Acts —

However all can better be judged tonight & tomorrow night. — If you hear how it goes off — pray let me know — of course it will be a thin House tonight —

Pray forgive this trouble —

231. BULWER TO FORSTER, [December 12, 1840]

I am exceedingly obliged by your kind note which gives much better news than I had expected — I have also to thank Blanchard for a very cordial & friendly note — & am greatly flattered by one just this moment received from Dickens.— I am laid up here by a violent attack on the Chest — as if I had swallowed a bag of Carpenter's tools — &. . . .

In regard to Websters Solicitation, I am unaware of the Etiquette's — whether to Chamberlain or Vice —. I know Mr Byng the Vice Chamberlain. — A very civil nice fellow, and if Webster likes w^d give him a note of introduction to him. He can then ask him the exact etiquette if he does not know it, & by putting the case well before him, get his interest with the Chamberlain, Ld Uxbridge who is his own brother in law —. . . .

232. BULWER TO FORSTER, 23 Bryanston St., Portman Sq., Tuesday morning, [December 15, 1840]

I cannot say how much obliged I am by your little volume upon Money in the Examiner[35] — It seems a little like the Immortal Bayes to compliment you on its style & manner — but I really must say that putting apart the pleasure I had in the partial praise — I had uncommon delight in the manner & spirit of the Criticism — I laughed much less heartily at any part of the Comedy itself than I did at your prophetic picture of Stout's ruin from the hour he

---

[35] Forster's review appeared in the Examiner on December 13.

became Benjamin — to Smooth — I envied you that most felicitous stroke — it ought to have been foreshadowed in the Comedy — it is one of those pieces of inspired knowledge in which Critics surpass the Author — I must have meant that Stout sh^d be ruined but by Jupiter I never exactly recollected it before — I was no less struck with the dim vision of Popkins that you have conjured up — It has really supplied me with an excellent idea should "the Public" ever find its way to the Boards — I think I see "the Public" Himself — after having been talked about like Popkins — after hearing of him — his grandeur & his wisdom & his power — & his wrongs & his rights, for 4 acts & ½ — yes I think towards the close of the 5th I see the folding doors at the back fly open, & "the Public" enter! — Confess that there is something very Aristophanic in the Notion — something that will remind you of the Demos of that great satirist — And yet — it came only into my head 5 minutes ago on reading your critique of the glimpse that was caught of Popkins.—

I went last night to the Haymarket with the intention of seeing the Play throughout — but tho' I was there at 7.— I could not get a place even in the slips & the private boxes were gone — So I went back again — However I am going this week with my brother.— I have an idea that a very slight touch — not above 4 lines might improve the end of Act 4.— by making Evelyn — propose at the last — to borrow of Stout!!! Which will give more zest to the father's violence.— I think they might be made irresistably comic — I want also to see the end of Act 2 on which I have written to Macready — . . .

I send to know how Macready's Boy is — What's your own opinion.

233. BULWER TO MACREADY, [*December 23*], *1840*

I send you your last speech Act 4 corrected — also the additions for Glossmore & Stout. May I inquire if Power is positively engaged for March when the House reopens. In that case I think we could ensure the permanence of the play — by altering Sir John for an Irish Blarneying fellow by Power. And I think I see by this a great effect for you in a new 4th Act — where a scene might come in, in which these 2 men have a thorough sharp Wits' encounter which shall take in the other? — in which there might be great fun & great interest.

[P.S.] I hope to hear new good news of the Invalid.

234. MACREADY TO BULWER, *Clarence Terrace, December 24,* [*1840*]

The alterations shall be attended to, and I think will improve the effect of the play. I understand that Power certainly returns in March, but I must refer you to Mr Webster for all information about him; as he is, I believe, singular in his view of characters, and wishes to be so in the pieces, that he takes part in. You must not hazard an expenditure of material without something like a security that it will make a return.

I called at Lord Lansdowne's this morning, but found he had left town for the Holidays.— I very much fear the Chamberlain will shut us up.—

I will speak to Mrs Glover. I am happy to tell you, with our united thanks, that our little invalid is going on very hopefully.[36]

235. BULWER TO MACREADY, *23 Bryanston St., December 31, 1840*

I congratulate you heartily on the improvement of your dear boy — such news gives me heartfelt delight.

So you have got the other month — I tremble for the awful length to which Money ought now to run. But as this precludes all future extended alterations, so we can only make the present Plot as clear & tangible as possible. I am glad therefore to hear that the alterations succeed — especially at the end of Act 4. I hear from many, before hypercritical, how much improved the play is — a large party were enchanted with you and the whole thing the other night. Still the one point of Evelyn borrowing from Sir John requires explanation & the enclosed few words (the last trouble I will give you) sets that right and will, by drawing attention to your dialogue with Sir John, serve perhaps to bring out some little of that Comedy which Mr. Strickland so resolutely buries. As the words are so few, I hope you will forgive them.

At the end of Act in your closing speech will you remember to say, you "WOULD" refuse me 10£ to spend on benevolence. Not you refuse me. The *would* is important.

---

[36] Henry Macready never properly recovered, but developed epileptic tendencies, and died at the age of eighteen.

chapter six

1841
1851

A Decade of Trial

Money was the last of Bulwer's plays which Macready performed, but it was by no means the end of Bulwer's experiments in dramatic writing nor of Macready's interest in them. Intensively during the next two years and sporadically thereafter, until Macready's retirement in 1851, negotiations between them went on.

A week and a half after the opening of *Money,* Bulwer swore to Macready, apparently piqued by some of the supporting actors, that he would "never write another play." But as early as January 6, 1841, Macready records that "Forster read me a sketch of characters, for a comedy by Bulwer." The sketch is preserved among the Bulwer-Forster correspondence in the Knebworth Archives (identifiable by its references to the character of Graves, in *Money,* and to the actor Tyrone Power, who had not yet sailed from America to his death in the Atlantic); it is curious for its effort to find a character suitable to Macready's personality and style.

236. BULWER MEMORANDUM

—— : Comedy : ——

Mr. Formal . . . . Macready

Mrs Formal . . . . Mrs Glover

Sophy, their daughter.   Priscilla Horton

Sir Francis O'Grady, a gay — dissipated — devil may care — but good hearted Irish Gentleman rich & the fashion in his way — a sort of Waterford — in love with Sophy & loved by her — always shocking the proprieties of Mr. Formal. . . . . Power

Mr. Jonathan Johnson — a decorous, sober, hypocritical suitor, whom Formal prefers. . . . . Wrench

Dr. Goodenough — an optimist, who thinks every thing for the best — the reverse of Graves — a friend of Formal .... Webster character for .... Rees

Character of Formal —

Very methodical & precise — severe outwardly — but full of the milk of human nature — affects to be severe to his daur — but doats upon her.— She very playful — & gay — afraid of her Father — but fond of him — Formal's humour comes out at first in his minute almost old maidish precision in small things —. w^d not stir out without his gloves & cane for the world — has a high regard for his character — for xternal respectability & decorum — very clever — but always liable to be imposed upon by the appearances he respects — the *pathos* of his character which I expect will be very great indeed — comes out Act IV. when his daur appears to have run away & be [*sic*] seduced by Sir Francis — Then he seems broken down — out of all his formalities &c His little habits and primnesses all forgotten — small touches of that kind — half comic, sh^d be very pathetic: Something it ought to be of Sterne's style — The *Force* of the character will break out either End of Act 4 or Act 5 — when he sallies out to find Sophy & meets the supposed Seducer — This if the story c^d bring it well round ought to be most startling — It sh^d be morally what Richelieu rising from his supposed Dying state is physically — Formal springs up from the chair of his *Mind*.

Mrs Formal is a good woman — very fond of Formal — but bullies him — He submitting to be slightly henpecked — ostensibly out of the respectability of the practice which he sanctions by historical precedent in reality out of kindness — he liking her Mrs F. more stern than he is — Won't hear of ever seeing her daur again when she goes off.— Her anger rouses Formal into passion agst *her* — this will make a fine scene —

Have no idea of the story other than that Sophy teased by her parents to marry Jonson — meets Sir Francis to wish him farewell — & he hurries her off.— He really means at first to seduce her.— And at the beginning of Act 5 — Audience must think that, to give effect to Formal's situation: — But — his own good heart & her innocence turn him from this.

Macready, probably not flattered by the sketch, "thought very poorly" of it. On the same occasion Forster revived the old subject of Cromwell, and Macready resisted that idea also: "that I think beyond all but Shakespeare." Yet Forster appears to have reported a more positive response than Macready intended.

237. BULWER TO FORSTER, *Knebworth*, [*January 7, 1841*]

. . . I am much pleased that Macready prefers Cromwell — But I can hardly think of the Plot till I get your papers which are at the Cottage.

But the great thing we must try & do is to get up a tender interest. How? — I think of giving him a Fool, as he had, who ought to be effective.

238. BULWER TO MACREADY, *January 7, 1841*

I am delighted that you prefer Cromwell — the other tho' containing a good character wanted lightness & brilliancy for a Comedy. In Cromwell, however, there are immense difficulties which with time, thought & patience may be overcome. Those difficulties are the Creation of strong interest. I send you a ROUGH sketch — Act 4 in it is the weakest. It would not do to begin till one has thoroughly matured the Plot — & got one clear, living, pervading interest. At present that connected with the daughter is not domestic eno', & her connection with Vane is too shadowy & subtle. Can we devise anything closer? Act 1. 3. & 5 as sent would have strong effect, but the pervading interest of the whole is wanting.

Shakespeare alone & he perhaps scarcely in the present day, can make History without love have universal & warm interest. Here, if we can connect a strong interest in the power & struggles of the . . . with some absolute tale or sympathy from first to last of the Dramatic kind — these should do very well. But the last is necessary. See well if from the Chaos I send anything can be struck & the cords round the heart drawn tighter. If not — it is best to abandon this Historical view altogether — & perhaps conceive a new plot of the time distinct from History — in which Cromwell may appear as an Agent, but not embracing his death or his great historical struggles. — Richelieu is somewhat done in this way, tho' there the story happily connects him with real events & characters, & we have an absolute Episode in his life (in the packet) to work on — & this made the Art & Success of the play: — I could not commence this till I saw all the scenes before me like a map. I shall hope to hear the best possible news of the poor little patient. I have ordered Saunders to send Mrs. Macready a copy of my novel. With kind regards to her and Miss Macready & best & most heartfelt wishes for the season believe me

[P.S.] Are the Houses *very* bad?

I have no copy of the enclosed. Could the Haymarket have the *mise en scene* of Acts 3 & 4? If I had "a Fool," who could act it — Miss Horton would remind the audience too much of the Fool in Lear — tho' the character would be very different. Besides, my Fool would have strong biting power. He ought to be deformed & have a hump. He is a dog that snarls & bites — but has a Dog's heart full of love for his Master. I *know* if I could get the actor, that I could make him most effective to Cromwell. But there is not a man I can think of, to be both pathetic & humorous.

Could Miss Horton be *made to do?*[1]

239. BULWER TO FORSTER, [*January 7, 1841*]

I enclosed to My. a programme of Cromwell tho' not more detailed than the one to you — In fact I cannot yet see my way through the Woman part of it. I don't much like the Vane & Claypole connection, for while eno' to

---

[1] An almost incredible question, since Macready's reason for casting Priscilla Horton as the Fool in *Lear* was that he conceived the Fool as a "fragile, hectic, beautiful-faced, half-idiot-looking boy." *Diaries,* January 5, 1838.

offend one's verisimilitude sympathies it cannot be strong eno' to have any hold on an Audience — There ought now a days to be a positive story   If I had *that* it would be all safe For I will answer for 3 Great & 3 true & telling characters in Cromwell Vane & the Fool, if I am permitted to have the last. But neither character, situation nor Dialogue suffice without more or less of an absolute Tale — And tho' many Writers can afford to lose the Audience, if backed up by a strong belief in the literary closet merit — you know that with all the Press Barkers at me my hold is the Audience & the Audience only — I don't want to fritter away Cromwell to a love interest — but still there must be some —. Could one do any thing with Henry Cromwell — & his death — one might claim him fairly for romantic invention. . . .

Will you allow me to hope for an early *precis* of your new plan for Cromwell —

[P. S.] You will find my programme at M's — Meanwhile I am again enlarging myself with Schiller[2] — A man gets bigger ideas on an Ocean — on a Mountain & more than all on a great Writers Soul!

The sketch or "programme" Bulwer sent is missing. Macready's private response to it is iron-hard resistance. "Received a letter from Bulwer with his sketch of a play for Cromwell, which I do not approve; it has no entirety, no object, and Bulwer is not the poet for historical scenes."

240. MACREADY TO BULWER, 5 *Clarence Terrace, Regent's Park,* *January 9, 1841*

I do not see how a beginning, middle, and end, is to be made of Cromwell, except in an Historical Play à la Shakespeare, or Schiller, which would be a fearful hazard. — The only way to use the character would be upon the plan of Richelieu — the various parts of his character working out an end, on which another interest, interwoven with that of himself, would depend. — Fine scenes strung together will never, in their result, satisfy you: for the effect on the public — i.e. in the theatre, will not be lasting. — The scope of the work must be dramatic effect; the History must be the happy accident, that heightens every scene. — I do not entirely agree with you that love is indispensable as a means of interest — I think the Oedipus tyrannus would be even now a play of rivetting interest — I think even the Philoctetes would have great interest. Did you see Sylla?[3] — *Query?* — is not there a hint? — Have you it? — I have, & can send it? — I merely mention it as furnishing a hint of the *position* of a man in power and those opposed to or depending on it. — It seems to me like the tracing of a noble and sure foundation — for Cromwell, or any other strongly featured character in power. — "I pause for

[2] In 1844 Bulwer published two volumes of *The Poems and Ballads of Schiller, translated, With a Brief Sketch of Schiller's Life.*

[3] Lucius Cornelius Sulla (138-78 B.C.), Roman general, consul, and dictator notorious for his cruelty. The tragedy of *Sylla* (Paris, 1821) by Étienne de Jouy (1764-1846), a study of Napoleonism, was played by Talma.

a reply", before giving further thought to the subject, for this has laid strong hold on me. — Our houses are to me wonderful, under the circumstances of no afterpieces, and *such* weather: — they have nightly advanced through the week — Thursday was a capital house & last night very good, but the wonder is how anyone leaves a fire under this temperature.

Our little Henry is progressing most satisfactorily — Mrs Macready joins her best thanks with mine and with sincere regards I am ever and always [P. S.] Pray regard my thought of Sylla — as merely the marking out places for scaffolding or the mere outline of the foundations of a building.

Oh — how bad — how atrociously bad — are Strickland & Webster! —

241. Bulwer to Forster, [*January 10, 1841*]

. . . I have heard from Macready putting an end to Cromwell in an Historical point of view — but leaving it open in the Romantic — like Richelieu — Will you thank him for his letter & say that I have thought of another character for him — a Comedy — What think you of it yourself — The subject of the Comedy — perhaps the title "Every Man, His price?" — Macready's character Sir Robert Walpole:[4] — The character itself may range in the high ground of Comedy — This skill in suiting the temptations of his corruption to the various characters of the piece would be comic — His thoro' contempt of the Honesty of Mankind — his contempt of poetry & literary men — his readiness, strong talents for hard business — his hardy short way of dealing with mankind — are all fine individualities — He is relieved by the one strong master purpose of his public life which must pervade the play — the keeping out Fanaticism & Despotism — in other words — the Stuarts — It may be placed at the time most interesting — in the midst of the Pretenders Plots on which the incidents may turn — & as at one period they were perilous, & but for Walpole (Note the year 49) might have been successful — dignity & truth may be here given. As one may take more liberties with Walpole's family & private life than Cromwell's I don't doubt that the anecdotes of the day may furnish me some subject of domestic interest — affording Comedy — & yet grave sympathy — I have not an idea of the plot or of one scene yet. But if he likes the character I will look seriously into the History & the elements it may afford when I come to Town. Macready doesn't like the Dress of that time. But his own would be very good with the dark crimson velvet — the Star & the Garter. Tell him I w^d write on this but as yet have nothing to say beyond the mere character.

When Forster read this to Macready the next day, Macready was delighted. "I caught at it," he exclaims. But, though Bulwer himself called on the twenty-ninth to discuss the subject of Walpole, nothing could develop of it in the immediate future. Parliament had opened, and, as Bulwer had written Forster on January 26, "it will be

---

[4] Here begins the long progress of a play eventually written in the 1860's, and published but never performed: *Walpole; or, Every Man has his Price. A Comedy in Rhyme, in three Acts* (London, 1869).

'rates riddles & botheration' for some time at least —.   Adieu Comedy — farewell Schiller! — No more cakes & Ale."

242. BULWER TO MACREADY, [*February 18, 1841*]

1st. Let me thank you for telling me to see the earlier part of Money. I saw your second Act last Tuesday. It was indeed admirably improved. In the scene with Graves especially. I still think that, however, you w^d make a much greater effect in the story of the Sizar, if you wound up & clenched the moral of it with the few words in the text — after career of a life blasted, "That is the difference between Rich & Poor. It takes a whirlwind to move the one, a breeze can uproot the other."

2ndly. May I ask you whether the enclosed refers to the Shakespeare Club you asked me to enter & if there would be any objection to my being a Vice-president at the Dinner. I ask this because the name of the Editor of the Satirist is in the List of Stewards — otherwise pour des raisons I wish to belong to the Dinner.[5]

3dly. Will you kindly get the Prompter to copy out for me the few alterations I made in "Money"? — Clara's words about the old nurse. Act I, your semi-explanation with Smooth, Act 3 & end of Act II, & observations to Graves, Act 5 — I am correcting a collected Edition of the Plays for Press & want it as soon as I can have it.

243. BULWER TO MACREADY, *Hertford St., Wednesday, [March 10, 1841]*

A Mr Richardson, the geologist & translator of Körner,[6] has sent me the accompanying Ms. of an afterpiece to transmit to you. He says it is a translation of a piece that makes the greatest effect in Germany.

I have looked over it — there is a great deal of fun in the idea, but it evidently wants a great deal of curtailment & a great deal of dressing up for the English Stage; in fact it should be put into the hands of a practised farce writer. Howbeit at all events you will do me the favour I know to send a kindly answer to the Author if declined altogether. His address is Geological Department British Museum.

244. MACREADY TO BULWER, *5 Clarence Terrace, Regent's Park,* *March 20, 1841*

I have promised to ask you if you are aware of the scene, that has sug-

---

[5] Matthews dated this letter October, 1840. On February 19, 1841, Macready recorded that he "wrote to Bulwer trying to dissuade him from dining at the Shakesperian Club Festival, of which that *scoundrel,* Gregory, editor of the *Satirist,* is the head." Barnard Gregory (1796-1852), editor from 1831 to 1849 of *The Satirist, or Censor of the Times,* was a libeler and blackmailer; he aspired to the stage but was hissed off because of his unsavory reputation.

[6] On March 18, Macready "dined with Bulwer and a Mr. ——————— of the British Museum an awful geological dust and bore." Karl Theodor Körner (1791-1813), poet, author of war lyrics called *Leier und Schwert.*

gested the enclosed — and if you recognize the subject, if you will honor the hand that traced it, by keeping it? —[7]

I have it from her in my instructions to ask you, if you will give Mrs Macready & myself the pleasure of your company at dinner on Tuesday March 23rd at a quarter before seven o'clock.

I further expect I shall have some news — important at least — to tell you in a very short time: — whether it is matter for me to rejoice in or no, only time can disclose.[8]

245. BULWER TO MACREADY, *March [21], 1841*

Lady Morgan[9] shewed the same design you so kindly sent me & I admired it extremely, so that I am peculiarly delighted to receive the drawing which I shall highly prize, nor the less so from having seen, I believe, the young Lady — with whose handsome face I was much struck. Pray present to her my best thanks, & my sincere appreciation of the Compliment with which she has distinguished my work.

I shall be most happy to dine with you, & hear your news which I hope turns on D[r] Lane. I saw L[d] Lansdowne last night who s[d] he had fixed tomorrow for our Committee on Mrs. Siddons &c.[10] — but c[d] not tell me the place or Hour.

Will you let me know?

---

[7] The Macready's had that day met a "Miss Meyer . . . a sweet girl." The enclosure was a drawing by her of a scene in one of Bulwer's works. The young lady was Eugenia Mayer (1814-1904), stepdaughter of Col. John Gurwood (the editor of Wellington's orders and despatches). She married William Brett, later Viscount Esher.

[8] Macready's "news" was his plan to take over Drury Lane for the next season.

[9] Sydney Owenson (1783?-1859), poet and novelist; after 1812, Lady Morgan.

[10] The "Committee on Mrs. Siddons" refers to a project which Macready labored at for at least sixteen years — to have a suitable memorial to Mrs. Siddons erected in Westminster Abbey. As early as 1833, two years after her death, he secured the promise of the great sculptor, Sir Francis Legatt Chantrey (1781-1842) to do a bust of her and negotiated with the Dean of Westminster to receive it. The Garrick Club agreed to sponsor the project, but in 1838 Macready withdrew from membership and lost that backing. His interest was roused again in November, 1840, when Samuel Rogers told him that Mrs. Siddons had said at the installation of John Philip Kemble's statue, "I hope, Mr. Rogers, that one day justice will be done to women." He began corresponding with influential persons in society and the arts to form a committee for the work. On March 22, 1841 (the day Bulwer here refers to), this Committee met at Exeter Hall under the chairmanship of the Marquis of Lansdowne, and passed resolutions to the desired end, including the proposition that the bust, or statue, be paid for by public subscription.

Macready worked very hard at seeking subscribers, but without much success. Failing this, in May of 1843 he persuaded his actors at Drury Lane to perform one night without salary in aid of the fund. Meanwhile, in 1842, Chantrey had died, and a sculptor named Thomas Campbell was asked to do the work. His first essay was a bust — presumably the one now in the National Portrait Gallery. Macready saw this bust and liked it, but the Dean of Westminster declined to allow a niche to be cut for it. Campbell then was commissioned to render a full-length statue. In February, 1846, the cast of it was placed in the position Chantrey had designated many years before, and all concerned approved it. In May, 1848, Macready staged another benefit performance for the cause

Early in April of 1841 Macready agreed with the proprietors of Drury Lane to take that theatre for the ensuing season.

246. MACREADY TO BULWER, *Birmingham, April 17, 1841*

Occupation has crowded so upon the event that I have not had time to tell you until everyone has heard of it, that cares about it — that I have agreed to take a lease of Drury Lane Theatre — you will say of course, quod factum felix faustumque sit!

Think of me therefore ever in your prayers, and remember that you are in the ship with Jason. Pray canvass for me & get me some Siddons names — I am hardworked, but have been very successful in my endeavours attirer la foule.—

"Remember me!"

Bulwer, in early June, proposed a fusion of two ideas for a comedy which he had thought of separately and earlier: *The Public,* which he had first mentioned from Germany on September 26, 1840; and *Walpole,* which had come into his mind in January.

247. BULWER TO MACREADY, *9 Pall Mall East, Saturday, [June 6?], 1841*

When do you come to town? I am delighted at what I hear of your prospects at Drury Lane.

Being seized with a profound disgust of both parties in politics — with the one for playing at fast & loose with the Credit and Finances of the Country, by daring as responsible ministers to leave them at the uncertain mercy of the 3 Party cries they call a Budget, & with the other side for not being either good eno' to support or bad eno' to excuse all measures that tend to keep them out — I turn once more to the Fair Life of the Ideal. Have you any idea for me? Will you give me any story or sketch for *"The Public"* A comedy — with Walpole for the hero? I am thinking of the experiment of a comedy in verse (Hexameter). Start not! I think I see my way to great effects in it. It is the very diction for epigram & wit & its suddenness as presented by an unexpected rhyme is dramatic & histrionic. But it would require rather an Artificial period like Walpole's and must be only adapted to the very highest school of Comedy. Give me a human interest & a good plot, and I promise you something sterling in that way. But I have no dramatic invention.

What a delightful book is Fleury's Memoirs The French Stage![11] It is the Gil Blas of Biography.

---

and in June Lord Lansdowne reconvened the Committee, but the appeal for funds brought poor response. At last, in September of 1849, Macready had the satisfaction of viewing the statue in its proper place — a dear satisfaction, for he had to make up nearly £200 of deficit from his own pocket. In our time, unfortunately, the effectiveness of the statue is completely ruined by the ugly clutter of other memorials that have been crowded around it.

[11] Abraham-Joseph Bénard, known as Fleury (1751-1822), an actor of the Comédie Française. His *Mémoires,* 6 vols. (Paris, 1835-38), were translated in abridged form by Theodore Hook as *The French Stage and the French People,* 2 vols. (London, 1841).

248. MACREADY TO BULWER, *Adelphi Hotel, Liverpool, June 7, 1841*

Shakespeare is always right — "There *is* some soul of goodness in things evil" — and I shall be more confirmed in my faith, if the miserable and selfish juggling of our politicians turn you from "all meaner things" to your proper destiny — to help and cheer your fellow-men in their improving progress. — I think great and salutary truths have very rarely been widely circulated by politicians — Let us look at some, which are made the texts of one party, and never even considered, in consequence, by another. — Let us have more Students, more such books as England & the English[12] — more novels, more plays — and no longer "to party give up what was meant for mankind". — How gladly shall I give my ruminations to the subject you start! — I do not exactly see my march with six feet, but I have confidence in Caesar. To dare is so often to do; and you must see much, before you would commit yourself to a hazardous experiment. — You will be sorry to hear that I am: — and have been very unwell: — I am over-worked, and must have some relaxation as my only chance of re-establishment. This I must have, if I *buy* it — a mode of obtaining goods the most repugnant to my feelings. — But it will be a delightful occupation for me to revolve the miseries & subsequent happenings of some creatures of Walpole, and perhaps some one thought may turn out a track towards your plot. — I think our company will be solidly good — capable of doing very well what we shall attempt. I have not read Fleury — merely seen extracts, and been amused with the narrow limits of the world, in which his mind moves, though they contained part of Voltaire. Could he have believed, that there was not a Theatre in Heaven? — I hope nothing will allure you back to low ambition & the pride of things — it is not through politics that the great work of the world's improvement is to be effected: — they only retard it — at least do not, as they ought, advance it.

Did you ever read Vanbrugh's Confederacy?[13] What humour — reckless fun — point — situation, and utter absence of all approach to morality! — If he had a moral purpose before him in what he wrote, he would have been our first comic poet, I think. —

Perhaps I may see you in town next week: — if I am at all pressed by work at the Haymarket, which I do not anticipate, I must put myself into my physician's hands, who, I know, will send me to the sea — and then I will give myself quite up to the subject of Walpole & the Public.

I blush for Rachel[14] — yet wish so much you had seen her *before her fall* — she was such a beautiful thing to see, believing in her as all did. —

Don't let them make you a Cabinet Minister, or spoil you in any way.

---

[12] Macready refers to Bulwer's *England and the English*, 2 vols. (London, 1833), and *The Student: A Series of Papers*, 2 vols. (London, 1835).

[13] Sir John Vanbrugh (1664-1726), the dramatist and architect. *The Confederacy*, an adaptation from the French, was produced in 1705.

[14] Rachel (born Élizabeth Félix; 1821-58), the French actress. She was at this time playing her first London engagement to almost universal critical acclaim, and she was

249. BULWER TO MACREADY, *105 Piccadilly, June, 1841*

It is, I find, quite hopeless to attempt getting y^r brother under the gallery during the Want of Confidence discussion. Every place has been bespoken many days & you know that the accommodation for strangers is considerably curtailed this year. But I enclose him an order for the gallery, where, if he go early, he will be just as well off. I have left the date blank, & he may fill it up either for Tuesday or Thursday (I have given away my order for Wednesday). If the debate last 3 days, Thursday will be the best day.

In the elections about the end of June, Bulwer was, somewhat surprisingly, unseated. In a note to Forster on July 9 he speaks of his relief to be out of Parliament, and wonders "Will Macready ever think of my Play." To Macready he announced himself ready for the theatre again.

250. BULWER TO MACREADY, *Craven Cottage, Friday,* [*July 9, 1841*][15]

Disengaged, perforce from the Political realities — that thou despisest — not unjustly — Behold me a-pluming my winglets for the Ideal.— If thou hast not yet thought of Walpole & Comedy — thou wilt find me soon lost in the highest Air of Empyreal Tragedy —. Wherefore, look to it & in thy capacity of Manager — forget not thy humbler duties of Prompter!

Thou hast never answered me touching Miss Villiers,[16] Discourteous & ungallant as thou art — Wilt thou now see her & where & when? — What days art thou & thy Family disengaged — so that I may fix one for meeting here while flowers yet bloom & the short lived strawberry yet buries its blushing bosom in the pure embraces of the Cream? —

251. MACREADY TO BULWER, *5 Clarence Terrace, Regent's Park, July 10, 1841*

If I was before disgusted with politics, I am not likely to be reconciled to that enlightening science after these elections. I wished to write to you, but as I could only tell you what you might have guessed, that indignation and regret has been echoed all around me at the self-stultifying conduct of the Lincoln Electors, I thought any mention of the annoying subject might have been de trop.— Well — I cannot help thinking that Guy Fawkes' reform of Parliament the best, when such sages as Col Sibthorpe [*sic*] — Captn Polhill, Charles Barry Baldwin — &c. &c. are returned as our legislators[17] — Oh C [*illegible*] and also the &c! —

---

the rage of society. Macready held a dinner for her on May 9, when there was "but one feeling of admiration and delight through the whole party." Queen Victoria entertained her at Windsor and honored her with gifts, including 15,000 francs and a bracelet inscribed *From Victoria to Rachel*. Rachel had indeed "fallen," and Macready had apparently caught some whisper of it. The gossip about the amorous liaisons (with Dr. Louis Véron, the Prince de Joinville, and others) did not become general until later.

[15] Original in the Library of the University of Illinois.

[16] Miss Villiers was apparently an aspirant to the stage, but is not identifiable.

[17] Colonel Charles de Laet Waldo Sibthorp (1783-1855), a notoriously reactionary Tory, who defeated Bulwer as M.P. for Lincoln.

Footnote 17 continued on page 198.

I have not been neglectful in my search for subject — but I have been ill, and very hardly worked. — An incident in Victor Hugo's Ruy [*illegible*][18] seemed to me capable of suggesting a good comic situation — La Calomnie[19] I have read again, and I think it very effective — I do not know, whether it is at all suggestive. — I must get a pile of papers off this table, and employ myself singly on the subject of a plot, before I can hope to think of any result.

I am here alone at present — My whole clan are at Eastbourne regaining the flesh and health they had lost. — M[rs] Macready comes home for a week on Monday — on which day and Wednesday I am hampered with Drury Lane appointments. — I shall be delighted to spend any day — free to both of us — in strolling over your beautiful lawn and, not "killing," but, creating "characters." I do not exactly know my days of Haymarket labor, but will learn.

You accuse me unjustly in regard to Miss Villiers: — I sent my Prime Minister Serle to bring me all needful intelligence about her, and I shall be too glad to find her bearing out Mr. Loaden's report. —

It would be most desirable to fix soon upon a subject, that you might have time to work it in your mind, and surpass what has been already done. — Be sure it is one of my most anxious thoughts, and I will very soon give myself exclusively to it.

I must let you know what we have been able to muster in shape of company, that we may not be over-tasked.

252. BULWER TO MACREADY, *Brighton, Friday, July 24, 1841*

I regret much that being absent from Town I cannot at present enjoy the opportunity of being introduced to M[rs] Adams.

I am shifting about at present from place to place — deep in Aristophanes & therefore little likely to be of any use. What a wonderful rascal he is.

[P. S.] My permanent address is always Fulham.

I have read L'Ambitieux.[20] Is it not sad stuff? Pray tell Forster, apropos of stuff, that his critique made me read Miss Sedgwick's book,[21] Le Scelerat! Her book is not only waste paper, but what is worse — it ought only to be used as such — by Rogers!

253. BULWER TO FORSTER, *Knebworth, Friday, [July 30, 1841]*

Thanks for your letter — I like you & Macready talking about the Comedy,

---

Captain Polhill was in the early thirties manager of Drury Lane, with Bunn as stage manager, where he lost £50,000 in four seasons; later proprietor of the *Age* magazine in conjunction with Bunn; M.P. for Bedford in 1841 and earlier.

[18] Presumably *Ruy Blas, drame en cinq actes* (Paris, 1838).

[19] Eugène Scribe, *La Calomnie* (Paris, 1840).

[20] Eugène Scribe, *L'Ambitieux* (Paris, 1834).

[21] Catharine Maria Sedgwick (1789-1867), American novelist. Forster reviewed, or rather, printed extracts from, Miss Sedgwick's *Letters from Abroad to Kindred at Home* in the *Examiner* on this day.

when Macready knows that I can't stir till he will sketch me a Plot — No not if it were January 9 times over. And it is too bad in him because I should really like to have time to finish a Comedy *ad unguem* — to lay it by — for final thought &c — as I generally do my novels — & not send out my first rough sketch as I have hitherto done.—. . . .

254. BULWER TO MACREADY, *Margate, Sunday, August 9, 1841*

Forster told me you w^d write to me about stratagems & plots. But your *libido tacendi* rivals that of the Philosopher in Juvenal.[22]

My researches on Athenian manners are carrying me thro' the whole range of antient comedy. There is nothing — but occasional witticisms to be gleaned from Aristophanes — but I have just concluded the 6 Plays of Terence, observing what Steele has made from the Andrea in the Conscious Lovers.[23] — I can't help thinking that a field is yet open. Phormio is capital, but there is no principal part for a high Comedian. What think you of the Heautontimorumenos? It seems to me that something very striking might be adapted from that idea — provided one could restore Menedemus that weight & passion which he must evidently have had in the original of Menander. Just see the opening where he is described. How fine a picture it is — the old man pinching & slaving himself for his Son. In a modern paraphrase he might be drawn not of course as a penurious agriculturist, but a tricky merchant — seemingly a miser — all from the same passion — love & penitence about his son.

The Courtezan, or rather *hetaera Bacchis,* would be a gay, dashing, extravagant widow, whose finery & expenses when introduced at the House of Chremes would be very droll. Chremes might be made a vain, curious, medling fellow — always thinking himself wise & always taken in — the Slave Syrus should not be a servant (for that is really foreign to our manners) but a friend to the 2 young men, & might be made very droll & effective. But the difficulty is how to draw out Menedemus. He is a mere shadow in Terence & ought to be your Part. If you have time, just think of this. I shall go thro' Plautus by & by. But I have him not here. Are there any of his comedies you could suggest? There are plenty of them.— Why won't you have Richelieu again? I would not have let Webster have it to lay on the shelf. Shall I write to him?

[P. S.] This is a most Enchanting Place — the Naples of England.

255. MACREADY TO BULWER, *5 Clarence Terrace, Regent's Park, August 9, 1841*

Yours just received has anticipated the fulfillment of my resolve to write to you today. I am delighted that you should have been caught by the charac-

---

[22] Juvenal, *Second Satire*, l. 14.

[23] Sir Richard Steele (1672-1729), the essayist, dramatist, and politician. *The Conscious Lovers*, his last comedy, was produced in 1722.

ter of The Heautontimorumenos — for I have always felt it to be most dramatic and touching and capable of noble amplification.— I will turn again to it — for it is a favorite of mine. In the meantime I have been hammering hard at Walpole — and have knocked some rough lumps together, that can scarcely be called ideas — about which I wished to talk with you, and purposed (thinking you were at Craven Cottage) urging you to come up to Town, or volunteering a visit to you to discuss the subject: — for to draw out a plot clearly, one must almost write down rough dialogue, and then it is not easy to convey all that might be desired.

When shall you leave Naples — or what are my chances of seeing you? — I think the hints of Terence — I have always thought so — very strong.

Mr. Webster would do nothing that he thought might be in any way agreeable to me — for it is his policy at present to devise all sorts of — what he supposes — annoyances to induce me to throw up my engagement in disgust — but my engagements at Drury Lane will not allow me; therefore I am obliged to say "a la bonne heure" to all that is proposed — For my "fourteen plays — *most of them to be studied* — to be acted on fourteen successive Mondays!!" — Such was the last requisition on me — to which I must say — as far as it is possible; — I do not think he *could* act Richelieu without Mr Phelps — and, if he thought I should prefer it, I think he would not, if he could.—

You do not say whether you are in the Chiaja — or Chiaturone — Toledo — or where — so that I write direct to Craven Cottage.

Do not lose sight of Terence — I have never read Plautus — it rests with intentions.—

256. BULWER TO MACREADY, *Margate, Wednesday, August 12, 1841*

Many thanks for your note forwarded from Craven Cottage. I am delighted to find you have some notions about Walpole.— By far the best subject if the story can be made to interest.—I shall be in Town to-morrow & will look in at the Haymarket after the play to see you.

Perhaps you can then give me your rough ideas of Walpole. I shall be but few days in town.

257. BULWER TO FORSTER, *[August 26, 1841]*

. . . I am coming to a close [*composition of Zicci*]²⁴ & could then, before I turn to Athens²⁵ — "do a play" — But Walpole won't shape itself. Do urge Macready to something else. I met young Kean at dinner yesterday — He is more agreeable & natural than I thought for — & explain about Knowles

---

²⁴ Bulwer published a sketch called *Zicci* in *The Monthly Chronicle* in 1838; he was now reworking it into a full novel to be called *Zanoni*, 3 vols. (London, 1842).

²⁵ Bulwer had published a study called *Athens, Its Rise and Fall* . . . (2 vols.) in 1837. Perhaps he now thought of returning to the subject.

whose play is only just penned.[26] He told me a scene hovering most critically between the ludicrous & beautiful — Very cockneyish, yet poetical. Knowles won't alter a word — & does not admit Kean to be "Fell Cibber!"

258. MACREADY TO BULWER, *5 Clarence Terrace, Regent's Park,*
    September 12, 1841

In the midst of cares — of all kinds — and toil at business, early and late — at bed and board — in the dust of Drury Lane, and the filth of the Haymarket — plodding my weary way through the streets, or indulging in the luxury of Cab No. 464 — a shadow haunts me — The furies of Orestes were mere blue devils to it.— It makes me miserable, and you aggravate its infliction by, as Forster tells me, complaining of my supineness.   This shadow is "a subject".— Fathers, husbands, brothers, friends — all sorts and conditions of men — are put through all kinds of scrapes and inconveniences, but to no result.

I think the *ground-work* of La Calomnie offers all the opportunities you require for the introduction of character.— The subject is not new — it is the Guardian — I think Garrick's[27] — and Mrs Inchbald's Simple Story — but what is new? — Whatever is originally treated. It seems to me, the only ground-work to build a good *popular* plot upon.— It appears to me to bring in the Public & the Press as well. I have been using every interval I could make in looking thro' biographies — plays & histories to get a glimpse of something. If I could only count upon a Comedy or mixed play, I should feel a great increase of confidence for the season.— My misfortune ought not to be charged on me as my fault — I would give a large reward for anyone, who will find the subject.

Is Walpole hopeless? — Bolingbroke would require more than any actor could give — But he might make a splendid intriguer. Roebuck[28] talks of bringing the Times to the bar of the House — I shall be going down on mine to beg of you to fix your choice.

I give every *off*-hour to you.— Let me have some news of comfort in return.

I have three plays of *deep* interest in my store.

259. FORSTER TO BULWER, [*September ?, 1841*]

I am haunted with visions of the Public . . . perhaps tis as I approach their ordeal.

---

[26] Presumably Knowles's *The Rose of Arragon, A Play, in Five Acts.* Performed with Mr. and Mrs. Charles Kean at the Haymarket on May 30, 1842, it ran for twenty-five nights.
[27] David Garrick (1717-79), the actor and dramatist. *The Guardian* (1759) is an adaptation of *La Pupille* (1734) by Christophe Fagan (1702-55), a favorite play of Voltaire's.
[28] John Arthur Roebuck (1801-79), Radical M.P. for Bath, but in later years a supporter of Disraeli.

That was too good an idea to be lost. I wish you would go back to it. The obvious contrasts it admits — I don't care whether embodied in Ministers, M[*illegible*], or M[*illegible*] — between the lofty indifference, the silent as the passionate suffering, the generally base and always amusing vulgarity — are high Comedy, with the relief & assistance of the pathetic interest, which such comedy (I mean with such agents) must supply. DO go to the consideration of it again. On *our* stage we have nothing of the kind. It might be made a School for Scandal of the year '41, without the least imitation or commonplace resemblance.

I cannot express to you how much I have felt this these last few days. In the silent watches of the night, I have seen English versions of Aristophanic sellers of Hides and Blackpuddings — I have been visited by an old father ΔΗΜΟΣ of this good city of London in the dominion of as fawning, flattering, cheating, lying slaves as ever enthralled the base old rascal in the streets of Athens — and I know that you only could realize such versions and visions. Oh, my dear Bulwer, do go back to that subject. Once fix your thoughts upon it, and a structure of humour and pathos will soon spring up, supported by such "flying" yet enduring buttresses of Wit, as all the light or heavy cavalry of our most infamous press shall batter at in vain.

— I will say more — that is, try to say and write more upon the subject — if you tell me you are disposed to entertain it in the least. For heaven's sake try to do so. I anticipate a *triumph*. The rhymed Comedy must wait — must follow after. . . .

260. BULWER TO MACREADY, [*September, 1841*]

I should have answered your letter before, but was in hopes that something might occur. Alas! the vein is still barren. Forster will tell you how he returns to my old Idea of The Public. He fancies he sees dignity and pathetic interest in the situations & his ideas seem very good. But I cannot find a clue to any plot. If you talk over this with him, some outline may suggest itself. It might embody a part of Calomnie. I have thought a little of a mixed comic classic play — Terentian — Scene Athens & subject taken from the favourite distress of the Greek Comedians — viz: the Law which obliged the nearest relative to marry an orphan. I think something serious & pathetic might arise here — & the Greek slaves parasites & boasters may furnish comic characters. But I don't see my way farther.

Unless a very good comedy suggest itself, a mixed play is safer, especially where the comic company is not so strong as the grave, which I fancy must be your case & indeed the case everywhere. A mixed play may centre itself like The Lady of Lyons in 4 characters.

261. MACREADY TO BULWER, *5 Clarence Terrace, Regent's Park,* *September 25, 1841*

Two days since I got Moore's Life of Sheridan to read in it the Sketch of an intended Comedy by R. B. S. to be called *Affectation*[29] — It is only the characters that are sketched — have you seen it? if not, will you look at it, it may touch a chord. — In the midst of my Herculean Labour — (I am turning the Alpheus into the stable) — I am "nettled and stung with pismires" in the vexatious reflection I have, that there is yet nothing in prospect from you. — I shall think *all is right,* when I know you are at work for us. — Are you revolving anything? — Some manna for starving people! —

262. BULWER TO MACREADY, [*circa October 4, 1841*]

I have rec'd yours on my return to Fulham. Alas, I cannot find any idea for what you desire. One indeed occurs to me which I fancy you would find invaluable as a Manager. But as an Actor you would not be wanted. Start not when I tell you the idea. Tieck[30] wrote in German a satirical play on Puss in Boots — it had immense success. This is my idea! — 3 Acts in rhyme like Bombastes Furioso[31] with songs — a sort of Beggars' Opera — full of allusions to the Present Day. I am sure I could make it witty. Aristophanes in his Birds will give you the idea of what I mean. The play to open with the Millers. Fancy their conversation on the Corn Laws! — Then think of the quiz on Charlatanism in the Marquis de Carabas seizing other people's property as his own. I propose a chorus of Rats — Radicals, whom Puss treats with great disdain. I shall introduce Homoeopathy — Magnetism — the Press — the House of Commons — Everything. Puss Miss Martin [Horton?] could do. The Marquis de Carabas w^d be a fine part! I am serious! I think I see something all the Town would run after & might alternate your grave plays. Celeste[32] would be the proper cat since Jenny Vertpré [Mme. Vestris?] is not to be had. But suppose we don't engage Celeste. It must be anonymous — full of travesties & burlesques. What say you? This is for your own thought alone. Don't mention it even to Forster.

[P.S.] I will read Sheridan's Remains.

263. MACREADY TO BULWER, 5 *Clarence Terrace, October 6,* [*1841*]

Upon the arrival of your note I encountered a most extraordinary piece of ill luck. — Forster was sitting with me after dinner — I was so amused and carried away by the humour of the idea of the satirical piece, that before I had read half of it — I laughed out, and turning back read it through aloud — nor discovered my blameable precipitation until I reached the last line — just in time to stop before "not even to Forster". — Of course I laid him under

---

[29] Thomas Moore, *Memoirs of the Life of the Right Honorable Richard Brinsley Sheridan,* 2 vols. (London, 1825), I, 212-18.

[30] Ludwig Tieck (1773-1853), poet, playwright, and critic.

[31] William Barnes Rhodes (1772-1826) was the author of *Bombastes Furioso,* a burlesque first performed at the Haymarket in 1810, and widely printed after 1822.

[32] Céline Céleste (1814-82), French dancer and pantomimist, settled in London and learned English in the 1830's, and for a time managed the Adelphi and Lyceum theatres.

the strictest promise of silence — but I have many regrets and apologies to make you for this unfortunate accident. I think the idea itself pregnant with wit and humour.— I would give anything that I had been alone in receiving the account of it.

What do you think of the suggestion of Glory — not Old Glory? — A man, with every *real* good about him, or in his reach — pursuing the shadow, that bears that name to him — attaining by intrigue — sacrifice of feeling — humiliations — abandonment of certain high principles — the various objects of his ambitious pursuit in the 1st, 2nd & 3rd Acts — His high-blown pride breaking under him in the 4th— and in the 5th some real act of domestic heroism imparting to him in the enjoyment of what is *really* good & great the knowledge of the secret of true happiness — Gracchus in history with a softer tumble — and Abudah in fiction for the talisman of Oromanes.[33]

Surely this would exactly dove-tail with your great thought *the Public*.— I pray so.— Have you seen my first Bulletin, dated from Head Quarters? —

I will find a Cat: — But think of Glory.— I am constantly thinking of you. I should be at ease, if you saw your way.— Forgive my incautious disclosure and believe me always

in truth & penitence

264. BULWER TO MACREADY, *Monday, [October 18, 1841]*[34]

With pleasure on Saturday at six.— Just as you please about Forster. I have no ideas to communicate with regard to myself. But wished to suggest to you an opera, that you might make a National hit.

265. BULWER TO MACREADY, *Craven Cottage, Tuesday, [October 19, 1841]*

I am unfortunately obliged to ask you to excuse me on Saturday. I had calculated on returning from a visit to Lord Cowper's[35] on Friday, but I have just had a letter that renders it uncertain whether I shall not be positively obliged to stay over Saturday. So that it will be better to defer our Meeting till some, I trust, very Early opportunity. As it was to be a *tête-à-tête* or nearly so, I have the less scruple in drawing on your Indulgence.

---

[33] Both Tiberius Gracchus (d. 133 B.C.) and Caius Gracchus (d. 121 B.C.) met violent deaths after careers devoted to governmental reform. Macready had played the latter Gracchus in the tragedy by Knowles in 1823.

Abudah, a rich merchant, sought for true happiness in fantastic dream-worlds of wealth, pleasure, power, and knowledge, finally to learn that true happiness is available only to the gods, and to content himself at last in the love of his family. See "The History of the Merchant Abudah; or, The Talisman of Oromanes," the first tale in the pseudo-Persian *Tales of the Genii* (London, 1764), by James Ridley (1736-65).

[34] The dating of this note and the next is tentatively established by reference to the notes of October 25. Matthews labels one of these 1838, the other 1843.

[35] George Augustus Frederick Lord Cowper (1806-56), Whig M.P., 1830 to 1834; succeeded to the Earldom in 1837.

266. BULWER TO MACREADY, *October 25, 1841*

I will dine with you on Friday with pleasure at 6 o'clock. With regard to the Comedy, I feel sure that I cannot see my way to it merely thro' the moral purpose w^h you so well indicate. What I want more is a view of the more physical progress of Plot as in the outline you suggested of Money. *There* I saw at once the effective scenes of the opening of the will — of the supposed reverse — & the domestic situation of Clara & Evelyn. In the play you suggest I see no scenes — & little comic situation — & I fear the Dialogue would be too much mixed with the politics of the day. What I should like most would be a Poetic Comedy that is a mixture of prose & blank verse as in The Lady of Lyons. With comic situations in Acts 1, 2, & 4 & grave in Acts 3 & 5 — I have so great an indisposition at this moment towards playwriting, that unless I can hit on something that would attract my fancy & excite enthusiasm, I fear I shall never get on. I like the idea of glory. But beyond this idea all seems to me cloud & darkness.— The operatic play I wished to point out to you is Robin Hood — the story might be made wild, interesting & yet lively & comic at times. The scene & name are National & it has this one great advantage, that it would incorporate the early English National music lately published by Chapel [*sic*].[36] Thus it might be made a *National Opera,* without borrowing a single foreign air.— Think over this.

[P.S.] Puss in boots can't take a step. His boots are not 7 league ones.

267. MACREADY TO BULWER, *5 Clarence Terrace, Regent's Park, October 25, 1841*

Our notes have crossed — your former one to me satisfied me, that if you could not be with us on Saturday, of course you could not on Friday *last week.* — This week I act on Friday, but if I have the good fortune to find you free on *Thursday* — my non-play night — shall be delighted, if you will take us in our homely way, and try if a tête-à-tête discussion is likely to "rouse a lion or to start a hare".— If Thursday, I shall suppose you will adhere to six o'clock.

Thus the summer and autumn passed in a frantic pursuit of ideas, but none of them, from Aristophanes' oldest to the newest of Scribe, could find a proper shape; and with the opening of Drury Lane on December 27, Macready was too deeply involved in the business of every day to pursue Bulwer farther. On February 8, 1842, Bulwer visited the theatre, to see the new operatic production of *Acis and Galatea* and Douglas Jerrold's *Prisoner of War.*[37] A few days later he reported to Forster:

268. BULWER TO FORSTER, [*February 12, 1842*]

. . . I saw Macready in all the Pomp of an overflowing House a most suc-

---

[36] William Chappell (1809-88): *Collection of National English Airs* (London, 1838-40).

[37] *Acis and Galatea,* adapted from Handel, opened at Drury Lane February 5, 1842. *The Prisoner of War* was added to the bill on February 8.

cessful afterpiece a most triumphant opera — & a most gorgeous private Box
But in his pomp was sadness! He sighed at Congratulations & complained of
the harrassments of greatness — & the uncertainty of success. — Unhappy
Man! When he gets a million, he will have arrived at the summit of his
sorrows —

I *had* thought at one time of a comic subject for him — But I feel that it
would be almost an insult to talk of Comedy — while his Melancholy overflows
with his Houses — By & by — if ever thinning Boxes lighten his heart — *nous
verrons!* —. . . .

269. BULWER TO FORSTER, *Knebworth, Saturday, [February 19, 1842]*

. . . I shall be at Fulham next week & shall be happy to fix a day then to
take a chop with you & if your avocations permit to see Gisippus.[38] I cannot
go the first night & the second is always flat — But I hope the third — . . .

I am thinking of turning into a Fiction what I once meant for a Drama —
had Macready been less overtaken with gravities — viz — The Last of the
Barons — Warwick the Kingmaker[39] — the time is full of philosophical movement, & I think I shall give a new reading of Richard the third's crimes &
character — new but I hope not untrue. Can you recommend me any Books
of that time for manners & costume? agst. we meet —

270. BULWER TO MACREADY, *Fulham, [Thursday?], February [24], 1842*

You, I am sure, will never impute to want of interest in your success that
abstinence from the enjoyment of the Acis & Galatea & Gisippus, with which
you kindly reproach me. Their complete triumph leaves me so easy on your
account, that I repose under your laurels, and the *vis inertiae* which in this
retreat weighs upon me of an evening, has kept me from all engagements I can
avoid. — Moreover I have had a great accumulation of business etc., but I
still hope to see both among my earliest recreations. And had either been
doubtful, my anxiety would have carried me to the scene of treat long ago. In
respect to anything from myself I roused my muse from an aversion She has
taken to further Dramatic composition, & essayed a Comedy, of which about
one Act was composed when, tho' pretty good, I perceived it would not be
striking & sparkling eno', & dropped it. Since then I have often tried to invent
a subject but in vain. I am sure, however, that whenever your resources fail
you, my zeal for you would refresh my invention. But you seem so richly provided for, & the literary Ambition of Authors is so much directed now towards
the story [stage?], that I do not feel any spur towards an effort which could
but substitute one play for some other just as likely to succeed. I wrote first for

---

[38] *Gisippus; or, The Forgotten Friend* was produced on February 23, 1842. The author
was the recently deceased Gerald Griffin (1803-40), Irish novelist, playwright, and
finally religious recluse.

[39] Published as a novel, *The Last of the Barons* (London, 1843).

the stage with the desire to set an example to others, & to serve you personally. Both these objects gained — my Fountain seems dried up, & its Nymph departed.

Howbeit, whenever you or my own reading suggests a subject likely to be brilliant you will, no doubt, revive the old impulses. Meanwhile I sympathize in the success of others & rejoice in the prosperity you so richly deserve.

271. BULWER TO MACREADY, *Craven Cottage, February 24, 1842*

I & Forster are going to see Gisippus Monday[40] & will look in on you afterwards — when if you think anything of my idea, I shall be happy to dine with you some day of your fixing & discuss it.

272. BULWER TO MACREADY, *St. James's, Charles St., Thursday, April 22, 1842*

I cannot tell you how grieved, sincerely and heartily, I am at the account I read this morning, of the reception of "Plighted Troth."[41] Tho' I never read the play, the outline of the story struck me as one of prodigious power, and the extract you read, convinced me of the presence of a thoro' and genuine Poet. I hope you will try it on, and that it may recover the effect of the First Night & I shall I trust be at the Theatre this Evening to judge for myself. Should I not see you, will you kindly do me the favour to say to the Author on my part, whatever you think may be received as the language of sympathy and encouragement. If I might venture allusion to myself, I would remind him of the fate of my best literary play, La Vallière — which did not present sufficient success on succeeding attempts to cheer on a man like the Author of Plighted Troth, in a path where he is, I am sure, able to achieve no ordinary triumphs.

[P.S.] Since writing the above I have been to Dr Lane & was disappointed to find the play put off.

273. MACREADY TO BULWER, *Theatre Royal Drury Lane, April 23, [1842]*

Many, many thanks for your kind note, which is so worthy of you. I was going to transcribe part of it, but could not resist sending it as I received it to Mr. Darley: — I have suffered more on his account than on my own.— We are hard at work to make good our retreat — our remaining weeks as little against us in figures as we can.— I am strong in hope for the future — auspice Teucro: — I shall read the subjects directly, and report to you upon them. — Oh! if we had but a play from you in hand at this writing! — but le bon temps viendra! —

---

[40] But a note to Forster on Sunday, February 27, cries off Monday and suggests Friday, March 4, instead: "I am delighted unfeignedly with its success."

[41] *Plighted Troth; or, A Woman her own Rival, a Tragedy*, by the Reverend Charles F. Darley, brother to the poet and critic George Darley (1795-1846), opened and closed on April 20, 1842 — the most crashing failure of Macready's managerial career. Not only Bulwer but all of Macready's circle had thought it a work of genius until the audience hooted it off the stage.

The play ought not to have failed — the causes of its ill success were several but not, I think, attributable to the author. I wished him to alter it for the second night, but he had not your indomitable nerve & resolution.

274. BULWER TO MACREADY, [*circa May 11*], 1842

It would be ungrateful not to inform you of the success of your Costume.[42] It went off with real *éclat*. I flatter myself that the accessories tended to heighten the effect. In especial I made a great feature of the sword, for judging the handle too rugged for the dress, I availed myself of a picture of the time to veil it in sword knots & drapery of Gold Lace round which was wreathed a chain of large Emeralds. I also took your hint about the chain for the cap, which was very good. I found the addition of a white & gold Embroidered Scarf with diamonds in the loop so effective that I recommend it to you for the stage.

So much for the reception of the Dress. I shall send it the first day I come to town, to Drury Lane & will you kindly desire the Tailor as I do not know his address, to send me in the acct.

[P.S.] Since writing the above I have received a request to sit for a portrait in the dress. May I keep it a little time longer or shall you want it? — if the latter, perhaps you can lend it after your Season.

Except that on April 3 Bulwer had left a couple of French plays for Macready to study for subject matter, there is no record of further effort at playwriting during the Spring months. Late in June, after the season had closed, he began to urge Macready to restore *Richelieu, Money,* and *The Lady of Lyons* to his repertory for the following season at Drury Lane. At the same time he submitted the manuscript of a verse romance he had written, *The Ill-omened Marriage,*[43] as possible material for a new play.

275. MACREADY TO BULWER, 5 *Clarence Terrace, Regent's Park, June 28, 1842*

I cannot attempt to produce Richelieu, until I have got such a surplus quantity of stock in the Theatre, as will enable me to do it justice in the decorative department without the very great cost its *getting-up* would now compel me to.

In our bare theatre this would not amount to less than £1,000 — and unless for the anticipation of a *great run*, such a sum could not be ventured: — When we have such a surplus of *stock* in the house as we can apply with little additional expense, I shall be too glad to have Richelieu in my list of acting plays. — The same arguments apply to Money with this still stronger one — that it does not give *me* a character of sufficient strength for a large Theatre, and for

---

[42] Bulwer had borrowed the costume of Ruthven in *Mary Stuart* for the Queen's fancy dress ball, which took place on May 10. Macready provided dresses for several of the guests, including Prince Albert.

[43] *Eva: A True Story of Light and Darkness; The Ill-omened Marriage, and other Tales and Poems* (London, 1842).

the comic characters of the play — Stout — Sir John & Graves — we have *no* representatives.

I shall like to talk to you on the subject of Richelieu & The Lady of Lyons, and let you understand my views in regard to them.

I have read "The Ill-omened Marriage" and "all the Mother came into my eyes" as they devoured the interesting and well-told tale. — I cannot imagine a much better subject for a mixed play — I see scenes in it of great tragic power — of great pathos — and opportunities for comic effect.

A new Play from you would be the thing to make a *sensation*. I feel confident it would greatly act upon the season: — I however still cling to something historical, if a subject could be gained — a known title is such an advantage. The reason too for my partiality to The Ill-omened Marriage is, that the man is not *young* — which I am not, as I feel and see. — Shall I see you before you leave town? —

On July 1 Macready records a letter from Bulwer — "discontented that I cannot afford to do *Richelieu* at present at Drury Lane Theatre."

276. MACREADY TO BULWER, *Clarence Terrace, July 1*, [*1842*]

I write on the receipt of your note to endeavour to explain to you in some measure (for I cannot hope except in conversation to do so altogether) the circumstances that control me in my movements at present in regard to Richelieu &c. — First let me say how very happy I should be to accept your invitation to Knebworth, if it were in my power: I am working my hardest to put things en train at the Theatre — in order to join my family at East Bourne, where I have the working of the season to prepare. Should you be in Hertfordshire about the beginning of Autumn, I should be delighted to run down and have grave discussion de omnibus rebus et &c. —

Richelieu cost £800 at C.G.T. — with no new material in the scenery — all was in the house, and very little in the dresses: — the furniture was, much of it, new, — Drury Lane has NOTHING in it — either of scenery — or dresses, except what I have put in — of furniture there is not enough for the ordinary stock plays. — Pray take these things into account, and you will see the fact, that Richelieu, if I had had it last season, or had it now in hand, would often be of very great service — but I could not present it as Mr. Webster did, and you must admit that to do it justice I must, in the present state of the Theatre, expend a large sum of money. — I should *certainly* wish to have the Lady of Lyons also on my stock list — but it is needful to *give it a rest* after Mr. Webster's recent treatment of it — acting it as an after-piece — and therefore I should not bring it out until the very end of the next season, if indeed I did not think it better policy to let it stand over to the following. These things must be *humoured* with regard to their attraction. — I think it very probable that you will not understand why this should be — I can only say, *it is*, and I am but consulting the interests of the play and my own (which are mutual) in my view of it.

I looked to the French Comedy as likely to furnish points of effect to the Ill-omened Marriage, and I do think a *most successful* play would come out of the subject. I cannot well imagine (unless from history) a subject affording greater opportunity for diversity of character and powerful scenes of passion and pathos. Surely to wish to make three thousand hearts beat as one and to carry suggestions and aspirations after the beautiful & true into corners of poor human nature, where else they might never have penetrated is not a mean ambition. — If a poet would rather write a people's songs than make their laws, I think it a still higher influence to make their drama.

Do not give up this subject. — You will put your own terms on the L. of L: — And let me add that I do not intend to lose Richelieu from my list of acting characters — but I am manager as well as actor — hinc illae lacrymae.

In February Bulwer had mentioned to Forster his notion for a tragedy on the subject of Warwick the Kingmaker, and his decision to turn it into a novel instead. By mid-July the novel was nearly completed and he longed to make a play of it also. Macready resisted this idea, recording privately his opinion that "I do not feel Bulwer's power to be in the high tragic vein."

277. BULWER TO MACREADY, *Knebworth, Stevenage, Herts.,* [*July 15, 1842*]

I have thought over your idea of blending The Ill-omened Marriage and the French Comedy — but cannot see my way to it. — The grave and comic do not seem to me to harmonize in it. If you have leisure for any ideas of the plot and Acts, pray chalk out your notion of the outline.

I should however much prefer a direct Comedy — or a direct tragedy — to a mixed play — and after all The Ill-omened Marriage must have the same interest as The Lady of Lyons — & Novelty w^d be wanting. — I have a superb subject for a Tragedy — if I can make you see it. "Warwick, the King maker — the last of the English Barons." I am finishing a romance on the subject, but I should treat it so differently as a Tragedy that that would not signify.

The Plot is full of domestic interest — almost as strong as Venice preserved. Judge for yourself. Warwick, the last & mightiest of the English Barons, has dethroned Henry 6 & placed Edward IV on the throne. — He loves Edward as a son, & wishes Edward to marry his dau'r, Isabel — but the King has chosen Elizabeth Woodville. Warwick, tho' disappointed, takes it well. He is sent by Edward on a solemn Embassy to Lewis XI to betroth Edward's sister to Lewis' son — meanwhile the Queen, who hates Warwick, has put on him a grievous insult, by persuading Edward to give his sister to Charles the Bold of Burgundy. — Play opens during Warwick's absence. He returns to find himself juggled. A powerful and stormy scene with the King — they quarrel. When Warwick leaves Edward the disaffected Barons come to offer Warwick (who is a Plantagenet) the throne; he refuses — partly thro' pride (he is an aristocrat who looks *down on* a King) — partly thro' love to Edwd & nobleness of soul. In the second act Warwick & the King are reconciled, & Warwick's daughter Isabel is to be married to Edward's brother the Duke of Clarence — but when Edward sees Isabel, who is wonderfully improved in beauty since he preferred Elizabeth Woodville, he falls in love with her & forbids the marriage with Clarence — finally he offers violence to Isabel — Warwick discovers it — his feelings. What! *his* daughter to be the King's *harlot* and Mrs Elizabeth Woodville the King's *Queen!* This drives him to rebellion — powerful scene with Margaret of Anjou and Henry 6th whom he had dethroned and whom he now would restore. He does restore Henry 6th, and Edward is driven from the country. Warwick is now at the height of power. His daughter is married to Clarence. But Clarence is discontented and listens to the intrigues of Edward to desert Warwick — Isabel placed between the contending duty to Father and husband. Edward lands, marches to London, and Clarence deserts with all his troops to him. The eve of the Battle of Barnet. Scene Warwick & his Daughter Isabel — & the final catastrophe of Warwick's death in the Battle. I have very roughly chalked it out — but I think it capable of strong domestic interest, while Warwick's character is very grand and absorbing — and a bold picture of the times may be given. This is the best tragic subject I can think of, but a pure comedy w^d be more popular if a thesis could be found. — But I have only to repeat that unless you could give me a subject, I shall never chance on one.

With regard to The Lady of Lyons. — It was only acted once as an after-piece — the night of Kean's benefit. I wrote to remonstrate with Webster immediately, & I don't think it can happen again. — I cannot agree with you that it should be laid aside a season, tho' I think it need not appear in the commencement. Would 100£ for it — for the next season after it falls due to me which is not until January — be too much? It certainly will be — unless you think of running it altogether from 10 to 20 nights. I have no scruple therefore in treating this wholly as a matter of business.

I really wish you could give me a comedy — for I should be most unfeignedly happy to aid your great experiment. — But I have no invention in plots — & a House must be founded before it can be built. Not a word of all this to Forster.

Warwick's death is affecting — Edward & Clarence sent to offer him terms and pardon if he would dismiss his army. His answer was full of lofty disdain & galled feeling. His brother Lord Montague & he killed their horses to fight on foot — in sign that they would conquer or die — embraced & fell fighting side by side.

278. MACREADY TO BULWER, *Cliff Cottage, East Bourne, Sussex, July 17, 1842*

I will give my earliest attention to the subject of the Ill-omened Marriage — but have so much on my mind in the preparations for the next season, that I find a difficulty in keeping my ruminations steady upon any particular thing. — I will also look, and anxiously too, for a comedy plot.

In regard to a Tragedy I have these two or three observations to make —
a tragedy is not so *valuable* in its success to the theatre as a comedy — its run
is not so long, its nightly receipts not so great: — The numbers of the fre-
quenters of the Theatre are very unequally divided between tragedy & comedy,
but the lovers of tragedy [comedy?] are the most frequent visitors. — A pure
tragedy would be accounted very successful, if it ran twenty nights, and those
nights would only be *good*, not great, houses — with the experience therefore
of its production, it ought not therefore to be put at a price above £300 — to
deal fairly by the Theatre: — The most *attractive* tragedy I have known was
Mirandola[44] — which for *nine nights* was played to *crowded* houses — from
the ninth it fell down beneath the *expenses* at Xmas time! — Ion,[45] with all
the prestige of previous laudation, was a very short-lived attraction.

My counsel would be, ware tragedy — I have already one, and really a very
touching one, and with scenes of great passion by Browning — one, the
Patrician's Daughter, of which I think highly, by Westland Marston — and
Athelwold, of which I also think very highly by W. *Smith* — (Parnassian
sound!) Darley — *G.* Darley — is also likely to throw off something — so that
my need that way is not urgent.[46]— I think it right to put you in possession
of all these facts.

The subject you mentioned — as far as the hero is concerned — I like particularly: — I have an absurd motive for thinking with interest on Richard
Nevil — but he already stands importantly in Shakespeare and is effectively
introduced in Franklin's [*sic*] translation from La Harpe:[47] — but I have one
objection — and one that I never get over — to your plot, and that is the
departure from a history, which I fancy is very well known — I think *that*
always disappointing, and when adopted, I always feel, that it would be better
the names were altered, and the story given as a fanciful one. — I have delivered myself of my scruples you will think in very abundant measure — but
you would expect me to do so. —

I think it would be fair to say £*100* for the Lady of Lyons *for a year* — from
the time at which you pass it over to me: — There is more expense attending
its re-production than you are aware of.— You must not regard a temporary
rest as a *shelfing* — any more than you should look upon a fallow as a sub-

---

[44] Barry Cornwall (Bryan Waller Procter; 1787-1874), minor poet and littérateur. His
tragedy, *Mirandola,* written with Macready's assistance, was performed by Macready at
Covent Garden, January 9, 1821.

[45] Talfourd's *Ion* was produced at Covent Garden, May 26, 1836.

[46] Browning's *A Blot in the 'Scutcheon,* produced February 11, 1843, for only three
performances, was the occasion of permanent rupture in the Macready-Browning friendship.

The Patrician's Daughter, by John Westland Marston (1819-90), critic, playwright,
and theatrical historian, was produced December 10, 1842, and ran for eleven performances.

William Smith's *Athelwold,* produced May 18, 1843, had but two performances.

[47] Dr. Thomas Francklin (1721-84) adapted *The Earl of Warwick* (1766), from La
Harpe's *Le Comte de Warwick* (1763).

merging, or destruction of the land by any other method. — Shakespeare's plays are not shelfed, or dead, because they are not brought every season on the stage, nor Sheridan's, nor Goldsmith's, *&c., &c.* — I shall not *speak* of the subject of your letter at all — certainly not to Forster.

I will set my brain on a blood-hound quest after a plot.

279. BULWER TO MACREADY, *Knebworth, Tuesday, July 19, 1842*

Tho' I do not think that Tragedy is to be estimated in its necessary attractions by the instances you would refer to, & I believe that a modern "Venice preserved" well acted would produce immense sensation & a continuous run, yet you say eno' on that subject to silence any suggestions of mine thereon. But with regard to Warwick, I must set you right as to an error you seem to have made. The outline I gave you is *precisely & literally* according to the true History.

The old notion that Warwick's quarrel with Edward was about the Princess Bona of Savoy — as recorded by Hume, whose history of that reign is the very worst part of his work — is unanimously set aside by better Historians. The dispute arose, as I stated, in the marriage of Edward's Sister to the D. of Burgundy — despite the embassy of Warwick to France, & was finally ripened by an attempt of Edward on a female relation of Warwick's. (See Hall's Chronicle.) This girl was supposed to be Isabel married to Clarence. But that could not be, for she was already wed to Clarence & not at the Court. It must either have been Anne or a niece of Warwick's — daughter to his brother Montagu. I have adhered exactly to the true History. The introduction of Shakespeare's very poor Sketch of Warwick, which has not a single trait of character, I think very immaterial. The splendour, the pride, the frankness, the passion of the stout Earl, ought to make a very distinct Portraiture. And the extreme love he had at first to Edward, succeeded by so fierce a hate, might be eminently touching. But, as this subject must be all buskin — high & gorgeous Tragedy alone, having thus vindicated my Historical accuracy — I leave it among the Embryos.

I meant to say a *year* for The Lady of Lyons, that is from January 15th to January 15th.

The sole thing left to think on is a *pure comedy* that might have some touches of pathos allied with humour.

Waste no time on The Ill-omened Marriage. What I feel about the success of any play of mine is this: — that, if it does succeed, its run would be greater than that of any less known writer (there being a prestige in these matters) whose work had equal merit. But that if it fail, its failure would be more complete. And in this — all depends upon the conception or plot. I have no fear as to the execution of the Play, provided the subject is popular & original. And so the Muses inspire your invention.

In Bulwer's last letter of the summer of 1842, one can sense a sort of dry gasping.

He rejects a story of Mrs. Opie's which Macready had offered; he rambles back over Scribe's *La Calomnie* and the various themes of Greek inspiration which had excited him so much the summer before; above all, he begs Macready to describe the sort of character he wants created for himself to play.

280. BULWER TO MACREADY, *Craven Cottage, Fulham, Friday, [August, 1842]*

Many thanks for your letter. I have been endeavouring in vain to recall my notion of the Heautontimorumenos, but all I can gather is the impression that it will afford one very fine scene or even Act — but I cannot see help for more. The German story from Mrs. Opie[48] will make a very pretty Inchbald sort of play — but lacks brilliancy, depth & effect for long & profound sensation. The more I think, the more I am persuaded, that since you dislike Tragedy, Pure Comedy would be the thing. And all, in this, I will ask you to do is to give me an idea of the sort of Comic Character which will suit yourself. No doubt, in your Stage xperience — you have often said — "If I could get such or such a character fully elaborated, I could make a great hit in it." Think but of this, & give me the fullest conception of it you can. What I want is — that all its pathos & height should not be apart from the comic, but belong so essentially to it (as in Don Quixote) that you should almost laugh & weep, ridicule & admire in a breath.

My fault is to separate the comic from the grave, but I think I could do much if I once saw how to blend the two in one conception. If I were writing a comedy for Farren, I should soon knock it off. But strange to say, you are my stumbling-block — I cannot raise myself up to that grave high Humour which would alone suit your dignity. My forte in comedy would be Farren Characters — I think it should be modern life — & introduce popular scenes — Kensington Gardens — the Stock Exchange Gradgrind agent etc. Yet I have often meditated on Athenian Comedy — & for the first time in Dramatic History, place the scenes & the life of that People on the English stage. The Law on which Plautus builds so largely gives half the Plot at once — viz: that the Nearest Relation must marry or find a Husband for, an orphan girl — once I thought of Pericles himself, who after passing a law to illegitimatize the offspring of the foreign women, intrigues to legitimatize his own Son by Aspasia. But this would require an Aspasia! & besides would be called Immoral.

Athenian Comedy abounds in character. The Parasite, the Demagogue, the plotting slave — the gay profligate termed Dandy — Philosophy & whoring — still, it would be an xperiment!

This is all I can say — I shall have one Month of Leisure — from the middle of September to the middle of October (my best period for the vein) — after that time, I have a most arduous engagement & shall be tied to Time. — Calomnie is excellent, but I have been so often accused of borrowing from

---

[48] Mrs. Amelia Opie, née Alderson (1769-1853), novelist and poet; married John Opie (1761-1807), the painter, in 1798.

the French that I had better avoid the charge, & unless I borrowed largely from Calomnie I should fall upon the School for Scandal.

281. MACREADY TO BULWER, *September 6,* [1842]

I cannot return you an answer to your enquiry about Mrs. Gore[49] without telling that I have carried your former letter about with me, wishing to answer it, but not knowing how. I have not time enough for the labour and needful thought that is required of me, and to think of a character — everything runs away from me, when I only in my mind look towards a subject. — Of all the modern plays in which I have acted Richelieu contained the character I liked best. — As comic characters Sir Oswin Mortland & Harmony in Everyone Has His Fault, both Mrs Inchbald's,[50] have taken me very much, and made me much wish that they had been more perfectly filled up — they are but sketches.

Do you know The Connoisseur of Marmontel[51] — if Celicour were not exactly a young man, but privately married to his Agatha — and suffering different sorts of patronage — his pride being obliged to swallow so much, and finding vent in satire & irony — I think both the higher and some of the low — the *lowest,* for where a litterateur is low he is generally of the vilest — might be very well displayed. I see in the distance many shadows of characters various & strong — but I know how often they dissolve as you approach them. — I think Marmontel affords capital hints for character & subject, but you have not fancied him as a suggester. Only do not desert us — this is really I think the trial of the drama's fate. We have much to hope from — but *want* a play from you. — Besides which, after being selfish, I should like a brilliant success for yourself. Do not let this precious time escape. — Try Marmontel once more. — My corps dramatique assemble to-day. —

Although Bulwer could bring no literary aid to the opening of the season,[52] he and Forster were working hard behind the scenes to bring aid of another sort, which was to present Macready a huge silver testimonial in honor of his stagings of Shakespeare. A long series of letters from Bulwer to Forster (not included here) is full of the details of the campaign. As early as June, 1842, Bulwer was troubled to learn that the subscriptions were not adequate to pay for the object (which is said to have cost £500), and began a campaign to raise more money. Somewhat later in the summer it appears that Macready was asked when he would like to receive it, and it was agreed that the presentation should occur soon enough to "have what action it may on the Ensuing Season." But the time of year — early autumn — was a poor one because "everyone is out of town," including the likeliest persons to serve as Presenter, such as Lord Lansdowne or Lord Normanby or the Duke of Sussex.[53] October 1, the opening night, came and went without the ceremony. Later in that month Bulwer

---

[49] Mrs. Catherine Grace Frances Gore (1798-1861), popular novelist and dramatist.
[50] Elizabeth Inchbald, *Every One has his Fault* (London, 1793).
[51] George Saintsbury, *Marmontel's Moral Tales* (London, 1895), pp. 206-32.
[52] Drury Lane opened on October 1 with *As You Like It.*
[53] Augustus Frederick, Duke of Sussex (1773-1843), sixth son of George III, zealous Whig and supporter of the Reform Bill.

reported that he had applied to the Duke of Sussex to officiate, and still later passed on a confirmation of the Duke's willingness, as expressed by his wife, the Duchess of Inverness. By now the event was being postponed to the end of January. On January 6 Macready notes in his diary the news from Forster that the Duke had "very pleasantly" consented to present the testimonial next month — and sourly adds, "So that my martyrdom is fixed." The Duke was old and crotchetty and hypochondriacal, however — much as his younger Liberal supporters loved him: he refused to go to the theatre for the ceremony, for fear of catching cold, and insisted on holding the affair at Kensington Palace. There followed an absurd series of postponements while Bulwer writhed and solicited more money. March 3, Macready's birthday, was displaced by March 7, and that date by March 15. For some reason that date failed too, and perhaps the Duke then withdrew from the affair altogether: in April he was ill of erysipelas and on the twenty-first of that month he died. The ceremony did not take place until June 19, 1843, five days after the closing of Macready's last season of management — a source of annoyance to the recipient, coming too late to do anyone any practical good.

By mid-December of 1842, ten weeks into the season, Macready was crying desperately to Bulwer to rescue him with a new play.

282. MACREADY TO BULWER, *Theatre Royal Drury Lane, December 14, 1842*

How should you suppose Pizarro and his thirteen comrades, who had remained on his side of the line he drew upon the sand, felt as they looked again and again towards the main-land for succour? — Much in the same state of hope and doubt do I look to you. — A hit from you would, as I firmly believe, decide the drama's and my fortunes. — Is nothing to be done? — The character you spoke of to me quite re-kindled my enthusiasm. — CAN you help us? — I regretted so much not seeing you, when in town. Do — give us some aid in our desperate combat. Do not leave me without hope — I am making the best fight I can, but must fall, if I have not some assistance.

I most earnestly hope, that your health is recovering, and that you will be our strong rock and tower of defence.

283. MACREADY TO BULWER, *5 Clarence Terrace, Regent's Park,*
December 18, 1842

Your kind note is the best exhilarator I have had these many days. — I have not shown the white feather in this business, but it has been a terrible hard fight against circumstances that were out of calculation's reach: — I think I have stood up to it pretty well in heart and work — still I have my moments of misgiving: at all events if I fail to accomplish what I had hoped, I shall not relinquish the effort with a crest-fallen or craven demeanour. — "There's life in a muscle," and I trust you will enable me to show there's enough for all our purposes.

On New Year's Day "Bulwer called and we talked over the subject of a play. He is my hope among authors." A week later Bulwer brought him a French play to think about, but he found it useless.

284. MACREADY TO BULWER, *Theatre Royal Drury Lane, January 11, [1843]*

My anxiety that you should be fairly engaged in my desperate cause made me sit up last night to finish Mediocre et Rampant[54] — I do not see how you (and if not *you*, who?) can work out anything for us out of Dorival —

The objects should be greater — the talent more — he is contemptible as he stands in the French Play, & no character can sustain a play, whose strength of wit or intellect does not hold the respect of the audience.— I *fear* it — I fear too the *experiment* of Nyac [?] — but of that I cannot speak until I see it.— If I could know you had a subject, I should really feel that there was hope for the prolongation of the *Drama's Life* — I declare, I look on it as almost DESPERATE without such an aid.— I hope that you will see King John tonight — but fear you will be dosed with the Theatre.—

The records of the ensuing months are sparse, but enough survives to reveal Bulwer determinedly struggling to fulfill Macready's need. The need was certainly intense, for every new play Macready turned to during this season went under. Marston's *Patrician's Daughter* was the best of them, but its attractiveness dwindled out in January after ten performances. February brought on the notorious and painful failure of Browning's *A Blot in the 'Scutcheon*. Knowles's *The Secretary*[55] and Smith's *Athelwold* were to collapse ignominiously in April and May. Before the end of February Bulwer could send encouraging news.

285. BULWER TO MACREADY, *36 Hertford St., Mayfair, February 22, 1843*

Will you send me *au plutôt* Dumas' Comedy Marriage sous Louis XV[56] which I lent you. In, I think, Act II, there is a scene I propose to borrow from — where the Husband finding the Lover & wife, tells them his position, & when one of them asks him — What did the Husband do — answers, "took up his hat & left them." Do you think you could make much of that position, if so I propose to place it in Act II of my own play. I am getting on, but have rewritten over & over again. However I hope in about 10 days to have a considerable portion to shew you. I think I see 2 very strong positions Acts 3 & 4. Some pleasant comedy — & a character for you, that tho' not very remarkable in itself, will carry the general sympathy with it & from its *position* have scope for fine acting — My eye is on *Stage* success as I write.

I expect there will be 2 capital parts for Keeley[57] & Miss Faucit.

[P.S.] Just returned from Brighton. 1000 thanks for your kind inquiries.

---

[54] Louis Benoît Picard (1769-1828), *Médiocre et Rampant, ou Le moyen de parvenu, comédie in cinq actes et en vers* (1797). See *Oeuvres* (Paris, 1821), I. In Toynbee's edition of the *Diaries* this title is misread as merely pejorative adjectives.

[55] Knowles's last play for Macready, produced on April 24, 1843, had three performances.

[56] Alexandre Dumas, *Un Marriage sous Louis XV, comédie en cinq actes* (Paris, 1841).

[57] Robert Keeley (1793-1869), low comedian; made his London debut in 1818; was a member of Macready's Drury Lane company; later shared the management of the Princess's Theatre with Charles Kean; retired in 1862. He and his wife (Mary Goward) were an extremely popular comedy team.

286. BULWER TO MACREADY, [*March, 1843*]

Do you still want my Play? Frankly yes or no.

I can now copy it fairly. I have heightened the individuality of your character — by what I think a happy afterthought & given to the whole play a purpose & philosophy it wanted before. This you may conjecture by the Title I now suggest

"The Egotists"

or

The Sin of the Century.

I propose carrying Egotism thro' many of its various Shades.

[P.S.] I have been ill again.

287. MACREADY TO BULWER, *Clarence Terrace, Wednesday night,*
    [*March, 1843*]

I answer your enquiry immediately, and, as I am obliged to do everything now, in haste. The scene in the play reads very effectively — experiment on the stage is the only certain answer, but I think it ought to be both interesting and striking.

I am *warping* the ship onwards, in hope of getting wind & tide with me, when under your auspices. It is difficult to say how anxious I am to have your M.S. in my hands.

Forster gave me the last news of you, who now is issuing bulletins himself, poor fellow!

Macready records that he called on Bulwer on April 3 and "talked with him on his new play, which he is to send me on Wednesday." Characteristically, Bulwer was generous in this crisis. "He spoke in a very honourable way about the remuneration for his piece, wishing only to be paid for it by its nightly success."

288. BULWER TO MACREADY, *Craven Cottage, Fulham, April 5, 1843*

I send you the 4 Acts, if they don't do, the 5th will be useless; if they do, the 5th must be well talked over.

The title I suggested will hardly suit.

Let me know your opinion *au plutôt.*

The sorry end of the affair is laconically set down in three entries in Macready's diary. Under April 5: "Received note and MS. from Bulwer. Read two acts of his play." Under April 6: "Read Bulwer's four acts to Catherine and Letitia. Not good — heavy and sentimental." Under April 9: "Wrote a note to Bulwer, declining his play."

The play thus rejected is to be identified with the incomplete *Darnley*, published posthumously in the Knebworth Edition of Bulwer's Works in 1882. *Darnley* deals with the theme of egotism. It contains in its second act the husband-wife-lover scene borrowed from Dumas's comedy, and a further scene of a wife offering her diamonds to bolster her husband's dwindling fortunes, which is borrowed from the same source. It is, like *Money*, a prose play of the modern scene, though rather more earnest than *Money*, being a serious representation of a painful domestic entanglement. The writing is in general superior to that of Bulwer's "successful" plays, and Macready's summary dismissal of it is not a credit to his judgment. In 1877 it was given simultaneous production in London and Vienna, with Ellen Terry playing the heroine in the English cast. Both productions were failures, mainly, according to Bulwer's son, because of the ill-advised fifth act supplied by a Mr. Coghlan.

Strange to relate, Macready seems to have urged Bulwer to try again. But after more than two years of trying, and so extensive an effort as this last, Bulwer had had enough, and firmly and frankly said so.

289. BULWER TO MACREADY, *May, 1843*

I had hoped ere this to have answered in person your letter. But I am as much oppressed by my business as you by yours, & therefore sit down to tell you fairly & shortly my views as to any aid I can give you. Putting compliment on one side & modesty on the other apart, I believe that I could be more useful than most other writers, & that a play of mine, if successful, would draw more than one of equal merit from Authors less known, or more hacknied in Stage Experience. But it would be idle to hope anything from me, unless you can find the leisure, to suggest and Chalk out your general suggestion of the subject — I cannot afford the time which may be wasted by writing, as it were in the dark, & you would perhaps count in vain upon assistance, which an ill-chosen subject would render a vain xpectation.

To speak frankly — no play can pay me in a pecuniary sense. For the least time it takes is about half the time of a Novel. The utmost pay it can receive is not half the profit derived from a fiction.

I might fairly value my time in the Last play I wrote for you — & which you thought hazardous — at 6 or £700. Now, I have not the least desire to make money the prominent object either in Dramatic or any other composition — less in the Drama while you are at its head than any other, but I *cannot* wholly omit its consideration. — I shall be delighted to write you a play upon a subject you suggest & think good, & leave the profits, in much, dependent on the run. — But it injures me, without serving you — to devote thought, time & toil to Vague experiments on which you cannot depend for your calculations, &c. Therefore, in brief, give me your subject & I will do the best I can — if not, "Sparta hath many a worthier son" & Forster will, no doubt, hunt him out for you, a Landor or a Tennyson of the Drama.

I am afraid you will think this letter somewhat brusque, but I hope at all events it will not offend you, & that you will clearly see that my sole wish is simply to put before you the real question. I am not fond of Dramatic composition. For no other man living with my present views & occupations would I write a play — unless greatly tempted & encouraged: I am willing to make any sacrifice of time or profit to serve you. — But then, I *want to be assured* that the sacrifice *does* serve you, or I lack heart and inspiration.

290. MACREADY TO BULWER, *Theatre Royal Drury Lane, May 29, 1843*

In the propriety and fairness of your views I most heartily concur — and thank you very warmly for your kind thought of me.— If destiny leaven the labour of next season, I shall be anxious to arrange with you in the way you refer to and hope to be benefitted by your aid, and that you will be won to a kinder liking for dramatic writing.

I will let you know as soon as anything is settled.

In the autumn of 1843 Macready took himself to America to make money, and the likelihood that he would want another new play was remote. Yet Bulwer kept him in mind, and as he worked over the materials of his novel-to-be, *The Last of the Saxons*,[58] he conceived it first as a play, "which I think," he wrote Forster, "with care might do good to Macready some day."

291. BULWER TO FORSTER, [*April ?, 1844*]

. . . My first notion was "an Historical Pageant" in 3 Acts — to group as it were all the manners & ceremonies of the time around one great simple figure — Harold the Saxon.— Afterwards I thought I saw stuff for a 5 act Drama — but both these plans fail on approaching them.— 1st because no versified language adaptable to the Drama suits the bold rough homely Saxon which ought to be the character. It could be chanted in rude rhyme — but blank verse seems to me dreadfully out of character.— The interest of the story too tho' it might be considerable in a Novel or an Ariosto sort of Poem wants the continuous thread of the Drama —

My programme was —

An introductory Act in which you would see the Norman Hunting Camp at Rouen — in the midst of which Harold is introduced coming to claim his brother hostage to W^m— The Act would end with his taking the oath to serve W^m & agreeing to marry his sister (He having then no idea of the Crown).— I meant this oath to hang heavy on him afterwards, when the crown tempts him —. He refuses the offer of it under the influence of the oath — & is quite *cowed* by that remembrance till he is suddenly made aware that W^{ms} object is to rule the Country not as a Saxon King, & Natural Heir to Edward but as a Norman Conquerer & Tyrant — then his mind leaps abruptly up from the oath. No oath can bind him to enslave his Country. I see a great Scene & moral effect here — & he accepts his Crown in order to preserve England —. Throughout these transitions I had meant to have a Saxon female — wife or mistress — a kind of inspired Prophetess who animates & angers but whose [*illegible*] he recoils from (tho' loving her) till he is freed from his oath, & then Love & Ambition are crowned in one.— This would be the end of the 3^d Act.— Then omens & superstitions would be at work — his brother revolts — (I meant to confound into one, Tostig the hostile brother, & Wulfrath the young Hostage brother, for whom he had put himself in W$^{m's}$ power — & made the breaking out of this fraternal War, touching as well as terrible — At the end of Act. 4. he would have conquered Tostig — & in the midst of his banquet

---

[58] *Harold, The Last of the Saxon Kings*, 3 vols. (London, 1848).

hear of W^ms Landing — All this in a story of the Epic form — or even in a Drama, long & loose like Shakespeares or Schillers. Historical plays might tell — But for our close & hard compact Theatrical Necessities it would be feeble — & I renounce it. — tho' with regret. . . .

I have just read Michael Kelly's memoirs[59]— How admirably written is the first vol. Reminds me of Le Sage — Was he good, in acting or singing?

Macready's long letter from America begins with an expression of sympathy for the death of Bulwer's mother, which had occurred on December 19, 1843. Bulwer's grief at this loss was profound, and it is said to have contributed to his subsequent breakdown of health.

292. MACREADY TO BULWER, *11 Warren St., New York, May 24, 1844*

If I could have persuaded myself, that any communication of mine beyond the length of those messages and enquiries, with which I charged our friend Forster, could have been worth to you the time of reading them, I should, when in Louisiana, have obeyed the impulse I felt, and have written to you. You will not think, I am sure, that I could be indifferent to the news of you, that has reached me. I learned with sorrow the calamity you had suffered, and could well understand, as it was reported to me, how much the loss, you have been called on to bear, would afflict, and shake you; and it was only on deliberation, that I with-held the expression of my sympathy. I held myself cheaper, than it seems, I had a right to do. I erred in judgement; and whilst I really grieve, that I did so, I am glad at my heart, that you should have desired it otherwise. You have been very often in my mind, and your name and doings have often been a subject of conversation with me even in the distant South and West.— I sent you a paper with a notice of Richelieu, that you might see, you were not unappreciated by the public here, nor forgotten by me.— Upon the Alabama river, I read your Last of the Barons.— Your book led me back to familiar scenes, over which you had built up to the fancy the gloomy and picturesque architecture of that iron time, and, with my eyes bent down upon the page, I could see in their "robes and furr'd gowns", the creatures of your pen, living, acting, feeling, and thinking before me.— The volumes were to me a series of tableaux vivans, in which the characters were as actual as those of dreams, and remain to me ideas of things, that have been. But to what distinct, what wild and strange realities I awoke from these visions of the past, as I turned my eyes from the romance to the scenes around me! — Rushing almost at a railway pace down the "proud river", which was far "peering o'er his bounds" in a gorgeous sort of ark, fitted up with all the conveniences of an hotel, and impelled by a high-pressure steam-

---

[59] Michael Kelly (1764-1826), actor, singer, and composer; *The Reminiscences of Michael Kelly of the King's Theatre and the Theatre Royal, Drury Lane, Including a Period of Nearly Half a Century*, 2 vols. (London, 1826) was actually written by Theodore Hook.

engine, that kept up without intermission its giant pant or roar (they call it the *"cough"* in the far west) like a Cyclops hard at work with his sledge-hammer in one of the forges of Aetna — except at any occasional stoppage, when it eased itself with a snort, in letting off its steam, that would possess an inexperienced ear with the belief, that it was his signal to make his peace with eternity! — This mode of transport is peculiar to the great Western rivers, and a very pleasant conveyance I found it. Making a journey of more than two thousand miles with the accommodations of good bed, board, and books — new, and grand, and constantly varying scenery to look out upon — variety and novelty of character to remark upon, and all varieties of manners to be amused with — and this without fatigue — to me without wearings of mind or body — is an economy of human life and labour, that the old world cannot parallel! — To be sure, on board the inferior boats you run the risk of being advanced on your way to heaven by occasional explosions, or having your downward course (should your destiny be to "the other place") accelerated by the intrusion of a snag: — but these accidents are of rare occurrence in the first-class boats. We were one night on fire on the Mississippi, and I had a summons from my accomplished valet — who thrust his head into my state-room, and in an under-breathed, mysterious, melo-dramatic manner — a sort of Mr. G. Bennett whisper — intimated, "Sir, there is something the matter with the boat; you had better get up."—It certainly was the best thing to do; for when I had, very reluctantly, left my warm bed, and dressed myself, and went upon the deck, I saw volumes of smoke issuing from the hold. Part of the hold, and some bales of cotton in it had taken fire; — we steered to the shore, and in about a quarter of an hour it was extinguished; — so after a short walk on the hurricane-deck, looking at "the chaste-cold moon", and the great illu-minated masses of boats, that with their fire-work chimnies were sweeping heedlessly by us in the middle of the stream, I turned in to my berth whilst our good boat went on, ploughing its way at thirteen miles an hour against the whirling, boiling, turbid, rushing flood of the great "Father of Waters".— They say here —*"they"* are the *"we"*—(the filthiest word, *so* used, in this country) — the *newspapers* — that you are coming out — actually coming out in prop. pers. here! — I send you a Republic of to-day, that alludes to the general belief; this paper is only echoing others, that have noticed, and com-mented upon it.— Is it true? — *Can* it be true? — There are here worlds, moral, intellectual, political, and physical, to engage, employ, and interest the man "Bulwer", but I am not sure how certain inevitable proximities would affect the gorge of "Sir Edward".— Oh, how I should delight in seeing you here! I mean for the selfish enjoyment of meeting you at such a distance from home, for distance from [home is?] like a central point to friends, drawing them closer to each other.— My time has passed as agreeably — as happily as it could from home: the purpose of my absence — the mending a few of the shattered planks in the crazy little bark, that bears my fortunes — has been most satisfactorily answered; and I have seen much in the political and social condition of this great country to please me greatly — very much in the wild grandeur and rich beauty of its surface to move my admiration and delight me. — Looking out from this land, which its cultivators possess and rule, (par parenthèse, — let me copy the head of a sub-poena for you — *"The People of the State of New York to William Charles Macready, greeting"* — is not that grander than the impiety and untruth of "——————— *by the grace of God" &c?*) — Well — to resume, glancing over the Atlantic to dear and lovely England, it is a nauseating spectacle to see the statue of Cromwell extruded from among the great spirits of our land, and that of George 4th set up in the same Square with Nelson's! — Bad taste is not confined to republics. You would deny its existence among them, if you could hear the Americans applauding Richelieu. The "gray doth something mingle with our younger brown" too much for my audiences to feel the same enthusiasm for Claude Melnotte: — or it may be, that the great popularity of the play has caused it to be hacked out in every theatre, and by every pretender to acting. — I do not expect, that I shall be able to return to England before September; and part of the summer I shall devote to the endeavour to see something, for hitherto I have been only casting random glances about me. Niagara I shall re-visit, and the Canadas: and perhaps go into Kentucky to see its Mammoth Cave and Mr Clay:[60] — Of the two the latter is to me the greater attraction. My acting, for the present, is drawing to a close. — Apropos — I play Cardinal Richelieu tonight, repeated from Monday last. It has been a great success through the Union. The native actors have done it: — Mr Forrest[61] and his imitators, representing the Cardinal as a hearty, jolly, hale, old fellow — and have had their course of triumph in it. — You may guess from my tone, that I look with different eyes, or come to different conclusions from Dickens. — I expect, that repudiation will soon be repudiated in every State — but one thing must, I think, be admitted here, that all movement is *advance:* I think the destinies of this country are great and certain. If you come I hope it will be Bulwer, and not the Baronet, who will pass judgement: — But I do not fear the result of your investigations. — I think I have inflicted letter enough upon you for some time to come, leaving myself scarcely room to say how very much and how sincerely I am always,

dear Bulwer, Yours

I earnestly hope, your children enjoy good health. ADDIO.

293. BULWER TO MACREADY, *Great Malvern, Worcestershire, June 29, 1844*

Your kind letter gave me real pleasure, perhaps the more so because I had

---

[60] Henry Clay (1777-1852), American statesman; in this year he ran for the presidency on the Whig ticket, and was defeated by James Polk.

[61] Edwin Forrest (1806-72), foremost American tragic actor of his time; during his next visit to London, in 1845-46, a quarrel with Macready was generated which ultimately caused the New York Astor Place Riot in May of 1849.

given up all hope of hearing from you. You greatly indeed underrate my interest in your career, if you suppose that under any circumstances I should not have been unfeignedly glad to hear from yourself, some account not only of your triumph, the fame of which finds other trumpeters, but of your health and prospects; your views of the United States are such as I should have predicted. O'Connell[62] once tauntingly complained that his conduct in struggling for a great people was viewed with the eye of a Master of the Ceremonies. With more justice may the young Titan of a Republic complain that almost every tourist has spoken of it in the mincing criticism with which a Dancing Master might favour the Farnese Hercules. They cannot screw its vigorous feet forever on the upward way into the affected grace of the 5th position. The last thing into which a manly & intelligent observer in examining America should search is the outward conventionality. He must mass together all the large facts connected with the greatest experiment in Government, since Greece shook off her brilliant tyrannies, and solve the problems of her surpassing energy — her public spirit — & her rushing progress. Of *manners* the Englishman is usually the most prejudiced judge. If he prefers his own to the Frenchman's, it is no wonder that he is vulgarly sensitive to vulgarity in the American. The wonder rather is that in a People without a court, without an idle Aristocracy, engaged thro' all its classes in anxious commerce & the rough strife of personal interest and political passions — the wonder rather is, that so much civility to strangers, so much courtesy to women, so forbearing an usage of legal equality — are the characteristics of the Population. The only points in which it appears to me the Americans are fairly exposed to censure are in their capricious and uncertain morality, which so often sinks character in success — their indulgence to "a smart man," & in that debasing appetite for slander & abuse without which their Press would long since have been reformed. The last has always been the character of Democracies — & doubtless the worst American paper is less calumnious than Aristophanes — the former is perhaps also a necessary consequence of the Trading spirit. By degrees the Americans may purify themselves of these blots, but in gaining some of the good qualities of an old country, they may lose much of the vigorous attributes of a new. Your letter which arrived two days ago, finds me under the Hydropathic Treatment. My painful & intense anxiety for some months, ending in the crushing grief, for the loss of my nearest & dearest friend, seemed to shatter into pieces a constitution never very robust. At last, finding all other means in vain, I came hither — anticipating more benefit from an entire and abrupt change of all my habits, than from the salutary tortures of wet sheets & mountainous blankets. Whether from the one or the other cause, I have derived great benefit from the water cure — tho' as yet in my novitiate I have been less than 3 weeks, & propose staying another month.— Some time in September I shall go abroad

---

[62] Daniel O'Connell (1775-1847), Irish political leader; after the Catholic Emancipation Act of 1829, an M.P. who supported Whig reform programs.

for the winter. But I hope to shake you by the hand with a hearty welcome before I depart.— All theatrical news you have doubtless rec^d from Forster & others, better versed in the Mimic world than I am.— I began at St. Leonards something for your return, but spirits & subject failed together. My idea was Harold, the last Saxon King, and I still think a most striking & impressive Drama might be worked out from his History & his Saxon qualities, by one quite up to the work. Which I am not. I heard somewhere that you were likely to go to Paris. Is it so? — I have lived quite out of the world for many months, & have nothing to communicate of its toil & turmoil. The Americans are never likely, I suspect, to find me upon their shores. The report circulated in their newspapers is without foundation. Me, the New World with its active hopes, has ceased to allure tho' not to interest.— I love more the holy day indolence, & dreamy reserves which the contemplation of States in which the Volcano is expended serves to nourish. At certain stages of life the Past has more delight for us than the Future. The creative Faculty, which is one with the true ideal, does not invent — it only re-creates. What can the imagination do to present before us and clothe with living interest the generations that may hereafter people the Alabona [Alabama?]? But the Poet & the Artist find their element in things that *have been*, & in Egypt, Greece, & Italy — we can bid the Dead live again. While we are practical men, Oeconomists, & Politicians, America attracts us. When we sink back into the second youth of Idealism — we prefer the old Titans to the new.— Adieu my dear Macready. *Vive, vale sis memor mei.*

After America, Macready made a triumphant visit to Paris,[63] and much of the year of 1845 was spent in provincial tours. Thus he and Bulwer (who was quite ill in 1845) saw little of each other. Somehow Bulwer came to imagine that Macready was offended at him. The following exchange of notes restored their friendship to the old level, at least for the moment.

294. Macready to Bulwer, *5 Clarence Terrace, Regent's Park, London,* *October 7, 1845*

Forster reported to me on Saturday the substance of a conversation he had with you last week.— I need scarcely allude to the surprise his information caused me; but I was in the main really glad to understand, that you had so far mistaken me, as to suppose I had taken umbrage at some imagined slight. It was a very great relief to me to know, that you had not, as I apprehended, conceived some cause of offence upon any unconscious act of *mine*. I could no more give my consent to any proceeding, that should create a minute's pain or annoyance to you, than I could entertain resentment or cherish coldness towards you, even if I could believe, you thought with indifference or anger of me. The years, that are before me are too few for the growth of many new friendships, and I cannot afford to part with that inestimable solace of un-

---

[63] The Paris engagement ran from December 16, 1844, to January 18, 1845.

happier thoughts, the affectionate remembrance of those, who are endeared to me by manifestations of sympathy, that are beyond all price. Pray believe, that it would be with unmingled sorrow, no feeling of selfish visitation disturbing it, that I should hear of your estrangement, and that I should still think of you with the same affectionate admiration & regard for your many noble qualities, that I have done since I had first the happiness of knowing you for a friend.

295. BULWER TO MACREADY, *Knebworth, October 7, 1845*

I am truly glad that your letter has served to remove any incomprehensible misunderstanding between us. In this Shallow Stream of life, there are constantly weeds and stones which fret the surface — we do well not to interrupt & chafe the current by hindrances of our own. Believe me I have never ceased for a moment to admire & esteem you — to value your friendship & feel a lively interest in your fortunes & career. I rejoice that you are going to appear again in Town. With you rests our Drama — & better things may come out of your return to us. With kindest regards to Mrs. Macready

Bulwer's next gesture toward Macready, however, did give offense, though obviously none was intended.

296. BULWER TO MACREADY, *36 Hertford St., December 6, 1845*

I called on you coming to town *en route* for Paris, & had the mortification to find you flown to Dublin. I wanted more especially a word or two with you on Dramatic subjects.

I shall have some leisure on my hands during my stay abroad, and if it can be employed with any advantage to you — the profit thereof will be doubly agreeable to myself. I have long had a belief that Sophocles almost purely & entirely in his own classic simplicity may be put on the stage.

And the success of Antigone[64] confirms my notion. What say you to the Oedipus (Tyrannus).

It was always the great histrionic part on the Athenian Stage, & is the most thrilling of the Greek Dramas, & I fancy it will succeed with us. Not a french Oedipe — but the old Drama, with Chorus & all as in the Antigone. In many parts literally translated, but in verse — and in short the original as much adhered to as possible. It will require the adjunct of fine music, but that can be obtained, either from English or German composers. I would not begin it, it is true, unless you see, which you probably do not, your way to purchase & represent it — unless indeed it were a partial engagement to purchase it — tho I should be quite willing in your case to let half the purchase money be contingent on the run as it is an experiment to both.

[64] A version of Sophocles' *Antigone*, said to be translated from the German, and accompanied by Mendelssohn's music, was being played at Covent Garden by John Vandenhoff and his daughter Charlotte (1818-60) in January of this year. Helen Faucit then performed it in Dublin, Edinburgh, London, and elsewhere to great critical acclaim.

I leave England on Wednesday after Post time. There is great time for me to have a yes or no, and if the former to look out the necessary books to take with me.— If it does not press you too much to answer this by return of Post.

If you don't write so immediately, you must then direct Poste restante Paris. Concluding the business part of the arrangement, supposing the price be 600£. I should be satisfied with half on completing the Drama — & the rest according to the run. If you dislike this idea, I own I have no other in my head but should be happy to receive any hints.

What are your plans and projects? I hear nothing of them.

297. MACREADY TO BULWER, *Dublin, December 8, 1845*

I much regret that I have lost the opportunity of seeing you in London, where I could have made all the enquiries necessary to a full and satisfactory answer of your questions. I think the Oedipus would produce a startling and striking effect, but I do not think the skeleton-like figure of the older drama would keep its place on our stage beside the flesh and blood of our great poets. — Still it might very well answer its experiment.— But — it should be produced — as regards acting and mise en scene to the nicest point of finish: — and how or where is this to be? — My engagement with Mr Maddox[65] stands for five weeks in January & February — five weeks in April — To enter on a new play I must make an entirely new engagement — this is not a thing, that lies in my will alone.— And then as to Mr Maddox' *getting up* or *laying out,* how is that to be guaranteed? What *bond* would hold him to the letter? — I myself, until I were in possession of a Theatre of my own, should be utterly helpless, my hands behind me.— The question can only be answered at present by the Knowledge of what Mr Maddox would do — This Forster could best ascertain, *if* — and there is MUCH virtue, alas! in *that* if — any reliance can be placed on Mr M.—

I cannot see any direct mode of dealing with the matter myself at present, but were I *in office* I should clutch at the experiment.

Can not you talk with Forster about it, before you start? — It ought not to be lost for want of moving in it.—I am here quite helpless to do anything.

I shall be in London in a fortnight, will you have anything respecting it for me.

I write in greatest haste, and am ever with warmest wishes most sincerely Yours'

Macready noted in his diary, with annoyance, the firm statement of the *price* asked, and being probably not at all aware of Bulwer's then rather straitened financial needs, took it perhaps as a threatened incursion upon his own treasury, which he was now desperately accumulating and hoarding against the foreseeable day of his retirement. "If I understand him rightly," he writes, "this is rather mingling the trader with the friend. Answered Bulwer, not accepting his offer." Two weeks later, in London, he

---

[65] Frederick More Maddox, manager of the Princess's Theatre, where Macready played several limited engagements in 1845, 1846, and 1847.

delivered his opinion to Forster "that Bulwer's expression, in his letter to me at Dublin, of 'desiring to *serve me* by writing a new play' was not very generous nor correct; that, understanding, as I believed I did, his position, it was certainly to '*serve himself.*' " Forster agreed that Macready was undoubtedly right, and was sure that Bulwer "would not use such a term in speaking or writing to him on such a subject." A strangely misleading conversation! Bulwer had not used the term to Macready, and Macready was perpetrating a morbid, if not vicious, misquotation.

Bulwer, writing from Paris, told Forster he would drop the *Oedipus,* and then immediately afterwards started up another idea — a tragedy of Brutus.[66]

298. BULWER TO FORSTER, *Hot. de Princes, Paris, December 15, 1845*

. . . I know not if I shall hear anything of the Oedipus — but if Macready had been more settled, I have thought of a splendid subject for him — A part that would (if I do it, as I conceive it) — make a prodigious addition to his great characters. It is a Tragedy & a Roman One — but not I think cold or stiff — But full of pother & terror, & the part itself while strictly historical thoroghly & peculiarly dramatic & of the highest order — But I say nothing more of it, tho' I have the whole tragedy mapped out, because I do not see any way to the arrangements for placing it on the boards.— I would not take less than 600£ for it when given.— But if any Manager where Macready performs will consent to give me that sum provided you & Macready approve & recommend it when written — without asking further guarantee or particulars — except my own responsibility I will set about & finish it at once — & very early in the Spring it should be ready & in England — Let me know about this as soon as you can —.   I dont like till then to mention the subject to anyone — Kean would give me 1000£ for it but unless I was very hard pressed for money I should not think of giving it to anyone but Macready — & prove that by taking 400 less than Kean has expressly offered me for any tragedy I please to write . . .

I should not go on with the Tragedy unless — there is a contract in writing for it —.   But, in that case would finish & bring it to England.— God willing.

By January Bulwer had, *pro tempore,* abandoned *Brutus,* and a month later announced from Naples that he had done the *Oedipus* after all.

299. BULWER TO FORSTER, [*Naples, January, 1846*]

. . . I can no longer delay thanking you for your remembrance of the absent & for your exertions about the play — I have laid it at present on the shelf, not being inclined to add to my collection of useless MSS — or to swell the dread Account of the Unacted Drama. Whenever I can learn that if written it will be accepted by the Manager on the conditions stated, & acceptable to Mac-

---

[66] Bulwer's *Brutus* was completed but not published. It was staged posthumously in 1885 as a five-act drama called *Junius Brutus; or, The Household Gods.* Several manuscripts of it are in the Knebworth Archives. L. Junius Brutus is the legendary hero who expelled the Tarquins from Rome after the rape of Lucretia.

ready — I will return to & complete it. Meanwhile the dolce far Niente gains upon me. . . .

300. BULWER TO FORSTER, [*Naples, February 5, 1846*]

Since writing to you in a fire of classical fervour I have *completed* what I had so long meditated — A Drama on the Oedipus Tyrannus, with the Choruses &c. More than this — I have arranged with the celebrated Mercadante,[67] the Composer for the Music to the Choruses & Overture. He is to receive 150£ for his work — & I am to pay him — He takes to it *con amore*, & I have little doubt that his Music will be very grand & effective —. Now can you arrange to sell this for me — to any Theatre where Macready performs. Surely it is a card in his hands to take it to any Theatre. — I am convinced that it is a part that will do him good — It always was the greatest part on the Greek Stage & if I cannot flatter myself that I have attained to the poetry of Sophocles — I think that I have improved the mere theatrical effect of the Drama — & I have certainly brought out the character of Oedipus in colours more adapted for a modern Audience —. I have followed the march of the antical plot almost exactly — with a few touches & additions here & there —. but I have not translated the Dialogue — I have rather *built upon* it. Also the choruses —. As a poem it is more uniform & restrained than anything I have written—. Produce it I must, now that I have both paid and pledged myself to Mercadante — for if it is useless to Macready or cannot be arranged with any manager for him — I must take it elsewhere.— I should say that its length is less than a 5 act play, not exceeding 1000 lines — but I can lengthen it if Macready thinks advisable. On the other hand to make up for the shortness — we must consider the time taken up by the Overture & choruses —. This including the Overture Mercadante reckons at 70 minutes which will bring the whole pretty nearly to the usual time of close.— Mercadante is the author of the Opera La Vestale [*illegible*] (Sappho) &c. & I suppose his reputation in England is not inferior to what it is here — He is considered the greatest Composer of Chorus & the most painstaking & classical composer in Italy —

What I want for the whole, including what I pay Mercadante is 500£ — down — If Macready does not have it, I shall ask more elsewhere — Mercadante will have completed his task before I can receive your answer. So that if you can succeed — the play, music & all will be sent over to you by return of Post.— But may I ask the additional favour of getting a positive Managerial answer immediately —. Otherwise as I leave Naples in a month I shall miss receiving it. Moreover as the Season is advancing I have no time to lose in selling it elsewhere if you fail which seems to me likely eno'— seeing that I have had no answer about my tragedy. I feel no hesitation in recommending it honestly to a Manager, as a good speculation. 1st the part is *made* for Mac-

---

[67] Saverio Mercadante (1795-1870), composer of many operas, of which *La Vestale* (1840) is his masterpiece.

ready — if Sophocles had written for Macready, he could not have thought of anything more adapted to him. 2^{ndly} the names of Sophocles & Mercadante suffice to remove the chance of *failure* & secure respect —

I ask 500£ which leaves only 350 for my self. The Manager must engage himself to have suitable Singers & Orchestra. — Rather than not conclude I would take off 50£ — making it 450 — but I think if a Manager will give 450 he will give 500 — & I believe I ought to have 600£. Mercadante proposes that the length of each chorus (5 in all) should average 10 minutes. — This however strikes me as too long for an English Audience — will you ascertain how long it ought to be on an average — so that I can get him if necessary to shorten them — 2ndly, will you inform me if it is necessary to have any peculiar form of specification to secure the copyright of the Composer as a Foreigner, to me or whether — the music being part & parcel of my production — it does not fall within the protection accorded to myself.

Pray kindly see to this at once & let me hear as soon as possible — it takes a fortnight to reach me — I believe it is best to put *via Marseilles et par Mer* on the address. . . .

[P.S.] The Tragedy is of course postponed — & on the Shelf.

Macready records on February 12 that Forster read him this last letter, but registers neither approval nor disapproval. Two days later he was infuriated to discover that Forster had been trying to impose the *Oedipus* on the Princess's Theatre manager, Mr. Maddox, sight unseen, and had imputed to Macready the responsibility for this condition.

Meanwhile the scandalous publication of *The New Timon*,[68] with its attack upon Tennyson, had broken upon the town, and gossip, for once correct, ascribed the authorship to Bulwer. On February 13 Macready wrote Bulwer, urging him, "if he could," to contradict the common report. Bulwer's answer is a flat lie, and it is curious that Macready never afterwards commented on being treated with such disingenuousness.

301. BULWER TO MACREADY, *Rome, March 3, 1846*

Many thanks for your kind & friendly note which I have only just received & which I answer in haste.

I was not aware of the groundless rumour you mention, — as I seldom see a paper & it was not alluded to in my letters from England. Except in one from Forster who implied rather his own suspicion — than mentioned any serious report. I have only seen the first part of the New Timon which was sent to me a day or two before I left England — but since your letter implies that it is no very creditable production, I am at a loss to know why Forster should pay me so bad a compliment. — Long eno', I dare say, before one's friends would suspect one of anything good! — I should feel much obliged if you would use *my distinct & most positive authorization* to contradict the report, wherever you deem it necessary. I wrote to Forster some time ago about my adaptation

---

[68] *The New Timon: A Romance of London* (London, 1846), published anonymously.

of the Oedipus, Mercadante having promised to write the music for the Choruses etc.— But I conclude from your letter, that you are not in a condition to think of such matters.

I am most truly concerned for the State of the Stage in England — & for your own imperfect connexion with it at this moment.— It is a disgrace to the Country that things should be so.

On my return to England I shall try & see you & discuss matters — I have an idea that a Company of gentlemen would agree in taking a suitable Theatre & placing it at your disposal — I should have little fear of the risk.

Nous en parlerons —

I came to Italy in a vague half-formed notion of selecting one of its cities for an habitual winter residence. I dismiss that illusion, my second visit has cured me of the enervating effects of the First.

I hope to be in London in little more than a month. With kindest regards to Mrs. Macready, Adieu.

302. BULWER TO FORSTER, *March 15, 1846*

. . . At all events let me thank you cordially for your troubles & kindness. The Oedipus will keep a little longer, seeing it has kept already 2000 years or so — something like the Woodcock reroasted for me today — & which I have no doubt was served up before to Lars Porsena[69] when that distinguished personage was traveling in this direction!

303. BULWER TO FORSTER, *[May], 1846*

> I go to Knebworth Tuesday
> pray write me word there,
> about the play

I send you the play.— On reflection I would never produce it (after it has been acted at Berlin) with borrowed music — I should lose all my claim to originality & the words must be allied to other Music — in fact it w^d be infra Dig.

But if you & Macready think it will do, I should make a push to get it out before the Berlin one which I am sure is best. It has not rec^d the last verbal finish

P.S. If the play should be acted I propose that the same actor who does Tiresias, should do the Messenger — as in the Greek Stage — for both parts require a good Declaimer — & I doubt if I could find 2 declaimers in the present state of the Stage.

304. BULWER TO FORSTER, *Knebworth, Saturday night, [May 10, 1846]*

I should be glad to know, as soon as you can, what you & Macready think of the Oedipus — of course much of its effect on the stage must depend on first

---

[69] Lars Porsena, semilegendary Etruscan king who conquered Rome c. 500 B.C.

rate music — But so far as I & the Acting are concerned — is it to be or not — according to your advice — & M's — I am obliged now to arrange my literary plans generally, & it enters into them & indeed into my *pecuniary* accounts to decide whether to put this play on the stage or quietly in my desk.— . . .

305. BULWER TO FORSTER, [*May, 1846*]

Will you now let Macready see the Oedipus as soon as he can, for I much fear that the Berlin success will forestall us here if there is any longer delay

Macready finally received the *Oedipus* on May 23, and it did not please him. "What I have read I do not like — it lacks simplicity of style and picturesqueness and *reality.*"

306. BULWER TO MACREADY, *19 James St., Saturday, May 24, 1846*

I congratulate you heartily on your new triumph in The King of the Commons[70] which I shall come to see next week. I have been wanting to get to you, but cruel business and much absence from Town have prevented it.— Forster has my Oedipus, & I wish much that you should see it as soon as you can, for I have little doubt that the great success of the same attempt at Berlin will add to the effect of the Play if brought out forthwith, while if there is much delay, we shall be surely forestalled.

On June 7 Bulwer called to discuss the *Oedipus,* on which Macready gave him his opinion "in part"; and "he seemed struck with some suggestions, but I showed him that there was no chance of its being performed, and I also gave my opinion it would not be attractive if performed." On this day too Bulwer reverted to his old notion that a theatre might be taken and run (for Macready's benefit) "by a party of gentlemen," but Macready was not interested. In his private reflections Macready was caustic on Bulwer's personal behavior: "I was sorry to see him so peculiar in his dress — most particularly extravagant in his attention to the costume of his face, which he makes unpicturesque and coxcomical."

Bulwer was disappointed at Macready's refusal of *Oedipus,* but undaunted. In a long series of letters to Forster from July, 1846, to March, 1847 (not here included), one may trace the steps of his negotiations to get it produced by Samuel Phelps at Sadler's Wells. Forster served as go-between, and at a meeting in Forster's rooms Phelps agreed to pay Bulwer £350 and Mercadante £150 for the overture and choruses, urging moreover "that not a day was to be lost" in getting Mercadante started at the composing. Mercadante agreed to complete the music by November 5, and wanted his money paid on receipt of it, but unluckily Bulwer had got no written contract from Phelps and the £150 could not be squeezed out of him. By October 20 Phelps wanted to get out of the agreement because Drury Lane and Covent Garden had monopolized all the available singers in the profession and the production was therefore impossible.

Two months later, Bulwer wanted to get out of it too. His latest novel, *Lucretia,*[71] had brought on a flood of hostile criticism because of its supposed immorality, and, as

---

[70] *The King of the Commons* was produced by Macready at the Princess's on May 20, ran for thirteen nights, and was later played in the provinces. The author, James White (1803-63), wrote a series of historical sketches on Scottish themes.

[71] *Lucretia; or The Children of Night,* 3 vols. (London, 1846).

he wrote Forster, "if so much indignation is produced by the written representation of crime in the Novel, what will be said of the actual, acted representation of homicide & incest on the Stage. True that this Drama is not mine but Sophocles's — still I may be liable to the charge of having selected & revived [it] for horrid & perverted purposes of my own." Without Macready's *"delicacy* and skill" to mitigate the horrors, Bulwer feared the worst and he preferred "to cry Hold, hold — to sacrifice the £150 to Mercadante, & withdraw the play." The affair dragged on unsettled into the next year, until, on February 8, Bulwer was pleased to know that Mercadante had been unable to complete the music and was willing to drop the engagement, taking a mere £50 for his pains. He wrote Forster that "considering the 'painful subject' — homicide & incest — considering that Phelps is not Macready — & hardly equal to the part . . . I shall now take advantage of the opportunity & back out. — I can hardly afford a failure & an execrating one least of all, at present." Bulwer and Phelps divided the £50 payment to Mercadante between them, and the *Oedipus* was shelved forever. It was never even published. Examination of the manuscript in the Knebworth Archives reveals it to be, if a little florid, a very decent rendering of the play for the stage of the time. "If Sophocles had written for Macready, he could not have thought of anything more adapted to him," Bulwer had said, and it is a pity that it went under to timorousness before the dread threat of decorum.

I can find no clue to the nature of the comedy Bulwer was working at in November of 1846, but the "4 Acts of a Domestic Drama" is plainly a reference to *Darnley,* and the following remarks about writing for Macready are eloquent of hope and despair.

307. BULWER TO FORSTER, [*November 22, 1846*]

You said in your last that you & Macready wished *he* had a part in my Comedy. What is meant by this? — My Comedy was intended for the Haymarket — & Macready has no engagement there, nor is seemingly likely to have one. Does Macready in short want a part in a play written expressly for The Haymarket, or does he want, (& is he in a condition to treat for) a play, which he could take himself where he pleased? I am very anxious to know this & to be clear on the point as soon as possible — For in looking over old Dramatic Attempts, I find 4 Acts of a Domestic Drama already sketched, in which the principal part (a sort of Provoked Husband) would suit Mac^y & could be acted by no one else — Now I have no idea of finishing this generaly for the Haymarket for that very reason.— The great stumbling block to a play at present is in fact having a part for Macready — & therefore I should lay it by — unless assured that he was in a state to undertake it himself or the engagement with the Haymarket — In the one case, I could finish off this thing in a fortnight — in the other I should write a more *complete* comedy without the *sentiment* which this has — & I should suit the parts to the Haym^t Company. In fact, except as a *kindness* to Macready — I should certainly choose the latter — & nothing but that remark of yours has made me revert to this play (which I rather think he or you must have seen some years ago —) which could, I see be an effective Domestic Sentimental Play, (not adding much to my reputation, because of its sentimentality) but *certain,* with some alterations to draw on the Stage

What I want to know is something definite — for the time I have lost in writing something for M. (entre nous) & then having cold water thrown on it, would have sufficed for volumes of plays.

I consider him — from the difficulty of a part to suit him &c — the great impediment to Activity & promoter of Despair!

308. BULWER TO FORSTER, [*February 10, 1847*]

. . . I have some little idea of making a Three Act Tragedy of my old plan of the Elder Brutus, ending with Lucretia's death — There is not stuff for 5 Acts — In that case, I think it would bear a Second Tragedy in 3 Acts, ending with the death of his sons —. The break in the interest caused by Lucretia's death does not allow, I find on going closely into it — the amalgamation of these 2 catastrophes into one Drama.— The Lucretia lately acted at the Theatre Francais has been very successful tho' my plan is different less classical & more Elizabethan — Brutus will remain a Fool till Lucretia's death —. His would be an immense part, but I doubt if any, save Macready could do it.—

Early in 1847 Macready, with Forster's advice and assistance, was investigating the possibility of taking a theatre of his own to finish out his career. The plan came to nothing, but Bulwer stood by to help if it had.

309. BULWER TO FORSTER, [*Gt. Malvern, April 15, 1847*]

I have been here ten days for my health. Voila why I could not meet you in Town. — I am ready to cooperate in any scheme for giving Macready [*illegible*] Theatre if to be sold.— I think a Subscription Company of Proprietors might be raised to build one & pay the ground rent. . . .

310. BULWER TO MACREADY, *James St., Saturday, May 22, 1847*

I got your note yesterday — it was returned from Malvern which I had left suddenly on urgent business.— I am obliged to run down to Kneb. but I shall be back Monday & delighted to see you on Tuesday if I can come in *the Evening* — mornings being occupied. I am rejoiced to find you engaged & cheerful.

In desperate haste.

On May 25 Bulwer and Forster dined with Macready. "Talked over the subjects of plays the whole evening," Macready reports, "and at last we seemed to settle down upon that of Sir Robert Walpole as the best that could be devised for a mixed play." Yet again nothing came of it. Bulwer reported to Forster on June 12, "I have been plagued out of my life & in no mood to sit down to a Comedy." That summer he ran for Parliament again, and was again defeated.

311. MACREADY TO BULWER, *5 Clarence Terrace, Regent's Park,*
    August 7, 1847

I must assure you of the annoyance and regret with which I read of the self-stultification of the Lincoln electors. It must be a satisfaction to you, under the disappointed [*sic*] of your just expectations, that indignation is felt, where-ever the news of the Lincoln Election is told. I wish I could have helped you with my Marylebone vote, which I had hoped I was to poll for you. We must hope for better sense and its day is coming to the constituencies of England.

Forster tells me, that you are going ahead: I must say to you with my addio in Moore's words "Oh, still remember me"[72] — or rather remember the play, you have been encouraging us to hope for. — It may make some amends in the pleasure of its success for the stupidity of Lincoln electors.

Trusting you may take and bring back health with you, and "give the stage one classic drama more". . . .

312. BULWER TO MACREADY, *Haymarket, April 27, 1848*

I send you the "Sylvia"[73] you were good eno' to lend me some time since.

I am most grieved to hear that Mrs. Macready has been long ill. I trust to have better reports of her soon.

I too have been much distressed by the long illness of my daughter.[74]

In the fall of 1848 Macready departed for his last visit to America. Arrived there, he found in the northern states the rising tide of anti-British sentiment focusing upon himself. Personal attacks against him, by or on behalf of the American tragedian Edwin Forrest, included among worser charges the assertion that Macready had tried to prevent Forrest from acting in Bulwer's plays. At Macready's request, Bulwer provided detailed denial of these charges.

313. BULWER TO MACREADY, *Leominster, December 16, 1848*

I have already written to you on the points named in yours — received to-day. I hasten to repeat the purport of my replies.

1st You never, directly or indirectly thro' yourself or others, expressed any wish whatsoever that M[r] Forrest should not perform in any play of mine, & it would have been so unlike you to have sought to influence me on such a point, that I should have disbelieved any one, who ventured to report to me that you had the least disinclination to M[r] Forrest's taking a part in my plays.

2nd You never had any communication direct or indirect with me or any agent of mine respecting any application from M[r] Forrest to act in my plays.

3[rdly] I not only do not believe you capable of any interference to the prejudice of the interests of another Actor upon such a point. But from a long & intimate acquaintance with you I should have considered it an insult to you, to have even asked you if you could object to any actor performing your parts in my plays: It is a proof indeed of that, — that I have always unhesitatingly given permission to M[r] Kean to play Claude Melnotte, even at a time when it might be thought that he pitted that performance against your own.

Furthermore, according to the printed statement from the Boston Mail,

---

[72] Thomas Moore, "Go Where Glory Waits Thee" (in *Irish Melodies*).

[73] George Darley (1795-1846), the critic, had written a "lyrical drama" called *Sylvia; or, The May Queen* in 1827, which may be the book referred to.

[74] Emily Bulwer (born June 27, 1828) died two days after this was written.

Oct. 30th, it seems that I did accord to Mr Forrest the permission to act the part of Richelieu & Claude Melnotte, for a less sum than I was, & still am, in the habit of receiving for them at a London Theatre — & a less sum than I should have asked from any manager with whom you yourself were engaged — viz 80 guineas for 40 nights, that is for a full season. My usual terms would be 100^{gs} & you know well that my reason for claiming pecuniary terms for the performance of my plays, no matter who the actors, is to set the example of enforcing my own act of Act of Parliament, for the benefit of poorer Dramatic Authors than myself. I am in the usual habit of leaving it to some friend of literary station & not to a mere agent to fix the terms, & I have little doubt but that as appears by the Boston Mail that the plays were offered to Mr Forrest upon more favourable terms than to an English actor, in order that as an American, he might have full chance of any benefit they could bring him.

The sum may seem high in America. But for performances fewer in number than 40 nights I shall receive this year a much larger sum from Mr Phelps as the Manager of a minor Metropolitan Theatre.

To the best of my recollection, at the time to which this matter refers, we were not in any personal intercourse with each other.

I have that confidence in the American Public, that I feel perfectly persuaded it will rally round you, with regret & even shame at so unworthy a calumny from a part of its population — unhappily misled — I can conceive that your high sense of honour may be wounded at the mere suspicion of practices so foreign to your nature. In England the injustice of such attacks seems as ludicrously glaring, as if we had heard a report that the Duke of Wellington had been broken for cowardice or the Archbishop of Canterbury sent to the Treadmill for picking pockets.

Your letter found me in the bustle of a parliamentary canvass — & you will excuse so hasty a scrawl from your sincere friend & brother Artist

[*notation by Macready*]
Sir E. Bulwer Lytton in reply to my direct question.

314. MACREADY TO BULWER, *City Hotel, Baltimore, M^d, December 24, 1848*

I need not assure you, my dear Bulwer, what deep gratification your most kind, most friendly letter afforded me. To judge of how sensibly I was touched by it, it would be needful, that a man should be, as I am, far distant from all that is most dear to him, and assailed as I have been by reckless opponents, carrying out in defiance of all decency, and to appearance, in despite of common sense, a scheme of mischief, that has only failed of its full effect from the blundering excess of malignity in its contriver. — The danger had passed over, when your letter reached me, but I was not the less affected by the consolation its affectionate heartiness afforded me. — What pleasure I have in thanking you for it! — I am in some measure indebted to the wickedness, that has been so active against me, for the solace and delight it imparted to me. — Since you wrote it, you will have received some direct questions from me upon the subject, to which, although they are really answered here, my lawyer thinks it well desirable to have your direct reply: — The newspaper libels are now assumed and published as direct charges by Mr Forrest: and although your name does not appear above what he has subscribed, yet it is within the previous list of accusations printed by the Boston Mail upon his authority and promised *endorsement.* How unintelligible it must be in England, that an illiterate and vulgar man, by mere assertion on his "belief" can induce a rabble to convene meetings to consider the question of driving a person away from a city, and actually instigate them to disorder and violence! — But with the low democratic press and its readers here, the question is not of talent or aptness, but they "*go in* for Americanism!" — This is a bad phase of this great community, and one which I did not suspect could ever show itself: but I have witnessed, and narrowly escaped its malignant influence, though supported by all of respectable and good that take interest in such matters.— You would have been greatly interested, as I was, in observing the perfect tranquility and good humour with which the office of Chief Magistrate of this vast country was transferred from one person to another.[75]

My visit here has been marked by heavy calamities at home.[76] — This has been indeed a year of affliction to me — but I thank God for the friends that are left me, and you, dear Bulwer Lytton, among the first.

The American visit was to terminate violently in May, 1849, in the famous Astor Place Riot, and Macready fled home. Bulwer, ill again, was reworking *The Sea-Captain,* ostensibly for Phelps. Yet, as he progressed with the revision, thoughts of Macready haunted him. Writing to Forster in November, from the Antibes, he said "I think it too good to throw away as an old play — on Sadlers Wells —. If it could be of any use to Macready himself, of course it is entirely at his service, irrespective of any pecuniary terms. . . . Better not speak to Phelps about The Sea Captain." About Christmastime he suggested that the revision be given to Charles Kean, but only "on the proviso of not acting it till after Macready's retirement."

Meanwhile on November 20 Macready took time to indulge in a rarely relaxed gossip to Bulwer, who was then at Nice.

315. Macready to Bulwer, *5 Clarence Terrace, Regent's Park, London, November 20, 1849*

Some days since — upon recollection I ought indeed to say, some weeks since — I mentioned to Forster my intention of writing to you, and to leave me no excuse for delay, he furnished me immediately with your address. But the idler's complaint of want of time has been, though perhaps not altogether without reason, mine: — or perhaps a consciousness, that nothing I could impart would be worth the minutes, that my letter may steal from you of

---

[75] Presumably Macready is referring to the succession of the presidency from the Democrat James Polk to the Whig Zachary Taylor.

[76] Macready's younger brother, Edward Neville, had died on November 4.

enjoyment in that delightful nook of earth where you are now, I trust, luxuriating, has betrayed me into the belief, that tomorrow would always suit me better than today. For what have I to say to you from the narrow world, in which I live and move and have my being? When I have expressed the earnest wish of my heart, that this may find you well in health, and fully enjoying the delicious atmosphere and the beauty of the little territory, in which the mountains wall you round, I seem to have expended all that has interest in my stock of communication. Alternate days of effort and lassitude make up to me the history of each week, as I wear through the last round of my professional course: and what care you now for the Haymarket Theatre, or how can you ever bring down your thoughts to its gas, and close-pent heat, and noise, from among the oranges and citrons of the garden, in which you live, and from the quiet shore of that deep blue sea, that spreads its beauty before you? What a vision of delight its recollection is to me, which I shall never look on, in its reality, again! My tent is set up, and early in the month of July (when my last "hour upon the stage" is noted down) we go to a little quiet town, called Sherborne, that looks nestled down to an everlasting doze in one of the valleys of Dorsetshire, where there are, as my temptations, one of Edward 6th's endowed schools, and some monastic remains, which are very superior specimens of Gothic architecture, an epitaph of Pope's in a beautiful church, and certain traditions of Raleigh, who lived there on the estate, which one of "our most religious and gracious" took from his widow to bestow upon the worthy Somerset. In addition to these notabilia, there is an old fashioned house, large enough to be an ark for us all — and what have I to do with more? — My large little family will not let me want occupation there; and except in aiding and preparing them for the world, whose evening shades will be beginning to close round me, I may say with Pope, that there

> "life will little else supply,
>   But just to look about us, and to die."[77]

In some weekly paper I shall probably read of the triumphant, or in legitimate Playbill phrase, "tremendous" success of Sir E. Bulwer Lytton's Comedy or Tragedy — or whatever he chooses it should be: — and perhaps there will be a passing twinge of regret, that I was not there to "pursue the triumph, and partake the gate."— In contemplating your range from King Arthur to the Caxtons,[78] there will be no cause for surprise in whatever your ever-busy brain may give forth. The Caxton Family came as a most especial boon to me. It is indeed a most charming book, full of the best wisdom, the noblest and sweetest humanity. I read one half of it in the bleared and blotted types of an American press, in the midst of the Atlantic, ensnugged in the corner of the Hibernia's

---

[77] A not quite accurate reading of the second couplet of *An Essay on Man*. The retirement to Sherborne did not occur in July of 1850, as here promised, but in March, 1851.

[78] *King Arthur* (London, 1848). *The Caxtons: A Family Picture*, 3 vols. (London, 1849).

cabin; and I wish I could convey to you a full idea of the delight it afforded me! The printed sheets gave me just half the story; it was ascribed to you, though published without your name; but its author was then disputed: it did indeed rejoice me to be certified at home, that the fame it so deservedly carries with it, is yours. Some little time since I finished it — at half-past four o'clock in the morning, which, from a man who usually keeps good hours, says something for its fascination and power.

Your son I perceive is gone to Washington with your brother. I was very anxious to have met Sir Henry at Forster's, to have talked with him about the country and the people, among whom he is going: but things kept me at home and I lost the pleasure of seeing him. The American Minister here, Abbott Lawrence,[79] is said to have taken Ld Cadogan's house at the full amount of his salary; so that he will appear more like the representative of California, than the frugal republic of the States. He is very wealthy and has made some most magnificent endowments and donations for the advancement of education in Massachusetts.— On the subject of education I am reminded of the young lady, about whom Forster undertook to write to you, which I trust he has done. He mentioned to me your enquiry, and we were quite happy to suggest Miss King, whom we think in all respects suitable — indeed the very person required by the Dss of Montrose[80] for her young boy or boys. She is quite equal, without exaggeration, to a degree in Classics at Oxford or Cambridge & is acquainted with Italian and French, has a pleasing modest address, and, I should think, would prove a *prize* to any mother wishing to exercise her children's minds at an early age.

You will not, I suppose, be here to take a farewell look at the Cardinal in his original representative; and when I turn recluse I must abandon all hope of seeing you; for not even a single-line railway penetrates to the depth of that seclusion, which is to be our home. But more of that "Family", to whom we are all indebted for so much gratification, will keep up our intimacy with *you* — with no unworthy representative of you — Let me not forget to tell you, that I have made free with you to debit you one guinea for the Siddons statue: it is now placed in the Abbey, and, to say the least of it, makes a much better appearance, than that miserable miniature of Kemble from the great hand of Flaxman.[81] I did not like the thought of the subscription list being closed without your name, and therefore took thus much upon myself.

---

[79] Bulwer's son, Edward Robert (1831-91), became first Earl of Lytton and was Viceroy of India; was a popular poet under the pen-name of Owen Meredith. The brother, Sir Henry Bulwer (1801-72), also an author, was a distinguished diplomat; minister to the United States, 1849-52.

Abbott Lawrence (1792-1855), American manufacturer, congressman, and philanthropist, was minister to Great Britain, 1849-52.

[80] James Graham, fourth Duke of Montrose (1799-1874), a staunch Tory; married Caroline Beresford in 1836.

[81] John Flaxman (1755-1826), sculptor and draughtsman; executed the statue of Kemble which is in Westminster Abbey.

With the hope, that you may live long enough to let your effigy find no room there — I mean the Abbey — where so very few places now are left, and with the kindest regards of Mrs Macready,

Macready's reference to his forthcoming retirement to Sherborne brought an astonishing offer from Bulwer. On December 13, at Shrewsbury, Macready received from him "one of the most delightful letters I have ever received — full of *bonhomie*, humour and wit, and what, of course, gives a zest to all, an offer of a house of his close to his park either to live in or to use as a place of occasional resort. Now whether this is only the generous and friendly impulse of the moment, or whether it is a pondered thing, it is most amiable, and I cannot but feel most affectionately and gratefully to the heart that could entertain such a thought."

During the winter, Macready's nineteen-year-old daughter Christina was declining of consumption. On December 26 she was too ill to attend more than an hour at the ball the Macreadys gave in her honor. By February 1, 1850, her case was desperate, and on the twenty-fourth she died. Bulwer, still abroad, was prompt with his condolences, but between grief, illness, and business, it was not until June that Macready responded.

316. MACREADY TO BULWER, 5 *Clarence Terrace, Regent's Park, London, June 14, 1850*

The length of time I have permitted to elapse since the receipt of your two letters makes it difficult to me to begin any acknowledgement of them. Your friendly sympathy will however readily suggest to you, under what I have been called upon to bear, a state of mind ready to find or frame excuses for itself in evading or deferring execution or employment. My health at last gave way under the weight my spirits have been called upon to bear, and I am only now beginning to see reasons for hope, that my strength will eventually be restored to me. It would be vain for me to endeavour to express to you what delight I had — I should say, have had in the frequent perusal of your letter of December last: — that of March came to administer comfort and relief in the thankfulness I felt under such deep affliction for the gift of such a friend. No one would better know, that words like those from you would be the best aid to a mourner, in his endeavour to subdue the violence of grief, that this world could offer. — All is tranquil now, and the memories and mournful thoughts that visit me I would not part with. —

How often I have read over your letter of the winter! — and how delighted I should be to be able to accept the offer it brought me: and for which I have never yet thanked you! But I am sure, though silent, indolent, and procrastinating you will not set down ingratitude among my sins. — Most deeply did I feel, and do feel, your kindness, and most happy should I be in profiting by the tempting prospect it held out of unceremonious intercourse and rural walks with you in your domain of Knebworth. But I have yet to make experiment of the future with an altered income, and I cannot yet form any accurate judgement of what surplus my economy of my fixed and limited income may leave me. Therefore I must be satisfied to mew my numerous tribe within the confines of the single ark, in which we are so soon about to launch our fortunes. But how heartily do I thank you for the mere thought of adding so much to our happiness. And certainly had I been able to have accepted your proposal, I should have thought it one way of testifying how gratefully I regarded it, by becoming a temporary retainer of yours for a portion of each year. I do not know whether this will seek you abroad or may meet you on your arrival in England; wherever it may find you, I trust it will be in amended health and enjoying spirits. Before my sick leave expires I shall try to see you either in London or, if you are not wholly engrossed, in Hertfordshire.

Forster is as active in enjoying himself, and in the service of his friends, as ever.— M^rs M^acready desires me to give you her best regards and kindest wishes, and with all that they can comprise, I remain ever . . .

Macready was one of a party of several to visit Bulwer at Knebworth on August 3 and 4, 1850. He found the house and gardens "a most finished specimen of a baronial seat. The order, the latest Gothic; the architecture, internally, in perfect harmony, though sometimes of different periods, with the outer ornaments of the building." Bulwer was extremely cordial, and a "very elegant" dinner was served in the great hall. Later in the day Forster arrived, and the three old friends sat up late, "Bulwer taking his long cherry-stick pipe and Forster his cigar." The next morning Bulwer took him for a long walk through the park, "discoursing on religion, the immortality of the soul, youth, marriage, and much interesting matter"— later, anecdotes of persons, such as d'Orsay and Lord Hertford.[82] Still later Bulwer showed him over the whole house with its pictures and library, and told him the story of the Knebworth Ghost, and again they toured the gardens and park. "I like him more and more," Macready exclaims. "I wish his health gave him more enjoyment. His place is beautiful." It was an outing for Macready to remember for ever after.

317. MACREADY TO BULWER, 5 *Clarence Terrace, Regent's Park,* *August 6, 1850*

I make no apology to you, my dear Bulwer Lytton, for the hurried words I send you: I seem always to be in transitu:— The few hours I have to spend here in my way from Ireland to Dorsetshire afford me an occasion of writing to you, which I cannot pass by.— On my leaving Knebworth, which I did most reluctantly, I wrote directly for the book I enclose to you — that which I spoke of in the interesting conversation of our morning walk.[83] — If I were to tell you, how anxious I am, that you should be touched by it as I have been, you would say something pleasant of it to gratify me — but I prefer the truth. — Our various differences of thought and feeling make it improbable, that we should agree *exactly* in judgement — and yet these churchmen would chain down every living soul each to his own particular and different belief! The

---

[82] Francis Charles Seymour-Conway, third Marquis of Hertford, (1777-1842), Vice-Chamberlain to the Prince Regent; was the original of the Marquis de Steyne in *Vanity Fair* and of Lord Monmouth in Disraeli's *Coningsby.*

[83] It was a book by James Martineau (1805-1900), philosopher and Unitarian divine; brother to Harriet Martineau; prolific writer on moral and theological subjects.

book I think to be purely Christian.— But I shall become apparently as zealous on one side as those to whose exclusiveness I so object.—

To another very different theme — I think I forgot to mention to you a
very earnest wish of a very warm-hearted friend of mine on the wrong side
of the Atlantic, that I should prevail on you to accept a copy of a comedy he
has published — I left it on the table, I think, of my bedroom — omitting the
intended formality of presentation.— The rogue Forster abuses it, but he is
too bad.— I however have only to commend it to you.

I hear your guests were all very happy on the occasion of the feste, and that
all went off most joyously and with great eclat, which I was delighted to know.

Your health I hope derives benefit from the country air: — it would be to
me such an enjoyment to go down to Knebworth, when you are alone, and
either talk or muse in wanderings through the park and neighbourhood —
but the future is always dim to me.—

318. Macready to Bulwer, *George Hotel, Perth, September 17, 1850*

I shall account among some of the most valuable privileges of my en-
franchisement that of going down to Knebworth and discussing, among fields
and flowers, fate and free-will and all those captivating subjects, which
charmed the fallen Angels into forgetfulness of pain. I am almost sorry, that
I raised your expectations so high in regard to Martineau; and yet I hold to
him, maugre my disappointment in your estimation of him, with all the
strength of gratitude. I admit occasional indulgence in figure, better refrained
from, and once or twice I have noticed obscurity of expression; but his faith
seems to me to impart its own enthusiasm, and I have never yet met with any
divine, who so well discharges the duties of his agency, who invites to him
those who labour and are heavy-laden, that he may give them rest.— Devout
Episcopalians who have failed to find rest of spirit from the writing of their
own teachers have to make acknowledged their gratitude to Martineau.— I
feel how much the charm of style would be required by you; and yet are we
to look for it in the apostolic writings? — The fathers I have never read, and
the extracts I have met with from them do not tempt me further.— But I will
reserve these matters for Knebworth Park if you should be welcoming the
flowers of Spring there — for before that time I see little chance of liberty.

I am here tonight to act the Cardinal, which was my business last night at
Dundee to an audience usurping the orchestra.

Your kind message I cut out of your letter, and that I might enrich him
with an autograph, whilst I gladdend his heart with your notice of his play.
I sent my friend, ipsissimis verbis, your acknowledgement of his offering.

If I *could* have run down to have made a partie carree I should have done
so; but no holidays for me until the close.

The year 1851 brought in Macready's last round of farewell performances before
retirement and Bulwer's last important effort in the drama, called *Not So Bad as We*

Seem.[84] This was designed not for the professional stage at all, but for the amateur players of the Guild of Literature and Art, a philanthropic organization of successful authors for the benefit of unsuccessful ones. Macready read it on January 8 and was delighted by it, though fearful that the amateurs (including Forster, Dickens, Wilkie Collins, Douglas Jerrold) would ruin it. "It requires actors to perform it, and actors to *produce* it," he says — "to know how to *work up* the scenes, where to omit, heighten. I fear their power of doing justice to it." On January 9 he scribbled Bulwer a hasty critique.

319. MACREADY TO BULWER, *Suffolk St., Thursday night, [January 9, 1851]*

I have read with very great pleasure the Comedy — I have the highest opinion — Alas! things of this sort would have kept me on the stage! —

I have thrown off illegible kinds of grunts, as I went on — for I could not make a consecutive review of the incidents & — which may serve you as leads, whereon to question and talk with me, as I learn from Forster, I am to look for you at half past one on Sunday morning. — He will send you this horribly rough piece of paper, and I have mentioned to him several hints, which I can repeat, and explain to you. — It will be best, that the M. S. should be sent here, when you can, that we may have it for reference. You will see that on one important alteration we jump to the same conclusion. Wilmot is a splendid part. It is very easy in a buoyant nature like his to give him a *burst of rapture* at his eventual success, and hits of good humour & wit, *right & left,* at the various characters, Softhead, Barbara, Easy &.c — around him, that will finish him off capitally. It is a splendid part. —

The comedy is a *hit,* and no mistake on that score — but I shall see you on Sunday.

Ever and always Yours

From the time occupied, and the feeling of weight in one or two scenes, I think the play must be LONG.

The Deadman's Lane *letter* is almost lost sight of in the course of the action — it should be KEPT IN SIGHT. — Query two — if some stronger purpose than mere charity could be the cause of the letter to Willmots —*"seeing him about the house"* might suggest him as a means to the parties of Deadman's Lane — &c. — as it *is,* it is *too much* of *chance.*

The first acts very good, but require, I think, compressing — I cannot see safety in the quantity of tragic emotion given to the comic Sir Geoffrey. —

I do not feel sure that the *"flowers"* will be universally understood — their language is not —

I think, if that figure had been seen by Sir G. before, if it seemed to be one of his *haunting* fears — if instead of the dog howling — (or let the dog howl too) — an air, that HE remembered &c. — had been heard at certain

---

[84] *Not So Bad as We Seem; or, Many Sides to a Character* (London, 1851).

nights played near his window &c — There wants *connection between the Deadman's Lane party & Sir G. — it comes too abruptly* — it should be *led to*

I doubt the scene between Lucy and Sir Geoffrey — if not pathetic it would be heavy, & I do not think it would *be pathetic.*

The idea of the drunken scene is VERY GOOD, but I fear the excess of Easy is a little too venturesome — if Softhead were quite maudlin & crying drunk & Easy rollicking as he is, insisting on his having his daughter — as a jolly old cock — the other self-accusing, and blubbering that he is not a jolly old cock, exceedingly remorseful & penitent AND Easy's consent to give Barbara might be brought up against her not ineffectively in last scene.

The chairing is capital and Softhead need not be carried off, better left crying behind — to him Wilmott.

Act 4.

I doubt *those flowers.*

I do not see the objection to Hardman's disclosure of himself to Sir Geoffrey — but I think, it ought to have been understood *before,* that Sir G. is acquainted with the mystery of Hardman's fate. ——

The *two stories* in one scene! — one shd be shortened and BROKEN UP into *dialogue.*

COMPRESSION in *last scene.*

Act 5.

Instead of Lady D — rushing out — Sir G. must *rush in!*

The reconciliation of Hardman and Wilmott might take place during Sir G's absence — Hardman meeting the parties — Sir G, Lady D, & Lucy, as they return, with his declaration to them of his surrender of his claims —

These rough remarks are I fear scarcely intelligible, for I have not time to go into each scene, but if I were in the working of the play, I knw I could show, how they would tell upon the acting.

I like the play EXTREMELY — think it will act excellently, is most lively and agreeable; I have been GREATLY PLEASED with it. For acting it will require, what we call, *bringing up* — compressing here & there —

Vale! — Plaudo.

Capital.

Bulwer called on January 12 to go over the whole of it, and Macready's apprehensions of the wreckage the amateurs would make of it intensified. He was too busy with his own affairs to help Bulwer as he wished to; but at another conference on January 19 he promised to read the play again, "and also to *arrange* it for him, with which he was greatly pleased." The play was strikingly successful all over England through the year 1851.

chapter seven

1851
1873

Last Letters

Macready made his farewell to the stage on February 26, 1851, playing Macbeth at Drury Lane. Three days later a ceremonial dinner, with more than 600 guests and with Bulwer in the Chair, was held in his honor at the Hall of Commerce. Macready had already established his family in beautiful old Sherborne House in Dorsetshire, and from March 2, when he went down to Sherborne, his retirement from the theatre was absolute.

Although this marks the end of professional interest in the Macready-Bulwer correspondence, letters were exchanged, in intermittent but friendly course, for many years longer. Bulwer, often troubled by bad health and by the scandalous attacks upon him by his mad wife, continued active in literature and politics. In 1852 he broke with the Whig party and was elected Tory M.P. for Hertfordshire; he sat in the Commons until he was elevated to the Peerage in 1866.

Macready's main preoccupation during the nine years he lived at Sherborne was the conducting of the Sherborne Literary and Scientific Institution, a night school for laboring children, attended by about 80 pupils from 10 to 20 years of age. Into this project he poured endless toil and a good deal of money, and he often called upon his old friends in literature and the arts to visit the Institution and give lectures. He was also much preoccupied by death. His wife, Catherine, was tubercular, and so, it seems, were most of their ten children. The three-year-old Joan had died in 1840, the nineteen-year-old Nina in 1850. Catherine herself died in 1852, and five more of the children were to die, at ages ranging from thirteen to thirty-nine, before Macready's own death. In 1860, at the age of 67, Macready married a very young woman, Cécile Louise Spencer, the "most intimate friend" of his beloved daughter Katie. The family, now much reduced, gave up Sherborne House and moved to smaller quarters in Cheltenham, where in 1862 Macready's last son was born. A complete list of his family is here appended:

Letitia Margaret Macready (Macready's maiden sister, who always lived with him), born December 4, 1794; died November 8, 1858.

Catherine Frances Macready (née Atkins), born November 11, 1806; died September 18, 1852.

Christina Letitia Macready ("Nina"), born December 26, 1830; died February 24, 1850.

William Charles Macready, (the "Willie" for whom Browning wrote "The Pied Piper of Hamelin"; attended Oxford and Haileybury; went to Ceylon as a Civil servant in 1854; married circa 1859), born August 7, 1832; died (in Ceylon) November 26, 1871.

Catherine Frances Birch Macready ("Katie," author of two volumes of poems), born July 21, 1835; died and was buried at sea during a voyage home from Madeira, March 24, 1869.

Edward Nevil Bourne Macready, born February 17, 1836 (educated at Addiscombe, joined the Indian Army, attempted to go on the stage); death-date unknown.

Harriet Joanna Macready ("Joan"), born July 13, 1837; died November 25, 1840.

Henry Frederick Bulwer Macready, born December 21, 1838; died August 12, 1857.

Walter Francis Sheil Macready, born June 27, 1840; died February 3, 1853.

Lydia Jane Macready, born December 26, 1842; died June 20, 1858.

Cecilia Benvenuta Macready, born June 24, 1847; by 1875 married to a Mr. F. Horsford; died 1934.

Jonathan Forster Christian Macready (became a surgeon), born March 24, 1850; died 1907.

Cécile Louise Macready (née Spencer, the second wife), born 1827; died September 19, 1908.

Cecil Frederick Nevil Macready (later General and Right Hon. Sir Nevil Macready, first Baronet), born May 7, 1862; died 1946.

The first letter announces the death of his wife, Catherine, which had occurred during a visit to Plymouth two days before.

320. MACREADY TO BULWER, *George St., Plymouth, September 20, 1852*

I have not written to you these many months: — to have done so would only have been to have intruded the anxieties and apprehensions I have been suffering upon your triumphs and enjoyments. I should not do so now, but that I am reluctant you should learn from any but myself the loss I have endured.— She, who made the happiness of my past life, is now no more. As she held you ever in the sincerest regard, her memory will have, I am sure, the tribute of your regret for her own sake, as well as mine.

321. MACREADY TO BULWER, *Nantwich, Cheshire, October 23, 1852*

I have wished to thank you for the comfort your letter gave me, but have not yet felt equal to the task: nor can I now read over again the precious truths its words of friendly sympathy convey, without emotion, that makes it difficult for me to fulfil my desire of acknowledging your kindness. How truly, how fervently my heart thanks you, none can know but they, who, suffering under a bereavement so desolating as mine, receive confirmation and strength to the hope, on which alone they can depend, their trust and consolation.

I have been too happy, have too large a debt of gratitude in the memory of my wedded life to repine or murmur at the decree, which has fixed the earthly limit of its course; but a change has come over me as to the feeling, with which I look on life and its duties. The elasticity of my mind seems gone. The object directly and conspicuously in sight, as I fix my regard on the future, is its end; and I have to reason myself into the necessity of giving attention to the duties, that may lie between. My children therefore occupy me as before, or perhaps even more; and I have determined to exert myself as actively as I can in the small circle of my neighborhood for any little good, to which I may be able to contribute.

Never was sorrow more devoid of bitterness than mine — Every remembrance, though mournful, is an indulgence, that has its own delight, and my hopes are comforting and assuring. Nor can I be insensible to the blessing I enjoy in the friends, that God has vouchsafed to me. It is with a deep sense of these bounties, my dear Bulwer Lytton, that I acknowledge your letter, for which I find words too weak to thank you.

I am absent from home on a visit of business to a relative here, but return to my occupations on Monday. My eldest son has left Oxford, where he was doing well, and is now at Haileybury, where he seems to continue his even course. My second is working in the hope of a nomination to Addiscombe, but I do not know, how far I may count upon his chance.[1]

You are girding yourself, I suppose, for the strife of politics. To me those once engrossing interests lose daily more and more their importance, but I may express the hope, that education will be a prominent subject of your parliamentary endeavours, for it will soon be a primary one of the country's. Adieu, dear Bulwer Lytton. . . .

Word of the death of Macready's fourth son, Walter, elicited the following note of consolation from Bulwer.

322. BULWER TO MACREADY, *Thursday night,* [*March, 1853*][2]

Your most interesting and manly letter gave me that kind of melancholy pleasure with which we admire the fortitude of a friend under affliction. And I sincerely believe as well as trust that time will gradually soften all sorts of privation into that holy alliance between present, past and future which the hopes that we cherish insensibly cement.

I have had here lately some of the American seers of whom you may have

---

[1] The eldest son was William. Haileybury College, at Haileybury, Herts, was a school where young men trained for service with the East India Company. The second son was Edward, to whom soon after was granted an Addiscombe cadetship for the military service of the East India Company.

[2] Matthews dates this letter November 19, 1866. It obviously belongs here, for Macready's next letter is a commentary upon it. The Earl of Lytton, in his biography of Bulwer (II, 42), prints two passages out of letters from Bulwer to his son, dated "about 1853," which are detailed descriptions of Bulwer's experiments with "the American rappers and Media with the spirit world." The reluctant reference to "change of parties" indicates Bulwer's recent switch to the Tories. "My little godson" may be the three-year-old Jonathan.

heard or read and who profess to be the mediums of communication between us and the spiritual world, thro' the medium of knocking or sounds. The phenomenon exhibited would have interested you. There is no deception, I am convinced, in the fact of the sounds being made without any known human or material agency — and these sounds reply to the Alphabet so as to produce an intelligible conversation with something or some being invisible. The conversations themselves so far as I have witnessed and participated are not, however, correspondent with our exalted notions of spiritual intercourse. Two or three predictions have been made to me and dates specified. I shall see if they will be verified. But my researches have lately occupied a very interesting ground viz: inquiring into the vestiges of Antient Magic & the old world belief in spirits, etc. I have convinced myself that there are in some organizations powers not to be accounted for by the senses, — and that in short there are more things in heaven and earth, Horatio, etc. Perhaps you will think from this that I am letting my fancy run very wild. But I have guarded myself against all tendencies to take any marvellous effect without strong evidence — And I must also add that with phenomena the most startling — much that is contradictory & fallacious is constantly found so far as I have gone. It is but peeps thro' the Blanket of the Dark. I look with distaste and reluctance to Politics & Parl^t. And my final position in the change of parties will be painful. If you come to town you will find me in trouble one of the Lone.

I suppose my little godson is thriving. Kiss him for me.

Adieu my dear friend.

God preserve and comfort you.

323. MACREADY TO BULWER, *Sherborne, Dorset, March 19, 1853*

Your letter, which Forster brought me, interested me very much.

I suppose we, most of us, work out in our minds some kind of scheme of connection between the visible and invisible worlds, and eagerly accept any facts or semblance of facts, that help to confirm the opinion, towards which we have tended. — In these startling phenomena you have lately witnessed, I fancy you discover some confirmation, if actually verified, of your own glimpses in the attempts you may have been making to fathom the infinite. I think however that the Creator has placed a barrier between the conditions of spiritual and material, which nothing beyond conjecture can reach; at the same time that I have faith in some of the guesses into futurity and "the world unknown," which clever and far-searching minds have made.

I am sorry not to have read Swedenborg,[3] who, from what I have heard, seems, with much that is wild and visionary, to have caught some faint rays of light from that far-off brightness, in which the privileged intelligences may exist. Still I am by no means sure of coinciding with his views, it being scarcely

---

[3] Emanuel Swedenborg (1688-1772), the Swedish scientist and mystic.

possible to find exact concurrence between any two minds in the realization of an idea, that has no earthly prototype.— But what you have listened to makes claim to superhuman agency.— I do not well know how to describe the seeming contradiction of the interest I feel in such pretension to supernatural commerce with the incredulity that accompanies it. Sound can only be produced by substance: spirit, we must think, would communicate by more subtle means.— Still, sceptic as I am, I should very much have liked to have been present on the occasion you refer to. With Johnson I would give all I could to *"see a ghost,"* or certify in any other way my belief in the undying sympathy between the living and the dead.

I had been indulging the hope, that towards the close of the winter or the beginning of spring I might have had a chance of finding you alone for a day or two at Knebworth, and have idly talked over some of these subjects and others in affinity with them. But I am becoming sadly schooled in disappointment. My eldest boy is at Haileybury (if I may still so flatter myself) and I had promised in compliance with his earnest wishes, that I would visit him there next term. He has been doing well during his short residence and I had great pleasure in the prospect of seeing him in his work; and had speculated on crossing from thence to you, if I should have known you to be entirely disengaged. But even whilst I was thinking of writing this to you, I received a letter from Dr. Watson impressing on me the necessity of taking immediate measures to arrest an incipient attack on his lungs. I have brought him home, and he is to sail for Madeira with his sister the 9th of next month. I persuaded myself that he is better since his removal here; but what I have already suffered by this insidious disease forbids me to feel secure, whilst the least remnant of it lingers in his system.[4] These many following cares and fears and regrets come to unloose one's hold of life. My interest in what is passing in the world seems daily to diminish, and will soon, I fancy, be constrained to the narrow circle of my own family and friends: I *hope* your cheval de bataille in politics will be the furtherance and diffusion of Education: it seems to belong to you, and is gaining ground so rapidly against the bigotry and selfishness of our clergy, that the triumph of the cause cannot be far distant.— These pomps of funeral obsequies have no attraction for me; I think Webster's funeral in his own grounds at Marshfield a better managed affair than the interment at St. Pauls; and the lying in state under his own trees and with the canopy of heaven above, his grand countenance offered for a last view to his surrounding friends, a nobler spectacle than the trophied coffin at Chelsea.[5] But these are heterodox opinions, to judge from the stir, which these ceremonies have made, and I suppose your prejudices run in favor of the heraldic display. I am in a very small minority, I fancy. . . .

---

[4] The invalid was William, and the sister Catherine.
[5] Macready is comparing the funeral rites of Daniel Webster (1782-1852), the American statesman, and Arthur Wellesley, first Duke of Wellington (1769-1852).

324. BULWER TO MACREADY, *No. 1 Park Lane, April 27* [*1853*][6]

I was delighted to see your handwriting again & to engage you in anything away from mournful thoughts, tho' you convey a sad intelligence about your son. I have known Madeira effect such permanent cures in consumptive cases that I am very sanguine of your son's complete restoration. "The spirits I have raised" I have no time to consult further, but I don't think their noises, if they make them, are conveyed thro' material that is substantial means but thro' electric or other fluid — which might telegraph from a great distance. I am now in for the theme of C —. What a life of evil passions & wearing drudgery! I repent of my whistle. If I can do anything in it I know not — if so, it will be with force and labour, & agst the grain.—

The sun for the first time shone in at my windows, but London smiles not — I detest it.

"O for a lodge in some vast wilderness."[7]

I don't know if we should quite agree about education. But tho' I would grant the utmost liberty to all sects, I would not have gov^t contribute to any education that excludes some religious culture. I never was better in the hour of temptation for what is called knowledge, but I have been saved from some sins by the Childlike habit of prayer.[8] And therefore I suppose others must be like me.

[P.S.] Saturday. I see nothing of Forster. He is so political that he always says something to hurt one's feelings.

325. BULWER TO MACREADY, *1 Park Lane, Saturday* [*August, 1853*][9]

I had not heard of Mrs Warner's sufferings a danger —. I have had so many demands upon me lately & such a rush of expense also what with an Election, the furnishing & repair &c of a new House — that the proposal of a subscription sounds in my ear much as the word 'Security' did upon Falstaff's[10] —. However so far as my mite of 5£ can go — I place it at your disposal & perhaps you will excuse my sending my cheque to yourself at once — to save further trouble.

I am so sorry to have missed you when you came to Town. I wish you would let me know before hand, another time.

---

[6] Matthews dated this letter 1848.

[7] William Cowper (1731-1800), *The Task,* Book II, l. 1.

[8] As early as 1850, W. J. Fox, the Nonconformist preacher and M.P. for Oldham, had introduced into the House of Commons a Bill for National Education, advocating purely secular education. This sort of program was what Macready believed in, and all his remarks to Bulwer, as well as the conduct of his school at Sherborne, point to this. Fox's bill had been defeated 58 to 287 and was denounced by all sorts of educationists and religionists as tending to revolution and atheism. Bulwer, having turned Tory, joined this hostile majority. The equivalent of Fox's bill was finally passed in 1870.

[9] Original in the Cecil Croft Collection in the Library of the Victoria and Albert Museum.

[10] Shakespeare, *2 Henry IV.* I. ii. 43 ff.

Of Forster I have seen nothing for months — He seems entirely to have renounced so conservative an acquaintance — Some people look on their politics as the Jews did on their religion — contented with their own sanctity as the Elect, they desire no converts — & have no objection to trade with followers of Bel & Moloch — Others rather resemble the medieval orthodox Christians & cannot regard with serenity the man who does not hold their own opinions as to a — Wafer.

Apropos of Politics — the Session has been woefully flat — & unprofitable — Two [*illegible*] & a bad India Bill — voila the result of the [*illegible*] wisdom of all the Talents. —

I have been interesting my self rather in examining into the researches which the grand thinkers of the early world carried into the Unknown — And I have convinced myself that there is no vanishing point on the Horizon of Nature — that where we would limit the Natural — we only [*illegible*] our own presumption by a Dogma as Faraday[11] has done about the Table Moving —

I propose shortly to try the effects of one of the German Spas my hand not having yet recovered its strength.

Believe me, I have sympathized fully in all your trials —. I wish however, that you had made your Home in or near a Capital amongst your friends — I think Solitude felicitous only while it nurses Hope — fearful when it is haunted by Memory — It is a wonderful thing in sorrow to be forced to live amongst the commonalty of men, & learn how easily the contact with others rubs away the rust that tears otherwise leave on the firmest iron.

God bless & sustain you, whatever your choice of life

326. MACREADY TO BULWER, *Bournemouth, Hants, August 8, 1853*

Many and hearty thanks to you, by dear Bulwer Lytton, for your kind help to my endeavour. I received your checque yesterday and remit it to Ransom's by this post.

My opportunities of leaving home are very rare, and the occasions of late have been most melancholy ones. Whenever, if ever, again business or the necessity for change should carry me to Town, I will not fail to try to insure a sight of you by apprising you in time of my intention to call.

I am sorry to learn that there has been such a distance between your interviews with Forster; but I am disposed to set it down rather to his incapabilitating illness, than to differences of opinion on political matters. He has been *very* ill, and fretted with the often deceiving promise of recovery; and even now, when I had believed him certainly regaining the full use of his limbs, his lameness has returned and he is again put on sick diet. On the question of politics you are aware I differ with you, but God forbid, my belief in a different mode of administering public affairs should affect my judgement in its high estimate of the superior qualities of your mind and heart, or should

---

[11] Michael Faraday (1791-1867), the scientist.

cool the warmth of feeling with which I regard them! — Several of my closest friends are what I should term red-hot Tories; but it would be a grievous deficit in my life's account, if I were to lose them for such a reason, for any reason. There is a wisdom of humility and charity, that especially delights me in these words of a writer, that you are conversant with, — "I could never divide myself from any man upon the difference of an opinion; or be angry with his judgement for not agreeing with me in that, from which perhaps, within a few days, I might dissent myself."[12] I had much rather see you in the Liberal than the Conservative ranks, and think you could have rendered better service in them. More than that, if I had been now living in Hertfordshire, I do not perceive, how I could, consistently with my views on our duty in politics, have given you my vote — which would have been a *very great* distress to me. But this is a very wide world, in which we can find ground for agreement, without fixing on that one identical spot in it to dispute upon. — Did I tell you, that it is to Mr. Herries I am indebted for a Cadetship which my second boy now holds at Addiscombe? My eldest, who was 21 yesterday, has been obliged to resign his Writership at Haileybury, and I am watching his health with trembling anxiety. I have therefore little disposition to look for care abroad. But in the cursory glance at politics I have taken, I find matter for exception in the India Bill, whilst I regard the Succession Duty as a means of raising income, which no one can really feel as an exaction unless expectation is to be counted as possession. I know we are at variance on this point, and it is natural perhaps we should be.

I shall like to have an indolent talk with you on your speculations into the invisible world; but of its connections with what we perceive, and the links, by which we ascend through it into relation with the highest, no human investigation can, I think, inform us — we must "wait the great Teacher" for satisfactory answers to our enquiries on such subjects.

Your remarks upon the loneliness of my present life (for there is nothing of congeniality or sympathy near me) are most just, but fluctuating between painful memories and hopes, continually sinking down to apprehensions, I should be out of place enough amongst those, whose intercourse has been formerly so gratifying to me.

I trust you will find speedy and permanent relief from your visit to Germany. My best wishes will attend you there. I suppose war, if there is to be war, will make no difference to English travellers. How much that limitation to Russian absolutism is required at the present moment, which has been the constitutional check in their government! —

---

[12] The sentiment is reminiscent of Lamb's declaration to Southey on friendship and difference of opinion, which Macready would have read in Talfourd's edition of *The Works of Charles Lamb* (see New York edition of 1849, I, 223). I cannot, however, find Macready's exact quotation.

327. BULWER TO MACREADY, *August 1, 1854*

M[r] Saunders, who some years ago published a few poems of remarkable sweetness & promise, has now written a play with the view of representation.[13] Would you do me the great favour to look over it & to tell him frankly 1st how far you think the play itself would do on the stage & next if you think it shows those attributes which (even supposing the play were not likely to tell with an audience) should induce him to continue the cultivation of the Dramatic Art.

I believe that he desires a *candid* opinion from a competent Authority — & there is certainly no Man living whose authority on such a point is equal to your own.

328. MACREADY TO BULWER, *Sherborne House, Sherborne, Dorset, September 22, 1856*

If in the tumult of your present stirring life a stray thought of me should ever flit across the ruminations and calculations, with which your mind must be so frequently engrossed, it must, I should fancy, come in company with the doubt, whether I have not been long since dead and buried. Though buried here, I am not yet actually defunct, giving occasionally faint signs of animation in feeble efforts to make myself heard in a Literary Institution, that I have fathered here, and in the cause of which I endeavour to enlist the services of such friends, as may be willing to lend their aid in enlightening the stolidity and stimulating the neglected intelligence of our semi-agricultural population.

Now, once upon a time — to be sure it is a long while ago — you talked of the possibility — probability — of your rambles as far as this little place; which is like one of the small towns among the Alps, on either side of which at some distance the mail-roads run, leaving it in its slow course of generating or vegetating, but knowing nothing and nothing of it known. — We are four hours from London. — What an impulse it would give to this Institution, which has really done and is doing good, if you would bestow a Lecture on it! — You do such kind things, stooping to conquer our good opinions! — Now is such a glorious event for the Sherborne Literary Institution within the reasonable dream of hope during the ensuing session, which begins with the next month, and extends to April? —

I could only attempt to bribe you, as Isabella does, with the satisfaction derived from imparting so much instruction and pleasure, and with the gratifying consciousness of having greatly contributed towards the permanent establishment of this Society, in which I take so deep an interest.

Perhaps it would amuse you to see, after the fitful fever of my former days, the state of still life, in which I continue to exist: and that too without the slightest wish of mingling again in the whirling movement of the busy world.

---

[13] John Saunders (1810-95), poet and novelist, wrote a blank verse tragedy called *Love's Martyrdom*, which was produced at the Haymarket in 1855.

I would not venture to say for myself, that "Wisdom's triumph is well-timed retreat,"[14] but I am quite convinced, that I should be out of place in any more ambitious home than this. I sit in this quiet old house, and hear of friend after friend departing. The lingering leaves, so few of which are left, drop one after another, teaching me the lesson, we all must learn.

What a delight it would be to see you once again! I am no longer so loco-motive as of old; and indeed it is an effort to obey occasionally the summons of business and peep into the world again: therefore my chance of meeting you *there* is very uncertain.

Will you add together these various reasons for a four hours run into Dorsetshire, and let us indulge the hope, that you will be disposed to confer a public benefit — I do not mean to say a great public benefit in such a little place — but I will say a very great individual pleasure by making the requisite sacrifice of time and trouble.

Excuse this lengthened request or invitation or application and believe me as ever, my dear Bulwer Lytton, affectionately Yours

329. MACREADY TO BULWER, *Sherborne, October 13, 1856*

For a retired gentleman to plead want of time in excuse for his omissions must seem strange; but I may truly do so. Your letter, received nearly a fort-night since, gave me so much pleasure, that I was resolved on telling you the very next day what gratification you had imparted; but the day came, and with it matters that would not wait; and so the next, and so the next, until I desperately determined that all other affairs should be postponed to the acquittance of my debt to you.

It was indeed a delight to me to hear from you.— Upon the subject of my retirement, I not only do not repent it, but am satisfied, it was the fitting step for me to take. If the absence of strong excitement sometimes induces a melancholy tone of thought, it is such as in life's sober evening one may natu-rally expect. But I may perhaps have to complain that even in retirement I have not altogether escaped the ill effects of a too ardent temperament. What Pope calls the ruling passion is a secondary cause in our destiny,— the mere accidental pursuit, in which our dispositions, be they impetuous or apathetic, are engaged. I cannot feel less in earnest now than of old.— Although with-drawn from the world, I cannot shut out its claims upon my interest. "Homo sum", and therefore cannot alienate myself from my kindred. The little efforts, to which this leads, the anxiety for their success, the sympathy with those, who on a grander stage are struggling in the same cause, all this creates excitement, and imposes on me, as an additional duty, the difficult task to still the internal tumult, that is awakened.— But I need the divine interposi-tion "componere fluctur".

I am striving to make the little active power of my later days serviceable

---

[14] Pope's *Moral Essays*, II, 225.

here in the same direction, as that I laboured in, when the poets' minister. But it is most prosaic work: I have weak and luke-warm supporters, and opponents animated with all the zeal of bigotry. Still I lose no jot of heart or hope, but. . . .

This next letter from Macready acknowledges condolences for the death of his son Henry.

330. MACREADY TO BULWER, *Woodhill, Portshead, near Bristol, September 4, 1857*

Your remembrance of me in my recent grief was received and felt by me as a great kindness. This is the only consolation, that in this world we can afford each other — the assurance that we participate in the afflictions that are severally alloted to us.

I was deeply concerned to hear in London of your son's illness. His talents and his amiability, of which I had most pleasing evidences, had excited the warmest interest with me in his welfare — independently of this consideration, that he would inherit, from me.— It was a great relief to learn from Forster, that you had happier news of him.

I used to promise myself an occasional visit to Knebworth, when you might be quite alone there: but with many other pleasing dreams, which years, and the feebleness they bring, take from me, I am forced to resign them: but though out of sight, I am not the less most truly and affectionately Yours

331. MACREADY TO BULWER, *Sherborne House, Sherborne, Dorset, June 6, 1858*

When I saw you had accepted the office of Colonial Secretary,[15] I thought to myself (as people usually do) that I would defer my congratulations to you, until you had not only actually taken your seat, but had had time to find yourself easy and at home in it: — and for this especial reason, that I could not, in writing to you, avoid intermingling a selfish object with the expression of my hope of seeing you eminently servicable to our country in your high appointment. God knows, she has need of good men and true in her present perilous condition! — and in that belief I trust I shall have to felicitate ourselves on your administration, as I now do you on the powers confided to you.

Our friend Forster it is, who has urged me to write to you at once on a subject of the deepest interest to me: and I have therefore anticipated the intended date of my application to you, which I should hesitate to press, if I could not most confidently make it with the conviction, that I should not commit you to any questionable step in acceding to my request.

My eldest son, whose health prevented him from fulfilling the expectations of Mr. Melville of Haileybury, received a Ceylon Writership from the Duke of

---

[15] Bulwer was Secretary of State for the Colonies in Lord Derby's Tory government in 1858-59, though by December of 1858 he was too ill to fulfill the duties of his post.

Newcastle.[16] Since he has been in the island, he has passed his examination in the language with very great credit, and has received the warmest testimonials from the officials, under whom he has served. His work is *very hard,* but he still perseveres in improving his knowledge of the language (which very few do) and has been looking forward to promotion, as some reward and incentive to his labours. This has been in some measure impeded by the unjust re-placement by Mr. Labouchere of a *civilian, Mr. Brodee,* who had left the service, I believe, five years before, and by him (Mr. L.) re-instated, after that lapse of time, over the heads of those, who had been working — *vainly* — upwards during that interval. It is from home, that men in that Colony, Ceylon, obtain the help onward they need. For ability, acquirement, and high character, I may safely assert, my son would not discredit your judgement in distinguishing him by advancement.

All assurances of my own sense of your kind thoughts on this subject would be superfluous. I am sure, *you know* them, and will only add, that, with my most earnest wishes, that your administration may add new honour to your name, I am truly and affectionately Yours

P.S. If your son is at home, pray give my very *kindest* remembrances to him.

332. MACREADY TO BULWER, *Sherborne House, Sherborne, Dorset, October 17, 1858*

I did not reply to your letter about my Son, because I was fully satisfied with your objections to any direct interference, and equally sure, that you would not pass by an occasion of rendering him a service. I should not have made the application but for a precedent afforded by Mr. Labouchere to the retardation of several of the Junior Civil Servants in Ceylon. But I quite understand and appreciate your ground of objections.

Do not think I am going to trespass in a similar way in mentioning to you the name of a *Candidate for a Writers' appointment in Ceylon, which will come before you, I believe, tomorrow. — As to his qualifications being far beyond the requisitions of the appointment I have no doubt; and as I think his case is a peculiarly hard one, and is entitled to consideration, I beg to make you acquainted with it. He is a gentleman, who has served for eight years in the Paymaster General's Office, and from whence I am assured he can take most satisfactory testimonials. Weakness of lungs, in fact incipient consumption, (my own poor boy's case) made leave of absence for a considerable period necessary. — The office could not extend the leave required, and he was, by his physician's order, compelled to resign and go to a warmer climate. Ceylon is among the very best refuges for one so affected, and his claims seem to me to be well deserving your attention. You might not have known these par-

---

[16] Henry Pelham Clinton, fifth Duke of Newcastle (1811-64), Colonial Secretary under Lord Aberdeen, 1852-54, and Secretary of War during the Crimean War after 1854.

ticulars but for my explanation of them, which will be sufficient to interest you without my admission, that his brother is a very highly and justly esteemed friend of mine.

[P.S.] I enclose his card.

> [*Notes*   *Mr. Leicester Bayly
>   *by*   90 Mount St
>   *Bulwer*]   Grosvenor Sqr
>   inquire if Mr Bayley is within the right age?
>   *Macready* in favour of MR BAYLY
>   Letter to Mr. B.
>   *(priv*t*)* 19 Oct
>   ansd 21 Oct:
>   Mr. B; name
>   will be placed on
>   list of Candidates

333. MACREADY TO BULWER, *Sherborne House, October 22, 1858*

I will not encroach upon your time — 'in publica commoda peccore' — longer than to say, how sincerely and heartily I thank you — not only for the act of kindness which excites my grateful acknowledgement most, — but for the unasked, undesired method of adding to the obligation by communicating my name to the recipient of the benefit, as interested for him. — I forgot to mention, what I am now glad of, that he is a relation of Mr. Bartle Frere[17] a man distinguished in Indian Government.

334. MACREADY TO BULWER, *Sherborne House, Sherborne, Dorset,*
October 27, 1858

I need scarcely say, how unwilling I am to seem continually trespassing upon you. The letter however, which I have received this morning, and which I can only, in explanation and in self-defense, enclose to you, leaves me no alternative. I think I told you, that Mr Leicester Bayly is nearly related to Mr Bartle Frere, and I should conceive there would be no doubt of his passing a good examination in Cingalese &c. after his tour of probation in Ceylon.

I hope you will think, that I had no other course, but to forward his letter to you; for *I* could not so clearly have explained his position. His uncle Sir Fred. Smith was to have presented his testimonials to you, I understand, had he not been anticipated by my application.

I am sure you will excuse this additional trouble given to you, seeing it is on my part unavoidable.

P.S. I ought perhaps to add, that my Son, on receiving his nomination from

---

[17] Sir Henry Bartle Edward Frere (1815-84), diplomat and colonial administrator.

the Duke of Newcastle, underwent no examination here, but passed a *most creditable* one in Ceylon.

[*Note
   by   *Ans^d 2d Nov.*
   Bulwer]   Can't be *done*

335. BULWER TO MACREADY, *Knebworth, Stevenage, Herts., August 21, 1863*

It is very long since we met & it would give me no small pleasure to see you again.

Can I tempt you & Mrs. Macready (whose acquaintance it seems to me I have a kind of right to make in my long friendship with yourself) to pay me a visit here for some days? I expect to be at Knebworth from now throughout the entire part of Septr. You will find no party but one or two friends and a cordial welcome.

I think you have one new addition to your family, if not more — whom this invitation will include.

336. MACREADY TO BULWER, *6 Wellington Square, Cheltenham, August 24, 1863*

The sight of your hand-writing this morning was a most agreeable surprise to me and the kind invitation it brought me, I need not say, added to the gratification it afforded me.

I have *very often* thought to myself, if my health would only warrant me, that I would write and enquire of you, when you were likely to be alone at Knebworth, that I might hope to enjoy a quiet ramble and talk with you there. But I have been in what we call a "shaky", or as some doctors term it, a "shabby", condition for some time past, and quite uncertain of myself. — I am thinking of a trip to London soon (though I am very hard to move) to consult some medical opinions, and, if I should find, that I should be authorized to inflict myself on a friend for a day or two, I shall be delighted to avail myself of the opportunity to see you once again — for I cannot now look into a very far future here. It will double the pleasure of my visit to make Mrs Macready my companion. We have one little off-shoot, who is big enough for his years, but not of growth for travel. — If the answers to my enquiries prove as satisfactory as I hope, I will write betimes to ascertain, whether you are still at Knebworth and not *companied,* for my enjoyment would be to find you, "your self alone."

337. MACREADY TO BULWER, *Cox's Hotel, Jermyn St., London, October 6, 1863*

In leaving home I had not expected to have returned to it without seeing you at Knebworth, hoping to find you without engagements there or company, and to enjoy a quiet evening's conversation with you. But I can no longer answer for my movements as once I could, and although I am no longer subject to the regular visits of my medical man, yet I do not feel that I can indulge in the liberty of perfect health, and am on more than one account, unequal to more fatigue and hurry, than I have already encountered. I must therefore postpone my intended enquiry, whether you could conveniently receive Mrs Macready and myself; but I hope, although deferred, it is yet a question to be asked and answered in the affirmative.— My journey has been productive to me of better results that I anticipated in the medical opinions I have received, and I am now anxious for the quiet and rest of home. On some not distant excursion from it I shall hope to include Knebworth among my halting-places, for I have been looking forward with great pleasure to seeing you once again, and introducing Mrs Macready to you, who joins me in every kind wish to you.

In 1866 Lord Derby formed his third Tory Administration and at once elevated Bulwer, then in his sixty-third year, to the peerage.

338. MACREADY TO BULWER, *Montpellier Terrace, Ilfracombe, Devon, July 16, 1866*

I cannot let so important an event in your life as your elevation to the Peerage take place, without assuring you, my dear Lord Lytton, that it is with the heartiness of true affection, I congratulate you upon it.— There are cases, in which political considerations might create a grudge of such well-won honours; but in this instance you have the satisfying assurance of the universal concurrence of your countrymen in the justness of the distinction Her Majesty has awarded you. May your life be prolonged to enjoy it many years, and may it descend through a long line worthy of you and it!

I have at different times thought of writing to you to enquire, if a disengaged week at Knebworth would allow me the opportunity of making you a quiet visit, which we might spend in rambles in the Park and in converse de omnibus rebus et quibusdam aliis; but my continually failing strength has kept me a prisoner at home, except under special requirements, when urgent business or the quest of health has, by my physician's order, forced me from my fireside.

General debility, aggravated by returns of asthma, make me sensible of the number of years, that have passed over my head; but I still "bear up, and steer right onward" with a cheerful spirit, remaining as ever, My dear Lord Lytton, with sincere affection, Yours

339. MACREADY TO BULWER, *13 Montpellier Terrace, Ilfracombe, Devon, July 27, 1866*

I have, as you will readily believe, very great pleasure in thanking you for your most kind letter and its tempting invitation to make a visit to Knebworth. But my visiting days are, I fancy, already numbered. Though, if I could persuade myself, that I had sufficient motive power left in me, I should certainly employ it in seeking my happy welcome from so kind a friend.

I have tried several recipes for my asthmatic inconvenience, but have found none more efficacious than the pure Havana cigar.

Will you let me use the occasion of this acknowledgement to trespass on your good offices for a cause, in which I am much interested? I am aware, there is considerable delicacy in officials interfering with the patronage of their several departments, but it has occurred to me, that the request I have to make is not of such importance, as to give umbrage to the First Lord of the Admiralty in its application.

Could you, without violation of etiquette, ask Sir John Pakington[18] for his nomination to a Naval Cadetship for a relation of mine, or, to be more correct, of my wife's? — The candidate is the son of the Revd Edw. Spencer, Head-Master of the Tavistock Grammar School, whose chance of entering the Navy does not extend beyond the current year.— This would be a serious obligation and a great service to me, if feasible; if not, I am still as certain of your ready will to oblige me and remain with all affectionate regard, dear Lord Lytton, Most sincerely Yours.

340. BULWER TO MACREADY, *Knebworth, July 27, 1866*

I am grieved to think that there is so little chance of my seeing you here.

I need not say how heartily any little interest I may have will be at your service for Mr Spenser. But I am at this moment prevented asking Sir Pakington for a nomination. The fact is that the very moment our party came into power I was beset by Claimants among Constituents etc. I have asked for their nominations at the various departments, till I can ask no more.

I have noted Mr Spenser's name as the first on my reserved List whenever I can decorously apply. But as you say this is his last year as to the requisite Age, it may be wise to apply to any other Conservative legislator you know and it may be well to observe that a Member of the House of Commons has much more influence than a peer in obtaining these nominations.

Of course you are aware that the person nominated has to undergo competitive Examinations.

341. MACREADY TO BULWER, *13 Montpellier Terrace, Ilfracombe, Devon, August 2, 1866*

I can well understand the pressure of applications that you must have to endure, and could hardly have expected to have found you free to undertake my suit; but I am not the less obliged to you, and thank you most heartily for your willingness to serve my friend's cause.

With every kindest wish I remain, dear Lord Lytton, always and most sincerely Yours

No later letters have been preserved, and probably none were written. As is obvious

---

[18] John Somerset Pakington, first Baron Hampton (1799-1880), M.P. for **Droitwich**, 1837-74; Lord of the Admiralty under Lord Derby in 1858 and again in 1866.

from the last here printed, the two old friends had little to say to each other. Bulwer, being shelved as a political figure after his ascension to the peerage, and being troubled by deafness and general ill-health, spent his last years productively in literature. He translated Horace, revised his verse-romance of *King Arthur,* and completed three novels, *The Coming Race, The Parisians,* and *Kenelm Chillingly.* He had by no means abandoned his interest in playwriting. In 1867 he made a prose adaptation of Plautus' *The Captives,* though Charles Fechter, for whom it was intended, apparently rejected it: it was never published. In 1868 he published his revision of *The Sea-Captain,* called *The Rightful Heir,* after its production at the Lyceum by Hermann Vezin. The rhymed comedy of *Walpole,* which had haunted him for decades, was completed and published in 1869. Four acts of *Darnley* were published posthumously as "an unfinished Drama." He died, after a brief illness, on January 18, 1873, in his seventieth year.

Macready's last years, at Wellington Square in Cheltenham, were sorrow-ridden and painful. The death at sea of his beloved daughter Katie in 1869 and the death of his son William in Ceylon in 1871 were hard blows to bear. His own physical decline was long drawn out. As early as 1867 his hands could barely hold a pen, and the postscript of a note to Mrs. Pollock reads "This is a sorry sight!" By 1871, when he made his last trip to London to consult a medical specialist, both hands were paralyzed and his voice was reduced to a choked whisper. "He is changed, and yet not changed," wrote Helen Faucit, who called to see him — "like a great ship, past its work, but grand in its ruin." His alert mind continued to work over the old roles he had played, particularly the Shakespearean, and on this same London visit he spoke to Mrs. Pollock of "some new ideas about Iago. Original, I am sure — true, I think." He survived Bulwer by some three months, dying at Cheltenham on April 27, 1873, at the age of eighty.